The Chicano Generation

The publisher gratefully acknowledges the generous support of the
Fletcher Jones Foundation Humanities Endowment Fund of the
University of California Press Foundation.

The Chicano Generation

Testimonios of the Movement

—

Mario T. García

UNIVERSITY OF CALIFORNIA PRESS

University of California Press, one of the most distinguished university presses in the United States, enriches lives around the world by advancing scholarship in the humanities, social sciences, and natural sciences. Its activities are supported by the UC Press Foundation and by philanthropic contributions from individuals and institutions. For more information, visit www.ucpress.edu.

University of California Press
Oakland, California

Library of Congress Cataloging-in-Publication Data
García, Mario T., author.
   The Chicano generation : testimonios of the movement / Mario T. García.
      pages   cm
   Includes bibliographical references and index.
   ISBN 978-0-520-28601-6 (cloth : alk. paper)—ISBN 0-520-28601-4 (cloth : alk. paper)—ISBN 978-0-520-28602-3 (pbk. : alk. paper)—ISBN 0-520-28602-2 (pbk. : alk. paper)—ISBN 978-0-520-96136-4 (ebook)—ISBN 0-520-96136-6 (ebook)
   1. Chicano movement—California—Los Angeles.   2. Ruiz, Raul, 1940-   3. Arellanes, Gloria, 1946-   4. Muñoz, Rosalio, 1946-   I. Title.
   E184.M5G374 2015
   305.868′72079494—dc23   2014033778

Manufactured in the United States of America

24 23 22 21 20 19 18 17 16 15
10 9 8 7 6 5 4 3 2 1

To Ramón Eduardo Ruiz, who believed in me

CONTENTS

Acknowledgments   *ix*

    Introduction   *1*

1. Raul Ruiz   *18*

2. Gloria Arellanes   *113*

3. Rosalio Muñoz   *211*

    Epilogue   *321*

Notes   *323*
Index   *333*

ACKNOWLEDGMENTS

I want to first express my deep appreciation to Raul Ruiz, Gloria Arellanes, and Rosalio Muñoz for their support of this project and their patience.

I want to thank my editors and staff at the University of California Press, including Niels Hooper, Eric Schmidt, Kim Hogeland, and Bradley Depew, for their assistance and helpful suggestions. Special thanks to Lynne Withey and Sheila Levine. The two anonymous readers for the press provided sage advice for improving the manuscript. In addition, I am grateful to Ellen McCracken for checking the Spanish used in the text. Additional thanks to Amber Workman, who helped me format the text.

I want to also thank my colleague Professor George Lipsitz for his support and encouragement of this project.

A number of photographers and archivists kindly gave permission to use the photos that appear in this book. They are acknowledged in the captions.

I especially want to thank the Guggenheim Foundation for awarding me a Guggenheim Fellowship, which was crucial at the commencement of this project. For additional funding support, I also want to thank the Academic Senate at the University of California–Santa Barbara and the Chicano Studies Institute.

Finally, as always, I am thankful to my wonderful and supportive family: Ellen, Giuliana, and Carlo. I hope and pray for many more years with them, God willing.

Introduction

"Viva la Raza! Chicano Power!"

I first heard these stirring words when I arrived in San Jose, California, in the fall of 1969. I had come from El Paso, Texas, to begin teaching as an instructor of history at San Jose State College (later San Jose State University). The rallying cry was my introduction to the Chicano movement. It had barely surfaced in El Paso, so what I encountered in San Jose was mind-boggling. I had heard about the movement, of course, and, in preparing a class on Chicano history, I had read up on it, discovering some of the emerging journals, such as *El Grito,* and movement newspapers in California. But none of this research prepared me for what I would personally experience.

I met militant Chicano students, Chicano studies faculty, and members of the Black Berets, the likes of whom I had never before encountered.[1] At first, I felt distant from them, and even a bit scared. But as I got to know some of these activists better, I came to identify with them and with the issues they were passionate about. I participated in marches and rallies against injustice to Chicanos in the schools and the community and especially against police abuse. (I had never seen such huge and intimidating cops—all white—as I did in San Jose!) It did not take me long to identify as Chicano and to align myself with the movement.

Of course, I knew the term *Chicano.* I had first encountered it in my all-boys Catholic high school in El Paso in the early 1960s. Mexican American kids from the hard-core barrio of south El Paso used it to assert pride. I lived, literally, on the other side of the tracks, in an ethnically mixed lower-middle-class neighborhood, and did not use the term myself but admired the students who did. Now, in the late 1960s, the term was connected to the Chicano movement and used politically by a

1

new generation to express the militant demands for civil rights, ethnic pride, and community empowerment.

Indeed, this is my generation—the Chicano generation. I too came of age in the 1960s and became politically conscious, first as a liberal Democrat and then as a participant in the Chicano movement. As a graduate student interested in Chicano history and as a professor of Chicano studies, I supported a variety of movement actions both on campuses and in the community. Through this oral history of Chicano movement activists, I have learned even more about my generational history.

It was the movement that provided the opportunity for me to advance my education, eventually obtaining a PhD in history and joining a university faculty. I owe much to the movement, and, as a professor of Chicano studies and a student of Chicano history, I aim to pass on to others the legacy of this struggle for social justice and ethnic respect. The cry "Chicano Power!" still resonates within me and is very much a part of who I have become.

I began this collaborative oral history, or *testimonio*, and the interviews with three key participants in the movement in Los Angeles in the early 1990s: Raul Ruiz, Gloria Arellanes, and Rosalio Muñoz. The text was more than twenty years in preparation. For this delay, I apologize to Raul, Gloria, and Rosalio.

This study is a collective testimonio of three major activists in the Chicano movement in Los Angeles during its heyday in the late 1960s and early 1970s. The years from 1965 to 1975 are especially critical in the struggle for civil rights, renewed identity, and empowerment by a new generation of Mexican Americans who revived the older barrio term *Chicano* as a symbol of new ethnic awareness and political power. The term *testimonio*, or testimony, comes out of a rich Latin American tradition of producing oral histories, or oral memoirs, through the collaboration of political activists or revolutionaries with progressive scholars or journalists.[2] The result is an oral testimony of the life, struggles, and experiences of activists who might not have written their own stories. While they focus on one life, testimonios are also collective in nature because they address collective struggles. Ruiz, Arellanes, and Muñoz are leaders, but they are group-centered leaders.

But more than just narrating life stories, testimonios are intended to educate others and inspire them to continue the struggles of the storytellers. Testimonios possess praxes: for readers to read, reflect, and act. That is what makes them a powerful teaching vehicle.

The Chicano Generation is in the testimonio tradition. It differs by concentrating not just on one subject but on three. This gives it a collective character, or what Jeremy Popkin calls a "coordinated autobiography."[3] I chose to focus on the Chicano movement in Los Angeles because the city represented the political capital of the movement. Every major political manifestation of the movement occurred in the City of Angels, including efforts in support of César Chávez and the farmworkers' struggle; the student movement highlighted by the 1968 East Los Angeles school "blowouts," or walkouts; the Chicano antiwar movement, including the historic National Chicano Antiwar Moratorium of August 29, 1970; the organization of La Raza Unida Party, an independent Chicano political party; the Chicana feminist movement; the organizing of undocumented workers; and the Chicano Renaissance, the flourishing of movement-inspired literary and artistic production. The life stories of Ruiz, Arellanes, and Muñoz touch on many of these manifestations. While each testimonio is presented here as a separate section, they speak to one another, since these activists participated in many of the same events.

I worked with my protagonists for a long time, interviewing them and recording their stories. Altogether, I conducted almost one hundred hours of taped interviews. I have many fond memories of driving to the Los Angeles area from my home in Santa Barbara to interview first Ruiz and Muñoz and later Arellanes. These were wonderful times. I learned about their lives and political engagements. Each of the three narratives is a life story, including family history, childhood, young adulthood, early school experiences, college years, and, of course, the individual's role in the movement. I also include material on postmovement years to the present. Each narrative is told in the subject's voice, based on taped interviews, which I edited for chronology and clarity.

The Chicano movement was a defining moment in the lives of Raul Ruiz, Gloria Arellanes, and Rosalio Muñoz. They were part of the Chicano generation that constituted the driving force of the movement—young Mexican Americans, mostly U.S.-born, who came of age during the 1960s and early 1970s and who were transformed politically from Mexican Americans into Chicanos. They discovered, or rediscovered, the term *Chicano,* used by hard-core barrio youth to characterize their ethnic identity, and they redefined it, retaining its countercultural connotations but infusing the term with a political consciousness. To be a Chicano in the movement was no longer just to be a *vato loco,* or street dude (a descendant of the pachucos and zoot-suiters of the 1940s and 1950s), but instead an activist in the movement. This was the new Chicano generation—La Raza Nueva.

The Chicano movement was the largest and most widespread civil rights and empowerment struggle by Mexican Americans in U.S. history. It combined the more traditional civil rights issues of the earlier Mexican American generation (1930–60)—which pioneered struggles to desegregate the so-called Mexican schools in the Southwest, where the majority of Mexican Americans resided—with efforts to break down discriminatory barriers in jobs, housing, the legal system, and political representation and to eliminate cultural stereotyping.[4] Although the Chicano movement was not aware of (or did not acknowledge) this precedent, in many ways it built on the earlier civil rights movement. Of course, the movement also has to be seen in the context of "the sixties," the period that, despite its name, actually spilled over into the 1970s. The black civil rights movement, Black Power, the New Frontier of President John F. Kennedy, the Great Society of President Lyndon B.

Johnson, the white student movement, the anti–Vietnam War movement, the women's movement, along with the youth counterculture and the general rebelliousness of that era—all affected the Chicano movement in one way or another. The movement found particular inspiration in Black Power, with its assertive identity centered on ethnic pride and self-discovery. Chicano Power, like Black Power, called for a new Chicano identity and change based on the rediscovery of Chicano culture.

Chicanismo, or cultural nationalism, stressed several themes. Central to chicanismo was the claim that Chicanos were an indigenous people because of their Mexican Indian and mestizo (Indian and Spanish) heritage. They were not immigrants but natives of the Southwest and of the Americas.

As indigenous people, Chicanos possessed a historical homeland: Aztlán. In their historical excavation Chicanos rediscovered this northern birthplace of the Aztecs before the migration south and the establishment of the Aztec Empire in the Valley of Mexico (later Mexico City). Chicanos asserted the controversial position that Aztlán had existed in what became the southwestern region of the United States, the area taken by the United States from Mexico in the 1840s. The exact location of Aztlán has always been disputed by scholars, but all acknowledge that it was north of the Valley of Mexico. Chicanos conveniently placed it where they lived.

But if Chicanos lived in their native homeland, they also lived in a lost homeland. This theme of a lost homeland led to the concept of internal colonialism, which held that, because of the U.S. annexation of northern Mexico, Chicanos were similar to third world subjects, with the difference that Chicanos were colonized within the United States.[5]

Chicanismo further advanced the notion that Chicanos represented La Raza Nueva, or the new generation of Chicanos, who would struggle against colonial oppression. In this struggle they would be fortified and inspired by their new awareness of, indeed, conversion to, an empowered identity based on rediscovering their indigenous and mestizo roots. Indeed, some exhibited the same missionary zeal as born-again converts.

The heart of chicanismo was *la familia,* or the Chicano family, the gatekeeper of Chicano heritage and culture. But the movement redefined *la familia* as the community—all Chicanos were linked in a collective cultural family. In this new and extended culture, *carnalismo,* or brotherhood, would further cement the movement. *Carnalismo* extended familial protection and proposed a new humanism, suggesting that Chicano culture possessed more humanistic and less materialistic values than Anglo culture.

If *la familia* was the repository of these values, so too were the barrios, the core Chicano neighborhoods throughout the Southwest and elsewhere. The movement upheld barrio culture as the essence of what it meant to be Chicano. Barrio culture protected and nourished Chicano culture.

In rediscovering Chicano culture, the movement also found a revolutionary heritage, appropriating certain revolutionary aspects of Mexican history, such as the Mexican Revolution of 1910 and the figures of Pancho Villa, Emiliano Zapata, and La Adelita. Seeing themselves as revolutionaries, Chicano activists found historical antecedents and support in Mexico's most important revolution.

Finally, chicanismo adopted the concept of self-determination from other social protest movements, most notably the Black Power movement and third world anticolonial struggles. Although the meaning of self-determination always remained somewhat undefined, it rejected assimilation and embraced community empowerment. The Chicano community needed to control its own resources and destiny.

Many of these themes of chicanismo are controversial and can be challenged historically and culturally. Indeed, they would even be tested in the course of the movement. Nevertheless, chicanismo provided an essentialist ideological foundation and inspiration for the developing Chicano movement. A social protest and political movement had to be built on opposition to the dominant liberal capitalist ideology. The concept of Chicano culture and identity represented an oppositional ideology that unified the movement.

Although informed by chicanismo, the Chicano movement was not monolithic. It manifested itself in different ways and in different locations. Still, certain movement struggles can be singled out. First and foremost was the struggle by César Chávez and the farmworkers. Although Chávez and his co-leader, Dolores Huerta, were not of the new Chicano generation, they and their movement had a major influence on the politicization of younger Chicano activists, not only in California but elsewhere. The courage of the farmworkers—the lowliest of all laborers—to challenge the economic and political domination of agribusiness was impressive. Beginning with the 1965 grape strike in the San Joaquin Valley and lasting five long years, what became the United Farm Workers (UFW) finally pressured the growers to recognize the fledgling union and to sign contracts improving economic conditions. Chávez, Huerta, and the farmworkers served as a beacon to younger Chicanos in the cities. Besides being impressed by the struggle of the predominantly Mexican and Mexican American farmworkers, the emerging Chicano generation was struck by Chávez's use of Mexican cultural and ethnic symbolism: the modified eagle on the union's banner, taken from the flag of Mexico; the use of terms such as *huelga* (strike) and *La Causa* (The Cause); the issuance of El Plan de Delano from the tradition of revolutionaries in Mexican history to first proclaim their plans or goals; the use of the figure of Emiliano Zapata, the agrarian leader in the Mexican Revolution of 1910; and, of course, the devotion of Chávez, Huerta, and the farmworkers to La Virgen de Guadalupe, the patron saint of Mexico. This was an early version of chicanismo, and it appealed to younger Chicanos. It sent the signal to them that it was okay to be Mexican and to be proud of one's heritage.[6]

Drawn to the farmworkers' struggle, many new Chicano activists, especially in California, received their political baptism by supporting the 1965–70 strike. In California many Chicanos, particularly students, made their version of a political pilgrimage to Delano to offer their assistance. There they met their Moses, in the form of César Chávez, who encouraged them to return to their home communities and assist the grape boycott. As a result, Chicano students and other activists led the mass picketing of supermarkets to convince consumers not to buy nonunion grapes. There is no question but that the farmworkers' struggle was a major catalyst in the Chicano movement. In turn, Chávez, Huerta, and other UFW leaders supported the urban struggles of the Chicano generation. In my opinion, César Chávez was the godfather of the Chicano movement.

Less well known, Reies López Tijerina of New Mexico was another role model for the Chicano generation. In the early 1960s Tijerina, a native-born Texan, or *tejano,* organized a land-grant movement in northern New Mexico. He called it La Alianza Federal de Mercedes. It focused on the loss of lands by Hispanos—the Spanish-Mexican people of New Mexico—to Anglos, or whites, after the United States conquered the area and the rest of northern Mexico in the U.S.-Mexico War (1846–48). Although the Treaty of Guadalupe Hidalgo, which ended the war, stipulated or at least recommended that the Hispano land grants be honored, land-hungry Anglo ranchers, along with the National Forest Service, usurped many of these lands. What remained were small plots worked by poor Hispanos. After researching the land-grant question in both Mexican and Spanish archives and studying the treaty, Tijerina promised to recover the grants that had been given to Hispano families as far back as the Spanish colonial settlements (1598–1821).[7]

Tijerina's fiery oratory, reflecting his background as an itinerant Pentecostal preacher, aided his campaign. An accomplished speaker in Spanish, Tijerina succeeded in organizing hundreds into a movement. To bring media attention to the issues, he staged public protests, such as the 1966 takeover of a portion of the Kit Carson National Forest, which he proclaimed a Hispano reservation. One year later Tijerina raised the ante by supporting a courthouse raid in the small town of Tierra Amarilla to carry out a citizen's arrest of the local district attorney, Alfonso Sánchez. Tijerina claimed that Sánchez and his deputies had been illegally harassing members of his group. The raid failed to detain the district attorney, who was not in the courthouse. Shots were fired and two officials wounded. The governor of New Mexico responded by calling out the National Guard in a manhunt for Tijerina. Resembling a Western drama, the courthouse raid and the search for Tijerina received national media attention, as NBC news, for example, called the land-grant leader "The Most Hated Man in New Mexico."

This search reminded Chicanos of the hunt for Pancho Villa by the U.S. military after Villa's famous 1916 raid on Columbus, New Mexico, during the Mexican Revolution of 1910. Although Villa escaped into the mountains of Chihuahua,

Tijerina was not able to elude his captors. Arrested and indicted, he served almost three years for both the courthouse raid and federal trespassing.

Tijerina's exploits and his militant rhetoric, along with the land-grant issue, soon caught the attention of young Chicano activists. Although many supported the nonviolent tactics of César Chávez, Chicanos were also impressed by Tijerina's confrontational and even violent style, reminiscent of the Black Panther Party and other Black Power advocates, who, like Tijerina, called for the community to defend itself with arms, especially against the police. If Chávez resembled Gandhi, Tijerina resembled Pancho Villa.

Tijerina's focus on land issues served as a lesson in Chicano history for emerging activists, teaching them that prior to the U.S. annexation of the Southwest, including California, people of Spanish and Mexican descent had a land base in the region that belonged first to Spain and later to Mexico (1821–48). Because Chicanos identified as indigenous, they felt they had a claim equal to that of the Native Americans who had controlled most of the territory. "This is our land," one Chicano leader later proclaimed. This claim to a native land in turn stimulated the concept of a historical homeland for Chicanos—the Southwest, but more. Led by the poet Alurista, Chicanos discovered Aztlán, which became the Chicano historical homeland, as proclaimed by Alurista in his "Plan Espiritual de Aztlán" at the 1969 National Chicano Youth Liberation Conference in Denver.[8]

If Aztlán was the historical homeland, it was also the lost homeland taken by the Yankees in 1848. This recognition focused the attention of Chicano activists and intellectuals on the historical importance of the U.S.-Mexico War and its consequences. Not only did Mexico lose close to half of its national territory (Aztlán) in this conflict, but also the history of Chicanos, or Mexican Americans, in the United States began with conquest. The initial Mexican American generation was a conquered generation. For Chicano movement activists this meant that Chicanos were a colonized people, which partly explained their marginalization in mainstream U.S. society and led to the movement's adoption of the concept of internal colonialism to explain the second-class status of Mexican Americans. Chicanos resembled those in the colonized third world, the only difference was that they were inside "the belly of the beast," as José Martí put it.[9]

Thus, while Tijerina's land-grant movement did not generate all these ideological implications, its emphasis on the lost Hispano lands resonated with and helped justify the developing myths and theories embraced by the movement.

Although the farmworker and land-grant movements could be considered precursors to the Chicano movement, they are in fact integral to it. Both Chávez and Tijerina became icons for the movement, and Chicano activists participated in both struggles. At the same time, the Chicano generation independently organized its own urban manifestations. Students, for example, reacting to a long history of educational segregation and discrimination in Los Angeles, walked out of their public schools in 1968, led by a dynamic and committed Mexican American teacher, Sal Castro. This series of protests became known as the "blowouts," or walkouts, as thousands of Chicano students left their schools in the first week of March. They demanded changes to make the schools more academically sound and to give the Mexican American community more control. As Carlos Muñoz Jr. correctly notes, the blowouts commenced the urban Chicano movement in Los Angeles and in California.[10]

The blowouts also helped coalesce the growing number of Chicano college students, some of whom helped Castro organize the walkouts, into their own campus-based organizations. In California, even before 1968, Chicano students had formed various groups, such as the United Mexican American Students (UMAS) and the Mexican American Student Confederation (MASC). Influenced by the 1969 Plan de Santa Barbara conference held at the University of California, Santa Barbara, which called for a unification of Chicano student groups under a common name, the Movimiento Estudiantil Chicano de Aztlán (MEChA) was born on most campuses.[11] Similar organizations also sprang up throughout the Southwest, taking on different names, such as the Mexican American Youth Organization (MAYO) in Texas.[12] These groups not only recruited more Chicano students to their campuses but also established Chicano studies programs to address the history, culture, and politics of Mexican Americans, which was then omitted in high school and college curricula. In many cases, this effort led to direct confrontations with university administrations, including mass protests and sit-ins. Chicano university students also participated in a variety of off-campus activities, such as support for the farmworkers, the blowouts, La Raza Unida chapters, and myriad other movement issues.[13]

Not all activists were students. Other political manifestations in Los Angeles included the birth of militant groups, such as the Brown Berets, who patterned themselves after the Black Panther Party with their military-style uniforms and command structure and their focus on community programs and protection against police abuse. The Berets were not committed to nonviolence in their tactics; at least rhetorically, they accepted Malcolm X's mantra about achieving their goals "by any means necessary." They illustrate that the movement was composed not just of high school and college students but also of community-based activists whose political work was in the barrios rather than on campuses.[14]

In Los Angeles and throughout the Southwest, community-oriented newspapers sprang up to form a communications network for the movement. They included publications such as *La Raza* in Los Angeles, edited by Raul Ruiz. Reflecting Benedict Anderson's concept of an "imagined community," this Chicano media network, along with movement conferences, helped create an imagined Chicano movement. Chicanos in different locations came to know that they were not alone but rather part of a larger struggle.[15]

Chicano activists in Los Angeles and elsewhere challenged the system as never before. They understood that it did not work for them or for other minorities. The American Dream excluded them. They also believed that the system would never change without confrontation. While activists used terms such as *revolución,* they did not necessarily mean armed revolution. Indeed, the term was used in an ambiguous way. *Revolución* could encompass anything from militant actions, such as those employed by Tijerina or the Brown Berets, to the blowouts demanding more practical educational reforms. What *revolución* meant—or at least what was accepted in common—was that nothing would change unless Chicanos mobilized for that change in their own organizations and employed "direct action," such as the walkouts. This attitude distinguished the Chicano movement from moderate Mexican American civil rights groups such as the League of United Latin American Citizens (LULAC) and the GI Forum, which believed that change could be achieved incrementally through established political and legal channels. The Chicano generation rejected this approach and believed that only confrontation in the streets would force change. Not all Chicano activists rejected the use of established institutions, but they understood that these institutions—the schools, the political parties, the legal system, among others—did not serve their interests and that countervailing community and people power had to confront the establishment.

With this oppositional spirit and politics, the Chicano movement clashed with many authorities—and not always the most obvious ones. In Los Angeles, for example, a number of Chicanos organized Católicos por la Raza to confront the Catholic Church, represented by Cardinal Frances McIntyre, to demand that the Church offer a larger share of its financial resources to poor Chicano communities, such as East Los Angeles. The confrontational politics of the Católicos included a disturbance at the cardinal's 1969 Christmas midnight Mass.[16]

Eight months later, also in Los Angeles, the most significant manifestation of the Chicano movement occurred. This was the National Chicano Antiwar Moratorium, led by Rosalio Muñoz, which highlighted how the Vietnam War negatively affected the Chicano community. Chicanos were disproportionately being drafted into the military to fight the war because their high schools were not encouraging them to seek higher education or preparing them for college, where they could get deferments from the draft. Funds used to pay for the war also meant money not used for antipoverty and job-retraining programs in the Chicano community. Recognizing that the war did not serve the interests of Chicanos, activists organized what came to be a regional movement. Never before in America's history had Chicanos so massively protested a war. Held on August 29, 1970, in East Los Angeles, the antiwar moratorium was the largest antiwar protest by any minority group at that time, with some twenty thousand protesters, mostly Chicanos, marching against the war. But the largest political protest of the movement and its biggest success also proved to be its most frustrating defeat. Determined not to allow

Chicanos to control the streets of East Los Angeles, county sheriffs, backed up by the Los Angeles Police Department, moved into the concluding rally and attacked the assembled participants. A police-inspired riot spread in the area, with many people arrested or wounded; three participants were tragically killed, among them Ruben Salazar, the leading Chicano journalist of his time. Salazar became an instant movement martyr.[17]

Other key manifestations of the movement, in Los Angeles and elsewhere, included the building of an independent Chicano political party, La Raza Unida Party (RUP), to oppose the traditional two-party system as unrepresentative of the Chicano community. RUP saw itself as more effectively representing Chicano issues and advancing Chicano empowerment than the established political parties would.[18] The growing controversy and alarm expressed by some in the non-Chicano community concerning "illegal aliens" also became an issue for Chicano activists, who formed an alliance with older community leaders, such as Bert Corona in Los Angeles, to defend and organize undocumented immigrants.[19] Chicano generation activists took up many other localized issues throughout the Southwest. No period in Chicano history had seen such intense, militant, and widespread protests by people of Mexican descent.

The Chicano movement proved the inspiration for a "new Chicano" and a "new Chicana" and for a new Chicano politics. In turn, writers, poets, theatrical groups, artists, and muralists were influenced by the movement's aura. The so-called Chicano Renaissance represented a flowering of Chicano literature, art, music, and scholarly production. Besides expressing a new Chicano aesthetic influenced by pre-Columbian, Mexican, and Chicano traditions, this artistic movement used art as a political weapon in service of the movement. The Chicano Renaissance helped inspire a new Chicano critical consciousness.[20]

The activism of the Chicano generation involved both men and women. However, as in other social movements of the period, women often found themselves struggling to assert their leadership. Despite the unfortunate presence of sexism in the Chicano movement, however, Chicanas exercised agency and emerged as leaders. Many Chicanas in both campus and community groups assumed key roles; hopefully, more localized studies of the Chicano movement will elaborate this part of the story. Chicanas became active because they shared many of the same grievances as the men concerning the racism and exploitation that Mexican Americans confronted. They embraced chicanismo and a new Chicano consciousness that recognized the historical and cultural contributions by Mexicans both in Mexico and in the United States. Chicanas first became involved in the movement as cultural nationalists, but, encountering sexist practices, some evolved as feminists. They organized Chicana feminist groups, such as Hijas de Cuahtémoc, which convened conferences and published newspapers and other materials reflecting Chicana feminist perspectives. While the white feminist movement of the 1960s influenced Chicana feminists, it did not absorb them. Chicana feminists sought to change gender relations within the movement rather than apart from it. They recognized that, unlike white women, especially the middle-class white women who led the second wave of feminism, Chicanas were triply oppressed because they confronted not only gender discrimination but also racial discrimination and, as mostly daughters of working-class Mexican Americans, class prejudice as well. While combating sexism by Chicano men, Chicanas focused not on men as their oppressors but on the American capitalist system that created the racial, class, and gender divisions facilitating oppression. Consequently, Chicanas, even against opposition, emerged as key players in the movement.[21]

The protagonists of this collective testimonio all played important roles in the Chicano movement in Los Angeles. Many other activists, of course, also participated. So how did I choose these three? I knew of them or had previous connections with them, although I was not personally acquainted with them during the movement years. Of the three, I have known Raul Ruiz the longest. In the 1980s, when I was chair of the Department of Chicano Studies at the University of California, Santa Barbara, I invited Ruiz to speak at our Chicano commencement. I knew of his work during the movement, especially his role with *La Raza* magazine. He is also a colleague in Chicano studies, having taught at California State University, Northridge, for many years. As for Gloria Arellanes, I knew less about her than about the other two, but I soon came to recognize her historical importance as the only female minister of the militant Brown Berets. I knew of Rosalio Muñoz's activism with the Chicano antiwar movement. Although I may have met him earlier, we were formally introduced in 1995, when we participated in a local Los Angeles TV program on the twenty-fifth anniversary of the death of Ruben Salazar and the moratorium of August 29, 1970. I had just published my edited volume on Salazar.[22]

I do not believe I could have chosen three better representatives of the Chicano generation in Los Angeles. Ruiz was involved in almost all the major manifestations. Arellanes was an outstanding example of strong Chicanas in the movement. And Muñoz was, without question, the key public figure, as well as organizer and leader, of the Chicano antiwar movement, although many others contributed to this historic effort.

Readers will discover their full stories in the text, but let me introduce each subject. As a student at California State University, Los Angeles, Ruiz first became involved when he joined the staff of *La Raza*, an early and important movement newspaper. He left that publication to work on other community newspapers, such as *Inside Eastside* and *Chicano Student Movement*. While working with these papers, Ruiz helped organize high school students for the 1968 blowouts. He served as a communication channel to the students about the problems in the schools and the need for drastic action. Ruiz himself was arrested but released without charges during the demonstrations. He also played a key role in the Educational Issues Coordinating Committee (EICC), which took up student demands and opened up discussions with the school board. In protest of the school administration's denying Sal Castro his teaching position at Lincoln High School in the fall of 1968, Ruiz helped organize a sit-in at the Board of Education offices that led to Castro's reinstatement. As a key movement journalist, Ruiz eventually became the editor of *La Raza* magazine, the most influential movement publication in Los Angeles and Southern California. Ruiz also emerged as one of the leaders of Católicos por la Raza. In the early 1970s he helped organize a chapter of La Raza Unida Party and became the best-known RUP candidate, running twice for the California state legislature. These are just the highlights of Ruiz's activism.

Gloria Arellanes first became involved in the movement when she joined the Brown Berets in 1967. In high school in El Monte, east of Los Angeles, she had become active among Mexican American students in combating racism in her school. Arellanes also had the distinction of representing her school in 1963 at the very first Spanish-Speaking Youth Leadership Conference, which later became the Chicano Youth Leadership Conference (CYLC), headed by Sal Castro. The Berets were a paramilitary outfit with a military-style hierarchical leadership headed by a prime minister and other ministers. The Berets focused on challenging police abuse and encouraging Chicano community empowerment through their programs. Possessing strong leadership skills plus a charismatic personality, Arellanes rose to become the sole female Beret minister. She also became the titular leader of the other female Berets. As a minister, her major contributions included editing *La Causa*, the Beret newspaper. But her greatest achievement was organizing and directing El Barrio Free Clinic, which provided health care to the Chicano community. Her leadership in these efforts, and more, marked her as a leading Chicana feminist of the movement.

One of the few Mexican Americans at the University of California, Los Angeles, Rosalio Muñoz first became involved in student politics on that campus. This involvement led to his being elected student-body president for the 1968–69 academic year, the first Mexican American elected to this high position at UCLA. He became involved with other Chicano students as they organized in UMAS and later MEChA. After he graduated in the spring of 1969, he had to deal with his military draft status. By now an opponent of U.S. involvement in Vietnam, Muñoz decided to reject his draft notice in the fall of that year. With the help of others, he organized a public show of opposition to his induction and to the draft. He opposed the racism of the draft, which targeted minorities, including Chicanos, and he equated it with genocide. On September 16, 1969—the actual date of his induction and coinciding with Mexican Independence Day—Muñoz rejected his draft notice in a public rally outside the Los Angeles induction center, the first in a series of steps that led Muñoz to organize a Chicano antidraft movement, which soon evolved into a Chicano antiwar movement. Muñoz and others initially staged two successful small- to moderate-size demonstrations at the end of 1969 and the beginning of 1970. With this momentum, he helped put together the National Chicano Moratorium Committee, which organized the massive Chicano antiwar moratorium in East Los Angeles on August 29, 1970. Muñoz would go on to participate in several other movement manifestations.

Although I have presented each testimonio separately, as an individual life story, together they compose a collective memoir, or autobiography, with certain common themes. All three activists reveal that their families or friends encouraged them to be proud of their ethnic roots and culture or to stand up for their rights. While insecurity about ethnicity and identity undoubtedly played a role in their coming-of-age years, parental socialization, or the influence of friends, as in Arellanes's case, countered this insecurity and made them receptive to the Chicano movement. Their family backgrounds and early schooling predisposed them to become activists.

Likewise, all three share a particular oppositional consciousness. Each is a strong person who stood up, and still stands up, against injustice and for the community. They are principled people. There is no hypocrisy or disingenuousness about them. They are what you see. They wear their colors on their sleeves. They are, as the saying goes, natural-born leaders. Such traits explain not only their community action but also their leadership roles.

In addition, all attended college. They were more highly educated than the large majority of Mexican Americans of their generation. Ruiz and Muñoz both graduated from college, with Ruiz later receiving a PhD in education from Harvard and becoming a university professor; Arellanes briefly attended college although she never completed her degree. As a result of their advanced education and real-life experiences, all three were exposed to ideas that further laid the foundation for their activism. Ruiz majored in history, with an emphasis on Latin American history, taught by radical professors at California State University, Los Angeles. Arellanes through her high school struggles against racism gave her exposure to civil rights issues. At UCLA Muñoz majored in history, with a focus on Western Europe, and took classes with progressive American historians. Muñoz also was exposed to movement views through Chicano studies. It has been claimed that the educated classes usually lead revolutions and social movements; this seems to be the case for the subjects of this study. More local studies of the movement need to be done to determine if it is true for other movement protests and locations.

Even though all attended college, for the most part they were not in the student wing of the movement. Many young Chicano activists went to college and, while supportive of community issues, focused on bringing about campus-based changes, such as Chicano student recruitment, student support services, Chicano studies, the creation of farmworker support groups on campus, and other activities, including cultural ones. By contrast, Ruiz, Arellanes, and Muñoz, although concerned about Chicano issues on campus, emerged as mainly community-based activists. As such, they are part of the nonstudent community wing of the movement. It is hard to make too sharp a distinction, because there was in fact a great deal of fluidity between student and community politics. Nevertheless, some movement activists spent more of their time on campus; others, in the community, especially after they graduated. Ruiz became active in almost every major phase of the movement in Los Angeles. Arellanes worked with the Brown Berets and in the Chicano antiwar movement. Muñoz organized the Chicano antiwar movement out of the community. Although some scholars conflate the Chicano generation with students, this generation was in fact more heterogeneous, as my project reveals.[23]

At times—and perhaps unavoidably so—the paths of the three activists crossed. They came to know one another, especially in the antiwar movement. Muñoz worked on the 1971 Ruiz-RUP campaign. Ruiz and Arellanes supported and participated in the Muñoz-led antiwar effort. Muñoz and Ruiz worked for undocumented immigrant rights. And Ruiz and Muñoz, at different times, ran for political office: Ruiz for the state legislature and Muñoz for county supervisor and other offices.

Let me also address issues of gender and memory in these three testimonios. It is interesting that while Ruiz and Muñoz, the two men in the study, acknowledge the involvement and even the leadership of Chicanas in the movement, they downplay or ignore the threats and potential violence aimed at some Chicanas for their strong roles. In her testimony Gloria Arellanes notes that this unseemly aspect of the movement, at least in her case, created the possibility of gender violence, including rape. Memory and gender experiences diverge in these narratives.

If they shared a common political struggle and the general tenets of chicanismo, these three activists were not one-dimensional. Like many other activists, as Jorge Mariscal has shown, they exhibited various influences and ideological leanings.[24] In *La Raza* magazine, Ruiz introduced readers to Latin American revolutionary movements such as those in Cuba, Mexico, and Central America. He published stories on the Black Power movement; the Puerto Rican movement, especially the actions of the militant Young Lords; and Native American struggles. Through her participation in the Poor People's Campaign in 1968, Arellanes developed contacts with poor whites and other Latinos. And in building the antiwar effort, Muñoz formed alliances with the white antiwar movement, especially in leftist organizations; later, as a community organizer, he favored coalitions with other ethnic groups. While all three were first and foremost Chicanos, they also understood the importance of other progressive movements. All possessed a third world outlook, and Muñoz gravitated toward Marxism. Arellanes admired Che Guevara and movements for liberation. Ruiz never joined a left political group and often expressed suspicion of the intentions of leftist groups, but he did not oppose socialist beliefs.

Despite these multiple political and ideological influences, what especially impresses me about the three subjects—*los tres*—is their pragmatism. None of them were ideologues. Yes, they espoused chicanismo and gave verbal credence to concepts such as Aztlán and internal colonialism, but in their day-to-day direct confrontation with the system, they displayed what might be called militant or radical pragmatism. They were militant in their use of confrontational tactics, such as mass protests and other forms of direct action, and they distrusted an American capitalist and racial system that hypocritically promised the American Dream while denying this dream to blacks and Chicanos. They were militant, but they were not blinded by their militancy. Like César Chávez, they worked within the system but not with it. They displayed pragmatic strategies and organizational goals. They did not organize to achieve rhetorical goals, such as reclaiming Aztlán, but fought for specific issues affecting the Chicano community and used militant tactics to achieve their aims.

Ruiz, for example, supported the school changes advocated by Sal Castro and the blowout students; he struggled to reform the Catholic Church through Católicos por la Raza; he ran for political office on a third-party ticket to represent the Chicano community more effectively; and he worked on a number of other issues, such as the campaign to incorporate East Los Angeles. As a Brown Beret, Arellanes attempted to address police-abuse issues and, most important, bring about health reforms in the barrios through her leadership in the free clinic. Muñoz focused on ending the war in Vietnam because Chicanos were unnecessarily dying in an unjust war and because federal funds that might better serve the Chicano community were being siphoned off to pay for the war. He also protested against police violence and organized around a variety of basic community issues.

All the struggles and issues engaged by these three activists used pragmatic strategies and had pragmatic goals, although articulated in militant, even radical, language—to be sure, language often tempered to reach people in the barrios. I suggest that they were Chicano radicals, American radicals, in the best sense of the term *radical*. Like Bert Corona and Upton Sinclair, these Chicano activists fought to change the system but recognized that the struggle would be long and had to be built on a series of successful changes and reforms. These efforts, in turn, would empower the Chicano community. They understood that freedom and liberation can be achieved only through action.

What all this means to me is that Jorge Mariscal's correct observation that the Chicano movement displayed multiple ideological tendencies must add radical pragmatism and even radical liberalism to the list.[25] Chicano activists such as these three did not see themselves as liberals and indeed denounced liberalism, even that of Mexican Americans. Yet in their own struggles, they aimed to achieve liberal reforms. They understood that, even though the movement might loosely use the term *revolución*, revolutionary conditions did not exist in the Chicano communities, much less in the country as a whole. Older radicals such as Bert Corona, Luisa Moreno, Emma Tenayuca, Josefina Fierro, and Ernesto Galarza, and others of the pre–Chicano movement years also understood this and worked to achieve practical changes. Ruiz, Arellanes, and Muñoz came to agree on this. Underneath the veneer of chicanismo was in fact a pragmatic liberalism that Chicano activists interpreted in more militant and radical ways. But this liberalism was focused not just on individual rights but on collective rights, as well as group self-respect. In the case of Muñoz, who later embraced Marxist beliefs and joined the Communist Party, these leftist connections were not irreconcilable with his pragmatic politics. The Communist Party had been active with Los Angeles Chicanos since the 1930s but had pursued a reformist and United Front approach to change in the United States, forging coalitions with democratic liberal groups and individuals and downplaying revolutionary goals. Although Muñoz sharpened his own class consciousness and radical critique of American society through Marxism, he still pursued liberal reforms as a party member.

Finally, what Ruiz, Arellanes, and Muñoz have in common is that despite their ups and downs in the movement and the toll on their personal and family lives, they never turned their backs on the movement and on their commitment to social justice, progressive change, and the empowerment of the Chicano community (Chicano Power!). They remained committed activists long after the heyday of the movement. Besides continuing to teach Chicano studies, Ruiz has remained politically engaged, opposing the U.S. role in the Central American wars in the 1980s and, more recently, protesting the U.S. invasion and occupation of Iraq. In the postmovement years Arellanes has expanded her community involvement to include working with California Indians, her ethnic legacy from her mother's family, and encouraging young Native Americans to be proud of their heritage. Muñoz remained in the Communist Party and has continued organizing on a range of community issues, including the outsourcing of industrial jobs from the Los Angeles area and racist anti-immigration measures such as Proposition 187. He too has protested the U.S. role in Iraq.

These were not just temporary movement activists. They remain involved and, in their continuing roles as activists, see the legacy of the movement. For them, the Chicano movement and Chicano Power still live because they have seen the changes that the movement and postmovement struggles have achieved in creating more and better educational and economic, political, and cultural opportunities for Chicanos and Latinos. They recognize that these are liberal reforms, but they also know that a wider spectrum of the Chicano and Latino population has been empowered because of these reforms. They still struggle for a new and better American society—perhaps even a revolutionary one—and they know that many changes are still needed. Even in their sixties and seventies, they are still fighting the good fight.

It is the struggle to achieve a more complete democracy that the Chicano movement and the other protest movements of that era have in common. While they may not have succeeded in all their goals and they made many mistakes, at their core all were responding to the unfulfilled promise of American democracy to their communities. We can no longer ignore or marginalize the history of Chicanos and other Latinos in this country; we must integrate the Chicano movement, as exemplified by these testimonios, with the civil rights history of this period and of other protest movements. The Chicano movement and the many others in the 1960s and 1970s remind us that the struggle continues. I am proud to present and preserve the stories of Raul Ruiz, Gloria Arellanes, and Rosalio Muñoz. This narrative is also a demonstration of Chicano Power.

Raul Ruiz

EL PASO

El Paso, to me, is where everything begins. I am from El Paso. It's in my blood, as it is for so many other *mexicanos.*

My family is not from El Paso. But like so many other Mexican immigrants at the turn of the twentieth century, they came to this border city from Mexico. They came from Chihuahua—*el norte.*[1] My grandfather on my mother's side, Miguel Bustillos, was a railroad man. He had little education and very early on worked on the railroads out of Chihuahua. It was the railroad that brought him to the border—*la frontera*—to El Paso. There he worked for the Southern Pacific Railroad. Starting as a laborer, he eventually worked his way up to the skilled position of a machinist. He was a union man. He became a leader in his union of machinists. He was not afraid or intimidated to go on strike.

Grandfather Bustillos was quite enterprising. He built his own home in El Segundo Barrio of south El Paso, the main Mexican settlement. Not only did he build his own house at Seventh and Florence right next to Armijo Park, but he kept adding apartments, where eventually his grown children and their families lived. For a while he owned some cantinas, or bars, in the barrio but lost them during Prohibition in the 1920s. Not to be outdone, however, he buried bottles of whiskey in the ground around his home. Later, as a kid, I would at times come across some of these bottles as I played in our yard.

Grandfather also learned English, and he could read it. His English was better than that of my own father. He was a proud and dignified man. I see pictures of him with a full head of hair; he was *alto y guapo*—tall and handsome. But my grandfather was also a tough guy. He would go to union meetings carrying a baseball bat because there was always a lot of turmoil. He even got into trouble with the law a couple of times.

Grandma Bustillos may also have been from Chihuahua. Her name was Angelita. She was already in El Paso when my grandfather met and married her.

I didn't get to know either my grandfather or grandmother too well since they both died when I was still young. I have fond memories of them, but I feel that I know them mostly through the stories my own mother passed on to me. My recalling them now is a way of keeping them alive.

On my father's side, the family also originated in Chihuahua. This was the Ruiz family. Grandpa Pablo married my grandma Margarita, and they had two sons— my father, Pablo, and my *tío* Andrés. Grandpa Pablo was an unskilled laborer and worked a bit on the railroads in northern Mexico.

Unlike my mother's family, my father's came to the border but lived in Ciudad Juárez, the Mexican border town across the Rio Grande from El Paso. Because this side of the family lived in Juárez, my siblings and I grew up closer to my mother's family since we lived on the U.S. side of the border.

My father was born around 1900 and grew up in Juárez. He had very little education, only three or four years. He worked in a foundry and then as a messenger for some business people. When he was about eighteen, he crossed the border and started railroad work at the Southern Pacific yard. I think the attraction was, why work in Juárez when you can make more money in El Paso?

My mother, who was born in 1901, was a beautiful and elegant woman, as were her three other sisters. She had a bit more education than my dad, but not much more, perhaps to fourth or fifth grade. My mother didn't attend the big "Mexican school" in the barrio, Aoy, which was the public school. She attended a small private one. My mother wanted more education, especially of a vocational type, but my grandfather didn't go for that.

My parents met at barrio social functions or at baseball games in the park. Actually, when they met they were about the same age, well into their twenties. My mother was thirty years old when she married my dad. She didn't work outside of the home but helped to take care of Grandpa Miguel's house.

My parents married around 1930. They then lived in one of my grandfather's apartments, next to what became their extended family. This is where my siblings and I were born. First came my two older brothers: Hector in 1934 and Fernando in 1937. I was born in 1940.

Although it was before my time, the Great Depression affected my parents as well as most other people. Of course, my parents and the extended family were accustomed to hard times. "*Ay chavalo tonto,*" my mother would later say. "Dumb boy, we've always been poor."

As working people we were not strangers to poverty. The impact of the Depression was that it affected even poor people's ability to work. My father began to experience layoff periods—*el layoff*—at the railroad yard. He was a proud man, so he never accepted help from my grandpa Miguel, who didn't have that much more but did have a few more resources. These seasonal unemployed times would even continue after I was born and growing up. Because of this, I came to hate the railroad even as a *chavalito,* a little boy.

FAMILY SOCIALIZATION

My brothers and I were raised in a strong family environment with strict discipline. In our family we did not misbehave. And if we did, we paid the consequences. We grew up with a sense of right and wrong. It wasn't something necessarily preached to us, but we got the point. It would never occur to me to steal or to vandalize someone else's property. It wasn't that we were cowards. We did all the barrio stuff. But we never got in trouble. As we grew up we never took drugs or even drank liquor. My father drank but only socially.

I grew up with a sense that my brothers and I were accountable to our parents. If we ever did get a bit out of line we were punished, including corporal punishment. This included *escobazos,* being hit with my mother's broom, or *cintazos,* being hit with my father's belt. This punishment didn't create psychological trauma or physical problems for us. But it did reinforce correct behavior.

Despite the stereotype of the father as the enforcer of discipline in the Chicano home, in fact it was mostly my mother who disciplined us. She was the chief disciplinarian and the primary policy maker in the house. My father was recognized as the ultimate authority figure—he had his *lugar,* his place—but in practice it was really my mom who made household decisions. She disciplined us by not permitting us to go out, by corporal punishment, or by denying us some material thing. This is not to say that my father wasn't involved. He was, but without giving up his titular role as head of the family, he allowed my mother to run the household as she saw fit.

While some people think that the woman in a Latino family is secondary in the decision-making process, I never saw that in my family. I never saw it in my cousins' families. Strong women such as my *tías,* my aunts, ran them all. I always saw my *tías* as extended moms, especially Tía Delia, who was even stronger than my mom.

There's no question but that my mother had the strongest influence on my early socialization. She was a very religious woman. There were santos in our home, but not excessively. My mother belonged to *las guadalupanas,* a devotional society to the Virgen de Guadalupe, at, I believe, both Sacred Heart and St. Ignatius Parishes. She made sure that within our home and at the barrio Catholic church we observed religious traditions and practices. During *cuaresma*—Lent—we fasted, especially on Good Friday. We never ate meat on Fridays, which was not then permitted by the Church. We ate fish instead. We also visited different churches on Good Friday.

My mother, of course, made sure that we were baptized, went to catechism classes, made our First Communion, and went regularly to Sunday Mass.

My father was not as religious as my mother, but he supported Catholic training for us. Later in his life, he became as devoted as my mother and prayed with his rosary every day.

Religion was always a part of our family's culture. It defined who we were and what we did. It was not something apart. It was never something forced on us. It was a natural family thing.

OUT OF THE BARRIO

When I was around six, my parents decided to move. Although my dad was at best a semiskilled worker at the railroad yard and had experienced many layoffs during the Depression, he was helped by the outbreak of World War II and full employment again due to the war effort, which ended the economic crisis.

He was able to save some money and at the end of the war had enough to buy a house of his own. Around 1946 he did so in an area beyond the south El Paso barrio. I think my parents decided to move for a couple of reasons. One, my father probably no longer wanted to live with the extended family in the *vecindades,* or apartments, that Grandpa Miguel had built. Actually, I think the rest of us felt the same way. Extended families are great, but sometimes there can be too much extended family, especially if you have cousins who run around beating the hell out of you.

Second, I think that my parents saw moving out of the barrio as a status thing. Buying a house, especially a sturdy one built of *ladrillos,* or bricks, and having Anglo neighbors was not bad for a Chicano. They also saw it as a way of helping us, hoping to provide more opportunities for their kids. There was always this thing of *mejorar,* of improving yourself. I think that this move was precisely that.

My father bought the new house—which was new to us, but others had lived in it before—for something like $6,000. I don't think that he needed a big down payment. It was what at the time was considered to be northeast El Paso up from El Segundo Barrio and north of the tracks. It was close to Alta Vista School, which became my school.

This was not a Chicano area, at least not then. There was a mix of people. Next door to one side of us was an Anglo family who owned a market on Paisano Drive, one of the main thoroughfares in the city. On our other side was an Anglo lady who was a pianist. I always saw her as a high-class lady, very refined, who played beautiful music. We used to sit on our porch and listen to her.

Next to the pianist was another Chicano family, the Riveras. The husband was a teacher. He probably taught music since he also played the piano. He was the only Chicano father I ever met who always dressed in a suit. He had a son, Carlito, a fat little kid whom every other kid on the block hated. They always used to beat him up. For some reason, I befriended him and became his protector. Señora Rivera used to visit my mother and ask, "¿Por qué le pegan a Carlito?" (Why do they pick on Carlito?).

I used to tell Señora Rivera that it was because of the way she dressed her son.

"Señora Rivera, don't send your son out with that little cap on because the guys are gonna want to knock it off. And does he have to play the violin?"

This was a neighborhood in transition. There were still many Anglos living there, but each year more Chicanos moved in as those who could afford it spilled out of the barrio. Within ten years, it became heavily Chicano.

This became our new neighborhood. My best friend was not another Chicano but a Chinese American boy, Gilbert Poo. Actually, Gilbert was half-Chinese and half-Mexican on his mother's side. There had always been a Chinese community in El Paso and Juárez. His father owned a neighborhood corner grocery store.

I learned English from Gilbert. In fact, I learned English not so much in school as on the streets with friends such as Gilbert. At home we spoke only Spanish, and like my two older brothers I began to pick up English playing with other kids.

EARLY SCHOOLING

I started first grade at Alta Vista School. That first year was traumatic for me. I didn't know English, and there were no bilingual teachers or aides. The teachers were all Anglos and knew little or no Spanish. But even if they did, it was prohibited to speak Spanish at school.

We were punished for speaking Spanish, including corporal punishment. We would receive a demerit for every word of Spanish spoken and be reported to the principal. A network of little snitches aided him. In some cases, the principal would administer corporal punishment, such as paddling us. Or he would send us to the coach who would spank us, swat us, or hit us on the head with the big ring that he wore. I didn't escape such punishments.

Because of the language gap, I and many other Chicanos in the first grade failed and had to repeat it.

But by the time I repeated the first grade and was advanced to the second grade, things were changing for the better. I was learning English if for no other reason than for survival. This transition was made easier because of my older brothers who had learned English before me as well as my English-speaking friends. My brothers and I began to speak English at home and to read comics in English.

By the second grade, I was no longer having a problem with English. In fact, I was becoming a good student. Still I had some rough edges and was still being disciplined in school. My mother became quite upset with me.

"Pórtate bien, Raul. Y si te portas bien te compro una bicicleta."

This was a bribe that if I behaved she would buy me a bicycle. It worked.

My parents were still facing difficult economic times, especially after the war as layoffs resumed at the railroad yard. After my dad paid the mortgage and bills and bought food, there wasn't much left. So the idea of getting a bicycle was fantastic. I shaped up.

"What did you do to this boy?" other parents would ask my mother.

I got the bike and was no longer punished in school.

Once I settled down and also became more at ease with English, I became an even better student. I liked my classes and did well. I wasn't a nerd, but I enjoyed learning.

My parents, primarily my mother, as well as my brother Fernando, who was also a good student, encouraged me in my learning. My mother wasn't always after me. I was becoming more self-motivated. I began to discover the library at Alta Vista and the public library. I particularly enjoyed reading biographies such as on Kit Carson and Davy Crockett and adventure stories. We didn't have any books at home except for an old encyclopedia, so reading involved taking out library books. I also read a lot of comic books.

Part of my becoming comfortable at school was the fact that I had good teachers. Some were quite tough and strict, such as Miss Brooker in the fifth grade, but I did very well with her, even though she was forever on my back. I didn't see these teachers as bad people or as racists. All of my teachers were Anglos. I didn't have a Mexican American teacher until I was in college.

As I look back on it now, especially on the language issue, I can understand that there was a certain insensitivity about this. There must have even been a certain institutional racism. But my memories overall are positive ones.

One of the noticeable things at school was how teachers transformed the Spanish names of the Chicano kids into English ones. José became Joe. Pedro became Pete. Rodolfo became Rudy. The names not only stuck but were accepted by *la palomilla*—the Chicano kids—because they didn't want to stand out. Not only were proper names changed but also the kids themselves invented English nicknames for one another, such as Shorty or Junior or Skinny.

But in these changes not all our Mexican culture was erased. For example, the teachers changed María's name to Mary, but among the Chicano kids she was "la Mary"—and there was "la Judy" and "el Frankie" too.

These name changes, to my disappointment, didn't affect me. You couldn't easily translate Raul or a name such as Mario. You could give it an Anglo intonation but not a literal translation.

Who knows? Maybe these name changes even made what we would later refer to as "ethnic relations" easier. Even though during my eight years at Alta Vista the school became more and more Mexican and less and less Anglo, it was still a mixed school. I don't recall any particular tensions between the Chicano kids and the

Anglo ones. We were in classes together, and we played together. El Paso has always had, at least on the surface, good race relations.

I was always in love with one *güerita*—blond girl—after another. I remember especially one, Gale Kunz, in either fifth or sixth grade. I was in love with her but never talked to her. Whatever happened to Gale Kunz?

Although we were becoming more acculturated at school, we retained our Mexican ethnic identity through our parents and our extended family on both sides of the border. Of course, in a border city such as El Paso it's very difficult not to be aware of the strong Mexican presence.

Besides visits to my mother's family in El Segundo Barrio, we would also visit my dad's family in Juárez. Our weekend trips across the border became part of our *salida,* or Sunday visit. Visiting, shopping, going to the movies, and eating at a favorite restaurant in Juárez became a weekly Sunday ritual. All these things were very cheap in the Mexican border town, so it didn't particularly strain my dad's limited income.

Even though my brothers and I were becoming more English dominant, we were able to retain some of our Spanish due to my parents and these family visits. Actually, among my peers we were mixing English and Spanish words, especially slang ones, together, such as "el nickel" and "el dime."

My mother did express some concern about our losing Spanish.

"Están hablando tanto inglés que están perdiendo el español," she would complain to our relatives. "They're speaking so much English that they're losing Spanish."

But I never lost Spanish completely. I was finding it more and more difficult to carry on an entire conversation in Spanish, but I still could communicate.

Later on as I grew up and began to get involved in the Chicano movement, I rediscovered my Spanish. I made a conscious effort to relearn it to the point where I could even deliver a speech in Spanish. Regretfully, I didn't pass this on to my own daughter. She understands Spanish but speaks very little. It's not automatic. Hard work is necessary to develop a bilingual facility.

Still, despite these changes, I didn't lose my sense of being *mexicano* or Mexican American—that was a term I recall hearing more as I grew up. I was Mexican American, even though I don't think I actually used the term. I recall the term *Chicano,* but we didn't use it.

Chicano was likely more used in south El Paso among the pachucos and gangs. There were gangs in the late 1940s and early 1950s when I was going to Alta Vista. There were none in our neighborhood, but I did know that they existed in the barrio.

Our neighborhood was becoming a Mexican barrio, but there was relatively little crime, at least that I was aware of. There were no car thefts, vandalism, or muggings. Of course, these were not particular to poor Mexicans but also to poor Anglos.

LOS ANGELES

In 1953 I graduated from Alta Vista School. I was entering a transition period that proved to be more than just going on to high school. It meant leaving El Paso and going to Los Angeles.

My father's job had always been a difficult one. Not only did he face periodic layoffs, but also his salary was limited since he was not a skilled worker. We never got allowances, and getting a treat such as ice cream was a rarity.

Things only got worse. The Southern Pacific by the early 1950s decided to scale down its operation in El Paso and began to lay off workers, this time permanently. My dad was one of these. He was already a middle-aged man.

Out of a job and with few other prospects in El Paso, my dad decided to go to Los Angeles to see if he could find work. He went by himself first to scout out possibilities. Fortunately, we had relatives in L.A., my tía Elisa. He stayed for a year by himself.

In the meantime, we rented out our house to secure an income and moved in with my tía Delia and her four children: Elvia, Nora, Benny, and Fred. Tía Delia, who was widowed, lived in our neighborhood, just a couple of blocks away from our house. Her husband, Tío Fred, had died at an early age. He had been in the military, so he left his veteran's pension for his family.

We struggled at this time. Our income was quite limited. I remember days when all we had to eat was frijoles: morning, noon, and night.

Fernando delivered the *El Paso Herald-Post,* and I would help him. But despite his promise to give me a small cut of his earnings, I never got it. It was just as well since my mother needed all of it. My older brother, Hector, joined the air force.

After about a year, my dad called for us to join him in Los Angeles. He had managed to secure a new job with the Southern Pacific there. This was fantastic because his seniority and pension were reinstated. But now it was our turn to leave.

I didn't want to go to L.A. All my friends were in El Paso. I was going to start high school. The move came at the worst possible time for me. I voiced my protests to my parents, but my dad put it to me straightforwardly: "Raul, this is what we have to do to keep the family together—¿entiendes?" Yes, I understood and agreed.

The family network already in Los Angeles eased our move. Besides my father already having spent time there, there was my tía Elisa and my tía Theresa, my mother's cousins, and their families. They advised us where to live.

"Don't go to East L.A.," they warned us. "There's too many gangsters and gangs there."

We, not knowing any better, accepted their advice. We moved into a rental in South Central L.A., close to our relatives. This was around the Normandy-Adams area near Vermont Avenue. South Central L.A. then, in the early 1950s, was primarily black, but Mexicans were beginning to move there in growing numbers, mostly Chicanos or Mexican Americans. They were not immigrants. Today, of course, South Central has dramatically changed, and it is largely an immigrant community of Mexicans and Central Americans.

Our first home was on Magnolia and Twenty-Third. This was a little apartment. After a while we moved to another rental on Vermont and Fifteenth. We then moved back to Twenty-Third after a few months. At this last place we lived for several years, until we bought a house in South Central Los Angeles at 2236 South Catalina near Vermont and Adams. My mother always disliked renting. She wanted a house of her own. One day she saw a house that had a sign in Spanish that read, *Se Vende* (For Sale). It was my mother's decision to buy the house. On her own, she met with the real estate agent and made all the financial arrangements. She knew that my father was loath to make such decisions. It was a three-bedroom house, and I later received ownership of it. This was about five years after we had moved to Los Angeles. By this time, we had sold our El Paso home, and with that money my parents made the down payment for the new house. It cost $10,000. Today it's worth close to $200,000, and I rent it out.

I had a difficult time adjusting to Los Angeles. I didn't like it. It didn't seem to have a sense of community, at least not in the way I was used to in El Paso. I still felt like an outsider. I couldn't fit in. This was unusual for me because I had always been the type of guy who fitted in and made friends. But here I didn't know the *onda*—the way things operated.

Although my brother, Fernando, attended a public high school—Manual Arts—I instead was put in a small Catholic high school, St. Agnes. This was more my mother's doing. She felt that since I still had all my high school years ahead of me that it would be better and safer for me to go to St. Agnes, which was closer to where we lived. The Sisters of the Holy Cross ran St. Agnes.

Even though it was a small school—my graduating class was about sixty—I still continued to feel like an outsider. Most of the kids, Mexicans and Anglos, had been attending St. Agnes since elementary school since it was a combination primary and secondary school. So I found it difficult to fit in. I also found the Chicanos very cliquish.

Even though I had been a good student in El Paso, I had more trouble at St. Agnes. It wasn't that I couldn't do the work but that I felt alienated. I didn't like the nuns, and they didn't seem to like me.

I was always in trouble and being disciplined. This often concerned my fighting with other students, especially the Chicanos. Discipline or demerits consisted of washing windows at the nun's convent on Saturdays.

Besides seeming to always get into trouble, I disliked the ethnic division at the school. The Anglo Catholics would all sit in the front of the classrooms, and the Chicanos sat in the back. Those at the front were in the A track, which was the college prep one, and those in the back were in the B track, the non–college prep one.

I had problems in high school, but they didn't drive me into gangs, drugs, or crime. I was never a gangster, never a bad person, never abused girls, or things like that. But I was always ready to fight if I had to. I wasn't a pushover.

I remember one time this nun was so harsh with a Chicana girl that she made her cry in class. "I don't think it's right what you're doing," I boldly and without thinking told the nun. Boy, was this the wrong thing to have said. I found myself again washing windows at the convent the next Saturday.

I had to work to help my family, and delivering papers was the way that I did. First on my bicycle and then later on the motor scooter I bought, I delivered the *Los Angeles Herald-Examiner* in South Central L.A.

Delivering papers was not an easy task. I was the only Mexican kid among black newspaper boys. On top of this, I was delivering the paper in a predominantly black area. I was often picked on by some of the black newspaper boys who didn't want me around. I had no option but to take them on. I was a little, skinny guy, but I never backed off. Sometimes I would have to fight every day. I used to hate getting up for my morning delivery because I knew that I was going to have to fight somebody.

After a while, these fights subsided as the black kids realized that they weren't going to drive me out and that I would defend myself. Some of these guys actually became friends of mine and would even come to my house.

I don't have many memories of high school, and what I have are not good ones. I played some baseball and ran a little track, but nothing big. I even considered joining the school band. But the day I went to try out I heard the other kids play, and it sounded like the Salvation Army band, and I said, "I'll never play in that!" I dated several girls, both Mexican Americans and Anglos, but nothing serious. I even went to my senior prom with the sister of one of my few friends. She was part German and part Guatemalan.

One thing that did affect me at St. Agnes was my religious feelings. I was very religious during high school. I even considered at one point becoming a priest. I was influenced by my Catholic education and by my parents, especially my mother's strong religious devotion. So even though these were difficult years for me, my religion and my parent's socialization kept me on a straight path. I had a sense of right and wrong.

I graduated in 1958. Even though St. Agnes prided itself on being a college pre-paratory school, I was never really encouraged to go on to a four-year college. It was not something that really crossed my mind. My two older brothers hadn't gone to college, so even within my family, I had no college role models.

Instead, I enrolled at the Los Angeles Trade Technical School, where students could learn a specific skill or craft. This was a technical version of a community college. I chose drafting in the hope of landing a job as a draftsman.

What I really wanted after I graduated from high school was to get a car—my own car. I asked my dad.

"You want a car?" he replied. "Well, you're going to have to work for it!"

I did. Instead of my paper route, I started to work at a post office branch. In time I saved enough money to buy exactly the car I wanted—a 1957 Chevy. What a beautiful car! It was a used car, but that didn't matter to me. It was two-toned, turquoise and white, with whitewall tires, and had lots of power.

I paid my car off as well as my tuition at Trade Tech by working as a clerk at the post office. I kept this job for several years. I would work at night and go to school during the day.

When I graduated from Trade Tech with an associate's degree, I looked for a job as a draftsman. I succeeded in getting one at Autonetics, an engineering firm in Orange County. It was a division of North American Aviation. But I still kept my evening job at the post office.

I hated my job as a draftsman. It was boring. I didn't mind the post office work but intensely disliked the drafting one.

Working was made a bit more tolerable by my social life. I was beginning to date more. I even started going steady with one young woman, Elizabeth Van Wyk. She was my first real girlfriend. I didn't notice or pay attention to any ethnic distinctions. We liked each other. That was all that was important. My parents also had no problems with this. The only ones who had a problem were Elizabeth's parents. They opposed her dating a Mexican. Elizabeth told me this, and I could pick up on their vibes. In fact, her father once called my dad and told him that he wanted to talk about my dating his daughter. My father told him to come over, but he never did. My relationship with Elizabeth never had a chance.

The big change in my life was when I decided to get married in 1962. I had met another young woman, Norma Bambila, whose family was from Guatemala, although Norma herself was born in Mexico and came to the United States with her parents as a young child. I met her at one of those beauty contests—*reinas de los pueblos*—sponsored by various Mexican social clubs, each sponsoring a queen candidate. Norma was *la reina de España*. The contest and dance was at the old Ambassador Hotel near downtown Los Angeles. A Latino friend, Harold Hartleben, who was part German and part Guatemalan, and I just went to it even though we didn't know anyone at the event. We went because we knew that there would be girls there.

The *reinas* would all line up and be presented to the judges and the audience. My friend and I kept saying to each other, "Which one do I want?"

"I'll take that one," my friend said.

"I'll take that one," I replied. Little did I know that I was selecting my future wife.

After the presentations, I followed Norma and saw that she was with her parents and didn't seem to have a boyfriend hanging around. So I asked her to dance and then talked with her and got to meet her parents. After that evening, we started to date. This meant going to the movies or to the parks. Since I had my car, I would pick her up.

Norma lived in the Santa Monica–Venice area where there had been a long-standing Mexican barrio. Her mother ran a restaurant there, and her father operated a gas station. Norma helped out in the restaurant. After about a year and a half, we decided to get married. Everyone thought it was a good idea, including her family and mine. For some reason her family liked me, although they were very traditional—much more so than my parents. They also saw themselves as more *mexicanos* and were more middle class. I had some reservations, but the families seemed so encouraging that I put aside my questions and went ahead with the marriage.

We had a big Catholic wedding in Santa Monica, with a big reception at the church hall.

We moved in with my parents for about a year until we rented an apartment in the same neighborhood. Norma worked at a hair salon and in her mother's restaurant. We went out with mostly my Latino friends. After about a year our daughter, Marcella Adriana, was born.

But despite our child, our marriage didn't work. Her parents expected that I would work in their businesses, but I wasn't interested. I was just starting to go to Cal State, L.A., and wanted to concentrate on my studies. My marriage also didn't work because we were just too young. Norma was a hardworking and a wonderful, beautiful lady, but neither one of us was ready for marriage. I knew that I wasn't. Both of us became very unhappy. About a year after Marcy, our daughter, was born, we divorced. Norma's parents arranged this in Tijuana, where they had legal connections. I don't think I even had to go there. Norma received custody of Marcy, but I visited her every weekend, and we've always had a close relationship. Norma later remarried but divorced again. I never remarried.

CAL STATE, L.A.

A year or so before I got married, I decided to go to college. I quit my job as a draftsman, which I hated anyway. But I kept my post office job.

I had never been encouraged to go to college. My parents didn't encourage me because they knew nothing about college. Fernando was taking some classes at L.A. City College, so that was probably some influence. Certainly the nuns at St. Agnes had never suggested or promoted college for me.

I chose to enroll at Cal State, L.A., because it was relatively close to where I lived. It was in East L.A. but not too far from South Central. It also was cheap, which was important to me.

I didn't have any sense of how one went about enrolling. I went to the Admissions Office, and they gave me a catalog and paperwork to fill out. There were no minority recruitment programs at that time. This was 1961, several years before the Chicano movement. There were no friendly faces to be seen.

I filled out the papers and submitted my application. I also had to take an admissions exam that was scheduled two weeks after classes commenced. But I wanted no part of such an exam. It intimidated me. So I didn't take it.

Since I had been notified that I could enroll in classes that fall, I did so even without the entrance exam. No one ever said anything to me about it. However, a few years later, as I prepared to graduate, it was called to my attention that I had never taken the exam. I was pretty arrogant by then and told them what they could do with it. But I couldn't graduate without it, so I finally relented and took it— ironically not to enter college but to graduate from it! To my surprise, I passed the damn thing!

I had decided to major in engineering. I had no idea what it meant to become an engineer. This proved to be a disaster. I had to take a number of math and science courses, and I flunked all of them. I remember taking a prealgebra class. The first day the professor wrote down all these formulas on the blackboard. *Pero ni papa*—I didn't understand any of it. So I got up and left and never went back. It was like this with the other courses. I was miserable. It was torture.

By the end of my first semester I was put on probation. They almost threw me out. I had no one to help me, and I was too shy to ask for help if I even knew where to get it. I had no one to say to me, "Raul, you need to take other classes where you can do better." Things like this we tell our students today.

I struggled through my first two years. I got bad grades, and I was under a lot of stress. All of this didn't help me with my marriage and undoubtedly contributed to its failure. So I was failing in college and in my personal life.

By the end of these two years, I knew one thing: I wasn't cut out to be an engineer. This wasn't for me. So I dropped that as a major. Fortunately, I also knew that I preferred literature and history. I changed to English as my major.

This didn't prove to be a bed of roses either. My background in English wasn't that much stronger than in math and science. I hadn't read too many books, and now I found myself with other English majors who had read so much more. Not only had I not read as much but also my writing was not very good.

I remember writing one of my first essays in an English class and the professor writing the comment, "You have a good mind, but you're basically illiterate." I thought about this and even went to talk to him. I said, "I don't understand your comment. You're saying that I'm smart but also that I'm actually stupid!"

"No, no, Raul," he replied. "It's just that you seem to be able to think well, but it's not reflected in your writing."

I agreed with him. I thought my writing was atrocious. But there was no way to get any help. There were no remedial classes as there are today. So I decided to just work on my own to improve my writing. I went to the library after my classes and wrote. I would write about anything that came into my mind but tried to write coherent sentences. I would then expand a sentence into a paragraph. Then I would try to connect these paragraphs together. I would do this for hours. Since I didn't have any friends at Cal State, L.A., I had plenty of time to do this in the library.

I also started to read a lot more. I would read not only the assigned readings for my classes but as much as I could outside of these assignments. If we were assigned to read a particular author in my English class, I would go to the library and select other books on this author by critics who would analyze his or her writings.

Through this process, little by little, my writing improved, as well as my ability to perform better in my classes.

During my junior year, I also started taking courses in history. This proved to be an inspiring experience for me. This was really the influence of one professor, Tim Harding. He was a professor of Latin American history, and I had never encountered a teacher like him.

Tim was the strangest guy I had ever met. I had always thought of professors as arrogant and distant. Tim was not arrogant, but he was somewhat distant, shy actually. He was a funny-looking guy with a scraggly beard and balding head and old-fashioned wire-rimmed glasses. Yet he was supportive of all his students. Tim introduced me to ideas that I had never heard anybody talk about. He was a socialist. I would sit in his class and think, "This guy is crazy, because nobody lectures this way."

Tim was also strange to me because I later learned that he was an accomplished musician in a mariachi band that he had organized. He knew all kinds of things about Latin American music, and he played it.

You would look at Tim and never think that he possessed a certain *espíritu de alma latina*—a certain Latin spirit. Yet he did.

I took several courses from Tim, including the history of Mexico. These were classes that intrigued me and that for the first time I had a real interest in. They seemed to speak to me in different ways about myself. What I learned to appreciate from Tim was how he presented history from the bottom up—about the poor and the oppressed. He opened our eyes to the realities of Latin America.

One of Tim's contributions was to get us to understand class conflict through a class analysis of Latin America. He got us to question why there were so many poor people in Latin America. Why the peasants were so bad off. Why there was so much economic crisis in Latin America.

I had never had anybody talk about history in this way. Tim's lectures were never bombastic or propagandistic, but he presented the conditions as they were and got us to think about why these conditions existed. He made us think. Who benefited from poverty? Why was there such a gap between rich and poor? Was this just the way life was? Was this the result of capitalism and imperialism?

I began to apply some of this analysis to my own life. Before this I used to accept things as they were. You work and work and never make much money, like my dad. But now I began to realize that maybe there were other circumstances that occur in society that hold back many people, that screw people, and that abuse them.

I also learned from Tim about the role the United States had played in Latin America that had contributed to these conditions. I began to see the United States as an intervener in Latin America, but one always on the side of the rich and the powerful and never on the side of the poor and oppressed.

Tim talked a lot about Cuba and the success of Fidel Castro and Che Guevara and the Cuban Revolution of 1959. The revolution was still a hot topic in Latin American studies at that time of the early 1960s. I became very interested in the Cuban Revolution and, in fact, would later—in 1968—travel to Cuba.

I learned much about Latin America, not only from Tim but also from the other Latin Americanists on campus, such as Don Bray. They were equally as effective as Tim.

As I took more classes with Tim and as he got to know me better, he would on several occasions ask, "Raul, what do you know about your Chicano past?"

"Not very much," I replied, "except what I know about my family. I've never read anything about Chicanos. I don't even use the word *Chicano,* even though I've heard it many times."

"Here, I want you to read this book by Carey McWilliams, *North from Mexico,* and let me know what you think about it."[2]

I loved the book. I couldn't stop reading it. I thought it was fascinating, and to this day I think of it as one of the best books written about Chicanos, and McWilliams wasn't even Chicano! I began to try to find more to read about Chicanos, only to discover that there was very little. I also began to ask more questions of my dad and mother about their experiences. All of this began to fill in some gaps.

Reading McWilliams and studying Latin American history developed within me a process of self-examination and self-awareness. Certainly taking Tim's classes awakened within me a certain political consciousness.

It wasn't that I was totally unaware but that my thoughts had not been very political. Up to this time, I was never very much, if at all, interested in politics. The election of John Kennedy in 1960, while it seemed to have excited many Mexican Americans, didn't affect me at all. I felt the same way about the civil rights movement headed by Martin Luther King. I couldn't relate to it.

Up to the time I started learning from Tim, I think I was more of an existentialist. I knew the term because I had read Sartre and Camus in some of my literature classes. I felt that what was going on in society was not all that important. What was important was our inner personal development. I wasn't interested in whether people liked me or not depending on my skin color. What was most important was to understand ourselves as human beings. But I never connected this to society or culture. I didn't think that this made me into some kind of reactionary but that such thought was sensitive and open. What Tim taught me was to connect human relationships to material realities. He made me understand that men and women—not only by knowing themselves but also by reacting to their social conditions—make history.

As my thinking began to change under Tim's influence and my study of Latin American history, I read another book that was very influential for me. This was Frantz Fanon's *The Wretched of the Earth*.[3] I thought his critique of colonialism and the effect it had on third world people, especially on their consciousness, seemed very applicable not only to Latin Americans but to Chicanos as well. This was the notion of the colonized mentality and how it affected the way we see ourselves and the world.

As part of these changes I was undergoing, I also began to pay more attention to the Spanish language. I had been raised speaking Spanish, but the more schooling I had, the more I lost my ability to speak Spanish—to the point that when I enrolled at Cal State, I was by no means bilingual. I had trouble making myself understood in the language of my parents.

I decided to change this, and I enrolled in several Spanish classes, where I met some other later Chicano activists such as Porfirio Sánchez and Alfredo Morales. Little by little my Spanish improved.

All of this began to affect my view of myself. I began to become more conscious of history, culture, and identity. It wasn't that I didn't know that I was Mexican or Chicano. I knew that. I came from El Paso and lived in L.A.—two very Mexican cities. I wasn't ashamed of who I was. As a result, I was never one who later during the Chicano movement became a super Chicano. The changes that I was undergoing at Cal State had more to do with my becoming politically aware. I was beginning to see the relevance of history and politics to my own reality. I had always seen myself as a loner, but now I was understanding the importance of being part of a group.

The problem was, what group? During my undergraduate years, there were political groups on campus. There were the few black students who demonstrated and participated in civil rights activities. There was a chapter of Students for a Democratic Society that involved radical white students demonstrating against U.S. military intervention in Vietnam.[4] But there weren't many other Chicanos on campus, much less Chicano political activities, up to 1966 when I graduated.

However, after I began to take graduate courses in history into the 1966–67 year, some Chicano activities developed. There was a group of students around Professor Ralph Guzmán, one of the very few Chicano professors. Guzmán was a professor of political science who had just started to teach at Cal State. Some of these students, such as Carlos Muñoz, Félix Gutiérrez, and Phil Castruitta, would become quite active in the Chicano movement. In 1967 these students, as well as

other Chicanos who were now being specifically recruited due to the early affirmative action programs, organized the first Chicano student group on campus: the
United Mexican American Students (UMAS). I began to meet these students and
to attend some of the early meetings. At that time, they discussed mostly how to
recruit more Chicano students, planning conferences and activities around Cinco
de Mayo. A good number of students attended the meetings. In fact, I saw more
Mexican American students there than I did on a day-to-day basis on campus.
Unfortunately or fortunately, I didn't really click with the UMAS crowd. I thought
they were a bit too arrogant and even anti-Anglo, especially toward a friend of
mine, Bob Ray, who had a confrontation with them and then, at my urging, tried
to reconcile it, but they ran him off. I couldn't work with people like this. Besides,
I was beginning to become more interested in doing something in the community
and not on campus.[5]

By 1967 I was now becoming Chicano in a political sense.

INSIDE EASTSIDE

As I became more politically conscious, I began to become involved in what were
the early stirrings of the Chicano movement in Los Angeles. Although I was still
taking classes at Cal State, I was more interested in activities in the community.
Bob Ray, who was a member of Students for a Democratic Society, told me that
there was going to be a meeting in the community to put together a newspaper, a
Chicano paper. This intrigued me, and I agreed to go with him to the meeting.
What intrigued me was putting out a newspaper written by and for Chicanos.

There were a few other Chicanos there, including Victor Franco, who became the
editor. The idea was to publish a Chicano community newspaper that would resemble the *Los Angeles Free Press,* one of the most important so-called underground
newspapers of the 1960s. The *Free Press* was a leftist and muckraking paper that
exposed and critiqued many of the social problems facing working people, students,
and minorities in California. It also was vehemently opposed to the Vietnam War.

We knew that we didn't have the resources to cover the entire Chicano community, especially of East L.A., so we decided that our focus would be the high
schools. We would publish an independent paper for the students of East Los
Angeles.

But none of us knew anything about publishing a paper. So we looked around
for help. Fortunately, there already was a Chicano community newspaper being
published. It was called *La Raza.* A couple of issues had been published. It was
being put out in the Lincoln Heights area of the Eastside out of the basement of the
Church of the Epiphany. This was an Episcopalian church whose pastor was Father
John Luce. A member of the prominent Luce family from New England, a proper
Boston Brahman family, Father Luce is an unsung hero of the Chicano movement.

Although not a Chicano, he supported Chicano issues and allowed his church to be used as an organizing center for some of the early activities, including the publication of *La Raza*.

I remember Victor Franco and I going over to the church to meet with the editors of *La Raza*. The key figure was a guy by the name of Eliezer Risco. He was a strange figure. He was not Chicano but of a Cuban American background. He had come to California from somewhere in the East and got involved with the farmworkers. I remember asking, "Who the fuck is this guy?" and being told by someone that he was some kind of Cuban commie. His key lieutenant was an Anglo woman, Ruth Gibson. They were a duo. Besides letting them use the basement of the church, Father Luce also secured for them a grant from the Interfaith Council to put out the paper. They bought typewriters and a typesetter. It wasn't such a big operation. They could publish an issue for about $150.

Our initial encounter with Risco was not a very good one.

"Why should we help you guys?" he, in an arrogant way, responded when we told him we were thinking of putting out a paper but needed help in starting. "No one helped us."

"You should help us because we're Chicanos!" I fired back. "And we're trying to do this for the community."

Risco just laughed at me. I left that meeting really disliking him. I took his rejection as a challenge. I told Victor, "Let's go out and publish a paper that will beat anything that these people can do." So we did.

This was the beginning of *Inside Eastside*. We worked out of our homes and out of Victor's garage, where we laid out the paper, although we had to have it published at a printer.

With no experience, a few of us organized ourselves into an editorial group. Each member was assigned a beat or a particular section of East L.A. and was responsible for covering the high school in that area. I got Lincoln Heights; that meant Lincoln High School. Others got schools in other districts such as Roosevelt, Garfield, and Wilson. Besides getting information on what was going on in the schools and the particular problems faced by Chicanos, each of us was also responsible for sales distribution in our areas.

This organization worked. After we put out our initial issue, for example, I would go to Lincoln High School and stand outside the main entrance and hustle the kids for a dime for the paper. Although some kids made fun of the paper or rejected it, a number began to buy it. I learned an important early political lesson. If you're patient enough, you in time will reach some people. Some kids would tell me that they had read the paper and really liked it. They had never read anything about Chicanos.

What many of them liked was our criticism of drugs and gangs at the school but also our sections on music and student activities. Some of the kids began to come around and to volunteer to sell and distribute the paper, including doing so inside the school. I soon had a core group of about twenty to thirty students to help sell the paper both in the school and in the community. After a while, I didn't have to do very much myself. We were beginning to distribute hundreds of copies of *Inside Eastside* throughout the barrio.

We also began to meet with some of the kids in their homes. These would be group meetings where the students would inform me about what was happening inside Lincoln High School. We would meet at different homes, and the parents were always supportive. Some of the issues troubling the students included racism at the school that they felt was particularly illustrated by the tracking system that pushed most Chicanos into the inferior academic classes and the noncollege track. They were also beginning to be concerned about the Vietnam War, as mass protests were being organized around the country.

Besides the students, one of the most significant sources of information about the high school came from a courageous and outspoken teacher by the name of Sal Castro. I had never met a teacher such as Sal. He had been teaching for a few years and had seen the problems firsthand at Lincoln and at other schools. Sal was very close to the students and was one of the few Chicano teachers in the Eastside schools. That was another bone of contention among the students: the lack of Chicano teachers and role models.[6]

As we began to put out *Inside Eastside*, I found myself going back to the Church of the Epiphany and to *La Raza*. I hadn't had a good initial impression of Risco, but I did come to understand that the church was a center of initial movement activities and that I as well as others from *Inside Eastside* needed to plug into it.

Besides housing *La Raza*, Father Luce opened up the church to other Chicano groups such as the Brown Berets, a paramilitary collection of barrio youth patterned after the Black Panther Party and focused, at least initially, on monitoring police abuse. This is when I first met David Sánchez, the founder and prime minister of the Berets.[7]

There would always be rap sessions at the church, many until the wee hours of the morning. We could show up at two in the morning and there would be something going on. They would talk about what was going on in the community, in the schools, among the farmworkers, about the Vietnam War, about gangs and drugs.

I wasn't ready to speak, but I was impressed with others who did, including Risco. He was very bright and seemed to have good political instincts. I also learned a little more about him. What particularly impressed me about Risco was how he had a way of looking at things that sort of turned everything on its head and made us think. I remember one time interviewing the vice principal at Lincoln for two hours and then later telling Risco about this great interview that I was going to write up for *Inside Eastside*.

"This is bullshit," Risco told me in no uncertain terms. "Don't you see that this guy is doing a sell job on you? He wants to use you and the paper to push his side of the story. He wants you to write what he wants. He's brainwashing you!"

Although this first put me on the defensive, it did make me think. Risco was right.

Soon many new people began to spend time at the church. The meetings or rap sessions were open, but you needed to know someone already attending. Some were students, both undergraduates and graduates, at UCLA, which was beginning to recruit Chicano students for the first time. This is when I first met people such as Juan Gómez-Quiñones and Moctesuma Esparza. Occasionally, some of the older community leaders came by, such as Bert Corona.

Another very interesting and important person was Joe Razo. He was a grad student at Cal State, L.A. He was from Los Angeles. Joe knew everyone. After meeting me, he kind of took me under his wing, even though he was just a bit older than me. But unlike me, Joe was experienced, and he was a tough guy. He was super honest. He was married and was *muy serio*—very serious. Joe became a mentor to me. To this day, I admire him.

Those who began to congregate at the church beginning in 1967 were interested in things that were going on in the community and looking to see how they might get involved. At first there was no guiding ideology or dogma, despite what the police would later say. No one was preaching a political line, such as a Marxist one. At best, people were pushing a civil rights agenda: stop police abuse, reform the schools, work on discrimination issues, and so on. Some ideologues were around but not many, and they didn't stay too long.

Those gatherings for me were highly stimulating and informative. I wasn't exposed to this type of community at Cal State. I lacked a base in college where I could meet people and exchange information and views. These were not exercises about abstract theories but instead about real issues that concerned real people. This is what inspired me as I began to write as a journalist for *Inside Eastside*. I had to write in such a way for students to understand.

I especially grew to like meeting and in time working with the different people at the Church of the Epiphany. I was more comfortable in this community setting. I was less comfortable with the developing Chicano student organizations that were more cliquish and exclusive. I was never part of the student movement.

Instead, I was more attracted to community-based groups such as the Brown Berets, although I was never a member of the Berets. Besides David Sánchez, the so-called prime minister of the Berets, I got to know other members such as Carlos Montes and Ralph Ramírez. Those guys had first organized what they called the Young Citizens for Community Action, which evolved into the Young Chicanos for Community Action, which in turn began to be popularly referred to as the Brown Berets. They became one of the most militant Chicano movement groups.[8]

The idea for using the brown beret actually came from Father Luce. David and the other organizers wanted to distinguish themselves by wearing certain jackets with the logo of the Berets, but Father Luce felt that this gave them too much the appearance of a gang. So he came up with the idea of a beret—a brown beret—which David and the others embraced.

The Berets first surfaced in 1967 around a particular horrendous incident in East L.A. involving police abuse by the county sheriffs.[9] Sheriff's deputies attacked and beat up a family—the Santoyo family—in their home without provocation. I remember that I and Joe Razo, along with some other guys associated with the church, became involved in helping the family. This in fact was one of my first involvements with a community action. I also covered the issue for *Inside Eastside*.

I remember that I suggested a picket—a picket of the sheriff's headquarters in East L.A. No one had ever done such a thing. At the picket, the Berets showed up to help. It was covered by one of the local television stations. The reporter and his cameraman quickly focused on the Berets and wanted to interview David. Afterward, the reporter turned to me and asked, "What are you doing here? What's this protest all about?"

I had never been interviewed before, much less by a TV reporter, and all I could utter was, "Well, well, well . . . I'm just here," or something to that effect. I was completely tongue-tied and embarrassed. I vowed then and there to work on my public-speaking skills.

Sometime also in 1967, the Berets opened up their own headquarters. Actually, it wasn't a headquarters at all. It was a coffeehouse—La Piranya at Olympic and Atlantic on the Eastside. They apparently received some funding from Father Luce to rent the storefront. Coffeehouses had been popular in the early sixties in the countercultural movements such as the beatniks.

La Piranya became another space to hold political rap sessions. Many of the same people who congregated at the Church of the Epiphany began to go over to La Piranya. It also hosted emerging leaders such as César Chávez and Rodolfo "Corky" Gonzales.

I began to go to La Piranya. Some of the high school kids that I was working with also started coming by. Here they discussed some of the problems in the schools, and it was clear that the tensions were coming to some kind of a boil. The Chicano college students likewise became part of La Piranya scene.

My days and weeks by now were becoming quite hectic. In addition to working with *Inside Eastside* and attending rap sessions, I was also still enrolled at Cal State, now working on my MA in history. Actually, it turned out to be a double MA because to get some college financial assistance I applied for an MA program in education. I received the funding but then had to also do a graduate program in education as well as the one in history.

In all, the year 1967 was an important juncture, not only in my life but also in the beginning of the Chicano movement in Los Angeles. In addition to the stirrings of the students on campuses and in the high schools, there were also certain community movements. These were centered on issues such as the police, the schools, and politics. Alicia Escalante had started an important welfare-rights group especially for women in the barrio. There were new associations forming as well as new life appearing in some of the older ones, such as the Community Service Organization, which had been formed back in the late 1940s by more established leaders such as Edward Roybal, who was in the U.S. Congress representing parts of East Los Angeles.

What was happening was the commencement of the Chicano movement in Los Angeles. The movement in other places of the Southwest, where most Chicanos lived, was also stirring. Much of this was being influenced by the inspirational struggle of César Chávez and the farmworkers in California, who had inaugurated their campaign to organize a union for farmworkers in 1962. Stressing the human dignity and rights of those who tilled the soil, predominantly Mexicans and Filipinos, and effectively utilizing ethnic and religious symbols such as the image of the Virgen de Guadalupe, Chávez and the farmworkers had captured the imaginations of urban Chicanos and inspired them to take up their own struggles in the cities. This was beginning to manifest itself in L.A. in 1967.[10]

While the farmworkers' struggle, as well as the black civil rights struggle, served as inspirations and to some extent models for us, in other ways those of us involved in the initial building of the movement in L.A. felt that what we were doing was something new. We didn't know or have a sense of a history of struggle before us. Some of the older groups, such as the Community Service Organization and the Mexican American Political Association, did have this sense, but those of us from the younger generation didn't.[11]

I think too that we felt that the older organizations were too focused on membership, which gave these groups certain exclusiveness. By contrast, the Chicano movement began with no concept of membership. You weren't a member of the movement; you were an activist in it. Our stress was on building not an organization but a community-wide social movement.

The movement was initially also not based on ideology. At our meetings at the Church of the Epiphany or at La Piranya, there was no discussion of history, of ideology, or of political theories. We talked about community issues, period. In time the movement developed an ideology that came to be known as chicanismo, or cultural nationalism, but not in the beginning.[12] We were issue-oriented, and if anything was influencing us, it was a sense of pragmatism. Consciousness and ideology would be built on action rather than ideology creating action.

The issue of terminology—what we called ourselves—likewise was not a big issue. Most of us had first developed an awareness of ourselves as Mexican Americans.

However, the more we got involved, the more we began to refer to ourselves as "Chicanos." We began to use the term as a sense of pride and affirmation. I think I was the first to use the term *Chicano* politically in a movement newspaper. This was a paper that I founded after I left *Inside Eastside*. It was called the *Chicano Student Movement*.

BLOWOUTS

Sometime into 1968 I began to get alienated from *Inside Eastside*. This had to do with criticism of my work from Victor Franco and others. We, along with *La Raza* group, were already facing certain pressures from the police, who felt that we were agitators among the high school and junior high school students. They didn't like us distributing our papers inside the schools. The result of this pressure is that Victor and a few others believed that *Inside Eastside* had to moderate its positions and to behave like a "real newspaper."

I disagreed and argued that the whole purpose of having founded *Inside Eastside* was to be a community paper, a barrio paper, and an alternative paper—a people's paper—that was on the side of the people and, in this case, the students. I felt that we had to continue to publicize the problems inside the schools, as well as the issue of police brutality. I began to realize that I couldn't continue to do this with *Inside Eastside*.

So I left. I and a few others who agreed with me and who also left decided to publish our own newspaper—a tabloid. We first called it *Chicano Student* and then *Chicano Student Movement (CSM)*. We were able to maintain many of our student contacts inside the schools who provided us with information and who helped to distribute the paper. I went back to Risco and *La Raza* and they gave us space, first inside the Church of the Epiphany to work on *CSM*. Then when Risco, with Father Luce's assistance, moved into larger quarters by renting a three-story building on Broadway, *CSM* also moved there into our own room.

The conditions in the schools were coming to a breaking point. This included the long history of discrimination against Chicano students; insensitive teachers, administrators, and counselors; high dropout rates; low reading scores; vocational tracking systems; and many more problems. For several months a number of us had been meeting with many of the high school and junior high school students. At the church and at La Piranya sometimes we had more than a hundred students at these meetings.

The students wanted action. They were ready to take action. Responding to this, those of us in the community, as college students, the UMAS groups, the people at *La Raza*, those of us in *CSM*, the Brown Berets, and others began to talk and develop a plan of action. We began to concentrate on a walkout. Here we were influenced by what was happening on many college campuses, where students were protesting about civil rights and changes in university life and especially demonstrating against the Vietnam War. The kids in the schools immediately embraced the idea. They were ready to implement it. As early as January 1968, they were ready to walk out. That month in my column in *Inside Eastside* (one of my last for this paper), where I used my pen name, Lázaro Q., I wrote a piece titled "Picket, Brothers, Picket," in which I wrote, "The ideas of walkouts, boycotts, and pickets are not against the law. You have the right under the first amendment of the constitution to assemble and petition for the redress of grievances."[13]

But we had to restrain them at first. We felt that we had to organize as many students as possible in as many schools as possible. One way of organizing the walkout was to continue to publicize the conditions in the schools and the student complaints through *CSM* and *La Raza*. Part of this strategy was to attack the administrations of these schools for being opposed to changes. I remember interviewing the vice principal at Lincoln High School for a story on conditions in the school. He was aware of our criticisms, but he agreed to talk with me. In fact, he sat for a couple of hours with me as I asked a variety of questions. None of his responses were satisfactory. So I wrote a scathing attack on him and on the school. The next time I ran into him during the walkouts, he said to me, "Wow, Raul, I thought you were going to be more objective. I gave you my time, and all you did was blast me."

I didn't feel at all guilty. That was my role—to blast him! We saw ourselves not just as journalists but also as activists. Our role was in fact not to be objective.

As part of our organizing strategy we also printed large numbers of leaflets about the conditions in the school. We distributed them outside of the schools and got our student supporters to smuggle them into the campuses. We stuck leaflets into the fences surrounding the schools. Sometimes we literally broke into the grounds at night and posted leaflets throughout the halls.

The administration tried to prevent this type of information from reaching the kids, but they couldn't. Students would walk into classes with leaflets in their books and distribute them everywhere. They would leave them in the restrooms and the cafeteria. This was a very well organized and subversive activity, and it went on for a couple of months into 1968.

We were focused on the schools, but in a way some of us also understood that the proposed walkouts would be a kind of coming out for the Chicano movement in Los Angeles. Our time had come. We had all been influenced and inspired by César Chávez and the farmworkers' struggle. We looked up to César. We were aware of the student and youth protests in the country and in Mexico. But this was going to be our thing here in L.A.! It wasn't just the school issue; it was also police abuse, the poverty, the lack of political power—all these things motivated us. The walkouts would be only the beginning.

While we helped to plan the walkouts, they would not have happened without the critical role that Sal Castro played. Sal was one of the very few Chicano teachers in the Eastside schools. He taught at Lincoln High School. He was a native of

L.A. and had been teaching in the public schools for several years. His role in the walkouts cannot be underestimated. Sal supported the students and was so discouraged about the ability of the school system to reform itself that he became convinced that drastic external action was needed. It was mostly his idea for the students to walk out. He met with us often, and he supported our activities.

Sal's involvement was critical because the students knew him and respected him. He was a leader and a role model. He possessed a great and charismatic personality. He was intelligent, smart, articulate, and good-looking. He was still in his late twenties or early thirties at the time. The boys looked up to him, and the girls were all in love with him. Sal was the first teacher I ever met who was candid and said exactly what he thought. His leadership and support for the kids were indispensable.

Over several weeks we, along with some of the student leaders and with Sal, plotted our strategy. We began to focus on the walkouts taking place sometime during the spring. We decided that we would first concentrate on Lincoln, which was one of the largest high schools. If we could get the Lincoln students to go out, the other schools would follow. However, this was not to be a spontaneous action. Besides our student contacts and leaders at Lincoln, we also had similar connections with the other schools in the Eastside.

In the meantime, we helped the students draft a list of complaints about school conditions that would be presented to the school administration. Sometime in February, these grievances and a list of demands were presented, but they were quickly rejected. With this rejection, we now also had another key issue around which to rally the students and the community.

In planning the walkouts, we, of course, had to take into consideration the reaction of the police. We already had been having some confrontations with both the Los Angeles Police Department (LAPD) and the county sheriffs. The police also harassed some of us, in particular, the Berets. We knew that it was likely that the walkouts would trigger conflict with the cops. This, however, did not deter us. We refused to be intimidated. Our concern was with protecting the students, and so we planned that those of us as community adults, as college students, and with the Berets, would form a defense shield around the students when they walked out so that if the police attacked, they would confront us and not the students. This was our plan, but we really had no idea if it would work.

By the end of February, we believed that we had everything in place. Working with our informal coalition, we planned the initial walkout to take place at Lincoln sometime in March perhaps, although we had no set timetable.

The students themselves, as it turned out, set the timing. Without our knowledge, the kids at Wilson High School decided to walk out spontaneously on Friday, March 1. In fact, it wasn't even the high school students who led the protest. It was the junior high school students. Some of those who had been working with us all of a sudden called us: "We're walking out!"

"Fuck it," I said to one of them. "You can't do this. Lincoln is supposed to be first."

"We're out, Raul. Five hundred students have already left classes."

There was nothing we could do now. What had happened at Wilson was that some of the kids were performing in a school production of *Barefoot in the Park*. But because of certain language in the script, the administration decided to cancel the production. This upset some of the students, who started throwing trash, yelling, and running through the school halls both in the junior high and the senior high, encouraging others to walk out in protest. Many responded. They literally had to break out of the school because the gates were locked. The police showed up, but there was no confrontation and the kids just went home. It was mostly the junior high school students and the younger kids in the senior high who walked out. The seniors were much less willing since they would be graduating that spring and didn't want to jeopardize their standing. They were more interested in their graduation and their prom. The real leaders were the crazy younger ones.

Once the Wilson students walked out, we now had no choice. The other schools would have to follow the next week. The walkouts, or what came to be called the blowouts, were on.[14]

We used the weekend to get everything ready. We, along with the students, had a phone bank, and we called as many students as possible to alert them to the walkouts. We also mobilized our UMAS students and the Berets, as well as a few community people. What we didn't do very well was to work with the parents and some of the older, more established community leaders and organizations. We were too brash to do that. We also used the weekend to write up signs to be used during the protests. While Wilson had been spontaneous, the rest of the walkouts would be well planned and well organized.

The following Tuesday, two thousand students walked out of Garfield High, followed the next day by Lincoln and Roosevelt. Lincoln, as we had planned it, was the biggest demonstration. The student leaders were instructed to begin the walkout at eight thirty in the morning.[15] At first they thought they just wouldn't go to school and start the walkout that way.

"No," we said, "you have to go into the school, to your first period classes, and then walk out. This will be more effective."

So they went to their classes. Outside, about a hundred of us milled around waiting for the action. There was also activity among the administrators and teachers who suspected that something was in the works. There were likewise some cops driving around.

Eight-thirty came, and the students hadn't come out. "Oh, my god," I said to myself. "It isn't going to happen." So some of us decided to take action and go into the school itself. Joe Razo, myself, Mangos Colorado, a huge big guy with no shirt on, and a few others ran into the building before the school guards who had been posted at the main entrance could stop us.

With the guards giving chase, we broke into the main hallway and started yelling to the kids to walk out. "Walkout, walkout," we called out. I remember one of the administrators, a Mexican American woman, running out of her office and upon seeing me, saying, "You, there, you're not a high school student!"

"Yeah, right," I shot back as I sped by her yelling, "Walkout, walkout!"

The kids started coming out. At first a trickle and then a rush of students. They also started to call, "Walkout, walkout!" However, some began to yell "Blowout, blowout!" I don't know where they got this term, but it stuck. I think that they wanted an even more dynamic term. More students started to cry, "Blowout, blowout!" The blowouts were now fully under way.[16]

Besides the students, Sal Castro, who himself was active in getting the kids to leave the building, and one other teacher walked out with the students. This other teacher was an Anglo by the name of Gordon. We called him "Flash Gordon."

In a few minutes about 1,700 students had walked out, almost the entire student body of about 2,000.

The next day Garfield once again walked out, as did Belmont High in the downtown area. On Friday of this historic week, Lincoln, Roosevelt, and Garfield walked out. About 5,000 kids were involved that day. Contingents of our group met the students as they exited and gave them protest signs. We then escorted them to nearby Hazard Park, where we organized a rally. A number of the students spoke, as well as some from our group. One speaker was Congressman Edward Roybal, who represented parts of East L.A. and was the only Mexican American representative from California. I didn't speak at the rally. It was a huge success and was conducted peacefully.

The walkouts at Lincoln and the other schools were without police incidents. The only exception was at Roosevelt on Wednesday. To assist the kids in walking out, we first had to contend with the fact that the school officials locked the gate entrances after the students entered the building. So that previous night, some of our guys broke the locks, which meant that the following morning all the kids had to do was to push the gates open, and they could leave the school. As it turned out, many of them also just scaled the fences to leave.

The problem at Roosevelt was not getting the students to come out but the presence of the police. Just down the street from the school, there was a police substation, so the cops were close by. I also think that once the walkout had commenced, school officials and the police were determined to prevent additional demonstrations by clamping down on Roosevelt. As soon as the kids came out, there were officers all over the place. They surrounded the school. We found it difficult to protect the kids because the officers were just milling around the grounds, making them easy targets for the cops.

We could feel the tension. I knew that something was going to happen. And sure enough, it did. Some of the students started throwing eggs at the squad cars. The officers immediately got out and gave chase to the kids. Other squad cars also followed.

I was just outside the school with my camera taking pictures. I had started using a camera with *CSM*. I found myself next to a girl who was visibly pregnant. Before I knew it, a bevy of cops descended on us, hitting everyone with their batons. I saw the girl fall down, and some cops jumped on top of her. I remember shouting to the police, "Why are you doing that? The girl is pregnant."

As I said this, the cop turned around. His face was all red, and he looked like a damn animal.

"You're not a high school student," he growled at me.

"Well, no, I'm not," I replied. "I'm a Chicano newspaper guy."

Boom, right away he arrested me and told me that I was interfering with an arrest. Before he grabbed me, I threw my camera to one of our guys so that the cop couldn't take it. He pulled my hands behind my back and escorted me to a squad car. He tried to throw me in, but the door was locked. So he just bounced me back and forth on the car door.

"Wait, why don't you just unlock the door," I said.

He finally did, and he and some other cop got into the car and drove around the street behind the nearby Safeway store.

"We're going to teach you a lesson, motherfucker, about you fucking around," one of them next to me in the backseat threatened me. They then pushed me around, although they didn't hit me in the face. They didn't hurt me very much, and after a few minutes they released me.

"If we see you again in any school," they told me, "we're going to do the same damn thing again."

This was the first time I had ever been arrested. Curiously, I wasn't scared or intimidated. In fact, I felt actually proud that I had been arrested. I guess I felt that this was a badge of honor. It showed my commitment.

Meanwhile, all around me things were getting pretty rough. Others, including students, were being beaten and arrested. Roosevelt proved to be a real battleground during the blowouts.

But the police attack at Roosevelt didn't deter the kids. That week about ten thousand students left the schools. This led to other police actions. At Belmont that Thursday, for example, I got arrested again. Like Roosevelt, Belmont was close to another police substation, the Ramparts Division of the LAPD. When the students walked out, the police were all over the place. I was there with Joe Razo and Guadalupe Saavedra, who was a poet and who always dressed in green army fatigues. He looked like a goddamn Cuban guerrilla fighter, and some people probably thought he was!

But I remember an Anglo girl who attended Belmont. As the cops were trying to prevent the students from leaving the school, she asked the police if she could borrow their bullhorn so that she could try to convince the kids to return to their classes. They agreed, but instead of doing what she said she would, she yelled into the bullhorn, "Walkout! Walkout!" She then ran away carrying the horn, with the cops chasing her.

While some of the police pursued the girl, others started arresting some of the students, as well as those of us who were there in support. Razo, Saavedra, and I were all arrested on charges of disturbing the peace, even though we were just standing on the sidewalk outside of the school. They took us down to the station, where they kept us for the rest of the day. They then released us with no charge.

Besides the Eastside schools, some of the predominantly black schools in Watts and other locations walked out in support, including a few Westside schools where mostly Anglos attended. The blowouts were not all in one week but over a two-week period. At some schools, such as Lincoln, the blowouts lasted only two or three days. At others, such as at Garfield, the students stayed out for almost two weeks.

The blowouts were a success way beyond our imagination. Although not covered very much by the media, or as much as we would have liked, still the actions sent an unexpected but strong message to the school administrators, the school board, and the city of Los Angeles.

In addition, the blowouts helped to create a new generation of student leaders at the high school level, many of whom would go on to become movement activists. This included kids such as Harry Gamboa, Patsi Valdez, and Gronk, all of whom became major movement artists. Still others were Paula Crisostomo, Mita Cuarón, and Vicki Castro, who years later would actually be elected to the school board.

And as we hoped, the blowouts likewise inaugurated the urban Chicano movement, in particular in Los Angeles. Not only would Chicanos in other urban areas throughout the Southwest emulate the blowouts by staging their own student walkouts, but also the blowouts in L.A. became the ignition that led over the next few years to many other protests associated with the Chicano movement. Los Angeles in many ways became the political capital of the *movimiento*.

Following the walkouts, we knew that to establish negotiations with the Board of Education it would be important to put together a committee composed of parents and community people who could speak for the students after they returned to their classes. For these discussions, we felt that we needed an even broader united front than we had in planning the blowouts.

Before and after the protests, we began organizing this parent and community group that we called the Educational Issues Coordinating Committee (EICC). On the surface, it appeared that the EICC was a reaction by parents who began to get

FIGURE 1. Raul Ruiz at a meeting of the Educational Issues Coordinating Committee, spring 1968. Courtesy of George Rodríguez.

involved once the blowouts started and that the EICC was separate from the movement and from more radical activists like us. But this wasn't true. We organized the EICC and for the most part controlled it, although it did mobilize many parents and community people.[17]

While we set the agenda for the EICC, we did have to share some of its leadership responsibility. I remember at one of our community meetings during the blowouts, when several hundred people attended, including many parents, that one very dynamic person got up and started speaking in perfect Spanish and English. He was a great speaker. We knew right there that we would have to share the leadership of the EICC with him.

This person was the reverend Vahac Mardirosian, a Baptist minister. He was of Mexican and Armenian descent and had been born and raised in Tijuana, I believe. However, at the time his ministry was in East L.A. In fact, Vahac was not the only Protestant minister supporting the blowouts and other subsequent actions. Several other ministers became involved, as they were in supporting César and the farmworkers—in some cases way before the Catholic Church did.

Vahac was this type of committed minister. Because of his stature as clergy and because of his speaking ability, he was elected chair of the EICC at one of our initial meetings. The people, including the parents, elected him. We initially didn't know who the hell he was. We were at first leery and suspicious of him. He was not part of our group, and, unlike us, he was of an older generation.

Yet it didn't take long for us to like him and to appreciate his leadership talents. It also didn't hurt that he agreed with our goals and strategies. Besides, we operated on consensus, and everyone agreed to the goals. We began to realize that to communicate with the parents, we needed Vahac. He spoke Spanish better than any of us could. It was hard to find people who could speak well in public. It's a hard thing to do. Most of us were inexperienced in this. If we had difficulties doing so in English, it was even worse in Spanish. I couldn't speak worth a damn in those days and especially in Spanish. So we needed someone like Vahac. He was very effective, and we came to have a good relationship with him. In retrospect, it was best to have shared the leadership with him because we came across as too radical for the community and the school board, whereas Vahac was totally reputable and had no radical baggage.

It was the EICC that filled the void after the blowouts. We began to meet with the Board of Education and assisted the students in presenting thirty-eight demands, which we helped to draw up:

Bilingual and bicultural education

New history textbooks that would accurately reflect the Mexican American experience

Smaller classes

More academic counselors

Less vocational education and more college prep classes

Teachers living in the barrios

More parental involvement in the running of the schools

New high schools to be built in East L.A.

The board readily accepted none of these issues, and most were relegated to various subcommittees. One demand that we were able to successfully force on the board was our call for amnesty for the students who had walked out. We felt that the students were exercising their First Amendment rights of free speech, protest, and freedom of assembly. The students should not be penalized for this. Despite the objections of some administrators, the board agreed with us.

At the board meetings, we usually engaged in confrontational dialogues with board members. One of our only supporters, although in a more moderate and cautious way, was Dr. Julian Nava, the only Mexican American on the board. Nava had been elected in 1967 with strong and enthusiastic Mexican American support. He had proved to be somewhat of a disappointment in advancing Mexican American issues, but on the blowouts he at least publicly sided with us in support of the students and their demands.

On the whole, I believe that the EICC was an important move forward in the Chicano movement in that it brought together the new movement activists and older community people such as the parents of the kids who walked out.

THE EAST L.A. THIRTEEN

At the same time that we organized community support through the EICC and by consistently attending board meetings, we still had to deal with the police. All the arrests that had been made during the blowouts had not led to formal charges against any of the students or anyone in our group. However, this didn't mean that the police or the district attorney were not still pursuing some indictments.

The DA went to the grand jury to seek indictments on felony charges of conspiring to cause the blowouts. This was aimed at members of our group. Several of us were subpoenaed to appear before the grand jury. It was very intimidating, but we all resolved to say nothing about the activities we had been involved with surrounding the protests. I was asked several questions, and I just responded that I didn't know or that I couldn't remember. Unlike an actual trial, you could be vague before a grand jury.

On the basis of whatever they discovered or perhaps made up, the members of the grand jury, egged on by the DA, issued an injunction for the arrest of several of our group on conspiracy charges. These felony charges carried maximum sentences equal to an armed robbery. In the first week of June, the police arrested thirteen Chicanos, including Sal Castro. Others included Carlos Muñoz, Moctesuma Esparza, David Sánchez, Carlos Montes, Eliezer Risco, and Joe Razo, in addition to six others. I was fortunate not to be one of these. I have no idea why I wasn't arrested, especially since I had been very involved with the blowouts. All the key walkout leaders at Lincoln High, for example, worked with me at *CSM*. I guess the cops had lousy intelligence. The arrested group came to be known as the East L.A. Thirteen.

The arrests were done on a Friday to prevent quick bail. The cops also broke into the offices of *La Raza* in search of individuals and material. The arrestees were kept in jail over the weekend, until the following Monday when bail could be arranged. The arrests meant that now besides continuing to work on the school issues, we had to shift gears and mount a community defense for the Thirteen.

Because Risco and some *La Raza* people were among those arrested, some of the *CSM* guys and I moved in and, using *La Raza*'s office, began to print leaflets and other materials protesting the arrests. We also organized weekend demonstrations outside of Parker Center, the main police jail in downtown Los Angeles. At one of these protests we had at least two thousand people completely surrounding the jail. We received support not just from Chicanos but also from other groups such as the Black Panther Party.

These protests and support campaigns went on for some time. After two years a judge dropped the charges. He concluded that it was not a crime to conspire to improve education. The irony, of course, was that whether legal or not, we had engaged in a goddamn conspiracy with the intent of disrupting the schools. For better or worse, we were guilty of this, and we were proud of it.

SIT-IN AT THE BOARD OF EDUCATION

The arrests led to still another related crisis. That fall, just before the start of the new school year, the school administration removed Sal Castro from his teaching position at Lincoln High School and transferred him to a nonteaching one outside of the school. They argued that they had no choice, because under their rules any teacher indicted for a crime, a felony, could not continue to teach until the legal issues were resolved.

This immediately became a hot button issue. Sal had been a key figure in the blowouts. He was one of the few teachers with the courage to support the students and to challenge the administration and the board. Of course, Sal had in fact been one of the instigators of the action. But we felt that this was a way for the school authorities to get back at Sal. We refused to accept this decision. We rallied around Sal and, through the EICC, insisted that it was wrong to remove a teacher such as Sal who helped make Chicano kids feel good about being Mexicans. One of the key issues in the blowouts had been that of having good and supportive teachers in the Eastside schools. Sal was such a teacher. We resolved to get him back one way or another.

After several protests before the board on behalf of Sal, we had had enough. After one of the September meetings at board headquarters, we were so frustrated that we just decided to have a sit-in and occupy the boardroom until Sal was reinstated. "Fuck it," we said, "we're not leaving." About fifty of us from *La Raza, CSM,* the Brown Berets, UMAS, and EICC, along with grad students from Cal State and UCLA, just stayed put and took over the Board of Education on Thursday, September 26. One of the persons who didn't sit in was Mardirosian, and I thought that was disappointing since he was the titular head of the EICC. He should have stayed, like some of us did.

The police were not called in right away, but after a day or so board officials locked the doors, preventing any additional supporters to enter. Before they did so, we received food and even a mariachi band to serenade us. Father Luce also came before the lockout and on Sunday said Mass using bits of tortillas for Communion. He was an Episcopalian, not a Catholic, but it didn't matter to us. He was one of us. After the gates to the building were closed, our supporters were still able to pass on to us through windows food such as tacos and burritos. We made ourselves as comfortable as possible. Some of us had reading material; some had guitars and played music; we all discussed our strategy.[18]

This strategy had to do with possible concessions by the school board, which informally began to make some overtures to end the sit-in. This included Julian Nava, who advised us to leave or we might be arrested. None of these possible deals involved reinstating Sal to his teaching job, and we agreed that this was the bottom line.

We staged our sit-in for five days. While we couldn't bathe, we used the bathrooms to clean ourselves as much as possible. Finally, by the fifth day, school officials told us that if we did not leave they would call in the police to forcibly remove us. We discussed this and decided that some of us should leave and some should stay and be arrested. Thirty-five of us volunteered to remain, including me.

The cops came in on the sixth day, October 2, and arrested us. Most of us spent the night in jail. We were released on bail. We were charged with trespassing, but the charges were dropped when we agreed to pay a fifty-dollar fine apiece.

More important, the sit-in at the Board of Education put more pressure on board members concerning Sal's case and helped mount even more community protests. The day following our arrests, the board voted to restore Sal to his teaching position. It was a sweet victory after a frustrating summer of arrests and of the board's avoidance of the key issues of the blowouts.

Over time, some of the demands were implemented. Others were not. The board did establish, with community input, the Mexican American Education Commission to continue the dialogue on the issues raised by the protests. The idea for the commission came from the EICC. Despite our increased militant rhetoric, most of us were pragmatists. We understood that it was not enough for us to be simply an advocate group outside the system. We needed to be also within the system to implement the demands. How do you put demands into existence? If there is no mechanism, you just continue to demand and protest with nothing else happening. We thought the commission would help bring about reforms within the schools. I think this strategy is basically correct, but it doesn't always work. In this case, it didn't.

The commission went into operation in 1969. I served on it at first and was quite vocal. But the problem was that the commission could only recommend; it could not enforce. Moreover, the board appointed those who served on it, and many became beholden to board members and hence reluctant to be critical. I think, too, that those of us who were more militant, as we became frustrated with the slowness of reform, rather than staying the course, we drifted off to other issues. The vacuum allowed more moderate and conservative voices to fill the gap and led to the release of pressure on the schools.

PERSONAL CHANGES

If the blowouts were a defining moment for the movement, they were certainly a defining moment for me personally. They represented my baptism by fire. It was a moment of conversion. I had been a listener up to that time. I had considered myself an outsider. I was not from East L.A. I had come out of El Paso and had gone to school in South Central L.A. As I became involved with *Eastside Inside* and *CSM*, I knew I had a lot to learn. I was becoming Chicano.

I was now an activist. There was no going back. My decision to get involved would have all kinds of personal repercussions. It would mean that for the next several years of my life, I would be totally immersed in various movement activities. The movement would come to represent the transforming historical event for me and for my generational cohort.

But I didn't necessarily at first see myself as a leader. Others were leaders. César Chávez was a leader. In the blowouts, Sal Castro was a leader. Eliezer Risco was a leader, as was Vahac Mardirosian. I was a journalist, an editor, a camera guy, but not a leader. At best, I was becoming a leader, and the blowouts accelerated that process. Other future events would speed this change in me even more and challenge my leadership capabilities.

My social life became the movement. My family life suffered, although not with my daughter. I always had Marcy with me, even on dates. Most of my dates by then were with women involved in the movement. But on dates, I took Marcy along. My girlfriends seemed to understand.

After my divorce, I rented an apartment in Lincoln Heights in East L.A. Although I no longer lived with my parents, I maintained a strong relationship with them. They were very socially conservative and religious but always very supportive of me. My mother never failed to bless me when I left her home. They were concerned about me but never tried to stop me in whatever movement activity I was involved in.

CUBA, 1969

A momentous experience for me that served as part of my political education came when I visited revolutionary Cuba over the Christmas season in late 1968 and early 1969. I was there to help celebrate the tenth anniversary of the Cuban Revolution, which had brought into power Fidel Castro and Che Guevara after the overthrow of the Batista dictatorship that had for many years been supported by the United States.

As part of the celebration, the Cuban government invited many representatives of the unofficial or underground press throughout the world, including the United States. As I recall, one of their contacts in this country was Elizabeth "Betita" Martínez, who was publishing a wonderful and militant newspaper in northern New Mexico called *El Grito del Norte*. It was through Betita that some of us in L.A. heard about the opportunities to go to Cuba. I was willing to go, and so I was chosen to represent the Southern California area. Other Chicano newspaper activists from other parts of the country were also selected.

I had studied Latin American history at Cal State, and I knew something about the Cuban Revolution. But what I knew came only from lectures and books. What was eye-opening to me was to see the country itself and the people.

We flew out of Mexico City on Cubana Airlines. At the airport a couple of American FBI agents came up to our group and identified themselves as federal agents and said they needed to take our photos before we left. I refused, but they still took pictures. We shined it all off as we looked forward to our trip. At the Havana airport we were greeted by our escorts, and we, or at least the men, were given free Cuban cigars.

We were allowed a lot of liberty to go where we wanted. We had certain supervised activities, but we were also given ample time to move around by ourselves. I took full advantage of this. Often by myself, I would walk around Havana with my trusty camera. I talked to people on the streets and snapped lots of pictures. I have some fantastic photos of Cuba as a result, although I have never exhibited them. Besides pictures of ordinary people, I likewise have several great shots of Fidel at some huge rally at the Plaza Martí in Havana to celebrate the anniversary.

I found Cuba to still be a poor country. But the poverty I encountered could not rival the poverty I would later see in other Latin American countries, including Mexico and El Salvador, and even in some parts of Los Angeles. Cuba didn't seem to have the alcohol and drug problems of many other areas. More important, I was impressed with how nice the Cubans were. They were extremely hospitable. I never felt that I was being manipulated or bribed. I just thought that most everyone we met, from officials to ordinary people, were all very good and decent human beings.

One of the things that also impressed me was that many of the Cubans that we talked to were aware of the Chicano movement as it was unfolding. They were curious about it and asked us many questions. Sometimes we found ourselves talking more about the movement than about Cuba.

I found a profound determination by the people to defend their revolution. They knew that this might mean war with the United States, which had already tried to overthrow the Cuban government and had imposed an economic blockade that is still in existence. But the people, at least when I first visited, accepted the consequences of supporting the revolution. I found a great deal of solidarity. They didn't seem to have the kind of cutthroat activity that would later affect the Chicano movement, to its detriment.

There was much about Cuba that I came to appreciate. The people were warm and generous. The music was incredible. You can't sit still and listen to Cuban music. You have to move and dance. And the women! Cuban women are among the most beautiful in the world.

But not all the U.S. visitors concurred. I got into an actual physical fight with this crazy Anglo guy who was there. He considered himself to be a super Marxist and took a hard line in his analysis of the Cuban situation, which he considered a failed socialist state. After we went to see the National Cuban Ballet led by the incredible Alicia Alonso, this leftist guy called the ballet an example of the continuation of the "decadent bourgeoisie." He said this in the elevator I was in, and this was the last straw! I took him on, and when the elevator door opened we rolled out on the carpet fighting.

Our Cuban hosts separated us. I was embraced for defending Cuba, and this guy was quickly sent back to Mexico and then on to the United States. I became a kind of instant celebrity. Our Cuban guides wanted to know if I needed anything in my hotel room. I was given plenty of rum and cigars. *Granma,* the major newspaper on the island, interviewed me, as did a radio station.

I'll never forget waking up on New Year's Eve and saying to myself, "What am I doing here? This guy from L.A., and I'm having this great experience here in Cuba. I'm actually spending New Year's in Havana!"

One of the highlights of the trip was meeting Fidel Castro. Our delegation met him at a big reception. I still have the official invitation in my collection. We were introduced as Chicanos "de los Estados Unidos." We met him in the reception line. I was struck by how tall he is. He looks like a walking statue. We didn't really talk to him, but he agreed to take a picture with us that I still have.

It was a wonderful and educational trip. I learned a lot about Cuba and, to some extent, about myself.

Upon returning, I wrote about my experiences in *La Raza* as well as talked about it with other movement activists. I received some criticism for this and hints that I might be a communist or that I had been brainwashed. The fact is that I have never been a part of any organized socialist or communist group. I was courted by the Communist Party, by the Socialist Workers Party, and by some of the Maoist organizations, which even wanted to send me to China for a visit.

I worked with some of these groups on later issues, such as the antiwar movement, but they never seduced me. At best, I was, and have always been, a Chicano nationalist. I didn't apologize for this, nor did I feel that it limited my political analysis. I felt that I could be a nationalist and also learn from other movements and ideologies. And I believe that I did.

As for being brainwashed, no one in Cuba told us what to say or what to write upon our return to the United States. I never felt that I was being duped or used. If anything, my Cuban visit energized me even more to continue my work in the Chicano movement.

What I took from Cuba, as I would later from trips to revolutionary Nicaragua and to El Salvador in the 1980s, was the commitment of people to issues of social justice and social change. I saw this in Cuba. They were committed to really building a new society. The common people exuded this great strength. They possessed a certain toughness and yet a personal gentleness to go along with it. Character building seemed to emanate from this dedication to cause. There was humanness in Cuba that I have not found elsewhere. I think that I became more of an idealist because of my trip.

This would not be my last trip to Cuba. I went again in 1975 and then in the 1980s. But my views on Cuba, on the revolution, and of the people have never wavered. The Cuban Revolution was an inspiration for many of us in the Chicano movement. It spoke to us in our language and from certain historical and cultural traditions that we could identify with. It was part of our time and the temper of our generation.

DENVER YOUTH CONFERENCE

A very important moment in the history of the Chicano movement was the First National Chicano Youth Liberation Conference held in Denver in March 1969. It was the first national gathering of movement activists and laid out a vision of the movement in the celebrated Plan de Aztlán. Rodolfo "Corky" Gonzales, one of the most dynamic and major leaders of the movement, hosted the conference. A few years earlier, he had organized the Crusade for Justice in Denver that spearheaded the movement in that city.

I already knew of Corky before the conference. Actually, I first came to know about him in a roundabout way. Just around the time in 1967 when I was thinking of becoming involved in community issues, I went into a Mexican restaurant in East L.A., on Brooklyn Avenue. As I was seated at a table waiting for my food, I noticed a newspaper on another chair. It was actually a tabloid, and it was one of the first issues of La Raza. I started to read it, and I was astonished to see that it was filled with news and information about Chicanos. I had never read such a paper. What especially caught my eyes was this poem titled "I Am Joaquin." No author was listed, but it was a powerful epic poem about the history of Chicanos and the search for identity. I had never read anything like this in my life. I later learned that Corky wrote it.

I also began to learn more about Corky and the Crusade for Justice. La Raza, for example, published stories about the Denver struggle against police brutality and about the school conflicts and Chicano student walkouts similar to the blowouts. Sometime in early 1969, we began to receive notices about a big conference in Denver. This was to be the Liberation Conference. Activists from all over the Southwest and from other parts were encouraged to attend. Some of us talked about going. By then I was with La Raza and had taken over from Risco as editor. Risco had a difficult personality, and others on the paper in effect pushed him out. I then merged CSM with La Raza, and it was just assumed that I would be the new editor. From the newspaper, Patricia Borjon and I decided to be part of the L.A. delegation.

I'll never forget the trip. We drove in a van with some students from Cal State, L.A., and from Sacred Heart College, a women's school in Los Angeles. We were a bit crowded, and it was a hell of a long trip. But we were young and enthused about going to the conference. This was a time when there was little internal feuding in the movement. It was all new to us, and most of us were political novices. We didn't know a lot, but our energy and confidence were infectious.

When we got to Denver, we checked in at the Crusade for Justice headquarters, where the conference was to be held. We were assigned to stay at one of Corky's chief lieutenant's home. We spent about four days there and appreciated the hospitality.

The conference was very impressive. I had never seen so many Chicanos together in such a setting. There were well over a thousand delegates. What was equally striking was that they came from different parts of the Southwest. The majority were from California, but many came from the other states, including, of course, from the host state of Colorado. All of this gave the conference a regional and, in some ways, a national scope. We could feel that we were not alone in our local struggles. We were part of a larger movement.

Part of this wider dimension was getting to meet Chicanos from these other areas. We exchanged information on what we were doing in our individual communities. We learned that many of us were using similar strategies and that we shared similar views. I was particularly pleased to meet other Chicano journalists. In fact, these encounters led to the formation of the Chicano Press Association, composed of the various Chicano newspapers springing up all over the Southwest and in other regions such as the Midwest.

Looming over all of the conference, with its different panels, workshops, and cultural presentations, was the figure of Corky Gonzales. He was the epitome of a leader—even of a godfather type. He looked and played the role. He was a tough guy, an ex-prizefighter. You would think twice about going against him. He was usually dressed all in black, although sometimes he wore a red shirt with black pants. His bodyguards always accompanied him. I have often wondered why he needed all those bodyguards. But that's the way it was then. I took it all in. I was observing and learning.[19]

One very important part of the conference was the caucus organized by Chicanas—the women. There were many Chicanas there, perhaps close to half of the participants. They also, despite later denials by some, were not docile or passive during the conference. They were quite active and involved. They organized a special caucus only for women. This was the first time this had happened in the movement. They discussed issues pertinent to Chicanas. They concluded that they, or at least the majority of them, did not feel comfortable taking a position separate from the overall work of the Chicano movement. They believed and asserted that their struggle as women was tied to the whole struggle and not separate from it.

As such, they did not want to organize a separate movement such as what was happening with the white women's movement. Out of this came the later controversial proclamation that Chicanas "do not wish to be liberated." This has been taken out of context by later Chicana feminists to mean that Chicanas were put down and not allowed a voice at the conference. This is not true. They did have a voice. What they were saying was they desired liberation but as part of the entire liberation of all Chicanos and Chicanas, men and women. They did not want to associate themselves with the white women's movement that Chicanas considered to be separatist and a narrow gender-based form of liberation. To this day, I think this was and still is a correct position.

I'm not saying that there wasn't sexism at the conference or in the movement. There was. But one has to remember that we were also all very young then. There were sexual feelings, and all of us, both men and women, were exploring our sexuality in a more "liberated" climate. We were not puritans, not the men or the women. But this was not necessarily sexual exploitation, or at least not in all cases. I don't understand how today themes of sexuality seem to be okay as long as they are applied to women and gays but not to straight men!

At Denver but also in Los Angeles, I was impressed with the quality of the female activists. I dispute the idea that women in the movement were simply treated as sex objects or as cannon fodder. I didn't see this. Instead, I saw them as integral to the movement. I don't believe the later rhetoric that Chicanas were basically repressed at this time and were just expected to serve the men, literally, as cooks. Frankly, it never occurred to me, "Oh, we're having a conference, and you women have to cook." This victimization theme that later Chicana feminists developed after the heyday of the movement is a bogus one, as is the false proposal that it's not until the 1980s that Chicanas become aware. That's nonsense! Yes, perhaps more men participated in the movement, and especially in leadership positions, but if you see my photos in *La Raza,* for example, you see many *mujeres* as activists. And you don't see them standing around with aprons on! They're *activistas!* Yes, there was sexism, but it's been distorted. There were also many wonderful and supportive male-female relationships. I saw women flourish as a result of the movement.[20]

I think more than anything else that the Chicanas at Denver recognized that our communities were under attack and that we had to react as a community rather than as just men and women. These Chicanas who took this position were criticized then and even now. But it was a very sophisticated analysis and, in fact, one that a lot of women in the third world possess today. A leader such as Rigoberta Menchú doesn't speak just for the rights of Guatemalan Indian women. She speaks for all oppressed Guatemalans, including men.

The Denver conference is, of course, linked to the drafting of El Plan de Aztlán. This plan is considered to be one of the most important documents of the Chicano movement. The poet Alurista from San Diego wrote the preamble to it, titled "El Plan Espiritual de Aztlán." Alurista was and is his pen name. His real name is Alberto Urista. He had been studying pre-Columbian history and cultures and introduced the concept of Aztlán to the conference and to the movement. Aztlán refers to the original homeland of the Aztecs before they conquered and settled in the Valley of Mexico, or the site of present-day Mexico City. Aztlán, so the legend went, lay to the north. Just how much north is still in dispute. Alurista and other movement writers and orators conveniently located Aztlán in the Southwest. This way it provided an origin myth for Chicanos and the concept of the historical and the lost homeland.[21]

El Plan Espiritual de Aztlán and El Plan de Aztlán were the first documents in the movement that defined Chicano nationalism by proclaiming Chicanos to be an indigenous people with a homeland and with the need to regain self-determination by reclaiming Aztlán from the gringos.

I was not particularly affected by this ideology. I think that it captured the growing ethnic and cultural nationalism of the movement. But Aztlán did not capture my attention or imagination. Unlike some activists and the more artistic elements, I was never too much into the pre-Columbian stuff. I was a nationalist but perhaps a more pragmatic one and more interested in our present-day realities. Frankly, I don't think that the concept of Aztlán, at least at the Denver conference, especially moved too many others either.

I think that more than El Plan de Aztlán, it was the so-called Plan de Santa Barbara that was more important in linking Aztlán to the movement. El Plan de Santa Barbara was drafted at a conference on higher education held at the University of California, Santa Barbara, shortly after the Denver conference. El Plan de Santa Barbara institutionalized the term *Aztlán* into the renaming of Chicano student organizations. These groups, especially in California, went by different names: UMAS and MASC (Mexican American Student Confederation), as well as others. At Santa Barbara, the call went out to adopt a new common name—MEChA, which stands for Movimiento Estudiantil Chicano de Aztlán, thereby incorporating Aztlán into the student movement. I never cared for the acronym MEChA. I think that UMAS was better and less ponderous.

These name changes, as far as I was concerned, involved a competition between *mexicanistas* and Chicanos. The former always favored Spanish names and terms, whereas the latter preferred English ones. This was a subtle and sometimes not-so-subtle internal rivalry within the movement.

I'm not saying that the term *Aztlán* didn't excite some at the Denver conference. It obviously did. In fact, one member of our group from L.A., Lupe Saavedra, who was also a poet, came back home quite enthusiastic about the newly learned term and concept.

But not everyone was so absorbed by Aztlán, as Lupe was.

The same could be said of the concept of a lost homeland, which is part of the myth of Aztlán. People did talk about regaining the land at the Denver conference, but it was very abstract. It was hard to grasp just what this would entail. The lost homeland theme became part of movement ideology, but it was more the artists, writers, and intellectuals who romanticized it. I don't think that community activists were affected by it, at least not directly. Motivated by a sense of community and ethnic solidarity, we saw problems in our communities, and we moved to correct them.

Still another vision that was part of El Plan de Aztlán was that of "La Raza Unida." This would later be translated into building an independent Chicano political party—La Raza Unida Party. But party building, although alluded to in the plan and at the conference, didn't at that time capture our imagination. I interpreted La Raza Unida more to mean, as the words themselves suggest, a people united. I always thought it ironic that the concept of La Raza Unida and the reference to organizing a political party came out of the Denver meeting, yet Corky Gonzales was never given much due as the originator of the idea. By contrast, José Ángel Gutiérrez from Texas, who was the first to actually build such a party and to implement it, was not at Denver and yet is seen as the founder of La Raza Unida Party.

I think that the most important thing about Denver was that it began to erase our political provincialism and that it provided an overarching purpose to our struggles. Denver promoted, like no other event up to that point, the notion of Chicano nationalism, or what came to be referred to as chicanismo. It tied us all into a larger purpose.

Denver forced Chicanos to broaden their local issues from a shopping list of grievances and demands to a more national perspective. This, above all, I credit to Corky. He really brought all of us together. He created a political ideology. This was ethnic, or what some came to call cultural nationalism. At Denver, Chicanos began to recognize themselves as a national group with a national heritage, a national orientation, and national goals.

This type of ideology was not coming out of any other source. It was not in New Mexico, Texas, or California. César Chávez was not doing this. It was Corky and the Denver people who were doing this.

However, this did not mean that we all returned from Denver as rhetorical nationalists calling for the liberation of Aztlán. Yes, we were nationalists, or becoming Chicano nationalists, but some of us at least were still focused, and rightfully so, on our immediate local issues. For example, we were still thinking about the blowouts and the ramifications of the school walkouts. What was happening was that there were two strands of ideology developing in the movement, but they were not necessarily contradictory or counter to each other. There was cultural nationalism, and there was also a strong pragmatic perspective. I could see the two converging in me. I think that it was important that both influences were there. We had to work on our local issues practically, and yet it was equally important that the movement have more meaning than local concerns. We had to recognize our history, our heritage, our culture, our oppression from a larger perspective. This linkage made us understand better the need for liberation, even though liberation was never concretely defined. *Revolución,* a word increasingly used after Denver, was also never spelled out. What we did know was that we in Los Angeles were not alone. We were part of a larger struggle, and this gave greater meaning to our struggle.

CHICANO PRESS ASSOCIATION

Besides the trip to Denver for the youth conference, I also went to Albuquerque later that year with Joe Razo to attend the first meeting of what came to be the Chicano Press Association. We represented *La Raza.* The key organizer of the conference was Betita Martínez.

I'll never forget the trip. It was just as long as the one to Denver. Joe and I drove in a van. First of all, it was a hell of a long drive. And second, we almost killed ourselves. It was snowing as we got to New Mexico. Then one of the tires fell off, and we almost drove off a cliff! Somehow we got the tire back on and reached Albuquerque.

It turned out to be a great conference. There were a number of editors of Chicano newspapers from all over the Southwest. They were all serious about making contacts, about learning from one another, and about establishing the Chicano Press Association.

Putting out a tabloid in the late 1960s was not a big problem due to the technology available then. For about $150 you could print several hundred copies. It was cheap. At one point during the movement, I counted more than a hundred Chicano newspapers. At Albuquerque, there must have been between thirty and forty papers represented.

In our case, putting out a paper and later transforming *La Raza* into a monthly magazine gave us a way of reaching people. We could influence them more than some particular activities of the movement. I think, too, that in a way publishing a paper prevented us from being too caught up in our own little petty views. We had to be out there with the people. We had to listen to people that perhaps we didn't always agree with, but at least we listened to them. As the movement in time became more intolerant of different viewpoints and more closed-minded, I always believed that those of us in the media remained a bit more open-minded. I'm sure some would disagree with this, but I believe it.

At Albuquerque, we all decided to cooperate with one another by forming the Chicano Press Association. It was an informal body. We had no officers or staff. It wasn't like the Associated Press. We met once a year to share experiences. We also mailed one another copies of our papers with permission to reprint stories. This all had to be done by mail since we didn't have faxes and certainly not e-mail or the Internet at this time.

What was also important at Albuquerque was that we validated one another. The conference recognized the importance of the underground press. We began to understand our role. At one level, we were functional. We reported about the movement, and our papers in turn documented the history of the movement. At another level, an ideological one, we existed to raise political consciousness. We saw ourselves as a political instrument of the movement. Unlike the *New York Times* slogan, "All the News Fit to Print," our unofficial slogan was "All the Chicano News Fit to Print."

We published Chicano newspapers. But we were also activists. We didn't see a contradiction. We never saw ourselves as simply journalists. We never accepted the false concept that a paper, or for that matter the media, should strive for objectivity. No paper or media outlet is objective. What passes for "objectivity" is in reality support for the status quo.

We were subjective, and we knew it, and we were proud of it. Our role was to report the news from a Chicano perspective. We never believed in giving both sides of a story. The *Los Angeles Times,* for example, would never print the Chicano community's side of a story. So our task was to balance the *Times.* This was our mission. This is what the Chicano Press Association was all about.

CATÓLICOS POR LA RAZA

By 1969 the Chicano movement in Los Angeles was going full force. That fall certain elements of the movement chose to take on one of the most venerable and established institutions, the Catholic Church.

The Church, of course, had been around for centuries and was a powerful and wealthy body. Most Mexican Americans and Mexican immigrants in L.A. were Catholics. Many of us, as activists, had been raised Catholics. But we in the movement were taking on all the dominant institutions, such as the schools, the political system, and the police. We decided to add the Church to our list because some of us believed that it was not on our side and that over the years it had dealt with us in a paternalistic manner. Moreover, we felt that the Church, despite its wealth, was not doing enough to help deal with poverty in barrios such as East Los Angeles.

The confrontation with the Church originated with a group of Chicano law students attending Loyola University Law School. A courageous, articulate, and charismatic young man by the name of Ricardo Cruz led them. Richard (as we called him), who would go on to become an activist community lawyer, was particularly incensed at what he believed was the Church's recalcitrant and right-wing politics. He criticized the Church for not doing more to assist the Chicano law students. He especially challenged Cardinal Frances McIntyre, who had ruled over the L.A. archdiocese for what seemed to be forever! About eighty years old, he was a former Wall Street broker and did not tolerate any opposition.

Richard believed that the Church with respect to the Chicano community was behaving like any other oppressive institution, the only difference being that somehow it was tied to God. He resented the fact that we were all raised as Catholics, but we were not really welcome as part of the Catholic family, even though we represented close to half of all Catholics in the archdiocese. Richard accused the Church of not providing any real economic or political support to Chicanos. He believed that the Church was racist. Richard pointed out, for example, the lack of Chicano priests in the archdiocese, including in the hierarchy. His goal was to humanize the Church and to make it relevant to Chicanos and to the poor.

Richard and the other Loyola law students, along with Chicanos in other California law schools, organized what they called the Chicano Law Students Association. They worked with the Chicano college students in the UMAS and, later, with MEChA groups. They also made contact with us in *La Raza*.

Out of these contacts, we formed Católicos por la Raza (Catholics for the People). We very deliberately chose this name to stress that we were neither anti-Catholic nor anti-Church but that we were concerned Catholics who wanted to reform the Church. This was liberation theology, East L.A. style.[22]

Many of us in Católicos had gone to Catholic schools; some, such as Richard, were in Catholic colleges. We had grown up during the time of Vatican II and its reforms of the Church, including a renewed emphasis on the Church's involvement in the modern world. Out of this came liberation theology in Latin America, which stressed that the Church's proper role was on the side of the poor and the oppressed. It reminded us that Jesus himself was a poor and oppressed man. We knew about liberation theology and were printing stories in *La Raza* about this movement, including the role of revolutionary priests in Latin America, such as Camilo Torres of Colombia.

I'm not saying that we were steeped in the reforms of Vatican II and liberation theology, but directly and indirectly we were influenced by the climate of change within the Church. Of course, the whole tenor of the times was oppositional.

Besides our overall critique of the Church, some concrete immediate issues motivated us. These included the lack of support for Chicanos to achieve higher education. There was also the case that the Church that fall had closed down Our Lady Queen of Angels School, a Catholic girls' high school in East Los Angeles. We felt this was unnecessary and evidence of the Church's lack of sensitivity to Chicano issues. At the same time, the Church was completing a multimillion-dollar new church, St. Basil's, on trendy Wilshire Boulevard, to serve the rich white people in that area. Then there was the fact that Cardinal McIntyre and the

Church in L.A. had refused to support César Chávez and the struggle of the farm-workers. All these issues triggered the protests carried out by Católicos that fall and winter.

We put out a list of demands that included more Mexican American lay representation to be part of the decision making of the archdiocese, especially as it pertained to the barrios. We called on more financial support by the Church for education, housing, and health in the barrios. We called for more recruitment of Chicano priests and clergy to service the barrios. And we called for the Church to support the Chicano movement, including the farmworkers' struggle. We issued various other demands, but this list provides a sense of our goals.

Our initial strategy was to meet with Cardinal McIntyre and other Church officials. We felt that we needed to go to the top, since the Church is really like a corporation. All power resides in the CEO, or in this case the cardinal. He ran everything. If any decision was made, he made it, and everyone else kowtowed to it.

We never actually got an invitation to meet with him. After several efforts to schedule a meeting, we decided to take things into our own hands. One day a group of us walked into the cardinal's chancery office in downtown Los Angeles.

"We're here to see the cardinal," we told the receptionist.

"I'm sorry, the cardinal is not here. In any case you need an appointment."

"We don't need a fucking appointment!" we shouted as we ran past her desk and down the adjoining corridor, opening doors in our attempt to locate the cardinal.

As we did, some of the resident priests came out of their offices and tried to restrain us. All this resulted in more shouting, more obscenities on our part, and some scuffling.

"That door! That's the one!" one of us yelled out.

Sure enough, we opened the door, and there he was, surrounded and protected by a number of other priests who must have thought we had come to lynch the prelate.

"What do you want?" they demanded to know. "Why did you break in?"

"We've been trying for weeks to see the cardinal," Richard Cruz shot back. "But he's refused to see us. We're here as Católicos por la Raza, and we're here to deliver demands to him."

Richard then quickly mentioned some of our demands.

As Richard did so, I could see Cardinal McIntyre getting redder and redder, as only a ruddy-faced Irishman can get. When Richard finished, the cardinal, who could barely talk since he was livid, said, "You're all crazy! I'm going to call the police!"

"Wait, wait," one of the priests interceded. After a short consultation with McIntyre, this priest informed us that the cardinal would consider our demands and get back to us if we left quietly.

"*¡Órale!* [Okay!]" we agreed and left yelling as we exited the chancery, "¡Viva la Raza! Chicano Power!"

But we never heard back from the cardinal.

In the meantime, to raise the stakes, we at *La Raza* decided to do some investigative reporting on the Church. Specifically, we wanted to support our contention that despite the Church's wealth, it was doing little for the poor in Los Angeles. We researched the Church's property holdings in the archdiocese. We simply went to the county recorder's office and asked to see the files on the Church. Since this was a matter of public record, the files were made available to us.

We were amazed at what we discovered. There were pages and pages of Church holdings. There must have been at least a thousand pages. We identified not only church buildings and schools but also a good deal of nonreligious property. This included apartment buildings and business offices. It also included slum dwellings and even cantinas.

We made copies of these pages and published some of them in *La Raza*. We couldn't publish all of them, but we did enough to point out to our readers just how rich the Church was and, by contrast, how poor the barrios were. It was a great piece and brought much attention to our publication, both positive and negative.

But we ignored the negative because we felt that we were now in a state of conflict with Cardinal McIntyre. Since he refused to listen to us and to establish a dialogue with us, we now moved to increase the pressure on him and to publicize our grievances.

Late that fall and into December, we organized a series of candlelight midnight marches and vigils outside the chancery office in downtown L.A. These were peaceful protests with a few hundred people each time, including some clerics, both priests and nuns, who had recently left their orders. We picketed the chancery as well as the newly constructed St. Basil's. We also had sleep-ins at both locations.

But our biggest and most memorable protest occurred on Christmas Eve that year at St. Basil's. The cardinal was scheduled to say the traditional midnight Mass there. We planned to protest and to disrupt the Mass. We organized a march to the church that included a few hundred supporters. Our plan was to first stage a counter-Mass at around eleven outside of the church as people entered it. We got Father Blas Bonpane, a Maryknoll priest who had recently been kicked out of Central America for his support of the poor and of oppositional movements. He said the Mass at a makeshift altar and offered pieces of tortillas for Communion.

Following the Mass, our plans were to enter the church and march down the main aisle and then present our demands to the assembled congregation, composed predominantly of middle-class and well-to-do Anglos. The church was packed. However, when our Mass finished and we tried to enter the church, we found the main doors locked. Inside the vestibule or lobby, we could see through the glass doors a number of "ushers," who later proved to be members of the sher-

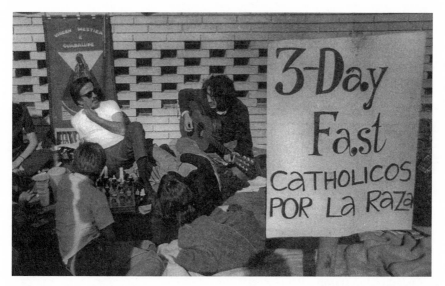

FIGURE 2. Ruiz at a protest by Católicos por la Raza, fall 1969. Courtesy of George Rodríguez.

iff's department. Everyone knew we were going to protest, and Cardinal McIntyre was ready for us.

We felt that we were Catholics and had every right to enter St. Basil's and to attend the midnight Mass. But despite our appeals that they open the doors, we were kept out, just as Mary and Joseph were not allowed shelter on this same night centuries before. So we started knocking on the door and shouting, "Let the poor people in! Let the poor people in!"

Meanwhile, the people inside the church began to sing louder and louder, "O Come All Ye Faithful," as a way of drowning out our shouts.

While the commotion was going on outside the church, someone from our group discovered a side door that was open and that went down to the bottom of the building. St. Basil's had two sacristies, a top and main one and a lower tier, where there was a second midnight Mass in progress. About twenty or thirty of us ran through the side door and entered the bottom sacristy at the side of the altar. Before anyone could stop us, we ran down the main aisle and to the back side so we could go up to the main vestibule and open the doors for the others. All of this was quite a scene. The people in the bottom were singing Christmas carols, and these crazy Chicanos were running down the aisle carrying banners and shouting, "¡Viva la Raza!" and "Let the poor people in!"

Then the real *chingazos,* or fights, started. As we exited the stairs and stormed into the main vestibule, who should be waiting for us but the "ushers"—these huge sheriff's deputies. And so we started going toe-to-toe with them as they tried to prevent us from opening the doors. In the meantime, our supporters increased their cries of "Let the poor people in!" It was an incredible scene.

Finally, we were able to force the doors open, and more of our people stormed in and more fisticuffs ensued. The "barbarians" had entered! But by this time an army of Los Angeles police arrived and surrounded the church. They pushed us outside of the church and began to arrest us. As they were doing this, someone picked up a big concrete ashtray and threw it at the glass doors, shattering them completely. It was crazy stuff.

I remember seeing Joe Razo being clubbed by the police. Then when they stopped beating him, they turned on me. I was arrested. Joe was arrested. Tony Salazar from UCLA was taken. Many of us were arrested and taken to jail. To make matters worse, as I was being arrested, a *Los Angeles Times* photographer took my picture, and in the newspaper later that morning, you see this skinny 130-pound Chicano being arrested by a huge LAPD cop. We spent Christmas Eve in jail.

My mother saw the paper that morning and was shocked. She called my brother Fernando. "Arrestaron a Raul."

Fernando went down to the city jail to bail me out. But by then we had been released. My parents were very relieved. I told my mother, "Look, don't worry about me. There's a way in which you're always going to know about me. If I'm really in trouble, you're going to hear about it. If you don't hear anything, don't worry, because it's okay."

Well, I don't think this ever worked. Like a good mother, she always worried about me.

The following day, Christmas Day, more protests took place outside of St. Basil's. This was marked by an unfortunate incident. Gloria Chávez, who was not really part of Católicos but who had been attending the protests, decided to personally disrupt one of the Christmas masses. While the Mass was being said, she walked down the main aisle, and before anyone could stop her, she took a golf club out of her coat and swung it around, knocking the priest's chalice and other blessed items off the altar.

None of this was our planning. Gloria was a loose cannon, but she was also expressing our frustrations with the Church hierarchy.

Other demonstrations continued for several days. Some of these activities were accompanied by violence, as certain St. Basil's parishioners tried to beat up some of the Chicanos. Cardinal McIntyre and the *Tidings*, the official newspaper of the archdiocese, also vehemently attacked us.

These attacks on us by the Church set the backdrop two months later into 1970 for an LAPD dragnet that arrested twenty-one of us associated with Católicos. Those arrested besides myself included Richard Cruz, Joe Razo, Richard Martínez, and several others.

We were charged with conspiracy to disrupt a religious assembly. We got off on bail but had to face a jury trial.

Oscar Zeta Acosta, the so-called Brown Buffalo, defended us. Oscar was a crazy and eccentric guy. He was originally from the San Joaquin Valley and later the Bay Area, where he had gotten a law degree. He went through a series of experiences, while trying to discover his identity as a Chicano, that he wrote about in his book *The Autobiography of a Brown Buffalo*. He had come to L.A. at about the time of the blowouts and opened up a law office downtown, which didn't have many clients. He later detailed these experiences in his second book, *The Revolt of the Cockroach People*.[23]

Oscar didn't really want to be a lawyer. He wanted to be a writer. I remember once going to his office and telling him that we really needed an attorney.

"I don't want to be a lawyer," he told me. "I'm a writer."

"We don't need writers right now," I responded. "We need lawyers."

But Oscar didn't really pay me any attention. He practiced law, but his heart was really in wanting to write.

Oscar was not part of Católicos, but he came to some of our protests. He was there at the midnight Mass as our attorney in case there was trouble. I think that I remember Oscar as being one of us who made it into the church and fought with the police. But others have disputed this. In *Cockroach People,* he claimed that he was inside. I do recall him being outside the church as the police descended on us. Even though Oscar was a lawyer, he also wanted to get arrested. He kept running around, yelling, "Arrest me! Arrest me!" But the police, knowing he was our lawyer, refused to comply, which agitated Oscar to no end.

Oscar was insane. He is perfectly described in one of Hunter S. Thompson's books. He possessed a very bright mind, but he was affected by the drug culture of the time. But crazy or not, on drugs or not, Oscar defended us, and he did a very good job.

Oscar mounted a brilliant defense. He didn't deny our activities at St. Basil's but instead focused on the procedures of the court itself. He did something that had never happened before. He challenged the process for selecting the county's grand jurors. It had been the grand jury that had issued indictments for our arrests. But what Oscar was saying was, "How were these jurors selected?" He noted the lack of minorities, including Chicanos, in the available pool of potential jurors. He documented that Chicanos had hardly, if at all, been part of that pool and consequently had rarely been part of grand juries.

This was only part of Oscar's defense. He also showed no deference to the judge or to the judicial procedure. In fact, he displayed nothing but contempt. We got a little concerned about Oscar.

"What the fuck are you doing, Oscar? You're going to get us convicted and put away for years."

But he reassured us that he knew what he was doing. We had no choice but to trust him.

I'll never forget his closing. He was all over the place, attacking the court, the police, and the jury-selection procedures, all of these using expletives. He ended up by quoting a Japanese haiku poem that seemed to make no sense. It was about a frog jumping into a pond and making ripples. What the hell was all this about?

And while he's doing this, I'm saying to myself, "I'm going to get hung. I'm going to die because of this crazy guy."

But Oscar wasn't that crazy. I've got to give him credit. He innovated a new strategy for dealing with a racist jury structure.

Oscar's ploy worked for some of us and not for others. Some were found not guilty, while others were found guilty. Richard Cruz, Joe Razo, and Richard Martínez were among those declared guilty. Cruz and Martínez did about three months, while Razo got only a couple of weeks. As for me, I was found not guilty of the conspiracy charge but did have to pay a fifty-dollar fine. The others wanted to know why I had gotten off so easily. "Well, I don't know. I guess I'm a good Catholic and you aren't."

The tensions surrounding the trial also reflected the fact that many in the community did not understand or support our opposition to the Church. This was in part the result of the Church's propaganda against us. But it was also due to our failure to convince Chicano Catholics that we were not anti-Catholic and anti-Church. We miscalculated how deeply faithful Chicano Catholics were and are to the Church despite its failures in the community.

Despite this concern and even opposition in the Chicano community, Católicos did achieve some results. Early in 1970 Cardinal McIntyre resigned. Although the Church never admitted it, we believed that our protests forced the Vatican to "convince" McIntyre to step aside. Rome, we believed, questioned, "What's going on with the Mexicans in Los Angeles?"

The cardinal was replaced by Archbishop Timothy Manning, who proved much more willing to take up our demands and issues. He even met with some of us and implemented some of the reforms we advocated, including support for the farmworkers, more Latino priests in the Church hierarchy, and greater involvement by Chicano laity in the decisions of the Church involving community issues such as education, health, and housing.

Irrespective of these new attitudes and changes, most of us remained suspicious of Manning and of the Church's intentions. We also believed that these reforms were only piecemeal and symbolic. To call attention to the Church's slow and minimal reforms, Católicos called on its followers to participate later that year in a baptismal certificate–burning protest. This took place in front of St. Basil's, where a number of Chicanos, including Richard Cruz and Pedro Arias, burned their baptismal certificates as a symbolic act of protest, similar to the draft card burning carried out by anti–Vietnam War protesters.

I didn't burn mine because of my mother's strong objection to such an action. This event received media attention, but it also represented the swan song of Católicos. By the end of 1970, it had ceased to exist. In fact, even earlier that year Católicos in reality was no longer functioning. We felt that with the St. Basil's Christmas protest we had brought to bear what pressure we could on the Church. It was now time to turn our attention to the next most pressing issue: the Vietnam War.

LA RAZA MAGAZINE

A year or two after I had joined *La Raza* newspaper, I became its editor. My idea was to transform *La Raza* into a magazine format. We would sell it for a dollar. We felt that we could also market a magazine better. It, we hoped, would pay for itself.

The other factor in shifting to a magazine was that I, and others, felt that we would produce a more quality publication. We wanted to use color and have an attractive magazine that people would subscribe to. A magazine would also give us more space to develop longer and more in-depth stories.

Well, we made the change in 1970, and we got a lot of positive reaction. People liked and appreciated the magazine. Subscribers increased the first couple of years. You have to remember that this was in the midst of tremendous movement activities, so people were hungry for news and analysis. *La Raza* became an eagerly awaited publication each month.

This reflected the fact that *La Raza* was more than just a magazine. It was an organization. We were one of the key groups behind the movement in Los Angeles. Not only did we report the movement; we were part of it. We were active in a whole slew of activities.

Another new aspect of the magazine was that we published articles not only about the Chicano movement but also about other social movements, especially about Native Americans and Latin American politics. Because of the mestizo heritage of Chicanos that brings into play the Indian heritage, I felt that it was logical for us to cover the Native American struggles in the United States. We saw ourselves in common alignment with Native Americans and their struggles. So we had articles, for example, on the conflict at Wounded Knee, as well as elsewhere.

Because of my own interest in Latin America, I knew all along that we had to have a section on it, whether on Mexico, Peru, or Cuba. There was a lot of revolutionary action and social protest at that time, and as Chicanos we needed to know and to learn from these movements. There was the Tupamaro movement in Uruguay. It was the period of the election of Salvador Allende and the socialists to power in Chile, and there were continued student and peasant struggles in Mexico. This type of coverage tempered the more cultural nationalism of the movement. It reflected a broader consciousness, including an internationalist or third world one.

It was also around this time—1970—that I got involved in a radio program about Chicanos. KPFK, the Pacifica station in L.A., wanted to do a Chicano program. They contacted or somehow were involved with Moctesuma Esparza, who is now a big-time movie producer. But Moctesuma had first started getting involved in the movement when he was a student at Lincoln High. He was one of the *grupitos,* or insiders, who gave us a lot of information about conditions in the school when I was with *Inside Eastside* and *CSM.* At the time of the blowouts, he was a student at UCLA studying film. He was one of many Chicano college students who helped organize the blowouts.

Moctesuma and I had a pretty good relationship, and he asked me to cohost the radio program. I didn't know anything about radio, but I felt it would help promote the movement, so I agreed to do so.

It was a crazy program with no real structure to it. It was every Tuesday at seven in the evening. It was half an hour each week and chiefly consisted of interviews. We called the program "La Raza Nueva." It was crazy because, among other things, sometimes I couldn't make it due to movement activities, sometimes Moctesuma couldn't be there, and then occasionally we both didn't show up.

Despite these problems, the program provided an opportunity for Chicanos to speak and to air their grievances. One of the first persons we interviewed was Reies López Tijerina, who was championing the militant land-grant movement in New Mexico to return stolen or expropriated lands to the poor rural Hispanos. Because of his exploits, including his arrests, Tijerina had become an instant folk hero among Chicanos. On one of his speaking tours in Southern California, we arranged to interview him on our program. It turned out to be almost a political catastrophe. This was because part of his bodyguard contingent on his trip was composed of a militant Black Power group called the US Organization. They had broken off from the equally militant Black Panther Party in Los Angeles. There was no love lost between these two rivals.

It just so happened that the Black Panthers hosted the program before ours. So as they were finishing their program, here comes Tijerina with his US bodyguards. Moctesuma and I just about freaked out. We thought that there was going to be a big gun battle right there at KPFK. To make matters worse, the cops, who seemed to be trailing Tijerina, also showed up at the station. This was beginning to resemble a poor comedy of sorts, except that it had the potential for real violence.

Fortunately, somehow violence was avoided, and we were able to get Tijerina into the studio before any fight took place. But it was a close call!

But after a while, the KPFK people began to play around with us. They began to preempt the program for other stuff and then changed the day of its airing without consulting us. They also put us at the late hour of eleven o'clock to midnight. Moctesuma and I were pissed. We decided to use the program to blast the station staff for what we believed was their insensitivity to Chicanos and their lack of interest and support. So on one program we just gave it to them. We also organized demonstrations outside the station. By that time, the program was canceled, and we left.

I don't know, as I look back, where the others and I got all our energy to do all this stuff. We were running around with these programs while at the same time publishing a fucking magazine and being involved in movement activities. Each day would be jam-packed with meetings with different people and groups. All of this wasn't made any easier when certain people got angry with us. Some threatened to beat us up; some threatened to kill us. To fuck with us. I got many threats on my life during this period.

These threats unfortunately came from other Chicano groups—always Chicano groups. As early as 1970 the movement was beginning to splinter into different political and ideological factions. One time there was an article in *La Raza* that apparently didn't go down too well with one group. At the time we published the piece, I had no idea that it would cause a bad reaction. But it did. I was pulled out of a meeting at gunpoint. These guys were going to kill me! They didn't, but they succeeded in scaring the hell out of me!

These weren't gangs, although they had a gang mentality. They were other political groups that didn't like *La Raza*'s coverage or our editorial positions. They operated like political gangsters. I called them "community gangsters." This was a bad side of the movement, and it was destructive. Not only were there ideological and political differences, but many groups were being infiltrated by cops and FBI agents who went out of their way to cause dissension and conflicts within the movement. This penetration became evident as we entered 1970, with the movement staging even larger protests.

THE CHICANO ANTIWAR MOVEMENT

There is no question but that the Chicano antiwar movement, protesting U.S. intervention in Vietnam, became one of the major issues of the movement. It led to the largest demonstration in the history of the movement on August 29, 1970.[24]

But the history of the Chicano antiwar movement goes back a bit further. By 1967 there already were some early antiwar expressions by Chicano activists. That year, Corky Gonzales came and spoke to a more general antiwar protest at East Los Angeles College. We were also quite aware of the antiwar efforts in the country and the large demonstrations, especially in Washington, DC. Antiwar protests were likewise taking place around the world.

But what really ignited the Chicano antiwar movement involved those early Chicano protesters who refused induction into the military. Some of this was taking place by 1968 and 1969. Here in L.A. the most celebrated case was that of

Rosalio Muñoz. He had been student body president at UCLA, and so he was known among the students. His refusal to be inducted was orchestrated to bring attention to the fact that Chicanos were being heavily exploited by the war effort. There was a report issued around that time by Professor Ralph Guzmán at Cal State, L.A., that indicated that Chicanos were disproportionately being drafted into the military and sent to Vietnam.

Initially, I was somewhat ambivalent about the antiwar movement being an issue for the Chicano movement. I wasn't uncertain about the war. I opposed it. I was also against the draft. Fortunately, I wasn't subjected to it because I was in school, plus I had a child. In December 1969 I wrote the following about the war and Chicanos: "There are many reasons Chicanos owe no allegiance to this country. One of them is that Americans are not going to Vietnam to liberate the people there from Communism, but rather to enslave them for the American economy. Why should Chicanos fight enslaved people when they find themselves in the same position in the United States."[25]

At the same time, I was ambivalent as to whether Chicanos would respond to an antiwar movement. I felt that most would not because Mexican Americans in all the previous wars, especially World War II and Korea, had patriotically supported and served their country. Many had been killed or wounded, and many had been decorated. I felt that history was against the idea of protesting the Vietnam War. I was both right and wrong. There was a generational divide. Older Mexican Americans either supported the war or were skeptical about the antiwar movement. Younger Chicanos, especially those involved in the movement, very quickly responded and supported the Chicano antiwar movement.

The idea of organizing a specific Chicano antiwar effort was strengthened when the general antiwar movement, led predominantly by Anglo activists, seemed to shun or ignore Chicano involvement. Few of those demonstrations had Chicano speakers, and little effort was made to include them.

As a result, Rosalio Muñoz, working with David Sánchez of the Brown Berets, organized what was called the National Chicano Moratorium Committee. It included representatives from many other groups. Those of us in *La Raza* participated. We went to the meetings and helped to publicize the committee's work. We also participated in the initial demonstrations staged in East L.A. by the end of 1969 and the beginning of 1970.

I thought that the Moratorium Committee was a good example of how the Chicano movement was definitely not just a student movement. True, Rosalio had been a student at UCLA, but not at the time he organized the committee. Moreover, he didn't focus on organizing students for this effort. He welcomed student support, but he was mostly targeting community involvement, including movement groups as well as the older Mexican American ones. Of course, the Berets were basically community based.

Rosalio and his colleagues Ramses Noriega and David Sánchez proved to be very good organizers. They worked hard and stressed inclusion. They networked not only in California but also throughout the Southwest and beyond. They succeeded in getting a wide array of Chicano groups, both community and student, to support the Moratorium Committee.

Beginning by late fall 1969, the Moratorium Committee began to organize local antiwar marches in East L.A. as a way of building up the moratorium effort and of laying the ground for a larger demonstration the following year. Both on December 20, 1969, and on February 28, 1970, the initial demonstrations took place. A few thousand people participated in each. We in *La Raza* participated in some of the organizing meetings and in publicizing the actions. I was not, however, part of the actual planning of these demonstrations or of the planned national one.

Having successfully organized the initial marches, the Moratorium Committee announced in the early part of 1970 that it was now organizing a national demonstration, to be held on August 29 in East Los Angeles. Intense organization followed during the next several months.

I had no idea how big such a demonstration was going to be, but I had a sense that it would be large. Our role at *La Raza* was to publicize the event and to encourage as many others to attend as we could. We also planned to cover it extensively. Since I was one of our main photographers, I personally planned to photograph as much of it as possible. I always had my camera with me and certainly intended to do so on August 29. This would be one of the most fortuitous decisions on my part that I have ever made.

None of us had any idea that there would be trouble at the demonstration. In fact, I took my five-year-old daughter, Marcy, with me. There were many other parents who did the same. If we were there to cause conflict, as the police would later allege, why would we have taken our children with us? Instead, many of us saw the demonstration as one big fiesta, a celebration.

We went directly to Belvedere Park. That was the staging area for the march. The march itself would wind its way through the main streets of East L.A., in particular Whittier Boulevard, and end up at Laguna Park (now Ruben Salazar Park). We arrived before eleven. That was the starting time for the march. It was like a day in the park. There was music, and people were having a good time. I wasn't planning on marching with any one particular group but instead to work the march and take photos at different points. Joe Razo and I both had our cameras, and we were both responsible for taking shots for *La Raza*.

At first it didn't seem to me that there were many people at Belvedere Park, but as the march started I was aware of many more demonstrators. The crowd seemed to grow and grow as we marched. All told, I later estimated about twenty thousand protesters, mostly Chicanos. It was not only the largest demonstration during the movement but also one of the largest assemblies of Chicanos in history!

We started on Third Street and went up Beverly to Atlantic, until we got to Whittier. That was the largest stretch of the march. By then all you could see was masses of people. You could look down Whittier for blocks and just see wall-to-wall Mexicans from one sidewalk to another. It was a totally peaceful demonstration, considering the number of people. I didn't see any problems.

At the same time, I was aware of many police officers, especially county sheriff's deputies, since East L.A., an unincorporated area, is part of their jurisdiction. They seemed to be well prepared. I would later learn that the sheriffs were reinforced not only by the Los Angeles Police Department but also by police units from other parts of Southern California. Why were there so many cops there? There had been no violence at the previous two antiwar marches. Were they preparing for something?

The sheriffs were everywhere, along the corners, the streets, the overhead crossings. There were helicopters. You couldn't put so many police in such a small area and not have a conflict.

It was somewhere along the march that I saw Ruben Salazar. He had been a reporter for the *Los Angeles Times* but was now the news editor for KMEX, channel 34, the Spanish-language television station in L.A. He was also writing a column for the *Times*. Ruben was a good reporter, and he had been covering the movement for more than a year. He was sympathetic to our cause, although, as a mainstream journalist, he insisted on keeping a distance. While Ruben and I differed about the role of journalists, I respected him and appreciated his work. The fact is that he was becoming more involved, especially at channel 34, where he was exposing on television various incidents of police abuse against the Chicano community.[26]

I briefly chatted with Ruben and then didn't see him again that day.

The march must have lasted a couple of hours. At the end, people streamed into Laguna Park for the rally. When I got there, it had not started yet. It would be another hour before everyone got settled in the park. People sat on the grass, facing the platform where the speakers and the music and dance groups would be positioned. I was at the front of the park close to the platform. It was at the back of the park where we noticed a disturbance. Soon the figures of the county sheriffs became visible. They were armed with clubs and with tear-gas weapons. I feared the worst.

"Take Marcy out of the park," I told a friend of mine. "I'm going to go back and see what's happening."

Without warning, the sheriffs shot tear gas into the crowd and charged into the park. Bedlam broke loose.

The sheriffs later claimed that they had intervened after a disturbance at a nearby liquor store, where some Chicanos, they alleged, had stolen some liquor or soft drinks. The owner panicked and called the sheriffs. The sheriffs also claimed that when they arrived, they were pelted with rocks and cans.

Almost immediately the park was surrounded, and the sheriffs declared the rally to be an "unlawful assembly." While it has never been conclusively proven what exactly happened at that store, there is no question in my mind that the sheriffs were looking for any excuse or incident to break up the demonstration. Even if the alleged incident took place, it was not enough for the overreaction by the sheriffs, who clubbed and teargassed the people.

A battle took place that day at Laguna Park. The sheriffs and the young Chicano men fought it out. Tear gas and mace were all over the place. Chicanos, including some of the women, were hit by the sheriffs' billy clubs. Demonstrators were arrested. I photographed a lot of this as I maneuvered around the conflict. Fortunately, I was not beaten or arrested. My mother later told me that I was spared due to her prayers that day that no harm would come to me. It's quite possible that this was the reason I didn't get shot or beaten, although I did get gassed. It's also possible that the cops thought I was a mainstream journalist because I had several cameras with me.

The melee in the park lasted about forty-five minutes. The sheriffs eventually pushed the demonstrators out of the park and into the adjacent parking lot. The conflict then spilled over into Whittier Boulevard, where for the next several hours the Chicanos ruled the streets. Store windows were broken, stores looted, and buildings and cars set on fire as the outraged people vented their anger and frustration. They pelted any police cars driving on the boulevard with rocks and sticks. It was a war. Maybe this wasn't correct, but there had to be a reaction to what had happened in the park. People felt that the police had gone in to beat them up, and they weren't going to take this stuff.

Some have referred to this conflict that afternoon as a "riot." To some extent, that's true. In fact, some have more appropriately called it a "police riot." The reaction of the Chicanos was not random and criminal. It was a political reaction to the unprovoked attack by the sheriffs and the disruption of a legal and peaceful demonstration. It was an assault on the Chicano community. I believe that it was a conspiracy. I believe that the police and the ruling politicians, perhaps even in Washington, did not want to see this massive Chicano antiwar protest succeed.

RUBEN SALAZAR

After the conflict spilled over into Whittier Boulevard, Joe Razo and I walked around taking photos for the next several hours. This wasn't easy because of the disturbance. It was a war zone. Although I didn't see Chicanos shooting guns, I did see some people with guns that they may have taken from the pawn shops that had been broken into. We walked down the boulevard toward the east. Little did we know that somewhere ahead of us was Ruben Salazar with his TV crew walking in the same direction.

After about an hour, we reached a place where there were no more disturbances and where the sheriffs were clearly in control. It was like a command post with several squad cars. We continued to walk a bit more. By then Joe and I were quite tired and thirsty. It had been a hot, smoggy day. We found a stand where we bought some soft drinks. We stopped to rest by sitting on the curbside. I noticed that we were right across the street from a bar that I later learned was the Silver Dollar Café. The bar was located about one and a half miles east of Laguna Park. This must have been around five o'clock.

Within a few minutes, I saw something happening. "Look, Joe, the sheriffs are going over to that bar."

One or two squad cars came by, and some deputies approached the Silver Dol- lar. At this point, I started shooting with my camera. I saw one of the sheriffs point his tear-gas rifle toward the open entrance of the café. Some customers were com- ing out, but a deputy forced them to go back inside. I never heard a warning from him for people to exit the bar. Then another deputy, Thomas Wilson, shot tear gas projectiles three times directly into the establishment. I didn't get photos of the actual firing into the bar, but what apparently happened was that Wilson couldn't shoot from outside since there was a barrier directly inside the door, with a curtain to the side, covering the actual entrance to the bar. He would have had to go inside and then open the curtain and shoot. Since he was that far inside, I couldn't take the photos.

But something else happened that was never reported, and that was what I did see and photograph. Another deputy by the name of Sparks shot from a handgun into the Silver Dollar. He shot from outside the bar, kneeling by his squad car. He was almost directly in front of me, and in my photo you can see the smoke from the gun. He shot prior to Wilson going to the front entrance with the tear-gas pro- jectiles.

It's hard to know what actually happened inside the bar, and we may never know. Guillermo Restrepo, who was with Ruben as part of his crew, later testified that he was sitting next to Salazar at the bar when he saw a tear-gas tumbler being thrown or shot into the bar. He thinks he remembers Ruben saying, "Let's get out that way," indicating the back entrance. Restrepo led the way, as others also began exiting through the back, and he thought Ruben was behind him, although he couldn't see him due to the tear gas. When he exited Ruben was not with him.

I don't agree with Restrepo's account. In my opinion, Ruben was hit by the first tear-gas projectile. It had to be the first, since if it was not he would have reacted to the first shot and either ducked or would have been able to leave, as did Restrepo. However, I don't believe that the initial shot killed Ruben. I believe that it hit him and stunned him and he went down but that somewhere during the next two hours that he laid on the floor someone entered and killed him. I may never prove this, but this is what I believe.

I didn't hear the shots because there was so much noise from the disturbance down on the boulevard, including sirens and helicopters overhead. But I saw what was going on and took pictures. I didn't even have to use a photo lens since I was so close. I also took pictures of the other deputies squatting behind their cars and behind a telephone post. They were right next to me.

I saw the smoke coming out of the café after the tear gas projectiles exploded. I walked around the squad car to get a photo of the car with the Silver Dollar in the background. We were never told to leave during all this time.

We were there for not quite an hour, and as more sheriffs descended on the area, we were now told to leave. We had no idea if anyone had been hurt. I had hoped that no one would come out of the café, because I was convinced that the deputies outside were waiting to kill someone. We didn't see them go into the bar. Wilson never went into the bar, but only to the entrance, from where he shot his projectiles.

The police were pissed because they had gotten their asses whipped at the park. They tried to intimidate the people, and the Chicanos said, "Fuck you," and fought back, toe-to-toe. The deputies were also pissed because they lost control of the streets. They were being pushed around, and you didn't do this in East L.A. Chicanos were not conforming to a stereotypical role. Instead of being passive, Chicanos were being tough and strong.

It wasn't until much later, after ten o'clock, that we heard rumors and then radio and TV reports that Ruben Salazar had been killed that afternoon. I was stunned. It was one more tragedy added to the awful events of that day. But at first I didn't connect Ruben's death with what Joe and I had witnessed that afternoon.

"Ruben Salazar was shot and killed at the Silver Dollar Café," the news reported.

"Goddamn it, we should have been there," I said to myself. "The Silver Dollar on Whittier?"

Then I had this flashback of the bar where we had witnessed the deputies shooting. Could this be the Silver Dollar? "Fuck, I'm going to find out."

After returning to La Raza's office and picking up my daughter, who had been there, and taking her home, I went back to the office, where we had our darkroom. Anxiously, I waited to see if we had been witnesses to the killing of Ruben. As the pictures appeared, sure enough, there was the Silver Dollar!

August 29, 1970, is a date that none of us involved in the Chicano movement will ever forget. It's impressed in our minds and souls. What at one level represented one of the peaks of the movement, at another represented the opposite. The largest demonstration of the period was suppressed, with many arrested, extensive damage, and three Chicanos killed, including the most prominent Chicano journalist of his time, Ruben Salazar. I later eulogized Ruben in my eyewitness report in La Raza: "Rest in peace, Ruben, and may the vengeance of the people seeking justice be vented against those that have cut short your life."[27]

I found it hard to sleep that night and for many nights thereafter. We lost something that day, not just Ruben and two other Chicanos killed, but something else less tangible that I wasn't as aware of then. It was our unfettered idealism.

MY PHOTOS

After I developed the photos, I decided that they should be shown first on channel 34, KMEX, since that was Ruben's station. I went to see Danny Villanueva, the station manager and former Dallas Cowboys football player.

"Danny, I think you should show these photos on your news program. They contradict what the cops are saying about warning the people to come out of the café."

Villanueva looked at the photos, and to my utter surprise and frustration told me that he couldn't or wouldn't show them. He gave no reason. I couldn't believe it.

"But he was your man! He died doing work for you! This is important. I'm not saying you should show the photos with my interpretation. But just show the damned photos!"

He wouldn't do it.

Instead, he told me that there were some people from *Alarma,* a Spanish-language sensationalist tabloid similar to the *National Inquirer* in his other office.

"They might be interested in your pictures."

I felt offended and told Villanueva where he could go.

I then approached channel 4, the NBC affiliate. I talked to a young reporter by the name of Tom Brokaw. Little did I know then that he would go on to become a big-shot TV news anchor. Brokaw came to our office. I showed him the photos, and he said that he would try to get the station to show them. Again, I was disappointed when he called back and said that channel 4 wouldn't let him do it.

"Something is going on," I said to myself.

It's then that I decided to hold a news conference and show the photos and *quien venga venga*—who comes, comes. We arranged to use the L.A. Press Club and sent out notices to all the media. A lot of reporters came and asked questions, but no one asked to publish or broadcast the photos. Except for one guy. He was an editor for the *Los Angeles Times* who sat in the back and asked no questions. However, at the conclusion of the news conference, he approached me.

"Look, if you want to come with me right now to the *Times,* we'll publish your pictures in tomorrow's edition."

"Okay," I said, "but only on one condition. I don't want any money for them. All I want is credit for *La Raza*."

He agreed, but this was a big mistake on my part, because after the *Times* printed the photos on September 4, they were reprinted all over the place and we never got any compensation or credit.

FIGURE 3. Ruiz with his photos of the Silver Dollar Café shootout, where Ruben Salazar was killed, early September 1970. Courtesy of Allen Zak.

Still, this was a first. The *Times* had never before given such attention to a Chicano perspective on the news. The photos with statements by myself and Joe Razo were printed on the front page and spread into the second and third as well.

Of course, I kept the negatives. In fact, shortly after the moratorium, the police broke into our office. This wasn't the first time, but I suspected that they had heard about the photos and were looking for them. But I never kept the negatives there for that very reason. I hid them in different people's homes for safekeeping. I still have them.

We used the photos ourselves and published a four-page special *La Raza* tabloid on the moratorium. It appeared right around the publication of the photos by the *Times*. We worked day and night on this issue. I still don't know where we got the energy.

We published about fifty thousand copies of the tabloid. That was a big job for us, but it sold out very quickly.

Later that month we came out with the regular issue of *La Raza* completely devoted to the moratorium, where we again published the photos. This issue had a big impact. It also included eyewitness reports by Joe and me. We printed about twenty thousand copies, and it also sold out quickly. Besides our regular subscribers, we sold the issue in the streets and in barrio stores. We also sent a good number to *pintos* (prisoners), although we knew that officials were censoring stories from *La Raza*.

THE INQUEST

The moratorium and the events of August 29 continued to be a trauma for the Chicano community. Within a short time, the district attorney organized a public inquest on the death of Ruben Salazar. A jury was impaneled to hear testimony as to the cause of Ruben's death. This was not a trial, and no attorneys were involved. An inquest officer, Norman Pittlock, was named to ask questions provided by the district attorney to a variety of witnesses, including the deputies who shot into the Silver Dollar. The jury would then determine if Ruben had died at the hands of another. But this decision would not be binding on the district attorney, Evelle Younger. Having heard testimony and weighing the jury's decision, Younger would then determine if he would seek indictments in this case against the sheriffs involved.

The inquest received a lot of attention and publicity. It lasted several days and was televised live locally on some of the stations. The entire day's proceedings sometimes lasted eight hours. The hearings proved to be a big farce. There was no real serious effort to examine the motives and actions of the deputies and why they had shot into the café. Why they had fired tear-gas projectiles into an enclosed area with people inside, which was against their own procedures, was never probed.

The claims of the deputies were also never questioned. For example, they alleged that the reason they went to the bar was because they had received a call that an armed man was inside the premises. But no witness was ever produced to corroborate this. They further claimed that they had warned the people inside to come out before they fired. My photos and my eyewitness account that suggested otherwise were never brought out. Why the deputies didn't enter the café for at least two hours after the shooting was never raised. All these questions went unanswered because the district attorney was there supporting the sheriff's department, even though the DA's office was supposed to be neutral.

None of these questions were asked of Thomas Wilson, the deputy who shot into the Silver Dollar and ostensibly killed Ruben by blowing a hole in his head, even though Wilson testified. All he was asked was to identify the weapon and the type of projectile used.

By contrast, when Joe Razo and I testified, along with others involved in the moratorium, Pittlock grilled us through questions provided by the district attorney.

Before our testimony, Joe and I agreed that we were going to be very strong in our claims about what had happened to Ruben. We believed that the sheriffs had deliberately sabotaged the moratorium and that they had targeted Ruben. They set out to kill him because at channel 34 he had been exposing police violence and abuse against Chicanos. This is what we intended to testify. We were not going to be shut up by the court.

I testified for two straight days for a total of about sixteen hours. Hour after hour, I was questioned. None of the inquiries dealt with my eyewitness account of the Silver Dollar incident. Instead, all the questions had to do with the demonstration itself and with the intent of casting doubts on my legitimacy as a journalist and on the reliability of my photos.

The DA used my testimony as a way of deflecting attention from the actions of the deputies and instead focusing on the moratorium itself. The suggestion was that the demonstration was communist-inspired and aimed at creating violence in the streets and that the sheriffs were there only to contain and prevent this. They accused *La Raza* of being a communist newspaper. They suggested that my photos had been doctored to cast a bad light on the deputies. One of my photos allowed into testimony showed a shot of the march down Whittier. It showed a number of Chicanos carrying signs such as "Viva la Raza" and "Brown Is Beautiful." But Pittlock was concerned only about one small sign in the photo that read, "Viva Che." This was a reference to Che Guevara of the Cuban Revolution, whom Chicanos regarded as a fighter for liberation and justice.

"What does Che mean?" Pittlock asked me.

"Che, Che," I responded, "stands for Che Guevara who fought for the rights of all people and for social justice in Latin America."

The Chicanos present in the courtroom broke into clapping and yelling in support of my statement.

"Isn't that Castro's man?" Pittlock came back. This was the DA's effort through Pittlock to red-bait the moratorium and to suggest that we were all communists who were sowing revolution in the streets of East Los Angeles.

But what they were really doing was covering up the deputies' actions and those of who knows else involved in the police attack on the moratorium. The inquest was a cover-up from start to finish.

We as Chicanos tried our best to expose this sham. From the witness stand we questioned the line of arguments and inquiries—all directed at the actions of the demonstrators and not the deputies. After all, this was not an inquest on the moratorium; it was about who killed Ruben Salazar.

"What does all this have to do with the death of Ruben Salazar?" I shot back at Pittlock.

During my testimony, Pittlock asked me to turn over the negatives of my photos.

"That's impossible. They're in Aztlán."

I was trying to be a smart-ass with him.

"Because you don't have them?" he asked.

"No, because the police have repeatedly broken into *La Raza*'s office trying to steal them, that's why not."

FIGURE 4. Ruiz testifying at the inquest on the death of Ruben Salazar, September 1969. Courtesy of the Los Angeles Times Photographic Archive, Department of Special Collections, Charles E. Young Research Library, University of California, Los Angeles.

I knew that if the police and the DA got hold of the negatives I would never see them again.

These were dangerous times. During my two days of testimony, death threats against me were phoned into the police. Whatever persons were calling in said that they were going to kill me.

"Do you want protection?" the police asked me.

Even though I took these threats seriously, I refused police protection. Who would protect me from the police? After all, it was the sheriff's deputies who had killed Ruben!

I declined the offer but tried to get some political mileage out of this. The next time I was on the witness stand and very aware of the TV camera, I announced, "I have just been informed that the court has received death threats against me. The court has asked me if I want protection from the sheriff's department. I'm formally refusing this protection because I'm more afraid of the deputies guarding me than about some weirdo taking a potshot at me!"

I could just see the anger in the deputies present when I said this. They got all upset, as did the district attorney. But then we were all upset as well.

The fact was that the inquest proved to be a circus. It was a joke. The jury, by a split vote, did conclude that Ruben had "died at the hands of another." But what the hell did this mean? We all knew this! We knew that Wilson, the deputy, had shot into the Silver Dollar and that this led to Ruben being killed, not by the projectile but by someone else, in my opinion. Ruben didn't trip and hit his head. His head was blown off, or so the autopsy concluded.

What we wanted to know was why Ruben was killed. Was there a conspiracy? And what was the DA going to do about Ruben's death? Was he going to prosecute Wilson and the other deputies involved?

Nothing came of the inquest. The DA, Younger, argued that because of the split decision by the jury he didn't feel that a sufficient case could be brought forth alleging that the deputies had willfully shot into the café with the intent of injuring, much less killing, someone. He refused to prosecute. But why had Wilson shot tear gas directly into the Silver Dollar almost at point-blank range? Did he not think that he would hurt anyone, especially after he had forced several people back into the café?

I have no doubt in my mind after all these years that the inquest was a cover-up. I also firmly believe that Ruben was deliberately murdered. Part of the cover-up was the coroner's report that stated that Ruben had died when one of the projectiles hit him in the side of the head and then exited the other side. Ruben had died instantly, Coroner Thomas Nguchi testified.

I have never believed this. If Ruben had been hit with the force of the huge projectile, his head would have been blown off. Look at the damage that a smaller bullet did to President Kennedy's head. Yet somehow we were being asked to believe that Ruben's head had not been blown off? But the head did remain. It was clearly visible at the funeral home, where there was an open casket. In fact, even though I felt uncomfortable doing this, as I walked past the casket, I took a photo of Ruben. There was a head, and it didn't show much damage.

So how did Ruben die? I believe that he was shot from the inside. I believe that one of the other persons in the café shot and killed Ruben after the tear-gas projectiles exploded inside the bar and possibly grazed Ruben, knocking him to the floor. Perhaps it was the alleged person who called the sheriffs about an armed person inside the Silver Dollar. I can't prove this. I know it's a conspiracy theory. But what I do know is that the failure of the inquest to really probe into the incident has left many unanswered questions and, as a result, spawned many conspiracy theories.

In retrospect, Ruben's family or we should have called for an independent coroner's report to examine the cause of death. But we didn't. Consequently, we may never know all the answers. Even today, every August 29, someone calls for a new inquest into Ruben's death. But I doubt that this will ever happen. Still, I and others will continue to ask questions and to investigate on our own. Why was Ruben Salazar killed?

MORE PROTESTS

Although angered and frustrated at the breakup of the moratorium, Rosalio Muñoz and the other leaders of the Moratorium Committee did not back down. Besides protesting against the war, Chicanos now had the additional issue of increased police violence against the Chicano community. More protests followed on September 16 and January 9, 1971. While the turnouts were more limited, unfortunately, they also once again were met with police violence.

August 29 and the subsequent events that were linked to violence—police violence—proved to be a watershed for the movement in Los Angeles. From this time on, we were more on the defensive, trying to explain that we were committed to nonviolence. But the damage had been done. August 29 didn't break up the movement; other issues would eventually do that.

But what did happen is that we as Chicano activists were pretty much on our own. We found it more and more difficult to include others in our struggles, in particular the moderate elements that were fearful of associating with the movement because they now linked it to violence. Our ability to participate in coalition politics, rather than being strengthened by the sheriffs' attacks, was instead weakened.

Intensified police and FBI surveillance and infiltration of the movement likewise influenced these growing tensions. Many groups were spied on. This was true of the Brown Berets as well as the Moratorium Committee. It's possible that *La Raza* was infiltrated, although I don't think it was. We were a pretty tight-knit group and a small one. We knew and trusted one another well. It was hard for a stranger to just come in and join. We were too focused a group for that. This was different from some of the other groups where people came and went and sponsored large community meetings where you didn't know everyone. These conditions made it easier for police and FBI penetration.

The police attacks, however, only encouraged further demonstrations. The next one was on January 31. Protesters from throughout L.A. and as far away as Long Beach converged on Belvedere Park. No confrontation occurred there, but at the conclusion of the march, several hundred Chicanos proceeded to a sheriff's substation in East L.A. Here is where the trouble started. One or more of the deputies shot at the crowd. This was heavy stuff!

Lots of people got shot. The cops fired live ammo. I was with the demonstrators, but when I saw the contingent of deputies waiting for us as we turned the corner into the substation, I left to a position where I could take better photos. I thought at the time that this was a wise decision, but it wasn't.

Somehow, as I was taking pictures of the riot, I got shot in the back. It may have been from a deputy's gun or from someone else's. I don't know. All I remember is that as I was reloading film in my camera, I felt something in my back. I asked a guy who was next to me if he could raise my shirt and look at my back.

"I don't know," he said, "it looks like a bruise."

I didn't think anything of it and continued to take photos.

However, when I got back to the office and took off my Levi jacket that I liked to wear because I could stick several rolls of film in the pockets, one of my staff members exclaimed, "Raul, you've been shot! You have all this blood."

Sure enough, my back was full of blood. I looked at my jacket, and there was a hole in it—what looked like a bullet hole. My shirt and my T-shirt also had holes. Although I didn't feel like I had been shot, my staff convinced me to go to the hospital.

"You're a lucky man, Mr. Ruiz," the doctor in the emergency room told me. "The bullet penetrated your clothes but caused only a scrape. It could have been a lot worse."

"No, Doctor, you've got it all wrong," I responded as I tried to be macho about the whole thing. "The bullet hit me, but my body stopped it."

The doctor didn't particularly appreciate my Superman joke.

Privately, I did feel pretty lucky. The same thing couldn't be said of some of the other Chicanos. One was killed and several others wounded. In all, about two hundred Chicanos were shot. At the scene, before I returned to my office, I had covered the body of the fallen Chicano.

That day was like the Palestinian intifada. The police possessed the guns, and they shot into the crowd. The Chicanos, like the Palestinians, had only the rocks and sticks that they hurled back. It was not an even match. Maybe the Chicanos shouldn't have thrown these things, but they certainly didn't desire or expect to be blasted by live ammo.

The January 31 incident and the previous ones took a lot out of the Moratorium Committee. The attacks brought only criticism of the committee and the movement as being reckless and provoking violence. All of this was unfair, but it was happening. What was clear was that these demonstrations could not continue without more police attacks and without the movement losing more credibility. Many of us desired to move on to other issues and struggles.

LA RAZA UNIDA

The idea or concept of La Raza Unida, which some people translated as "The United People," first came to my attention at the 1969 Denver youth conference. But it wasn't linked to a political party movement. It was just the idea of a united Chicano movement. At least this is the way I remember Corky Gonzales referring to it. It's possible that Corky and others already then envisioned an independent Chicano political party. But what I took from the conference was more a sense of ethnic solidarity.

The linkage of La Raza Unida to a political party didn't really begin to surface until the events in Crystal City, Texas, following a school walkout. In late 1969 and early 1970, José Ángel Gutiérrez and the Mexican American Youth Organization (MAYO) began to organize electorally around what they called La Raza Unida Party, or RUP. In the spring of 1970, the RUP won several local elections in some of the small south Texas towns, including Crystal City, where Chicanos gained control of the school board.[28]

We read and heard about these events and were excited about them. The newspapers referred to these victories as a "revolution in Texas."

Soon some activists in L.A. began to talk about organizing La Raza Unida in Southern California. A couple of guys, Gilbert Baca and Reggie Ruiz, helped put together a meeting about it. I went to it and sat in the back and listened. I thought it made a lot of sense to organize our own Chicano party. Why not? If they could do it in Texas, we could do it here!

I thought this was particularly important at this moment because, ever since the moratorium, we seemed to have become more on the defensive. We were reacting to issues rather than promoting them. La Raza Unida was a way of becoming proactive again in a very concrete way. Chicanos needed more effective political representation that would not sell out to other interests. La Raza Unida would provide that representation. It was a way of gaining Chicano power. It also made sense from an organizational perspective. East L.A., for example, represented a largely Chicano barrio or series of barrios that, I believed, would respond to an all-Chicano party. We had found a new issue!

We decided to organize the party right out of our *La Raza* headquarters. We felt that we had the experience and the community contacts to do so. We were a known entity.

Fortunately for us, at this very time in 1971, a special election was being held to fill a vacancy in the Forty-Eighth Assembly District for the California legislature. The previous incumbent, David Roberti, a Democrat, had been elected to the state senate and his assembly seat had to be filled. The Forty-Eighth District covered a good chunk of East Los Angeles. We felt that this was perfect for us. We would use the special election to organize and promote La Raza Unida.

I agreed to be the candidate for the party in the election, which consisted first of a primary, open to all candidates irrespective of party, where those with the most votes would participate in a runoff. I felt that I could articulate the issues that we wanted to stress as a way of building the party. Our headquarters was in the Forty-Eighth District, but the candidates also had to live in the area. My parents didn't, since they lived in South Central L.A. Some people asked, "How can Raul run in this district? He doesn't live there."

Fortunately, I did. I was living in the City Terrace area of East Los Angeles. I was renting a guesthouse from my friend Danny Zapata. I lived there for about five years.

The Democrats had always held this assembly seat. It was a solidly Democratic area. The Republicans didn't have any chance of winning. So the real issue was who was going to run for the Democrats. There was some real tension and competition as several individuals announced their candidacies. However, the real competition pitted two big Democratic honchos against each other: Walter Korabian, the state senate majority leader, and Bob Moretti, the speaker of the assembly. Both supported different candidates. What was interesting was that Korabian was endorsing a Chicano candidate, Richard Alatorre, one of his aides. There is no question but that Korabian was reacting to the pressures from the Chicano movement. Moretti also felt these pressures and supported another Chicano, Ralph Ochoa. This was the first time that the Democrats had endorsed Chicano candidates.

On the Republican side, the key candidate was Bill Brophy. No one expected him to win. The Democrats, on the other hand, worried about me and the impact my candidacy might have on the election. Sometime just as the campaign got under way, Alatorre approached me.

"How come you're running?"

"How come you're running?" I arrogantly shot back. "After all, you haven't done shit in the community."

As far as I was concerned, Alatorre was just another political wannabe who had no movement credentials. Richard had participated in the blowouts to some extent but then had gone the establishment route. He wasn't a bad person, but he just wasn't a movement person. In fact, Richard, although of Mexican American background, couldn't function very well in the barrio. His Spanish was lousy.

By contrast, Brophy, although a Republican, was an Irish Catholic who spoke perfect Spanish and had lived in Mexico. He was also a millionaire. When all the candidates were interviewed on television, Brophy would have fun off camera with Richard by cursing him in Spanish—"*pinche puto*," motherfucker. Richard couldn't understand what Brophy was saying. What Richard did have was a lot of money from the Democratic Party.

We knew that challenging the two-party system, and in particular the dominance of the Democratic Party, in the Forty-Eighth District was an uphill battle. Still, we weren't interested in practical politics, at least with respect to the Democratic Party. We were idealistic and purists on organizing our own party. We honestly believed that we could win. We believed—naively in retrospect—that since the district was overwhelmingly Chicano, they would vote for a self-identified Chicano instead of for the other candidates who didn't stress their ethnicity.

We were into movement politics. This was ethnic nationalism, and we believed that this would carry us to victory. We weren't interested in running a campaign simply as an educational process, as some La Raza Unida activists in other places did. We felt that we could do exactly what José Ángel Gutiérrez and the RUP had done in Crystal City and other small towns in south Texas, and that was to win elections by appealing to ethnic solidarity.

Our platform for the campaign zeroed in on the lack of effective and grassroots political representation for Chicanos in East Los Angeles. We raised other issues, of course, such as police abuse, school problems, and the Vietnam War, but the main thrust was Chicano political empowerment. We stressed that as Chicanos we had to start relying on ourselves rather than on others, outside people, to represent us in Sacramento and in Washington.

"What has this gotten us?" we asked. "Nothing! We have lousy schools, lack of opportunities, bad housing, and the worst of everything."

We, as Chicanos, had to come together politically and to harness this great potential that we had not exercised before electorally. But we had to do so now in a new independent fashion. The Republican Party had never cared a damn about us. And the Democrats took us for granted. If the Democrats, who had historically represented Chicanos, had really done something, we would not have been in the bad circumstances that we faced. If we could blame anyone, it was the Democrats. It wasn't until we started to protest some of these conditions that the politicians began to try to do something. This reinforced our central argument that only through an independent political party, La Raza Unida, could we expect action from the establishment.

The campaign lasted several weeks, and we were fortunate to have a lot of volunteers from a cross section of people: movement activists, students, and community people. Overall, it was primarily nonstudents who volunteered. This is another example of how the movement was not just a student movement, as some contend. It was not, although many students were involved. But so too were many community people. This was certainly true in L.A. and in our campaign.

With our volunteers and with *La Raza* staff, we engaged in a variety of electoral activities during the campaign. One of the most important was registering voters. We canvassed most of the district. We went door-to-door. We set up our tables in shopping areas and at public events. We encouraged people to register as members of La Raza Unida or as independents.

We didn't have much money to publicize our campaign. In fact, I used a lot of my own money. By contrast, Alatorre had quite a lot. We certainly couldn't afford the big billboards that Richard had all over the district. Some of these were spray painted or destroyed. While we weren't responsible for this, Richard still blamed us.

Fortunately for us, we had *La Raza*, with its printing capacity to turn out thousands of tabloids and leaflets. We couldn't afford to mail these, so we distributed them by hand. In all our materials we used the name La Raza Unida. We also got the endorsement of other Chicano movement papers such as *Justicia O!,* published by the Abogados de Aztlán (Lawyers of Aztlán) and La Raza Students' Association. In its endorsement, the paper stated, "But there is something happening in the Southwest and in Los Angeles, Raza, that may make our votes mean something. That may make it worth our while to go to the polls on October 19, 1971. For the first time a man is running for a political office—for State Assembly—under the name of El Partido de La Raza Unida. His name is Raul Ruiz. He is a Chicano. And he does not believe that the democratic or republican parties will ever do a damn thing for the betterment of our peoples."[29]

The regular media also brought attention to our campaign. We didn't get a lot of press, but enough stressed our effort to build an alternative party. Most of this reporting was hostile, but at least we got La Raza Unida in the papers and on television and radio.

We likewise organized rallies and neighborhood meetings. We were a very community-oriented campaign. We were on the streets with the people. We got good turnouts at our gatherings. Many people were excited about us. In these barrio meetings, I spoke in both English and Spanish. If the people were older and Spanish speaking, then naturally I spoke Spanish. If it was a mixed audience, young and old, then I reverted to a bilingual format. It was still a bit difficult for me to speak Spanish in public, but by this time I could give a pretty good rap in Spanish. I was a much better speaker than Alatorre and the other candidates.

In the primary election that involved several candidates, we worked hard to bring out our voters. We did very well. Because there were ten candidates in all, including me, we all split the vote. I received 4 percent, which I felt was very good, given the large field. For someone to win outright, 51 percent or more of the vote was necessary. Given the large field, this was unlikely. The candidates of each party who received the most votes would then move on to a runoff.

Since I was an independent representing La Raza Unida Party, all I had to do was get more votes than the other independent candidates, such as the one from the Peace and Freedom Party. I was able to do so. The runoff consisted of myself, Alatorre for the Democrats, and Brophy for the Republicans.

For the next month, before the runoff on November 16, 1971, we doubled our efforts. On election day we again worked hard to turn out the vote. We had a list of registered voters, and we either called them to encourage them to vote for us or went door-to-door to see if they had voted. If some needed help to get to the polls, we helped them. We did as much as we could, and there was a good turnout.

Up to and including election day, I felt that I could win. I won 2,778 votes, or almost 8 percent of the total. In a surprise upset, Brophy triumphed over Alatorre. The Democrats were stunned. We were ecstatic. We didn't win, but we proved to be the margin of victory. We didn't aim to get a Republican elected, but we punished the Democrats for their years of neglect. Besides, in our cocky and naive way, we honestly believed that there were no differences between the Republicans and Democrats.

We had wanted to win. We had set out to win, but we were very pleased and encouraged by the results. It proved to us that voters would respond to an all-Chicano party. We vowed to do even better next time.

By contrast, Richard Alatorre was fit to be tied. He felt that I was personally responsible for his defeat. He was *llorando* (crying) and *chillando* (complaining), "Oh, my God, my future is lost!" His attitude created a backlash by some Democrats, who tried to pin on us the title of "the spoilers." They claimed that because of my candidacy that the right-wing Republicans got elected. In fact, they went further and suggested that there was some kind of collusion between Brophy and us.

This was all nonsense. We had nothing to do with Brophy and the Republicans. In fact, he won the expected number of votes that usually went to the Republicans. He didn't get any extra ones. We helped increase voter participation, and we got many of the new votes. We didn't deprive Alatorre of victory. He and the Democrats lost the election. Richard ran a weak campaign. He didn't distinguish himself, despite all the money he had from his mentor, Korabian.

As far as we were concerned, La Raza Unida had arrived in Los Angeles.

One year later, our chapter of the RUP, the City Terrace one, decided to challenge a Chicano Democrat, Alex García, who represented the Fortieth Assembly District, which also took in part of East Los Angeles. By this time, I had bought a house in that district and qualified as a candidate. I had started to teach Chicano studies at San Fernando State, and that provided me with the income to meet my mortgage.

Running in the Fortieth was different because here all the major candidates were Chicanos. Besides García, the Republicans put up someone named Aguirre. There were no Anglo candidates, so whatever happened, the district would be represented by a Chicano.

As we did in the previous campaign, we organized to win, not just to educate the voters about the evils of the two-party system. I felt that we could win, especially because García was a weak candidate. He had a horrible absentee record in the assembly and had voted against education and minimum-wage legislation that would have helped Chicanos. On top of this, Alex had a drinking problem that, we felt, would hurt him.

Our biggest obstacle was just getting on the ballot, but not as La Raza Unida. It would have taken too many signatures to do that. I just had to get on as an independent. But that still required two thousand signatures of people who would have to state that if the election were held at the time of their signatures they would vote for me. At first it seemed pretty difficult to do this, especially since we had to do it in three weeks.

But we again had the help of many volunteers, including the other local RUP chapters. We went door-to-door and put up tables wherever we could to push our petition. Working long hours, our staff and volunteers pulled it off. On the deadline, we turned in the required signatures, with some to spare. At least my name would be on the ballot.

The campaign started that summer in 1972 and went into the fall for the November election. In the middle of this period, I went off to El Paso for the national convention of the RUP (which I go into later). I was actually criticized for doing this. "Where the hell is Raul?" some of our people asked, criticizing my leaving for a few days. But it was important to be in El Paso for this historic meeting. Afterward, I resumed my campaign.

We pushed the same agenda, attacking the Democrats for not really representing the interests of Chicanos and emphasizing the need for an independent Chicano political party. We especially used the presidential campaigns of both President Richard Nixon and Senator George McGovern to attack both candidates. We asserted that there were no differences between the two. They were both equally bad. In retrospect, this was not true. McGovern was more liberal and against the Vietnam War. But in the heat of the moment, we believed otherwise.

I debated Alex García during the campaign. I felt that I won each time. He was usually drunk. He could hardly speak Spanish. He was an awful campaigner.

Going into election day, I felt that we had a chance. We got a good voter turnout. But I didn't win. I received a larger vote than the first campaign. I got more than five thousand votes, some 13 percent of the total. The problem was that the Republican Aguirre did horribly, and, as a result, García won some 56 percent of the vote.

Many of our supporters were quite happy with our performance. We had significantly improved in one year.

But as far as I was concerned, I wasn't happy. In fact, I was very disappointed and discouraged. I felt that we could have won. Perhaps this was wishful thinking, but I believed that with more of an effort we could have pulled off an upset. I was particularly concerned because I felt that most of our supporters were content with just a good showing and using the campaign to politicize and educate Chicanos. I wasn't against this strategy, but I felt that it also led to a certain lethargy. Educating voters about issues and using the RUP as an educational vehicle was not the same as organizing an electoral campaign aimed at winning and taking political power. I didn't want to just educate voters; I wanted to empower them!

I took out my frustration in a piece I wrote for *La Raza*, in which I attacked this more limited strategy and focused on three key issues: (1) our failure to appreciate the deep loyalties of Chicanos to the Democratic Party, (2) our failure to truly politicize the people, and (3) our inability or unwillingness to embed ourselves in the community on a more permanent basis. This is some of what I wrote:

> No matter how we rationalized, it was a disappointment not to receive more votes—especially from the Chicano community. . . .

Now this does not mean that we are wrong in the establishment of a new political concept and structure. But it does mean that we have a difficult road ahead. We cannot expect to do away with a political party that has been using and confusing our people for many years, for over half a century, with a few months of campaign activity. . . .

It is true that winning the office for the sake of winning is not the all-consuming reason for our political existence because we believe that the political consciousness that the people receive from our contact with them is more important. This, though, cannot be employed so loosely as to imply that anything we do in our political activity in fact increases the awareness of the people politically. If we say, for example, we didn't win but we did politicize the people, then why didn't we receive the vote of support and confidence from this newly politicized block of voters. The fact of the matter is that we not only lost but we failed to politicize the people to any meaningful depth, at least the Chicanos in our district anyway. . . .

The partido needs to establish a stronger base in the community; campaigns are good, but campaigns in and of themselves are not enough to politicize the community. . . .

Our partido is not as our name states, but rather, it is a goal that all of us should strive to attain.

La Raza Unida is still a dream.[30]

THE NATIONAL RUP CONVENTION

Besides our own local RUP campaigns in L.A., other RUPs in other states, including Texas, were also running candidates. However, the biggest development in this early history of *el partido* was the organization of a national convention to be held in El Paso over Labor Day in 1972. The convention, of course, also would occur in the midst of the presidential campaign that year. The Democrats chose Senator George McGovern as their standard-bearer, and President Richard Nixon ran for reelection.

I was also involved in my second campaign, and even though I was quite excited about the national convention, I was too busy to be part of the preconvention meetings that took place in L.A. that summer. Perhaps I was also too arrogant to participate. As it turned out, I was the only representative from our RUP City Terrace chapter to go to El Paso. The rest of our members were too busy with our campaign.

I arrived in El Paso expecting to play little or no role in the convention. I felt that I had to put in an appearance and then as soon as possible return to L.A. to resume my campaign. I didn't even arrange to stop at the convention hotel—the old Paso del Norte in downtown El Paso. Instead, I stayed with my tías and my *primos*, my cousins. Little did I know what was in store for me.

Either the day I arrived or the day before, a young RUP delegate from Colorado, Ricardo Falcón, was shot and killed by a gas station owner in Orogrande, a small

New Mexican town just north of El Paso. Falcón was with part of the Colorado contingent driving down from Denver. Apparently, there had been some dispute between Falcón and the owner, and for no apparent reason, the owner shot and killed the young man.

So the convention began with all this tension and anger. It was an ominous sign. It put a cloud over the proceedings.

The tension was increased by what quickly became a power grab by the Texas delegation, on the one hand, and the Colorado one, on the other. Even before the convention came to order, both sides lobbied for their positions. The most controversial issue was whether the convention would run a presidential candidate or possibly endorse either McGovern or Nixon. Actually, there was no way the delegates were going to support "Tricky Dick."

Since the idea of running an RUP presidential candidate did not get off the ground, the real issue was whether the convention would endorse, albeit critically, McGovern, who represented the more liberal and antiwar wing of the Democratic Party. The other choice was for the meeting to refuse to endorse either candidate and remain independent of both parties. It was clear that the Colorado delegates, who not so subtly suggested that the Texas people might be sympathetic to McGovern, were pushing the no-endorsement position. I knew that the endorsement position wouldn't fly, and it didn't.

This competition between Colorado and Texas was further driven by the growing rivalry between the charismatic leader of the Colorado RUP, Corky Gonzales, and the equally charismatic leader of the Texas RUP, José Ángel Gutiérrez. Corky was the ideological guru of many Chicanos due to his sponsorship of the Youth Liberation conferences in Denver. Beginning in 1970, José Ángel had already successfully organized RUP campaigns in south Texas, including in his hometown of Crystal City, where the RUP took control of both the city council and the school board. At El Paso, both men put forth their candidacies for the chair of the national RUP.

Part of the rivalry between Corky and José Ángel was the question of who was the "founding father" of the party. Some claimed that it was Corky because the first call to organize an independent Chicano political party came at the 1969 Denver youth conference. On the other hand, José Ángel put the RUP on the map since he was the first to successfully organize the party in his home turf of Crystal City. I thought this debate was ridiculous. Both of them were key founders of the *partido*.

I had the utmost respect for both Corky and José Ángel. Both had done great work in their communities. But, at the same time, I had my doubts about both of them as national leaders. Part of the problem with the RUP was that there were leaders such as these two, who were trying to be national leaders but in fact weren't operating nationally. They were quite sectional in their operations and in their perspectives. Curiously, the same thing could be said of César Chávez. He focused almost exclusively on farmworkers in California. We really had no national leaders comparable to Martin Luther King Jr.

Of the two RUP rivals, José Ángel attracted the most opposition, although that came primarily from the Colorado people and perhaps half of the California delegation. They didn't trust him. They felt that he was an opportunist prepared to sell out the party to the highest bidder, whether McGovern or Nixon. They also believed that he had only the interests of the Texas RUP in mind. Still, some in the California group supported José. It was a split delegation, as were some of the other ones. I stayed out of this dispute since officially I was not part of the California delegation. I had come to El Paso on my own.

Neither Corky nor José Ángel seemed to be able to rise above this petty bickering. Neither seemed capable of producing consensus. I thought both were very limited as leaders. I felt like telling them, "You don't deserve to be national leaders, because you don't behave as national leaders."

But I didn't tell them this. Perhaps I should have.

I also felt that both were too individualistic, ego-driven, and provincial. Corky had a greater breadth of understanding. He had a sense of the people as *la raza*. Yet he was very much tied to Denver. Still, at least, Corky had a Chicano nationalistic ideology—chicanismo—while José didn't seem to have an ideology at all. He made fun of ideology. I would ask him, "José, what's your ideology?" He would respond by making a wisecrack. You couldn't talk ideology with him.

However, this didn't mean that José was devoid of any type of political consciousness. He was what I would call a pragmatic nationalist, as opposed to Corky, who was a romantic or ideological nationalist. José would say, "Don't talk to me about your ideology, about the liberation of Aztlán. Talk to me how you propose to put in a new drainage ditch or a new sidewalk and build new schools in the barrio. How is my embrace of Aztlán going to do this?"

José Ángel was right. Many of us at the time were too caught up with this vague nationalist Aztlán ideology, while José talked about the nuts and bolts of concrete social change.

I liked José, but he was very arrogant. He knew that he was a good politico. He could talk. He was a great speaker, in both English and Spanish, an advantage that he had over Corky, who found it difficult to give a good speech in Spanish. José *tenía presencia el muchacho*—the guy had a presence about him. I admired José, as I did Corky. Still, I didn't think that either one was doing a good job nationally for the RUP.

Although the differences between Corky and José were to a large extent not ideological but personal, there were some differences regarding political strategies. José Ángel came to the RUP from the position of electoral politics. Corky, by contrast, saw electoral politics as a way of organizing the community. The differences were based on the reality of their experiences. José had a legitimate position because of his electoral successes in Crystal City and other south Texas towns where *mexicanos* predominated and could use ethnic politics to gain political control.

This wasn't the case in Denver, Corky's base. A Chicano couldn't do anything—electorally speaking—in Denver. Chicanos were too much a minority to gain political representation solely on the basis of ethnic politics. As a result, Corky saw the RUP in his area as a way to raise consciousness and organize the community but not necessarily to elect candidates.

In L.A. some RUP members supported Corky's views. I didn't. I felt that we could elect candidates. What I was pissed about after my second campaign was that we didn't win or raise consciousness.

Since José Ángel, who had done most of the spade work for the El Paso convention, and Corky, who had become a living icon of the movement, were both contending to be elected chair of the national RUP, neither could serve as chair of the convention. So who would do so? Who was not already committed to either man and could be "objective" and "neutral" in running the meeting? Little did I know when I arrived in El Paso that this person would be me!

I don't know who first suggested my name. It might have been Corky's people. But both he and José, and their aides, had to agree on a convention chair. I had pretty good contact with both of them. I got along fine with both. They both liked me. When my name surfaced, people apparently said, "Yeah, Raul." I was unanimously accepted. People, I guess, felt that I could be fair and impartial. If I had known what I was getting into, I don't think that I would have accepted. It was a no-win situation.

Once I was named and accepted by the delegates as convention chair, I worked hard to stay above the growing feud between Corky and José. I didn't participate in caucuses sponsored by either faction. I felt that it would hurt my neutrality if I did. The moment that I would go to either a Texas or a Colorado meeting, I would have been accused of favoring one side. For that reason, I was glad that I was staying with my tías and not at the hotel. Besides providing me with a nice bed, my tías shielded me from the brewing convention storms—at least from some.

Despite these tensions, I was determined to run the convention openly and fairly. I remember telling José Ángel, "If I make a mistake, I make a mistake, but it won't be because I'm influenced by one side or another."

That's another reason why I didn't participate in meetings of the California delegation, in addition to the fact that I wasn't an official delegate. I was the chair of the convention, and it was inappropriate for me to attend any of the state caucuses.

But I was put in an impossible position. I had to appear to be totally disinterested, neutral, and unbiased. And I think that I was. I don't think that anyone can say that I tried to control or manipulate.

There is no question that the most difficult task I faced as convention chair concerned the voting procedures of the meeting. The issue was whether each

FIGURE 5. Ruiz with José Ángel Gutiérrez at La Raza Unida Party National Convention, El Paso, Texas, early September 1972. Courtesy of Oscar Castillo.

individual delegate from the several states represented from the Southwest and a few outside the region would have an individual vote: one person, one vote. Or would the delegates vote by the unit rule? That is, majority rule would result in all of the state's apportioned votes being cast in favor of a particular resolution or candidate. If this wasn't confusing enough, the issue of voting became a political football between Corky and José Ángel. Corky's faction favored the unit rule; José's, the one person, one vote. I was caught in the middle of what became, next to selecting a national chair, the most contentious issue at the convention.

The motion to adopt the one-person, one-vote procedure was made by José's people. They were convinced, and I suspect had already done a head count, that in this way José would be elected chair. The motion was made and seconded. However, at this point, Corky's delegates challenged the motion as being out of order. It fell on me to rule. From the podium, I felt the tension rising. I first tried to duck the issue. We had a rules committee, so I said, "Okay, guys, you got it. This is your job!"

The motion had been made at ten at night, and that's when I turned it over to the committee. For the next five hours, while the convention was in recess, the committee and I debated what to do. Members didn't want to touch it. It was a hot potato. Everyone understood the stakes involved. How we ruled would determine whether Corky or José got elected. This was high drama—literally smoke-filled room politics—Chicano style!

The committee in the end refused to resolve the challenge to the motion.

"You do it, Raul," they said.

"Bullshit, thanks a lot for nothing, *cabrones* (assholes)."

It was three or four in the morning, but I went back to the convention delegates who were still milling around and from the podium announced that as chair of the convention I was ruling that the motion was in order and that the delegates could vote on the motion. I thought I was going to be lynched at that moment, but enough sanity prevailed for the vote to be taken. Each state caucused and recorded each of their delegates' votes. A roll call of the states was taken and the votes recorded. A majority voted for the motion, and it passed. We would henceforth vote in the convention by individual delegates.

I survived that night and that ordeal, but I became quite unpopular with Corky's people and with the majority of the California delegation that had voted against the motion. These delegates felt that I had betrayed them and that I was doing José's bidding. I thought that I would be physically attacked. But I did what I felt I had to do. Since the rules committee chickened out, I had no choice but to make the ruling myself. I then and still now believe that I did the right thing. But I was sure glad that I had the sanctuary of my tía's house to go back to that night!

Fortunately, the adoption of the platform did not elicit the same fury. There was consensus on almost all the issues: an end to U.S. involvement in Vietnam and support for the farmworkers, more antipoverty programs, affirmative action, and a range of other national, regional, and local issues.

While the tensions abated over the next day or so, it mounted once again as we neared the final day that would focus on the selection of a national chair. There was already a lot of lobbying for both Corky and José. Both sides were involved in forms of character assassination behind the scenes. I felt that all of this was regrettable and reflected the lack of political maturity among many of the delegates.

Things began to turn into a frenzy. Both sides were totally polarized. You would have thought that the delegates believed that the future of all Chicanos was at stake by who was selected as chair. I thought this was nonsense. Some of these Chicanos were crazy and out of their fucking minds! I didn't think it was a big deal who became chair. Perhaps we should have acted like the PRI in Mexico.[31] We could have named either Corky or José as chair, and then the other would succeed. Either that or we could have flipped a coin. The winner would serve four years and then the other guy. This way we could avoid tearing ourselves apart.

But there was no desire to compromise. Everyone, including the two candidates—with their immense egos at stake—was on their own *ondas*—their own deals.

While voting for the chair was filled with drama, it was also, at least to me, anticlimactic. It became clear once we had adopted the one-person, one-vote rule that José had the votes. Not only had he personally organized the convention, but also in the months prior he had done a lot of traveling and speaking in some of the states outside of the Southwest, so he could organize support for himself. He went to the Midwest and even to some eastern states. The result was that some of them— Illinois, Wisconsin, Kansas, and even the District of Columbia—sent RUP delegates even though they had no real party chapters. José made sure that each of these delegates received a certain number of votes. Individually they weren't a lot, but they added up in José's favor.

When I counted the vote for the chair, it was no surprise, at least to me, that José won. I was totally exhausted by then. But for the sake of what party unity could still be salvaged, I called for both José and Corky to come up to the podium to address the convention. They both did: José with his rolled-up sleeves and thick glasses and Corky in his usual black clothes, although he may have had on a red shirt that day, and with his bodyguards. Reies López Tijerina, who was at the convention but played no significant role, joined them. He had just been released from federal prison for his actions related to his New Mexico land-grant movement, and in a pathetic way was hawking sales of his autobiography, recently published in Mexico. Tijerina, in a show of unity and to place himself in the limelight, stood at the center of the podium and raised high the arms of the other two. The next day this picture appeared in numerous papers throughout the Southwest and in other parts of the country. It was like the four horses of the Apocalypse minus one.

Despite the appearance of unity, and the pride from having met in their own political convention, you could see in the faces of Corky and José the intense rivalry and even stronger dislike of each other. They were like the chieftains of the Mexican Revolution of 1910—Pancho Villa and Emiliano Zapata. They were leaders, but they could not compromise with each other. What was at stake was not really ideology or even political strategies. It was pure ego. Each one wanted to be the big *chingón,* or boss. This defeated the dream of a national RUP. The El Paso convention was the first and the last national convention. Postconvention efforts to organize nationally failed due to the continued rivalries between both sides and especially Corky's bitterness over his defeat.

Corky's feelings spilled over to me as well. After the voting for chair had finished, I went over to see Corky to explain to him that I had nothing to do with the results. I didn't talk to him because one of his lieutenants, Ernesto Vigil, a tough young man and a friend of mine, intercepted me. He was very, very angry with me. I thought he was going to punch my lights out. He didn't, but I knew that the Denver people, including Corky, believed that I had sold out to José Ángel. I couldn't convince them that I had done nothing of the sort. I acted honestly, even though it cost me my friendship with Corky. He would have nothing to do with me for many years.

Some have suggested that the RUP convention in El Paso was one of the major highlights of the Chicano movement. But I don't buy that. It represented a failure, not a success. The movement became even more fractured after the meeting. The RUP was totally polarized. The convention had no impact on the community. The provincialism and petty personality splits of the RUP contributed to its demise.

There is no question in my mind that the problems and failures of the RUP could be traced to the lack of effective and strong national leadership, and I include myself in that indictment. Everyone was trying to protect and expand his or her own turf. There was no way Corky was going to leave Denver, nor was José going to leave Texas, and yet they both wanted to be national leaders.

I think, too, that those of us in the RUP overestimated the ethnic nationalist appeal of the *partido*. We felt that Chicanos or Mexican Americans would positively respond to an all-Chicano political party because they were Chicanos. This was naive and showed our political immaturity. Even though Chicanos had historically faced discrimination and segregation, they still were part of, and affected by, the larger society. They wanted mobility and security like any other ethnic group. They were also pursuing the mythical American Dream. We underestimated how attracted Chicanos were, for example, to the Democratic Party, the party of Franklin Roosevelt and John and Robert Kennedy. Chicanos, and here I'm referring to grassroots Mexican Americans and not movement activists, might support some of the ideas and views of the RUP, but that didn't mean that they would vote for it.

Having said that, I think that the legacy of the RUP is threefold. First, it represented one more vehicle to promote the movement's message of ethnic pride and solidarity through political organization. It helped to get people to think about a community identity. We were the first to really begin to focus on the Chicano community as a community that had a certain uniqueness of background, traditions, heritage, and culture. Through the *partido,* we tried to build some kind of political network.

Second, although the RUP, like most third-party movements, did not survive, it forced both the Democrats and the Republicans to pay more attention to Chicanos. The significant gains in Chicano and Latino political empowerment during the past four decades can, I believe, be traced to our efforts.

And, finally, the RUP was an instrument whereby many of the grievances and problems of the Chicano community could and were articulated. Locally, statewide, and nationally, we took strong positions on a whole range of issues. In the case of the Vietnam War, the *partido,* after the attack on the moratorium, became the most significant group that highlighted Chicano opposition to the war.

In L.A., we continued our City Terrace chapter for a while after my failed 1972 campaign, but for all practical purposes after that year, we no longer built the party. We went on to other issues.

INCORPORATION OF EAST LOS ANGELES

Although I had become somewhat disillusioned about electoral politics following my second RUP campaign in 1972 and the decline of the *partido* in general after the El Paso convention, I made one more run for office in 1974. However, this was an unusual circumstance. It had to do with the move to incorporate East Los Angeles, which had been an unincorporated part of the county for many years. East Los Angeles is a specific district east of the Los Angeles River. It does not incorporate all of what is commonly referred to as East L.A.—barrios such as Lincoln Heights and Boyle Heights, both of which are within the city of Los Angeles. East Los Angeles had no local government, despite being one of the largest Chicano barrios in the country. So it was an issue of self-governance for the predominantly Chicano area.

The move to incorporate East L.A. did not come from our group, *La Raza* magazine. It came from a more moderate group of East L.A. leaders, such as Esteban Torres, an organizer for the United Auto Workers. Torres and a few others had put together a community development agency called TELACU (The East Los Angeles Community Union). It promoted economic development for the area and had gotten some grants from the county and other sources. Although TELACU was doing a pretty good job, its organizers believed that a future change in county government might jeopardize their funding. If East L.A. could become a city, Torres and the others felt, then TELACU would no longer be reliant on county largess. TELACU believed that it could dominate the politics of a new city government.

So it was TELACU that organized the election that called on residents of East L.A. to vote for or against incorporation. In addition, candidates for the new city government would also be on the ballot. If incorporation won, the top five candidates would become the city council and the candidate with the most votes would become the mayor. TELACU, of course, fielded its own slate of candidates called the Good Government ticket.

The issue for us was whether we would participate or not in the election. *La Raza*'s office and what remained of our City Terrace RUP office were located in East L.A., so we would be affected. We listened to the TELAC arguments for incorporation. For us the telling point was that East L.A. should be self-governing instead of being run by county supervisors, none of whom lived in our area. It was a self-determination issue that resonated with chicanismo ideology. Other, much smaller areas of the county had been incorporated and done well. Why shouldn't East L.A. be incorporated?

We—*La Raza* group—decided to get involved. We came up with our own Raza Unida slate. I felt that despite the failure of our last campaign, this one was different. I wasn't going to be the only candidate. I would be part of a ticket. It wouldn't be a campaign to elect me but to elect our group in the hope of gaining self-governance for our barrio.

FIGURE 6. Ruiz, early 1970s. Courtesy of the Los Angeles Times Photographic Archive.

Our slate consisted of me, Arturo Sánchez, Jorge García, Daniel Zapata, and a wonderful woman, Celia Rodríguez. She was a longtime community activist and the sister of Julia Mount, who was also a key community person. As a ticket we promoted the idea that incorporation was a viable issue and that East L.A. had the tax base to sustain cityhood. We pointed out that East L.A. should not remain so totally dependent on the county and the one supervisor, Ed Edelman, who represented the area. Edelman wasn't bad, but he represented a district that stretched from Beverly Hills to East L.A., and there was no question which sections of his district he favored, since he drew most of his campaign financial support from the Westside. Edelman knew where his bread and butter was, and he threw us only the crumbs.

In the campaign, we tempered the strong *raza* nationalist rhetoric and instead stressed the need for the community to take control of its own resources and its future. We pointed out that if incorporation was not adopted that more and more of East L.A. would be gobbled up by adjacent cities such as Monterey Park and Montebello or the city of Los Angeles itself. We stressed that if we were concerned about the integrity of our community, we should support incorporation. We weren't asking people to support us because we were Chicanos. That didn't make sense since all the other tickets were composed of Chicano candidates. Instead, we represented our ticket as the best one to lead the community because we had been involved for several years.

Our main rival was the TELACU group and their Good Government ticket. We couldn't compete dollar for dollar with them. We knew that they had overwhelming bucks and could swamp the community with their campaign literature. But we weren't particularly concerned about this. Our strategy was to ride the TELACU crest, because they were doing the job of convincing people that incorporation was a good idea. Their propaganda in effect became ours as well. All we needed to do was to add that we felt that our ticket would serve the community better.

Realistically, we didn't believe that our entire ticket could be elected. The field was too crowded. There were at least three other slates, plus *un choro de independientes*—a whole bunch of independent candidates. Our hope was that at least two of our own would be elected. We thought that it was possible. After all, we were no slouches. We knew how to get our message out. We had *La Raza* and we had our printing press. As we did in our previous campaigns, we turned out literally thousands of leaflets and flyers. We also used our informal distribution system composed of volunteers to canvass neighborhoods and distribute our literature.

Moreover, people knew us. We had a good image and reputation. Some might consider us too radical, but by and large most acknowledged that we worked for the community.

In the campaign, the key voters we were all targeting were the many resident home owners. Many outsiders have an image of East L.A. as a transient area composed mainly of immigrants and renters. In fact, this is not true. There has always been a large and stable group of Mexican American home owners, many of whom have lived in the area for years. As home owners, they were first and foremost concerned about the economic implications of such a change, in particular on property taxes. Frankly, we underestimated these concerns, but so did the rest of the tickets and candidates.

However, the opponents of incorporation did not. They directly targeted the issue of property taxes and argued that incorporation would increase taxes. The main opponents were many of the businessmen, both Mexican Americans and Anglos, in the area. They were aided by the *East L.A. Sun,* a community newspaper. The opposition was well organized and effective. We kept telling people, "Don't worry; we won't raise taxes." But many didn't believe us. We further argued that we felt that the tax base was already sufficient to run a city government and that if additional resources were needed, industrial parks could be established to broaden the tax base. But it still was a tough sell.

Although I think we ran a good campaign, this fear on the part of home owners and small business owners was hard to overcome. In the end, incorporation went down in defeat. It was close, but the measure lost by about eight percentage points.

One consolation was that in the ballot for a potential city council, which was now meaningless, I got the most votes of all the candidates. If incorporation had passed, I would have become the first mayor of East L.A.! This proved to be the first and the last campaign that I would ever win.

The failures of incorporation made me think a great deal of what it was going to take to bring real social change to the Chicano community. What was beginning to sink in was that as radicals and militants, we were too far ahead of the average community person. This wasn't a good thing. Most Mexican Americans, although they had grievances, were primarily concerned about survival and trying to provide a decent life for their families. They were not gamblers or risk takers. This was evident in the incorporation vote. They had to look after themselves.

I began to realize that social change takes time and patience. It's a long haul. The movement had made some changes, but they were only the beginning of a long struggle that was needed. This was a sobering process for me and for some of my colleagues. We began to recognize that on our own we were not going to change the world, or at least our own part of the world. I felt the need for time to reflect rather than just act. I wasn't just right then ready to take a sabbatical from the movement, but I began to think about it.

CHICANO STUDIES PROFESSOR

During the early 1970s, I also had the opportunity to begin a career as a professor of Chicano studies. The movement spawned Chicano studies on a number of campuses in California and elsewhere. This was the result of the early outreach or affirmative action programs that led to a steady increase of Chicano students at all California public institutions of higher education: the University of California campuses, the Cal State system, and the community colleges. As these Chicano students found one another, many of them pushed for Chicano studies, especially as they saw the implementations of black studies programs. This was the origin of ethnic studies at these institutions.

I was finishing my MA at Cal State, L.A., and after Chicano studies was started there around 1969, I hoped to get a job in the new program. It was also a way of adding to my income. I had continued working at the post office, but not on a full-time basis, so I needed more income. It was not unusual in those days for faculty in ethnic studies to be hired only with an MA and not the standard PhD. In some cases, even those with only a BA were hired! The fact was that there were very few Chicanos with a PhD.

I applied for a position in Chicano studies at Cal State, L.A., and was accepted by the Chicano students and faculty. However, to my misfortune, the academic vice president of the campus was Dr. Kenneth Martin. He and I had both served on the Mexican American Education Commission, which had been set up following the 1968 blowouts as a way of following through on the student demands. Martin and I did not get along, and he regarded me as some kind of crazy extremist. He literally told the Chicano students and faculty at Cal State that he approved of hiring a new faculty member in Chicano studies but that it was not going to be Raul Ruiz. I couldn't believe that he would say this! Unfortunately, the students and faculty, for the most part, just accepted Martin's decision and hired someone else.

Soon thereafter, I heard about another opening, this time in the newly created Chicano studies department at San Fernando Valley State College (now Cal State University, Northridge). I heard this from Dr. Rudy Acuña, who had also served on the Mexican American Education Commission and who was one of the first faculty hired in Chicano studies at San Fernando. He strongly encouraged me to apply, and I did.

Chicano studies, along with black studies, was the result of student protests in the late 1960s at campuses such as San Fernando State. These protests got quite militant. In fact, at San Fernando the police and National Guard had to be brought on campus to quiet the disturbances. But it wasn't only student pressure; it was also community pressure. The result was that the administration was forced to establish ethnic studies.

What is important is that Chicano studies at San Fernando began in a big way. The problem with many other Chicano studies departments or programs was that they started small but never really expanded. This wasn't true at San Fernando. The students demanded and got something like eight faculty positions right off the bat. By starting big, the department was able to grow even larger.

It was the students who recruited faculty such as Acuña. I believe that Rudy at the time was teaching in a community college. He, along with the students, then recruited other faculty.

By the time I applied, the department was already quite developed. It offered a range of courses, including Introduction to Chicano Studies, Chicano Culture, Chicano History, Chicano Literature, and writing classes, along with others. Chicano studies at San Fernando was, as far as I know, the largest Chicano studies department in California and in the country. I think it still is.

Another important factor about Chicano studies at San Fernando was that it had a strong community outreach program. It operated with a philosophy that the department was worth only what it gave back to the community.

When I interviewed, the department operated through a *junta directiva,* or governing junta, composed of students, faculty, and staff. This is the group that interviewed me. I had a positive and supportive meeting. What helped was that they knew me. My editing *La Raza* and my other community involvements were well known. The line of questioning focused on how I would teach certain courses and how I would help involve students in community issues. Apparently, they liked my

FIGURE 7. Ruiz, professor of Chicano Studies, California State University, Northridge, 1983.
Courtesy of the Los Angeles Times Photographic Archive.

responses because they recommended to the administration that I be hired, which
I was. I started teaching full-time in the fall of 1970.

I taught and continue to teach a number of classes at San Fernando or Northridge, including a course on Chicano ideas that I developed. My students started
calling it "Raul's Ideas." It is a combination political science–sociology class. I
focus on key contemporary political and social issues affecting the Chicano and
Latino communities. I also bring in issues from Mexico and Latin America. It's an
interdisciplinary course. I have also taught Chicano history, Latin American history, Chicano culture, and Chicano literature.

Moreover, what made our classes interesting, especially during the period of
the movement, was that there was also a lot of political tension. Students would
disagree with one another, Chicano versus Chicano. Sometimes they would yell at
one another. And, occasionally, they would fight in the classroom! I myself wasn't
immune from engaging in these arguments.

The issue of whether to be active on campus or in the community reflected the
overriding political and ideological issue confronting Chicano studies in those
early years. What was the relationship of Chicano studies to the community? This
was the key question. Of course, it was understood that the faculty had to function
within the campus and had to legitimize the program to the academic community.
But beyond that, it was expected, certainly by the students and community leaders,

that Chicano faculty also had to play a role in the community. The same went for students and staff.

But this was not necessarily a problem, because there were so many things happening in the community. Students, who were very active then, unlike today, especially put pressure on faculty to do things in the community. These pressures were not acute for me since I was first and foremost a community activist. While I never used my classes to recruit students into my political activities, I did encourage students during my office hours and outside of classes to support various issues. For example, during my two RUP campaigns, a number of my students worked as volunteers.

One activity on campus that I very much became involved with was the organization and publication of *El Popo,* the Chicano student newspaper. This involvement originated from a class I taught on Chicano journalism. The class was basically designed to publish a newspaper, and the students got credit for it. I started the class due to my own journalistic experience. The name *El Popo* comes from one of the major volcanoes in Mexico. I named the paper. I don't know why I liked the name *El Popo.* I just did. Our first editor was Frank del Olmo, who went on to a position with the *Los Angeles Times* and who became a columnist and associate editor until his tragic early death a few years ago.[32] I even wrote some initial opinion pieces for *El Popo.* The paper focused on both campus and community issues. It is still being published today.

POSTMOVEMENT YEARS

Throughout all my political activism during the Chicano movement, the one thing that remained constant was my journalism and my work with *La Raza.* There's no question that we had elevated our magazine to becoming the major Chicano publication in L.A. and one of the best, if not the best, in the country. But like everything else associated with the movement, there was a beginning, a middle, and, regrettably, an end. As the movement declined in intensity by the late 1970s, it became more and more difficult to put out the publication. Many staff members were moving due to personal and family responsibilities, including myself. People had just burned out after so many years of intense engagement. In addition, there wasn't a critical mass of activists out there any longer who could not only provide us with information about community activities but sustain the magazine. While we weren't a business in the strictest sense, we did need to sell enough issues to get *La Raza* out. It had served its purpose as a movement information organ, but we were now in a different period, where even the mainstream media was reporting more on Chicano and Latino issues. *La Raza* was born out of the movement, and when the specific historical movement ebbed, so too did *La Raza,* as well as many other political publications. It was a great ride as long as it lasted.

As the movement declined, I had to confront my own personal situation. Unlike many other activists, whose personal and family lives were shattered due to their deep political involvement, I was fortunate that I had the strong support of my parents. They always were there. Even though I was living on my own, I saw them all the time, and later, as they became older into the 1980s, I moved back in with them in our South Central home.

I had many ups and downs with women, and I never remarried, but at least I had my parents. The one major regret that I have is that I didn't spend more time with my daughter during her growing years. Still, I came out of the movement emotionally and psychologically in one piece.

What helped me, in particular, was my teaching position at Northridge. I received tenure and had economic stability. But I also knew that if I was going to advance more in the university system, I needed to get my PhD. I was encouraged to do so by my department and by the administration. I further recognized that I hadn't taken a sabbatical from the movement all those years and that leaving for a few years to study would represent a welcome respite. I needed that. I needed some distance and time to reflect on what I had gone through and where I was in my life. I was ready to leave L.A., at least for a while.

I got that opportunity when Harvard offered me a graduate fellowship. Someone had told me to apply, and I did. To my amazement, I was accepted as a graduate student in the Administrative Planning and Social Policy Program of the School of Education. I accepted and began in the fall of 1977. My department and dean gave me a leave of absence and even continued to pay me some of my salary.

Harvard proved to be a good experience. I studied under Professor Nathan Glazer. As a Chicano, I wasn't totally alone. By this time, Ivy League schools such as Harvard and Yale were recruiting minority students, especially at the undergraduate level. There weren't many but enough to form a type of community.

After completing my course requirements and passing my PhD qualifying exams, I had to choose a dissertation topic that Nate Glazer would direct. I decided to take advantage of my location at Harvard and do a study of Chicano students in Ivy League schools. I wanted to study their adjustment and their degree of success and failure. I started first by interviewing students at Harvard. I also visited campuses such as Yale, Columbia, Princeton, and several others. I made several visits to these schools. Students started to say, "We don't know if Raul is visiting us or studying us!"

I accumulated a great deal of data. In fact, I had so much that Glazer became concerned that I would be overwhelmed.

"Why don't you just focus on Harvard?" he advised me.

Although I wanted to do the full project, I agreed that it would be more practical and certainly more expeditious to do just the one campus. So I did. I'm glad that I did, because it actually took me several years to write the dissertation. After

I returned to full-time teaching at Northridge in 1980, I found it difficult to make the time to work on it. As a result, I didn't finish until 1989. Although it took me longer than it should have, I was pleased with the result and happy that I now had my PhD. I was now Dr. Raul Ruiz!

Even though the movement had pretty much come to an end by the late 1970s, at least in its intensity and its organized activity, there were still many other issues around. After returning from Harvard, I felt more refreshed and ready to resume my own political activism. However, I decided to focus more on broader Latino and Latin American issues rather than just Chicano ones. I had always been interested in Latin America. I had concentrated on Latin American history both as an undergraduate and then as a graduate student at Cal State, Los Angeles. So it was not unusual for me to be drawn into the Central American issues so paramount during the 1980s. The civil war in El Salvador and the coming to power of the Sandinistas after their overthrow of the Somoza dictatorship in Nicaragua in 1979, plus the U.S. interventions in both countries in support of right-wing groups, caught my attention and inspired my involvement in support of the revolutionary struggles.

Like many others on the left, including many Chicanos who had been part of the movement, I was outraged by the efforts of the Reagan administration to support, first of all, the repressive military-dominated government in El Salvador and its death squads. Instead, I supported the insurgents. I was especially livid about Reagan's attempt to overthrow the revolutionary Sandinista government in Nicaragua by funding and training right-wing counterrevolutionaries known as the Contras.

To protest U.S. policies in Central America, I joined Central American support groups that organized protests, marches, and rallies. I also went to Central America, specifically to El Salvador, with a group of other Latinos activists, such as Armando Navarro. We were the first Latino peace group who went to El Salvador. We met with opposition leaders and even traveled into the mountains, where we met with the guerrillas. I almost got killed doing this, because while I was there, the Salvadoran army attacked. I was lucky to get out with my life. I went back several more times to El Salvador during the 1980s.

I also became involved in the politics of Mexico following the 1988 presidential election, when Cuahtemóc Cárdenas of the PRD was cheated out of the presidency by the corruption of the PRI.[33] The PRI had dominated Mexican politics since the 1930s and had developed into a powerful but corrupt institution that won election after election through coercion and fraud. The PRD and Cárdenas represented a reform and democratic movement and the strongest opposition to PRI rule.

Following the election, some of us in the Latino community, such as Pedro Arias, organized a chapter of the PRD. I became very involved in it. We served as an information network on the PRD in Los Angeles, and we organized meetings and rallies, including some with Cárdenas himself. I served as the chair of this group.

My political involvement at this time also extended to issues such as the Gulf War in 1991. I strongly opposed the U.S. military intervention in the Persian Gulf against Iraq because I believed that it was principally done to support U.S. oil interests in the region. I didn't like the idea of U.S. soldiers, including Chicanos and Latinos, dying or being wounded for the benefit of oil corporations. I became cochair of the Chicano Mexican Committee against the Gulf War. We were the only Chicano group against the war. We did a lot of protesting in L.A., even though it was difficult because of the strong support for the war and the anti-Arab reaction that followed. Some thought that we were Arabs, so we experienced some of these racist attacks. But even though we were a distinct minority, we held our ground.

In 1992 I witnessed the so-called L.A. riots in South Central Los Angeles. This followed the decision in the Rodney King case, when the jury voted not to convict the police officers charged with repeatedly beating King, a beating graphically caught on videotape. Many blacks in the area rioted in protest, and many others opportunistically engaged in random violence and looting. My parents still lived in this area, and I was concerned for their safety. My father was quite ill and my mother was incapacitated, and so I instructed the women who cared for them to get them ready to be evacuated. Fortunately, I didn't have to do this. In the meantime, I went into South Central with my camera and took many photos of the rioting. In fact, some Korean store owners whose businesses were under attack and who thought I was one of the looters almost killed me. It was a mess. I saw and photographed many Latinos—Central Americans and Mexicans—regrettably engage in this violence, especially by looting all kinds of items, including Pampers for their kids. But Latino small businesses also got looted and some of their stores burned down. Latinos did this, not just blacks. I did not see all of this as some kind of political rebellion, as some on the left suggested. I saw it for what it was: opportunistic rioting and looting that made absolutely no sense. The L.A. riots to me didn't have a political orientation. What it did show was people—blacks and Latinos, especially immigrants—living in poverty and in desperate circumstances.

Into the rest of the 1990s and into the new century, I've continued teaching, including doing courses at Santa Monica College. As I get older, I'm not as involved politically, but I stay engaged where I can help out—including sponsoring Mexican and Latino cultural events. My political time may have passed, but I try to inspire my students and younger Latinos. I tell them that they now have to seize their time to advance not only the issues of the Chicano and Latino communities but also the great issues of war and peace.

POSTMORTEM ON THE CHICANO MOVEMENT

There's no question but that the movement changed my life. In fact, it became my life during those hectic and crazy years of the late 1960s and early 1970s. I participated in almost every aspect of the movement in Los Angeles. I lived the movement day and night, week after week. I had little time and less energy for anything else. I met wonderful people in those years—lifelong friends—but I also met some whom I'd rather not have met.

Throughout all of this, my parents remained my bedrock. They always supported me and loved me. They worried about me but never once questioned my commitment to the movement. I was only glad that in later years, when I became more settled, that I was able to give more back to them and help them. Both are dead now, but they'll always be with me.

Of course, one major regret is the little time I spent with my daughter, Marcy. She grew up mostly with her mother, although I would see her occasionally. All this didn't bother me much then, but it does now. The only problem is that I can't go back and change this.

It's not that I didn't have a personal life. There were many girlfriends, although nothing serious. The movement was in part also a sexual revolution, in keeping with the changing mores of the sixties. We were all experimenting—both men and women—with our sexual lives. At one level, it was liberating. At another, it was exploitative. It's not the part of the movement that I choose to dwell on. Some might believe that opening up our personal lives is what's really important, although I doubt that those who argue in this vein would open up their own lives for such scrutiny. This isn't for me. The movement to me was first and foremost political. I was and am a political animal. Whom I slept with and when is no one's business but my own.

As I look back on the movement, I recognize its contributions and its drawbacks. For me, as a movement journalist, one of the biggest contributions was the movement newspapers. They, like La Raza, helped create a new consciousness among Chicanos, as well as provide attention to a group that the mainstream media had mostly ignored. During those years, the media paid attention only to the black civil rights and Black Power movements. That was true even in Los Angeles, where blacks represented a smaller community compared to Chicanos. In L.A. the Chicano movement was much more dynamic. We were the civil rights movement in Los Angeles. We were also the antiwar movement.

What the Chicano newspapers did was to legitimize the movement, at least to activists, and to link the movement in different regions together. Through the movement papers, activists imagined a community. These newspapers are still important because they contain the history of the movement. They represent now key historical documents. They serve as an invaluable tool for historians. It's a shame that they don't seem to be utilized very much.

The movement created a force and a presence that nobody could deny. For the most part, it was a very positive contribution. Chicanos became more reflective and aware of social problems. They began to address issues pertinent to the community. We recognized that, like blacks, we were also a minority group that had rights and a social contract with the larger society. This contract assured our rights. We likewise found our voice to articulate our grievances and our dreams. But our actions likewise spoke when we protested on a variety of issues: education, the war, the police, the Church, politics, and many others.

But we didn't just march in the streets. The movement didn't just cause Chicanos to yell and scream. It also inspired people to greater heights of cultural and artistic expressions. The movement spawned not only activists like myself but a whole new generation of writers, poets, novelists, musicians, artists, filmmakers, and drama groups. This is the so-called Chicano Renaissance. More books about Chicanos written by Chicanos were published at this time than ever before. More artistic *centros,* or centers, were opened than ever before.

In addition, the movement opened the doors to higher education. For the first time in our history, more Chicanos attended colleges and universities. This led to new recruitment and retention programs as well as Chicano studies on many campuses. These changes encompassed not only undergraduate education but graduate as well. The movement produced the first significant generation of Chicano PhD's. The appointment of Chicano faculty and staff in the Cal State system and in the University of California is directly linked to the movement.

Politically, educationally, and culturally, the movement, directly and indirectly, effected positive change. Certainly, the recognition of Chicanos as national political actors and the overall political empowerment of Latinos in California and elsewhere is traceable to the movement. It created a new Chicano and Chicana, and this legacy continues.

On the downside, I think what the movement failed to establish was a lasting organizational structure, such as La Raza Unida Party, which would have provided continuity. In its heyday, the movement seemed to have a sense of unity and coherence throughout the Southwest. We had succeeded in creating not only an imagined community but, through contacts at conferences and demonstrations, also a real political community. We spoke with one voice despite some internal differences. Maybe this was because we were still very much on the outside of U.S. society. When you have nothing or very little, it seems like you have more unity. Once you actually acquire a stake, it seems that unity begins to weaken.

I think that this is what has happened. We became victims of our own successes. Yet, in some way, these were unintentional successes. While we were not revolutionaries in the classical sense and certainly not armed revolutionaries, we did believe that the system was rotten and had to be changed. We saw ourselves not as reformers but as social rebels. We wanted to remake society. We weren't clear what this meant, but we did know what we didn't want. We never achieved that goal of a new society. The more militant we became, the more, ironically, we pushed the system to reform and to recognize, albeit not willingly, many of our demands for change: in the schools, with respect to political representation, on police abuse, and for cultural recognition. We weren't reformers in the liberal tradition, but we succeeded in reforming society to the extent that today Chicanos and Latinos have a much larger stake in the system than before the movement commenced.

But part of that success is that we now have a less focused leadership. At the political level, for example, we have many political groupings. Some are still grassroots ones, but many more center on the growing numbers of Latino elected officials. The results are many more political communities and voices. There doesn't seem to be much consensus on what to do with political empowerment. Achieving elected status seems to be an end in itself. Somehow and at some point, recognizing the many remaining problems facing Chicanos and Latinos, we have to get back to that élan of the movement that sought more than just reforms and personal advancement. We believed in revolutionizing U.S. society to eradicate the roots of racism and economic exploitation. This is part of the legacy of the movement that I hope we'll never forget.

Does the Chicano movement still live? This is a question often asked by my students. Not in the sense of a specific historical movement set in time. We were the products of our time. We were influenced by all the national and international movements for social change. Our struggles and organizations were part of this history. All of this can never be replicated. Time changes, and so do circumstances. A new Chicano or Latino movement looking into the twentieth-first century would look very different.

However, what I think still lives is the spirit of the movement. That spirit, in my opinion, embodies a sense of self-respect and self-dignity and a sense of community and self-sacrifice for the community. I still see some of that spirit. I try to pass this on to my students. If I can do so to even just one young Chicano or Chicana, then I've remained true to the movement's legacy.

2

Gloria Arellanes

RELIVING THE CHICANO MOVEMENT

As I parked my car in a lot adjacent to Olvera Street, the old Mexican cultural center in downtown Los Angeles, I felt a lump in my throat. Apprehension and even fear crept up on me. I didn't really want to do this. Why did Rosalio Muñoz call to invite me to the fortieth anniversary of the Chicano Antiwar Moratorium?

"Gloria, you have to come to the opening day of the exhibit on the anniversary," Rosalio told me on the phone. "You were an important part of organizing the moratorium, and it's important that you be recognized."

"I don't know, Rosalio. I haven't been involved in some of the earlier commemorative events, and I'm not sure I want to go through this. I have some bad memories of my involvement in the Chicano movement, and I don't want to have to revive them."

But Rosalio, as usual, could be very persuasive, and he persisted in trying to get me to agree to participate. Probably as my way of trying to stop him, I finally agreed, although still thinking I might back off as the date grew nearer.

"Now don't forget," Rosalio concluded, "it's going to be at the Mexican cultural center right there in the plaza by Olvera Street. We'll start at three, and I'll introduce you, along with the other former Moratorium Committee members. It'll be fine, and others will be glad to see you again."

I wasn't so sure. I really didn't fully identify anymore as a Chicana. After I dropped out of the Brown Berets in 1970, then worked with Rosalio on the antiwar effort, and then opened my own free clinic in East L.A., I moved away from movement politics and later began to identify more with my Native American roots from my mother's side. In fact, I even became an active member of my Tongva tribe and am now an elder. This is where I continued my activism. I don't resent my involvement in the Chicano movement, but, at the same time, I was hurt by it and felt I had to go in another direction.

As the day of the event came in late August 2010, close to the actual date of August 29, 1970, when perhaps as many as thirty thousand mostly Chicanos protested against the Vietnam War, I began to get cold feet about attending. Who else was going to be there? What would I say? Would I even recognize some of the other former movement activists? I just wanted to stay in my home in El Monte and not have to drive into L.A. Why did I need to go?

But I felt I couldn't disappoint Rosalio. I've always had the utmost respect for him and consider him a dear friend, even though we didn't see each other that often. I knew that he had never lost his commitment to the movement and to the Chicano struggle for social justice. I knew that he had worked hard to organize the commemoration, and he expected me there.

And so I went. I'm glad that I did. Everyone greeted me with such warmth and respect. I was moved almost to tears in reuniting with former colleagues in *la lucha*, in the struggle. It was a reunion in the best sense of that word. Like all reunions, you go back to the past. You relive the past; you are the past. But that's okay, because the past is important. It's important that the new generations of Chicanos and Latinos know who we are and how we struggled under very difficult circumstances for the rights and empowerment of our people, not only men but also many women.

I was part of that struggle, and I now want to tell my story as a Chicana—as a woman—in the movement. My hope is that my story will inspire other Chicanas who were also in the movement to tell their stories. Stories are powerful. I get this from my Native American community. Stories educate and inspire. I hope my story does this.

FAMILY STORY

My father was César Barron Arellanes. His parents were from Chihuahua, and his father was a musician. They first migrated to Texas, where they had some of their eventual fourteen children. My dad was one of the oldest. He was born around 1924. My mother was also born around that time. From Texas, my grandparents moved to East Los Angeles where my grandfather owned and operated a wrought-iron shop. They lived right across from the Maravilla Projects, a large housing court with mostly Mexican tenants. But my grandfather died very young. I don't remember him at all—I just have stories that my dad and uncles told me.

My grandfather, for example, would play his violin outside of his shop, and he would attract many passersby. I understand that he was a very strong man with a strong personality. My dad inherited that, and I think I did too. When my grand-father died, his sons took over the business, and my father wound up running it. He made wrought-iron fences. I remember seeing the anvil, if that's what it's called, and my dad hammering away.

My father was a very difficult person. As I matured, I would clash with him over his hardness. He was not a very affectionate man. My mom was the complete opposite, very affectionate and very loving. My friends would say, "I wish my mom was like your mom." My dad, on the other hand, was very demanding.

My paternal grandmother was Catalina Arellanes. For a grandmother, she dis-played no emotion. I've never seen a grandmother like this. She just never showed any affection, no hugs, no kisses. By contrast, I smother my grandchildren. My grandmother was very cold. My mom would tell me, "don't eat any of her food." I was quite obese as a child, and so I would peek into my grandmother's refrigerator to see what I could eat. But all she had was zucchini and carrots—yuck! She was a diabetic, as I would also become years later. And so she had to be on a diet. I remember that she spoke only Spanish. I wasn't raised speaking Spanish, but somehow we communicated.

My grandparents had a big house because they were more middle class due to my grandfather owning his own business and doing very well. I later heard that he did wrought-iron fences and other projects for famous movie stars such as Lucille Ball.

Although my grandfather was a difficult person, he seemed to have had some social conscience. I heard that he would periodically drive a trailer up north and bring back fruit, which he distributed to poor Mexicans living in the projects. This was during the McCarthy era in the early 1950s, and, as a result, my grandfather was called a communist by some.

My grandmother lived much longer than my grandfather. She was in her seven-ties when she died, but for some years she was very senile. She couldn't even rec-ognize her own son. They called my dad "Chicho," but she had no idea who Chicho was. But my grandmother, like my grandfather and my dad, was a very difficult person. She never called me Gloria. In fact, I don't remember her even calling me by any name. I did not have a very close relationship with her. I grew to despise her based on how she treated my mother. Most of this, I later learned from my mother.

Once after my brother and I had been born, my parents lived with my grand-mother. During this time, my father was hospitalized due to a very bad auto acci-dent. My mother was pregnant, but after my dad's accident, my grandmother told my mother, "You can't live here and have more babies. You need to get rid of it."

As a result, my mother had an abortion and lost the twins she was carrying. When I later learned what my grandmother had done, I had nothing but contempt for her. My mother had to go to an alley butcher, and she was lucky that she didn't die. My mother listened to my grandmother because she felt she had no choice.

She was living in her mother-in-law's home, and my father was seriously hurt. But I also blame my father because my parents must have discussed this. My mother would not have acted without her husband's consent. She lost a boy and a girl.

My mother had always had a distant relationship with my grandmother. She would later take us for visits to see our grandparents only because of my father. Part of this tension had to do with my grandmother's racist views. She was light skinned, as was my father, and she looked down on dark-skinned Mexicans, even my mother and my brother. Ironically, her own husband was dark skinned! Because of my mother's Native American background, she was darker.

I later learned another story about this. After my dad's military service during World War II, he got a loan through the GI Bill to purchase a new home in El Monte, east of Los Angeles—in fact, the same house I inherited and still live in now. But at the time in the late 1940s, El Monte, or at least this neighborhood, was predominantly white. Because my father was very light skinned with hazel eyes and his surname was not a typical Mexican one, the realtor probably thought he was Italian. However, on the day that my dad had to sign the final papers for the house, he took my mother with him to see the real estate agent. When the realtor saw my mother, he must have almost fallen out of his chair.

"You can't buy this house. They won't accept Mexicans in this neighborhood."

My father went into a rage. He reminded the agent that he had already given the down payment and had proof of this and would go to court and sue him. The agent backed off and we moved in, but that's how racist this area used to be.

My dad, who was born in East L.A., didn't go beyond the eighth grade. He attended Garfield, which was a combined middle and senior high school. My mother also went to Garfield, and that's where my parents met. However, my mother graduated from high school. Although my dad didn't have much education, he was very intelligent and self-educated. He constantly read. The reason my dad didn't continue his education was because he had to work in my grandfather's shop. My dad was in the army during World War II, but didn't see combat. He was stationed in either North or South Carolina.

MY MOTHER

On my mother's side of the family, her father was named Antonio González and my grandmother was Sandalia López. My grandfather came from Guanajuato. He was about thirteen when he crossed the border. He was some kind of a tribal person, and so he was much more indigenous. He was very dark skinned with high cheekbones. My grandmother was even more indigenous. She traced her heritage to the Gabrieleño-Tongva community here in Southern California. I prefer the name Tongva. Gabrieleño refers to the San Gabriel Mission. So, on my mother's side, my ancestral roots come from Asuksagna, which is present-day Azusa. The term *Azusa* comes from Asuksagna, which means grandmother. Asuksagna refers to the place of the grandmothers, which must have been very powerful. My grandmother was actually born in Alhambra, as was my mother, who was one of sixteen children although a number of them died at birth. My mother was the oldest of the daughters.

I learned of this California Indian heritage that I belong to only much later in my life, because my mother never told my brother and me that she was Tongva. I remember asking my mother if we were Indian, but she would deny it.

"You're Mexican," she would say.

It wasn't until after my mother died that I learned from one of her sisters, my aunt, the connection to the Tongva. I also learned that my mother and her siblings denied that they were Indians because in school they were punished for saying that they were Indians. It was safer to say that they were Mexicans. When the Spaniards first came they not only conquered the California Indians but also took their away their names, religion, songs, dances, and they made us dress like them. But we never lost our memories. In fact, the Tongva community persists. It's quite large, and we've been able to bring back our language and other aspects of our culture.

My maternal grandfather was a construction worker. He must have been a cement mixer because when I would see him he would always be in a painter's kind of white work clothes. My grandparents lived in the Pasadena-Alhambra area. However, they were asked to move out of there for reasons I don't want to go into. It's not a very pleasant thing. They moved to East L.A., down the street from my father's house. My mother would pass my dad's home every day, and that's how they got to know each other better, besides the fact that they went to the same school.

My mother's family was very poor, and it didn't help that my grandfather was sent to prison for reasons that I don't know. So it was my grandmother who raised her children. My mother told me she had only two dresses to wear as she grew up. She never made oatmeal for us because she would get nauseated smelling it since she had to eat it all the time as a child. They also ate mostly potatoes and beans. I don't think that my grandmother worked, and so they must have been on welfare.

My mother first attended public schools in Pasadena and then in East L.A. She graduated from Garfield High School. After school, she went to work in the military-related industries as a riveter. She was Rosie, or Rosa, the Riveter. After marrying my dad, she continued to work as a riveter. She never talked much about her work experience. My parents got married around 1944 or so.

Growing up, my father spoke both Spanish and English. However, my mother spoke only English. I used to make fun of her when I was a teenager when she tried to say something in Spanish. She couldn't enunciate properly. She couldn't roll her r's, as in Arellanes. But I was no better than my mother, because I also didn't learn Spanish. My father forbade my brother and me from speaking it. I later learned

Spanish in school and from just listening to other Chicanos. My dad didn't want me to grow up with an accent, because he felt this would hurt my work opportunities later.

While my mother was raised a Catholic, she was not a regular church-goer. I don't know if my father was raised Catholic, but he always said that he was an atheist. My brother and I were raised Catholic because of my mother, but not in a very strict way.

GROWING UP

I was born on March 4, 1946, in the Mayo Clinic on Soto Street. Up until I was about five years old, with the exception of when we briefly lived with my paternal grandmother, we lived in the Maravilla Projects. The only memory that sticks in me about that time was my father reading all the time and the number of books he read. I later identified those books as ones about history and about other countries such as China.

My earliest memories as a child really begin when we moved to El Monte. I remember so many other kids in the streets, and I would always be running, playing, and rough necking with them. These were all white kids, since my neighborhood was all white except for a Hawaiian gentleman across the street, with his white wife. I don't really know the reason why my dad wanted to move to El Monte, except that he probably thought it was a good opportunity, and he thought the schools were a little better. He was very concerned about our education. He wanted my brother and me to be as educated as possible.

I actually started kindergarten twice—the first time in East L.A. and then another one in El Monte. I started at the Cogswell School in El Monte and then for the rest of my elementary years attended the Parkway School, which was built just a couple of blocks from our home. I went through the sixth grade at Parkway. The one main thing I recall about elementary schools had to do with the fact that I was already quite overweight and, as a result, got picked on by the other kids. I was tall—taller than my classmates—but also much heavier. Because of my physique, I got teased or what we now call bullied. The boys did this to me. This bullying, in turn, made me very shy. I just didn't want to be noticed, but it was unavoidable due to my big body. I was very overweight until my late thirties. So, for a period of my life, I faced people reminding me of how big I was, like I didn't know this.

My bigness was from both genetics and diet. Both of my parents were big, but not as big as I became. I got all the way up to between 250 and 300 pounds in high school. I'm tall, big boned, and then overweight. I just stood out. Beginning in elementary school, my mother had to sew my clothes because I couldn't fit into store-bought ones.

Our diet at home didn't help. In my parents' time, the feeling was that a fat baby or child was a healthy baby and child. People wanted to see big cheeks and fat legs.

My mother cooked both Mexican and American foods. She cooked what my dad demanded.

Although my dad fished, he was basically a meat-and-potatoes man, although he insisted on having *frijoles de olla* (fresh-cooked beans) every day with salsa, which my mother would make. My mom also made the biggest and most delicious flour tortillas. Of course, she, like most other Mexicans, made them with *manteca* (lard). She also made the most delicious tamales cooked in manteca. They were heaven. She also made refried beans, again with manteca.

At the same time, my mother did believe in good nutrition, and she always made sure that we had vegetables along with meat or chicken. I just remember having really good food at home and obviously lots of it. My parents never restricted how much food I ate. The one food I really detested was liver—liver and onions.

With this type of diet, I got bigger and bigger as I grew up.

FAMILY HOME

After we left East L.A., I grew up in El Monte in the house my father bought. It cost him only $10,000, but that was a big amount then. It's the only home I have known. In fact, I still live there. It's a small house with just two bedrooms, but it was adequate for us. Three generations have lived here, including me, my dog, and my cats today.

In my home, there was no question but that my father was the dominant figure.

"Cuca, bring me my food!"

I remember hearing him sometimes when he would come home early, not feeling well, and went to bed. He called my mother Cuca for some reason, even though her real name was Laura. Actually, it was Aurora.

"Cuca! Bring me this!"

He would snap snap, and my mother would comply.

Once, as I got older, I asked my mother, "Why do you do that?"

"What?" she replied.

"Why do you jump for him like that?"

"Because I love him."

I couldn't, and later didn't want to, accept this. Her exploited relationship with my father impacted my life with men. No men then or now place any demands on me. I have carried this my entire life.

At the same time, my father loved my brother and me, in his own way. We didn't have a horrible relationship; it just wasn't an affectionate one. I think all children want affection. I think that reinforces that you're okay. My mom gave us that absolute love, but not my father.

My mother was a soft, gentle person, and my father was very conservative, harsh, and unemotional. He never showed emotion. He was like my grandmother.

Yet he loved his little doggy. He installed a fence around our property, not for our safety but for his dog.

He occasionally screamed at us, but it was crushing to me. He didn't really hit us, but once he came close to doing so with me. I don't know what I did, but he put his hand on my leg, and he slapped his own hand over mine. It hurt and I cried. That was the only time he hit me, and it was an indirect hit. Still, it crushed me, and it affected me emotionally.

On the other hand, my mother was more capable of hitting us when we misbehaved. She used a stick and it hurt. She also occasionally spanked me. She could get away with doing this in those years. She hit me more than my brother, because he was the *consentido*—the favored one. Although both my parents disciplined me, I was much closer to my mother. My father wasn't around that much. When he wasn't working, he'd spend his social time at the Elks Club, where he was a member. On the whole, despite these limitations, we had a good home. My parents tried to give us a good home. My father did drink, but never at home. He did his drinking at the Elks Club or at the local bar, the Sonic. I never saw liquor at home, not even beer. He also was a diabetic, and all this, I'm sure, contributed to his early death at age forty-nine.

But there was also some time for family activities, especially after my brother, William César, was born five years after me. We went camping in the San Gabriel Mountains. A lot of my father's family would join us. These were fun times, until we got older and I couldn't handle my dad yelling all the time. He was always yelling at my poor brother. I don't remember going to the movies or other forms of recreation with my family.

Ethnicity was part of my growing up, but in an interesting way. My father always told me, "You're Chicano!" He used that term to include both males and females. He was politically conservative but identified as a Chicano from his own growing up in East L.A., where he knew pachucos and zoot-suitors who used the term. In fact, one of my mother's brothers, Uncle Sonny, who was really Uncle Reginald, was a zoot-suitor.

"You're a Chicano," my dad would insist.

"No, Dad. I'm American!"

Here I was going to elementary school, where I recited the Pledge of Allegiance, but my dad was insisting that I was a Chicano, not an American. I cried and said, "But they told me I'm American!"

"No, you're a Chicano!"

I really don't know why he said this. Ironically, much later, when I became involved in the Chicano movement, he hated my doing so.

An additional aspect of our ethnicity was that even though I was of light complexion, I knew that I wasn't white. My Anglo friends were white but not me. In part, this was because of my father's insistence that we were Chicanos. My brother had a dark complexion, as did my mother. I inherited my dad's lightness. Of course, the fact that we sometimes ate Mexican food also said we were Mexicans. But in those days we didn't take our burritos to school for lunch since the Anglo kids made fun of us if we did. Now they beg for that kind of food.

But even as a young girl, I saw much more striking ways that brought attention to my Mexican background and the racism directed against Mexicans. I remember a scary moment with my mom. We went to a Thrifty's drugstore, where they used to serve food. I especially liked their banana splits.

"Let's sit over here," my mom said as we entered the store.

In that section, there were these white women sitting there. They were big, slobby-looking women. They gave a look to my mother like, "Don't you dare sit near us." I remember my mother grabbing me. You always feel your parent's fear when they grab you in that certain way.

"Honey, let's sit over here."

We just went to a different counter. I remember this so distinctly. I was around six or seven years old. I'll never forget that look those women gave us.

Religion further played a role in my young life, but not in any major way. My parents were raised as Catholics, but my father really didn't practice this religion. My mother did, but she wasn't obsessed with it. In fact, because of my father, my parents were married in court and not at church. My mother did make sure we were baptized and made our First Communion. To prepare for the latter, she sent me to catechism classes at our local church, the Church of the Nativity. All I remember about these classes is how scary the nuns were. They were scary and mean. They slapped kids' knuckles with rulers and screamed at the top of their lungs. I was afraid to mess up in any way with them. Somehow I got through these weekly lessons and made my First Communion, but I have no memories of it except for a picture and a certificate. I must have been about ten at the time. At home, the only religious figure we had was a picture of Jesus. I don't recall an image of La Virgen de Guadalupe.

During my elementary school years what stuck to me was the bullying that I encountered, especially from the white boys who teased me about my size. Mostly whites attended the school. I was one of the few Mexicans. My teachers never intervened to stop this. Many days I came home crying because of the taunting. My parents must have been aware of this, but they never confronted the school. Parents didn't seem to do this then. The bullying consisted of the boys laughing at me and calling me names. I don't remember what they said, but I don't think they had any ethnic connotation. It was just about my body.

All of this deeply affected me until later in elementary school, when I began to realize that the boys were actually afraid of me because I was so much bigger than them. Eventually, as I entered middle school, I started to use this to my advantage. In fact, despite the bullying, I was a good student. Some of the teachers, such as

Mrs. Miller and Mrs. Wade, were very supportive and made me comfortable. I couldn't say the same about some of the other teachers.

Despite the bullying by the boys, I did have some white girlfriends. I've always gotten along with people very well. I played with them at school and in my neighborhood, but I never went to their homes. The only time some of them came to my home was when I had a birthday party. Birthdays were a big thing in my family. I would have a piñata, and, I guess, this represented another expression of my family's Mexican background.

Although I was physically large, I grew up with a feminine attitude. I was never a tomboy. I had dolls. I wore dresses with huge amounts of petticoats. In fact, once, while playing tetherball at school, my petticoat slipped down, and one of the boys made fun of this. But instead of picking up my petticoat, I just turned to this kid and said, "Isn't it pretty?" This was my way of not only expressing my femininity but fighting back and not allowing the boy to humiliate me.

JUNIOR HIGH

Junior high, or middle school, was not particularly memorable for me either. I've blocked much of it out of my memory. I attended Mountain View Junior High, which was maybe about a mile from our home. I walked there, as I had walked to my elementary school. Like my elementary school, junior high was predominantly white, but there were more Mexicans there. One of the things I remember best is that I made many new friends, and they were primarily other Mexicans. I was gravitating more toward people of color. One of my female friends was called "Moose." She was bigger than I was, and I was very big!

Classes at Mountain View were not memorable. I did okay and received mostly Bs and Cs. I was an average student. If I had a favorite class, it would have been art. I liked to draw. I also didn't have a close relationship with any teacher. I think they were all white. I didn't struggle with my classes. I did all my homework with no assistance from my parents, who didn't offer to help anyway. My dad, in particular, wasn't too involved in my school. This was my mom's area. She didn't go to PTA meetings but probably did meet with my teachers.

Bullying wasn't as much of a problem in junior high, or perhaps by then I had become numb to it. I'm sure it was there, because I was still big. I was so big that my mother still had to make my clothes. There probably was a Lane Bryant, which is a store for big women, but it was too expensive. Besides, my mother was a great seamstress, as was my maternal grandmother, who made clothes for my dolls. My mom didn't work, so as a housewife she had time to sew. Girls didn't wear pants to school then, because the school didn't allow it. I wore dresses. This only made me look bigger.

Of course, junior high is also puberty time. Part of this change involved a certain moodiness and an "I want to do this" attitude and probably a "no, you can't do that" response from my parents. They did let me go to the movies on weekend afternoons with my girlfriends, but they still wouldn't let me go over to their homes. They were pretty strict with me. I was also getting interested in boys and had crushes, but because of my size I wasn't going to put myself out there and be humiliated.

My parents never warned me about boys, and I never got "the talk" from my mother. I learned from my girlfriends. But my mother never talked to me about menstruation; it just happened. When it actually did, she just told me, "You have to wear these."

Junior high was a blur. I just remember walking through those halls and my girlfriends and I having fun.

HIGH SCHOOL

High school represents both good and bad memories. I attended El Monte High School, which was much farther from my home, but I still walked to school. It had a very large student body composed of a majority of whites, but with a significant number of Mexicans or Chicanos. All the different barrios, such as Flores, Basset, Hayes, and Hicks, fed into the school. But this changing demographics also led to a lot of tension between whites and Mexicans. The whites felt that they were losing control of the school, and they reacted with a lot of hostility toward us.

"Hey, beaners," they would call out to us. Or they would taunt us by calling us "dirty Mexicans." This occurred both at school and when we walked home.

There was very little interethnic or interracial mixing. We attended many of the same classes, and most of the time the seating was alphabetical. Since my last name started with A, I usually sat in the front. But beyond this, we could feel and hear the racism.

The other Mexican students and I reacted by creating our own sense of community. We started hanging out together and acting in a defiant manner in the way we looked and talked. Each morning, for example, all or most of the Chicanos would go to a park right across from the school. This included both boys and girls. We assembled there, and we stayed there talking and mixing with one another until the bell rang to start classes. We did this for our own self-protection and to make us feel good about one another.

We now started to call ourselves "Chicanos," and this was some years before the Chicano movement, since I attended high school from 1960 to 1964. We also dressed in a countercultural fashion. Once a week, we dressed all in black. This was usually on Fridays, and so we called it Black Friday. I used to wear these black skirts that came up to the "empire," or to the bosom, with straps. They made me seem to have a waist. I wore white blouses. My mom sewed this outfit for me. The other girls had similar black skirts and white blouses. Our skirts were below the knee, not miniskirts. We sometimes wore an artificial red rose on our sweaters, which were also black. Although, in general, women didn't like to dress like one another, we did. As part of our attire, we wore these big shoes that were called "bunnies." They were big, wide shoes that made our feet look huge. They were called bunnies because they had these two pieces of leather that stood up and looked like bunny ears. They would be called wedges now. We wore them all the time.

Besides Black Fridays, we also had Blue Mondays, Green Tuesdays, and so on. This meant that on those days the girls in my clique favored those colors in our school clothes.

We, the girls, also "stacked" our hair—like two feet tall! The style was not a pompadour like the 1940s pachucas wore. Ours was cut in layers, with a *colita*. We curled our hair in pin curls but left one strand of hair straight in the back, which was longer than the rest of the hair. It was a *colita*. It was a pre-*chola* (gang) look. But we weren't a gang. Our look was our identification and our way to stick together.

While the girls had our particular look, so too did the guys. They wore the khakis and plaid shirts just like they do today—the *cholo* look.

While I also wanted to wear big hoop earrings like those of the other girls, my parents wouldn't let me. They didn't even let me pierce my ears.

Although we might have looked like gang members, few, if any of us, in school belonged to gangs, although there were some gangs in El Monte.

We also came up with names for ourselves. We decided we were going to name ourselves in defiance of how the teachers either mangled our names or changed them to an English version. There was Watusi, Zombie, and Duck. These became our *placas*, or nicknames. I was called *china*, using the Spanish pronunciation. I once wrote my *placa* on the wall of one of my classes, and the teacher caught me and made me wash it off.

While we spoke predominantly English, we did use Chicano slang—*caló*, which had been invented by the pachucos.

Unfortunately, the racial tensions at school led to actual conflicts, in the form of fights between whites and Chicanos. There was a place where everybody used to stand between classes, with a clock by the intersection of four hallways. That's where some of the fights broke out. These were fistfights or hair pulling and involved boys and girls on both sides. I never saw any knives or other weapons used. These became free-for-alls. I myself never engaged in these fights, but my girlfriends did. I wasn't a physical fighter, despite my size. I fought with my mouth and verbally challenged the racial slurs aimed at us by the whites. I also didn't need to fight because all I had to do was give that dirty look and others left me alone. They were afraid of me because of my size. But I witnessed these fights in the hallways and even tried to protect some of the Chicanos, especially the girls.

I remember one particular fight between the white girls and the Chicana girls. It was in one of the lounges, and for some reason both groups were practicing dance steps there. However, each were dancing differently, although to the same music. The white girls were dancing to what was called the Surfer Stomp. Part of this dance involved putting their butts out and doing some steps. But as they did this, one or more of them butted into the Chicanas, and that's when the fight started. The girls used their fists and pulled one another's hair.

When these fights broke out—and they were on a regular basis—the teachers and the principal never tried to stop them; they usually just called the police. Many times the police entered the school. On one occasion, they drove their motorcycles straight into the school and into the hallways. Mostly they arrested only the Chicanos, usually the boys, and handcuffed them and took them to jail. They never arrested a white student that I can recall.

I did okay in my classes but was not highly motivated. This in part had to do with the racism on campus, including that of my some of my teachers. I loved history, but in one of my history classes every time I raised my hand to respond to the teacher's question or comments, he refused to acknowledge me. It was like I was invisible.

"Choose me, choose me, my hand, my hand," I thought to myself, but to no avail.

Here I was trying to participate in class, and the teacher refused to let me do so. After a while, I just gave up and didn't raise my hand again. "Well, screw that!"

Chicanos, on the whole, were tolerated in classes but not significantly encouraged. Many were shuttled toward vocational classes in our tracking system, such as homemaking for the girls. I wasn't one of those students, but I couldn't help but notice that it was mainly Chicanos in those classes. I became, as did many other Chicanos, alienated from the school. Many dropped out. They should have stayed in, because the school didn't keep any students from graduating, including Chicanos, even if they failed classes. They just wanted us in and out as fast as possible.

If they didn't drop out, some got into drugs. I saw Chicano kids sniffing gasoline from gas tanks at school. Some passed out in the parking lot. Some took reds, or barbiturates; or whites, also called "bennies," which were amphetamines.

All my teachers were white. I never had a Chicano teacher, not even for Spanish. I got a D in one of my Spanish classes. Not only did I not know the language, but the teachers emphasized a Castilian Spanish, which I was even less familiar with, as opposed to a Mexican Spanish.

I was also terrified at the idea of doing PE because I was so fat. I couldn't see myself wearing shorts. My legs, especially my thighs, were humongous. I refused to wear shorts. I wasn't going to be humiliated, because I knew how people would react. My mother tried to help me by sewing me a white pleated skirt with a white shirt that she and my dad requested to my counselor that I be allowed to wear instead of the shorts. He agreed, but when I tried the outfit on at home, I looked like a big mattress. I refused to go to PE. Finally, the administration backed off, and they allowed me to work in the school office during my PE time. To my relief, I didn't have to do PE.

RECONCILIATION

But school wasn't all bad. Some things began to change by my senior year. This was largely the result of one of our counselors, Mr. John Bartan. He wanted to do something about the fighting and the racial tensions, and so he organized a Human Relations Club. He talked to us, the Chicanos, and to the white kids and brought us together in a series of encounters. Well, at first, it was tense and we all shouted at one another, but finally, perhaps out of exhaustion, we began to listen and attempt to reconcile matters. We began to treat one another respectfully. The local El Monte newspaper wrote this about our encounters: "Some of the new leadership has come from two groups that reportedly had been causing concern: the khaki-clad Mexican-American students who have habitually clustered together at the park across from the school and the Surfers, an Anglo group whose most obvious characteristic is long bleached hair."[1]

What Mr. Bartan accomplished was a miracle. The fighting stopped. This didn't mean that all of a sudden our school was a racial paradise, but we had gotten over a huge hurdle. In the club we elected officers, and I was chosen as secretary and a Chicano guy, Pat Reyes, was selected as president.

Just as important, Mr. Bartan recognized that, as Chicanos, we needed to have an outlet, one that would develop our leadership. Since we were never represented in the student council, he helped us organize a Chicano youth council, Los Unidos, where we elected our own officers. We would meet and plan Chicano-sponsored events on campus, such as dances or cultural activities. At our meeting we also discussed our school experiences. This was important in giving us a voice. I was the only female officer of the club, and it really empowered me. I could give a good rap even then, and the leadership role helped.

What also helped in my development was when Mr. Bartan chose me and three other students to represent our school at what was being called the Spanish-Speaking Youth Leadership Conference, to be held at Camp Hess Kramer in Malibu. This is the famous Hess Kramer, where Sal Castro got his start in working with Chicano kids as one of the camp's counselors.[2] I was the only Chicana representing my school and in 1963 attended the first conference, which soon was renamed the Mexican American Youth Leadership Conferences. It was a great experience and a beautiful setting. For the first time I met many other Chicanos from the Greater L.A. area and had an opportunity in the organized discussion sessions, and outside of them, to learn the conditions of Chicano students in other schools. I learned that we were all in similar situations, in which the schools didn't respect us and failed to develop our potential. Although I was one of the girls there, I was not intimidated, and I furthered my leadership skills. I'm honored to be an alumnus of Camp Hess Kramer, which became better known later due to its influence in the 1968 blowouts. My parents were very supportive by allowing me to attend.[3]

These initial leadership opportunities helped me overcome what shyness I still had due to my weight. I started developing a new attitude of "if you're going to look at this outer part of me and not take what's in my heart and my head, then I don't have time for you." Once I developed this attitude, people who might have earlier bullied me backed off. I came to realize that I wasn't afraid to say things and to speak out and have some impact.

Things clearly had changed for the better by the time I graduated. At the same time, socializing between whites and Chicanos remained limited. Most everyone went to the school dances and proms, but few whites dated Chicanos and vice versa. The few Chicanos that did were not part of our group. We considered them to be coconuts or Oreos, that is, brown on the outside but white on the inside. They were *agabachados,* or Anglicized. We frowned on interethnic dating, which, as I look back, was wrong for us to do. I personally did not attend my prom because I considered it to be a white thing. I dated only a little and that was with a Chicano boy. In high school I also started going to parties, with my parents' permission. These were just Chicano parties.

One social activity that I particularly liked was going to rock concerts at our local community center and seeing different groups perform. Concerts were a big thing in the sixties. The most popular venue was the El Monte Legion Stadium. I saw greats such as Richie Valens, Ike and Tina Turner, and Ray Charles. I started going when I was fourteen, because my aunt took me. While I was in high school, my parents allowed me to go to these concerts with my friends, but I had to be home at a certain hour. But they also realized that I was getting older and needed to enjoy that social part of my life.

Through high school I also began to dress differently, as I started to blossom. I was still quite big, and I think I weighed around 250 pounds in high school. People would often tell me, "Gloria, your face is so beautiful." What they meant but didn't say was "you're fat." But by then I started to develop a shell for myself. "You know what?" I thought to myself. "I don't care what you think of me." I started to get mean. I wasn't going to take any more teasing or bullying about my size, and I didn't.

In high school I started buying some of my clothes, although my mom still made some for me. In fact, I learned how to sew and made some of my own clothes. I dressed in skirts and dresses because this was the norm for girls at schools. Miniskirts were beginning to come in, but my friends and I didn't wear them. For one, I was too overweight to wear one. I also never wore pants because we were not allowed to in school.

Besides being involved in trying to improve race relations at my high school, I, in general, was becoming politically aware due to both national and local conditions. I knew about Dr. Martin Luther King Jr. and about the black civil rights movement. I cried when I saw on television how blacks were being treated with fire hoses just because of the color of their skins. Some of my cousins on my mother's side are half-black, and so I had a personal reaction to this form of discrimination. I was raised to not be prejudiced. That's one thing my parents taught me, including never to use the "*n*-word."

But racism also affected Mexicans in El Monte, not only in the high school but in the community as well. There were few, if any, blacks in El Monte, and so race revolved around whites and Mexicans. Some whites hated Mexicans; they even formed a Nazi group. I never actually saw the Nazis, but I knew about them and they scared me. I also knew of actual conflicts between Nazis and Chicanos. In fact, many Chicanos sought out the Nazis to beat them up. Eventually the Nazis turned on one another and disappeared.

My parents were Democrats, and although they were not politically active, they did vote. I'm sure they voted for John F. Kennedy when he was elected president in 1960. We loved JFK and were shocked by his assassination. On November 22, 1963, I cried in school when the principal announced that the president had been shot and killed. Many others students also cried. It was frightening. What was going on? They've killed the president, a good one. Like most other Americans, we were riveted to our television, watching the events following the assassination.

But my politics, such as they were, had to do with issues of race. I was very aware that I was treated differently because of the color of my skin and the fact that I was of Mexican descent. I was aware that there were inequalities and that education wasn't catering to me. In high school I was already developing a social conscience.

I graduated from high school in 1964. I wore a cap and gown over my big beehive hair. In my graduation picture, the top of my head was cut off due to my beehive.

My parents, of course, were very proud of me. My mother had a high school education, but not my father. My dad wanted my brother and me to be educated. He wanted me to go to college, but he also wanted me to get married and have children.

The biggest thing about my graduation was that my parents—specifically my dad—gave me a brand-new light blue Volkswagen bug. I loved it and had it for years. My dad had taught me how to drive, and as a senior I often drove to school with him, but he would take over as we got close. I think I got my driver's license the year I graduated. I learned to drive a stick shift since that's all we had. My mom didn't drive.

That summer I became involved in what was called the Mexican-American Youth Council, and, in fact, I became president of it. It was mainly a social club, and we sponsored dances for youth in El Monte. María Ávila, an older woman involved in local politics, organized the club, and we met in her garage. I think some of our dances were also held there. We played records and danced. We did the Stroll.

In the fall I enrolled at East Los Angeles College, which was the closest to my home at that time. It took me only about twenty minutes to drive there. Going to community college was more to please my dad, because my heart wasn't really in it. This wasn't my aspiration. I would sit in classes that would just go over my head because I had no interest in them. One of the few classes I somewhat liked was one on juvenile delinquency, which probably was a sociology class. I wound up quitting school during my first year. My father was quite upset with me.

But I was okay because I started doing community work. I got a full-time job with an antipoverty program, the Neighborhood Adult Participation Project on Brooklyn Avenue (now César Chávez Avenue) in East L.A. I wound up working there for several years. I did clerical work but moved up administratively. The agency served both the Chicano and black communities. I worked for a while in our south central office, which dealt primarily with blacks. It was the first time that I ever met black Muslims, and I was so impressed with them. They were very proper and treated me with respect. Among other things, we did voter education. I also continued to live at home, even though my dad and I, more and more, didn't get along. I got older and more politically involved. He was just very conservative and unaffectionate, at least toward me.

THE BROWN BERETS

I first became aware of the Brown Berets about three years later, in 1967, when they began to organize and were transitioning from being the Young Chicanos for Community Action. The Brown Berets became perhaps the most militant group of the emerging Chicano movement. They started a coffeehouse called La Piranya on East Olympic Boulevard, and they hung out there.[4]

My girlfriends and I got into the habit of cruising on Whittier Boulevard, the heart of East L.A., in my little VW or in one of my friend's cars. Hundreds of people cruised on Whittier on weekend nights. It was the thing to do. Many of the cars were lowriders, but not mine. I didn't want to lower it like the others. I cruised with two close friends from Santa Fe Springs who were sisters: Andrea and Esther Sánchez. Somehow we wound up one evening at La Piranya. I just remember walking into the place and it being pitch-black. Our eyes had to adjust to the darkness.

"Why is it so dark?" I asked someone.

I learned later that the Berets kept it like this because the L.A. county sheriffs began harassing them by coming by and shining their floodlights into La Piranya.

While the place used to be a coffeehouse, under the Berets La Piranya served no coffee. It was just a meeting place with a few tables and chairs. There were many

Chicanos there the first time I went. They were mostly young guys but a few young women were there as well.

Later some lights came on and one guy came up to me and introduced himself.

"Hi, I'm David Sánchez. Welcome to La Piranya and the Brown Berets."

"Oh, nice to meet you. I'm Gloria Arellanes."

Little did I know at the moment that David would become the so-called prime minister of the Berets. He explained to me who the Berets were and how they were working in the Chicano community, especially in confronting police abuse. He called the police "the pigs." He also used terms like "revolution." When I first met David they had not yet officially become a paramilitary outfit that wore military-style uniforms. They would shortly thereafter.[5]

"You and your friends should join us," David said.

"Well, I think I need to know more. I like what you're doing and what you're saying, but I need a little more information."

I didn't tell him that I thought all this sounded very radical and different to me. The Berets, from what I could tell, seemed very nationalistic (a term I didn't use then but would soon enough learn) about how Chicanos were being treated and how the Berets were organizing to confront racism in East L.A. These were things that I hadn't been involved in, although I was aware of discrimination and racism, having experienced it in high school and in my own community. But no one was talking in such militant fashion as David was on police abuse, educational problems, and efforts to deny Chicanos their own identity and culture.

My initial impression of David Sánchez was that he was interesting. He came across as very intelligent, seemed to know what he was talking about, and knew what his goals were. I would describe him as having a vision and pursuing it, although in those days we didn't talk like this. But I did see that he was goal-oriented and that he was trying to bring Chicanos together. He was able to recruit people like myself. I wouldn't call him charismatic or electrifying, but he was a leader. If he had been charismatic, I think I would have jumped right away and said, "Wow! I have to follow this guy." Corky Gonzales, for example, had charisma; David didn't. I found him very reserved at times. He was very dry and stiff and lacked a sense of humor compared to the rest of the Berets.

I also related to David because he was about my age or just a bit younger. In fact, all the Berets—men and women—were quite young, some of them in their late teens or early twenties.

Although I wasn't ready to join the Berets based on our visit to La Piranya, my girlfriends and I did agree to attend some of their meetings. Some were held in La Piranya, but some also in member's homes or when the Berets participated in community meetings. I had heard that the Berets sponsored speakers at the coffeehouse such as César Chávez and black militants such as Stokley Carmichael, but either I didn't attend these meetings or they had occurred before my visit to La Piranya. However, the Berets soon left this location because, I think, they lost their lease. They also were being harassed there by the county sheriffs. They then opened up an office on Soto Street in the Boyle Heights section of East L.A.

These visits with the Berets allowed me to ask the questions I was interested in such as "what are you about?" and "what are you planning?"

What I considered was how different the Berets were from anything I had been involved with and that they were very radical. They especially took on the police because of their harassment of Chicanos and their brutality. Did I want to participate in this? How dangerous was this? Could I get into trouble? Even arrested? At the same time, the Berets were taking on issues that few others were fighting for. That attracted me.

I also liked that the Berets advocated no drugs and no drinking for their members. I never dabbled in those things myself, but I knew how devastating drugs and drinking could be. I saw this in my work and my own father, who drank too much. So the discipline of the Berets attracted me.

After attending some of these meetings and community events, plus weighing the pros and cons, my girlfriends, Andrea and Esther, and I decided to join the Berets. This was sometime in late 1967. The Berets had just organized earlier that year, and so we became part of the foundation. I don't recall any specific formal membership process, although there was an application form of sorts. There also were no dues. It was just a verbal agreement.[6]

"Okay, we'll join," we told David and the other leaders—all men. The Berets took anyone that was interested in what they were saying and doing. We then followed and proved ourselves. It was up to the individual to decide— "this is for me or this isn't for me."

This was a big step on our part, but, at the same time, it seemed natural, as we wanted to do community work, which I was doing anyway in my antipoverty job. Joining the Berets would make it possible to expand this work. I loved the idea that it was a community organization and geared toward battling injustices and inequality. I was also affected by the ethnic and cultural nationalism of the Berets, which promoted our ethnic and cultural pride as Chicanos.

When we joined, there were about twenty active members, including some women. This number would grow to about seventy overall by 1970, but there was always a smaller key core. However, after we became members, other women also joined, and we became an important nucleus within the group. These women included Arlene Sánchez, David's sister, and she recruited some of her friends, such as the Leyva sisters, Elena and Yolanda Solís, and Hilda and Grace Reyes. Lorraine Escalante, the daughter of Alicia Escalante, who headed the East L.A. Welfare Rights Organization, also joined. This became our clique. We were more

or less the same age, in our late teens or early twenties. There was no age requirement for joining the Berets, as far as I know. The only requirement, and it was an
unstated one, was that you had to be a Chicano, man or woman.

My younger brother, Bill, also later joined the Berets

In general, the Beret's position was that we were in East L.A. and not many
whites lived there, so it was only natural that we were a Chicano group.

Because the Berets came to consider themselves to be a paramilitary organization similar to the Black Panther Party, they eventually wore military-style uniforms at public events such as marches, demonstrations, meetings, and conferences. The men wore bush jackets with epaulets, along with their brown berets. I'm
not sure where they got their jackets—probably at some used military store.

The brown beret was the most distinguishing part of the uniform. According to
the Brown Beret manual, "the brown beret was chosen because it is a symbol of the
love and pride we have in our race and in the color of our skin. The Brown Beret
also acts as a symbol of unity among the Chicanos."[7]

In a lecture David Sánchez once said, "A representative of Father John Luce at
the Church of the Epiphany, who was one of our sponsors, gave me a blue beret
that I started wearing. But it didn't go over very well—a blue beret? So I bought a
brown beret and that seemed more attractive and appropriate for our group, and
so I went out and bought twelve brown berets and distributed them to some of our
group, and this is the origins of the name of the Brown Berets."[8]

The berets had the Brown Beret logo, which consisted of a yellow-and-brown
design of a cross topped with a beret and draped by two bayoneted rifles, and on
top of that the term "La Causa," borrowed from the farmworkers' struggle. The
yellow represented the land Aztlán, a land stolen by the Anglo-Americans, and the
brown symbolized la raza—Chicanos. The cross represented the Catholicism of
most Chicanos, and the rifles stood for self-defense and the use of violence as a last
resort. I don't know who designed the logo.[9]

The women's uniform was different. Hilda and Grace Reyes's mom had a friend
who ran a garment factory. In fact, I think that their mother worked there. We
went there and got measured for our outfits. We didn't wear classic bush jackets,
but more of a blazer that still looked like a bush jacket, but it was a darker brown
than the men's khaki color. Our blazers buttoned down the front and had pockets,
but no epaulets like the men's. They were lined and done very nicely. There was a
definite feminine touch to our uniforms, and we wanted them that way. We didn't
need David's or the other ministers' approval of how our uniforms looked. We
approved of them ourselves. Along with our blazers, we wore black skirts and, of
course, our berets, which had our logo, "La Causa," on it. We, along with the men,
wore our uniforms with great pride.

Later, as we recruited some even younger women, they started wearing miniskirts, bush jackets, and long black boots. I never wore this look. For one, when

you're overweight, you don't want any big, fat legs hanging out. My skirts, and those of some of the other women who, like me, were big, went below our knees. I also didn't wear pants as part of our uniform, although some of the younger and thinner women did. I also don't recall paying for our outfits, in particular the blazer. I think the factory manager donated them to us. I don't know if our uniforms were supposed to emulate those of the Black Panther Party. I don't recall anyone ever saying, "We need to look like them." Maybe it was in David's mind.[10]

At the same time, we admired the Panthers, and in L.A. we developed good relations with the local Panthers. We supported their struggles, and they supported us, even though there were no instances, that I can recall, of both groups actually cosponsoring activities. But we respected each other's jurisdictions and knew that we were similar in style, ideology, and politics. We knew that we both especially hated the cops and the cops hated us. Part of the informal relationship that we had with the Panthers consisted of a mutual pact that if we found ourselves in black neighborhoods such as Watts or South Central L.A., the Panthers would protect us, and if the Panthers came to East L.A., we would reciprocate. The leaders of both groups occasionally met, but I, and for that matter other female Berets, was never included in such meetings.

I wasn't aware of it then, but as I look back on it I know that our uniforms were aimed at two audiences: the police and the community. The police, both the Los Angeles Police Department (LAPD) and the Los Angeles County Sheriff's Department, wore uniforms, and so did we. In other words, our uniforms were a direct challenge to the cops. In effect, we were saying, we now represent the real security and police for the Chicano community. In fact, our whole organization mirrored the hierarchy and military style of the police. They had a chief of police or county sheriff and we had a prime minister. They had their high-level subordinates and rank-and-file cops, and we had our different ministers and our rank-and-file Berets. They drilled and marched. We drilled and marched. They had guns; we had guns. So our uniforms, organization, and style were a direct confrontation with the cops, or "pigs."

On the other hand, our uniforms were also aimed to impress on the Chicano community that we represented their security and that, unlike the cops, we were there to protect and help Chicanos and Mexicans in the barrios. But this wasn't easy at first. It was hard for the community to accept our appearance. We looked like an invading army. Some people probably thought, "Are they going to bring army tanks in here or what?" They didn't trust us at first, and some never did. They thought we were trouble. At the same time, some probably thought, "Wow, they really have it together—look how nice they look." I think that through some of our programs, especially the free clinic that we started, we gained the confidence and support of many in the barrio.

But we really antagonized the cops. We called attention to police profiling and abuse. They hated us and we hated them. I'll never forget one incident. In 1968 at the Hollywood Palladium, the Greater Los Angeles Urban League decided to give the Berets the Ghetto Freedom Award for our community service. David couldn't go to the award banquet, and so he had me go and represent the Berets. By this time I had been elevated to minister of finances and communication and the only Beret female minister.[11]

"You go, Gloria," David said.

"Okay, I'll go."

I went with two other Berets in their uniforms, who acted as my bodyguards. I didn't wear all of my uniform, only a brown dress with my beret and blazer. When I went up to the stage to receive the award, I looked out at the audience. The only face I zeroed in on was that of chief of police Tom Redden. His face was beet red. He looked like he was going to die because we received the award. He looked livid. He got even angrier when the L.A. Black Panther Party also received a similar award. Redden detested us as much as he did the Panthers and saw both groups as nothing but revolutionaries or worse. But I loved our "in your face" approach to the police.

I still lived at home, and, needless to say, my father hated my joining the Berets. He hated what I did but didn't kick me out. Although he accepted the term "Chicano," he felt that the movement and especially the Berets were too radical and maybe communists. My mother didn't say anything, but in her quiet way supported me. I was a free spirit and very independent, and she respected that. My dad didn't.

HIERARCHY

As a paramilitary organization, the Berets had a top-down hierarchical governing structure, just like in the military. At the top was the prime minister, David Sánchez, and he was surrounded by his other ministers, of defense, discipline, information, communications, education, and public relations. These included Carlos Montes, Ralph Ramírez, Richard Díaz, Ron López, and two others. Below the ministers were the rank-and-file Berets. The ministers, especially the prime minister, made all the decisions. This was anything but a democratic structure. The ministers rarely challenged David, although they discussed issues among themselves and most often came to a consensus. They hardly ever discussed issues with the rest of the Berets. David and his ministers were a tight group, a clique. They were very close and always together. I became one of the ministers and will discuss this later. While, on the whole, David did not relegate authority easily, he did at times, such as when he later appointed me to direct the Beret health clinic.

Ideologically, the Berets focused on community empowerment, and we clearly were an oppositional group to the status quo and against racism toward Chicanos. Our motto "to serve, observe, and protect" stressed that our role was to serve our community, to observe conditions in the community such as police abuse and lack of social services, and, finally, to protect our community against the police and, in a larger sense, against racism.

We had a Ten-Point Program, although it later expanded to a Thirteen-Point Program. I sometime later learned that this was patterned after the Ten-Point Program of the Black Panther Party, which the Panthers referred to as their "survival program." Most of our motto was centered on the program. The ten points included the following:

1. Unity of our people regardless of age, income, religion or philosophy.
2. We demand the right to bi-lingual education as guaranteed by the Treaty of Guadalupe Hidalgo.
3. We demand the true history of the Chicano be taught in all schools of the five Southwest States.
4. We demand a civilian police review board made up of the people who live in our community.
5. We demand that all police officers in the Chicano community must live in the community and speak the Spanish language.
6. We demand that all Chicanos whose homes get removed by Urban Renewal be given job training to acquire employment that will enable them to live in the new homes built in their barrios.
7. We demand a guaranteed annual income of $5,000, for all Chicano families.
8. We demand that all juries that try our people be composed of an equal number of people of each race: whites, blacks, orientals [sic], and Chicanos. And that the jury be just of the same economic and social status as the defendant.
9. We demand that the literacy text for voting be given in the Spanish language, and that persons who speak only Spanish be given the same voting rights as any other person.
10. We will keep and bear arms and use them against any threatening elements from outside our community such as the police or right wing extremist groups and we will also use them against any traitors from within our own community.[12]

Of course, the most controversial point was number 10 on keeping and bearing arms. We believed in guns and the right to bear them. But, frankly, I don't think even then that I believed wholeheartedly in this. I certainly wasn't going to carry a gun around in public.

We also had a Brown Beret manual, which David titled *The Birth of a New Symbol*. We were encouraged to learn and memorize it, although I didn't and I suspect others didn't either. Some of the key points of the manual included the importance of organization. "Organization is a form of people power," it stressed. It also specified three steps in applying pressure on the system. These included communication, demonstration, and "alternatives," which meant "by any means necessary."[13]

Despite these perspectives and the fact that David was quite ideological, the Berets as a whole did not focus on ideology or political philosophies. We never had session around these issues. We were an action-oriented, grassroots organization. We didn't sit around talking politics; we acted out our politics. That politics was, as our motto indicated, to serve our community, the Chicano community. We were nationalistic, radical, and militant because we opposed the racist system that exploited Chicanos. We confronted that system: the police, the schools, the government, and the Mexican American *vendidos,* or sellouts to the system. As our manual noted, we believed in protecting our community and ourselves "by any means necessary." Did that mean carrying weapons? Yes. Did that mean starting violence? No. We would never initiate any violence, but we pledged to counter violence against us or the community by counterviolence if necessary. Fortunately, that never came to happen. Despite our harassment by the police and conflicts with other Chicanos, we never used violence, at least while I was in the Berets.

We saw ourselves as part of the Chicano movement, but we believed that we were even more radical and militant than the rest of the movement. Although, for the most part, we had good relations with other movement groups, our more strident attitude sometimes caused tensions. Quite frankly, I don't think that we were the favorite people of other activists, such as Eliezer Risco and Raul Ruiz. They looked at us as younger and probably thought we were somewhat foolish. I don't know if that is true, but this is what I felt. I think they and possibly others looked at the Berets as being irresponsible at times. But I think this may have been age more than anything else. It wasn't that people like Risco and Raul were a generation older, but compared to most Berets, they were already more mature, into their twenties.

MEMBERS

Like so many other Chicano movement groups, the Berets was predominantly a youth movement. We were part of the new and emerging Chicano generation. Most of us, as noted, were in our late teens or early twenties. I was about twenty-one when I joined. In fact, I was one of the older Berets. We included those who were still high schoolers or who had recently graduated from high school.

The Berets attracted young people because it gave them a place to be acknowledged. I think they lacked that in their homes, and the Berets gave them a feeling of self-importance. That came from doing good things for the community, so other people came to believe in them. The fact was that despite the movement's rhetoric about *la familia* and its cultural importance, many of us came from dysfunctional families, with abuse, alcoholism, or drugs. This didn't include most families, but you could see it in a lot of the young people who came to the Berets, including the *vatos*, or gangbangers. Some joined the Berets or hung around us. A gang member could belong to the Berets, and we did not make it mandatory that they had to drop their gang affiliation. I actually enjoyed being with these vatos and got along fine with them. I even dated one. But they were tough. You didn't mess with them. If they meant something, they meant it.

While we got along well with some vatos, we did have tensions with some of the more prominent gangs. This is interesting because a popular notion is that the Berets were composed principally of vatos or the so-called vatos locos, or crazy dudes. This was not the case at all. Most were not vatos. Perhaps this is why we had conflict with some of the actual gangs in East L.A.

One of these gangs was the Primera Flats, or First Flats gang. They came by their name because their turf included what was called Primera Flats, or the First Street section of Boyle Heights in the Greater East L.A. area. Because our first Beret office was located in that area on Soto Street, the gang saw us as encroaching on their turf. One day they stormed into our office like thugs and demanded that we leave that community not only because it was their territory but because, they accused us, we attracted too many cops to that area. I was in the office and tried to challenge them, but they quickly shouted me down. I decided that under the circumstances and with the possibility of violence, this was a time to be quiet. But there were some instances of fistfights between Beret members and gang members. We never resolved these tensions with some of the gangs, and later, when our office was firebombed on Christmas Eve 1969, we suspected Primera Flats.

The fact of the matter was that the majority of our members were not vatos, and this included both men and women. We were high schoolers or high school–educated and not dropouts. Most of our guys, including David, were more of what I would consider to be college-boy or preppy-school types even though most were not in college, but they had that college or preppy look when they didn't wear their Beret uniforms. David had graduated from Roosevelt High School but didn't go on to college. In fact, the manual stressed dressing simply when out of uniform.[14]

At the same time, the Berets distrusted college students and those considered to be intellectuals. I'm not sure why this was, and I didn't feel this way. I think it had to do with these types not understanding or appreciating us and thinking that they knew better. We were uncomfortable with them. We also considered them to be removed from the grassroots since they were in college. Yet, despite these differences, David supposedly had a saying: "Every Mexican American is a potential Chicano." I say supposedly because I never heard David say this. But it sounds like David. I think he was referring to more middle-class Mexican Americans who didn't live in the barrios and who believed in the American Dream. He would include students and professors in this category. But the point I believe David was making was that these Mexican Americans could become Chicanos. They could be converted, perhaps not by the Berets but by the movement. In a way, David was his own example. He was first a suited-up young Mexican American who was recognized as a youth leader by archconservative mayor Sam Yorty. Then David went through his own conversion and became a Brown Beret.

I've been asked whether we had gay members. My response is that if some were gay, which I doubt, they didn't reveal themselves as gay, and none of their behavior revealed them as gay. This seemed to be the case throughout the movement.

Unlike gang members, who probably didn't work, most of our members, especially those out of high school, had jobs. After I joined the Berets, I kept my job with the antipoverty program and would do so for all my tenure with the Berets. Of course, others were still in high school, but some of them probably had after-school jobs. In fact, to reach out to high school students, in 1969 we organized a Brown Beret Student Organization in East Los Angeles.[15] A few here and there attended college or took college classes, like Carlos Montes, who attended East L.A. College and actually became involved in Chicano student politics there by helping to organize a more radical group, La Vida Nueva, to oppose a more moderate MEChA one.

IDEOLOGY OF THE BERETS

We saw ourselves as revolutionaries, although we never really identified what this meant. What it meant to me was that we were in the forefront of combating, in a militant and radical way, those, such as the police, who were messing with the Chicano community.

While we weren't that steeped in ideology, we would have some meetings where primarily guest speakers discussed political issues and, for example, the role of Chicano culture with us. There is no question but that we were especially influenced by chicanismo, the cultural nationalism of the Chicano movement. We were affected by it, and we used it as an organizing tool. Chicanismo gave us an identity as Chicanos. My dad had told me that I was Chicano, but growing up I had no idea what this implied. The school told me I was "American." Then I learned that I was Mexican American, but I still didn't know what that meant. Chicanismo helped me and others reconcile all these identity issues by simply saying, "You're Chicano. You're Mexican and you have an indigenous and mixed or mestizo background. Accept this and be proud of it. You have a rich history and culture." It gave us pride in asserting that we were Chicanos. It led us to use this new identity to organize around our culture and traditions, or at least those we had grown up with or had some familiarity with. Part of our cultural nationalism, as David often asserted, was that our main interest was first and foremost to organize our own backyard, which was the Chicano barrios.

Part of chicanismo was the concept of Aztlán and the idea that it represented our indigenous historical homeland. It asserted that Aztlán was the original homeland of the Aztecs, and it coincided with the Southwest, where most Chicanos lived. We lived in our ancestral lands. I later came to reject this as I learned about my own family indigenous background in California that had nothing to do with Aztlán. Still, in the late 1960s, I accepted Aztlán. It gave me an identity and pride in being Chicano. I especially was attracted to the idea that we were a mestizo population, a combination of indigenous and Spanish to represent a new people. This was a beautiful concept, and it was real to me. Perhaps it was a myth, but not for me then; it was real. There's something satisfying and enriching when you've been deprived of an identity and then you find it. We had been told that we had to be Americans, not indigenous or mestizo people. Supposedly, we were part of the "melting pot." We couldn't speak Spanish in school; we were punished for doing so, and that's why my dad, I think, also didn't want me to speak Spanish.

Chicanismo changed all of this.

Although chicanismo represented the core identity or ideology of the Berets, we were also influenced by other perspectives. This included a third world view. For example, we had a lot of communication with the Black Panther Party in L.A., and even though they in part promoted Black Power, they were gravitating more and more toward a third world position. They endorsed other struggles, including the Chicano movement and liberation movements in Africa, Asia, and Latin America. We also had some relationships with Asian American radical groups. Of course, we were affected by the Vietnam War, which we came to oppose. We saw the Vietnamese as our brothers and sisters and not our enemies. We compared the Vietnamese Revolution to our "revolution." One article in La Causa, our newspaper, stated about this comparison: "Let us learn from their example that to resist is to survive a free man and to submit is to be a puto [asshole] and then a slave."[16]

We idolized Che Guevara as a revolutionary hero, in addition to the fact that he was a gorgeous-looking man! There was a third world influence, but only partially. We were a local movement trying to go national, so we had to concern ourselves primarily with Chicanos. In our newspaper, David wrote, "We are not left wing or right wing, we are Chicanos, and we denounce all white foreigners who try to put any other jacket on us."[17]

Along those lines, I don't recall much of a Marxist influence on us. I think we had been affected by the anti-Marxism of the Cold War and the fear of communism. We learned these things in the schools. I don't remember anyone in the Berets saying that they were Marxists, much less communists. I knew some, such as Carlos Montes and Raul Vega, who read Mao's Little Red Book and believed in some of those concepts and quoted Ho Chi Minh and Angela Davis. But we were not a Marxist group, and most of us didn't want to be. We saw it more as something outside of the community. It was a philosophy, but we weren't enchanted by it. The fact was that there weren't too many Chicano communists or socialists at the time. Later, when I got involved with the Chicano antiwar movement, I dealt with a few in the Socialist Workers Party who supported our position against the Vietnam War.[18]

I've heard it said that David was very anti-Marxist and suspicious of Marxist groups. That might have been, but I don't recall him preaching about this. I never heard him denounce Marxists, and I was never aware of anyone in the Berets being disciplined about reading Marxist literature or accepting some Marxist views. I also don't remember David warning us about staying away from groups such as the Communist Party or the Socialist Workers Party. At least he never said that to me. I got along well with everybody, including those who called themselves Marxists.

While we weren't a Marxist group, we, as noted earlier, admired Che Guevara, a Marxist revolutionary. We had posters of Che in our office and later in our health clinic. We pinned Che buttons on our uniforms, and we put his image in *La Causa*. We didn't embrace Che as a Marxist but as a revolutionary and, in particular, a Latin American revolutionary.

While we had occasional discussions about political ideology, we didn't do any common reading as a group. I think we once started to organize a library, but it didn't work out, although we did collect some books in the Soto office. I was familiar with Malcolm X's autobiography and the writings of Frantz Fanon, but I didn't really read them. Perhaps some of the other Berets did on their own; we were just too busy to have study sessions, much less time to read on our own. We weren't ideologues. Our manual stated, "Do not get hung up on theory and ideology for you may alienate yourself and your thinking from the people in the street and thereby fail to communicate."[19] I did occasionally read movement newspapers such as *La Raza* and other movement literature.

At the same time, we did see ourselves as a revolutionary group. But we defined revolution more in social terms that meant fixing all the ills of the community by being militant in attitude and appearance. However, some Berets, mostly males, actually believed they could accomplish a political revolution. I never bought into this.

"How silly, you really think we can win a revolution? We're what? A membership of how many?"

Still, David saw the Berets as a revolutionary elite. He called us "Chicano prophets" and claimed that Chicano nationalism was the only nationalism that was "authentically revolutionary" due to centuries of our indigenous and mestizo ancestors struggling for liberation from white colonizers.[20] In an article in *La Causa*, he wrote, "Since we are the vanguard of the Chicano movement, we must continue to build an organization that will not win the battles, but an organization that will win the war."[21]

Most of us, certainly the women, instead focused on making changes in the community to improve it. We had a more practical approach to revolution. We weren't just going around mouthing off about it. We aimed our rhetoric based on our audience. If we were around other militants, then we talked more militantly; if we addressed community groups, we used a softer tone.

Some always reference the Berets by the idea that we accepted Malcolm X's mantra of achieving our goals "by any means necessary." This is interpreted to mean that we would use violence and guns to achieve our goals. That was the philosophy, and in theory we accepted it; however, we never used it. The reality was that we weren't just ready to pull out guns and take over by any means necessary. I think we were saying, "We will do our revolutionary thing by any means necessary." If that meant guns, then it would be guns. If it meant talking, then it would be talking. The fact is that we favored the second approach. I didn't have to carry a gun. I used my mouth.

On the other hand, we did have to take an oath when we joined the Berets to "kill a pig." That meant that if we had to we would use our gun to kill a cop. I vaguely remember taking this oath, but to me it was just a part of the Beret rhetoric. I never took it to heart. Kill a pig? To me that was insane. I would never consider killing a human being or an animal! That's just my nature. I also could not imagine most of the other Berets really believing this, and certainly not the women. Perhaps I could imagine some of the guys, but it would have been reckless to fulfill this oath. We all would have been killed, and I certainly didn't want to die. And, as far as I know, going out to "kill a pig" was never part of any Beret initiation. I think this oath was just wishful thinking. It was more bravado. It was people saying, "yes, I can do this (but in reality I'm not going to do it)."

In a way, we had a certain sense of innocence or purity. I've heard it said that David had a focus on purity. I'm not sure what this means. However, by purity I mean that we believed in the righteousness of our cause—La Causa. We had to believe that in order to be a Beret. We believed that what we were doing was right and in the best interests of the community. Now, did that mean that we thought we were better than other Chicano movement groups? Perhaps some of the Berets believed this, but I personally didn't. I respected other groups; at the same time, I believed that we had the best approach and vision in dealing with community issues.

As I became influenced by chicanismo and the Berets, I became more conscience of my views of American society. The racism against Chicanos was horrible; it still is. We couldn't get a good job; we couldn't get a good education. People lived in lousy housing projects. Too many Chicanos lived in poverty. That's how I saw it then. I still see it like this to some degree. I didn't see myself as a patriot if that meant wrapping myself up in the red, white, and blue and then treating others in a racist way. In that sense, I've never been a patriot. But my sense of patriotism was questioning a system that allowed racism and other forms of oppression. A good citizen raises questions; a bad one doesn't and accepts the status quo. At the same time, I've worked all my life, I pay my taxes, and I vote. These are forms of patriotism. Despite my criticism of the system, I would not live in another country.

Why should I? This is my country, but I struggle to make it a better one. I saw myself as a rebel. I'm still a rebel. I'm a woman warrior and was so in the Berets. I was and still am outspoken and will speak up for something I feel is not right. I've always been for the underdog. Did I see myself as a revolutionary? I think for the time I was revolutionary in going against the norm and creating awareness. But I don't believe in violence.

OFFICES

Besides La Piranya coffeehouse, the first real office of the Berets, was the one on Soto Street near the corner with Brooklyn (now César Chávez Avenue) in Boyle Heights. We rented the space for a certain amount each month, which we paid out of our fund-raisers since we had no dues. The office consisted of two large front rooms that faced the street. There was a back room plus a bathroom. After it was firebombed, we had to move and rented another office on Olympic Boulevard near the Long Beach Freeway. This one had just one big room. When we opened our free clinic in 1969, it was on Whittier Boulevard. The clinic didn't function as a Beret office, although some of the guys tried to use it as one, especially in the evenings, causing a lot of friction with those of us working in the clinic.

We didn't really have formal or regular meetings. We met when we had to, depending on the circumstances. If there was a police-abuse issue such as the beating of a Chicano or a possible killing of a Chicano in jail, then we would meet to discuss how we would participate in any protests. Of course, we didn't have e-mail or text messaging then, so we communicated by phone or just got the word out that we were meeting. I don't even think we had an office phone. When we met there wouldn't be a formal agenda. It was just what David and the other ministers wanted to discuss. Everyone could participate in the discussion, and people jumped in and out of the dialogue. We called our discussions "rapping." Rapping meant talking. We didn't use *Robert's Rules of Order* or even have to raise our hand, but somehow we conducted business. I don't ever remember raising my hand to speak. I would just listen and then interject, "I have something to say about this" or "I have a question" or "What do you mean by that?" There was also no time limit to our meetings; we met for however long we needed to. Usually, we met on weekends during the day since most people would be available then, unless there was an emergency. Of course, we also attended many other meetings in the community that were sponsored by other groups.

We conducted all our meetings in English. Most of us couldn't speak Spanish very well. We weren't bilingual. I never heard David speak Spanish. In fact, I don't think he could speak it. Only Carlos Montes could speak Spanish. All the women, like me, spoke only in English. However, some of the men used *caló*, the particular language of the vatos.

Not speaking Spanish sometimes could be embarrassing, such as one time when *La Opinión,* the leading Spanish-language newspaper in L.A., sent a reporter to interview me on the Berets or on some related issue.

"I don't speak Spanish," I had to tell the reporter.

"You should learn to speak it," the reporter replied.

"I know I should, but my father didn't want me to speak Spanish."

So we conducted the interview in English.

Of the women, even before I became a minister, I would speak up the most. While some of the men may have disliked or felt defensive when women spoke out, that was not usually the case. Carlos Montes always had very positive feedback or input when women spoke, as did Ralph Ramírez. David often didn't comment when women spoke. He didn't open up to others easily, including women. He was always very serious.

But, in general, the men, especially the ministers, dominated the meetings.[22]

DISCIPLINE

Because we were a paramilitary group, we practiced discipline, or at least as much as we could. As mentioned earlier, we did not tolerate using drugs or drinking alcohol, although sometimes that was not fully enforced. We stressed a certain proper behavior not only among ourselves but especially in the community. We needed to show the community that despite our uniforms and our confrontational style, we were good and decent people. We didn't tolerate behavior that went against this. If somebody didn't follow our rules of behavior, they were disciplined. But this was done informally. There was no coming before a tribunal and being chastised or anything like that. If anything, we pushed self-control so that we disciplined ourselves. We believed that discipline of the mind led to discipline of the body.

Image was very important. How we presented ourselves in the community was critical. That is why, for example, David was always very clean-cut and so were all the other men. The only beard that I recall was worn by Carlos Montes, but it was always nicely trimmed, as was his hair. The men did not support those men that they referred to as "longhairs" or hippie-types. Some of these would come around, but the men made it obvious that they didn't like them. I think the male Berets associated long hair for men with femininity. But this was not true for me and the other female Berets. Some of these Chicano longhairs sometimes came around to our free clinic, and the other women and I enjoyed their company. We had fun with them, and some became good friends. Most were college students who wore their hair long, which was then the style for men.

The women also paid attention to their appearance. Outside of our uniforms, we always dressed nicely, and many of us, like me, always wore skirts or dresses. We had long hair, which was the style then in the late sixties, but it was always nicely combed. All of this was David's way of not alienating ourselves from the community. In our Brown Beret manual, which David wrote, he laid out these forms of behavior and appearance.

Another way we practiced discipline, as well as expressed that we were a paramilitary group, was in our drills. We learned how to march in military formation. Every Sunday, or nearly every Sunday, we went to Elysian Park and for an hour practiced our drills.[23] "About face!" We marched up and down the park. The ministers—the *chingónes* (big shots)—always drilled separate from the rest of us. We also practiced parade rest. We became pretty good, and in protest marches in the barrio, we'd show off our drilling skills. We didn't wear our uniforms when we practiced, just whatever clothes we wanted. I should have worn pants to these drills, but I didn't because they didn't make pants, or at least comfortable pants, for big women. I still weighed over two hundred pounds. My thighs were thunder thighs. Just big! So I didn't want to show them off by wearing tight-fitting pants. As I learned how to drill, I became a drill master for the women. It's so silly to think that I was telling other women how to behave.[24]

Ironically, we learned to drill from one of the Berets, Robert (Bob) Acosta, who turned out to be an undercover cop. He knew about drilling because he was an ex-Marine and had also learned it at the police academy. He was the only one of us who knew how to march. He was a U.S. marshal.[25] Not only did he teach us, but every time we practiced the police always showed up in their black-and-white cars to watch us. I guess they thought we were practicing to engage in a violent revolution, which was pretty far-fetched.

In addition to drilling, some of us had guns. We didn't carry them openly, but some of the men, including the ministers, had weapons. I never saw them, but I knew of them because the guys talked about their guns. As a paramilitary organization, we believed in arming ourselves. I mean, we talked revolution, although unrealistically, I understand now, but we believed in revolution and uprising and defending ourselves even with the use of weapons, especially against the police. But I never saw Berets openly carrying weapons and certainly not at any of our meetings. We also didn't carry weapons out in public since we knew that we always faced the threat of being arrested or harassed by the cops, and so it wasn't a smart thing to be armed around them. If they stopped us and we had guns, it would have given them even more reason to arrest us or worse. Fortunately, we never engaged in a gun battle with them or with anyone else for that matter.

I was the only woman with a weapon. I bought an M1 carbine. I just went to an army surplus store and bought it with cash. There was no background check or anything like that. I didn't need to get a legal permit to have the rifle. My receipt was my legal document. Those of us in the Berets who had weapons were responsible for learning how to take them apart, clean them, and put them back together. No one instructed me how to do this. I just learned it myself, but not very well. I kept it at home except for one time, when I put it in my car and drove up to the mountains with Andrea and two guy Berets for target practice. Andrea didn't have a gun. I think this was the only time I shot my rifle. It's a powerful weapon with a strong kickback that just throws your shoulder. I shot it a few times. It was target practice, but we didn't shoot at any targets. We just shot at the mountains. It was almost like a game. I'm not a violent person, and I regret having that rifle. Later, when I became pregnant, I got rid of it. I became very aware that I didn't believe in guns.

As part of the Berets' stress on being a paramilitary group, we sometimes provided security for certain events, such as being bodyguards. However, it should be said that such activity involved only the men. This was considered to be "men's work." One such example occurred around February 1968, when Reies López Tijerina, the militant and charismatic leader of the land-grant movement in New Mexico, came to L.A. to speak. Some of the male Berets served as his bodyguards during his visit. They protected Tijerina, but, as far as I know, they did not carry guns to do this. We never carried guns in public because we didn't want to attract the cops. Guns for us were more of an underground thing. The male Berets, in particular, idolized Tijerina for what he did and for his confrontational politics, including bearing arms. Many movement activists gravitated toward him because of his fiery oratory and dynamic personality. I don't recall where Tijerina spoke, but I think it was at UCLA. I attended but, as noted, was not one of his bodyguards. I know that he didn't visit our headquarters. I would encounter Tijerina later when I went to the Poor People's Campaign in Washington, DC.

BLOWOUTS

One of the first major actions that the Berets got involved with after I joined was the 1968 "blowouts," or walkouts, in the East L.A. public schools. The Berets functioned as part of the security that Sal Castro, the key teacher who inspired the kids, requested.[26] I didn't actually participate with the other Berets as the thousands of students walked out of their schools because I worked during the day. I wanted to be there, but my boss, Mr. Ed Bonilla, warned me about getting involved.

"Gloria, if you go out to those demonstrations and you're not back in time from lunch, you'll be terminated."

It was ironic that the head of a program in Boyle Heights that was supposed to help Chicanos didn't want to support the blowouts. I was tempted to go anyway, but in the end I felt that I had to protect my job and that I could be supportive in other ways. So I didn't go to the schools. However, my friend Andrea did and got arrested. But she was arrested because this Sergeant Armas of the Special Operation Conspiracy Force of the LAPD thought that Andrea was me. Armas's goal in life was to get the Brown Berets. Since by then I had become one of the ministers, he had it out for me.

"Oh, I finally got you, Gloria," he told Andrea.

"I'm not Gloria."

"You're Gloria Arellanes!"

"Call me whatever you want man, Santa Claus, I don't care," Andrea, with her insane laugh, responded.

Armas really thought he had arrested me, but I never got arrested. He later released Andrea after they fingerprinted her and discovered she wasn't me.

Although I couldn't go to the actual protests, I supported the walkouts by attending the community meetings at the Euclid Center. Sal Castro spoke at these meetings of parents and community leaders, which later became the EICC (see Raul Ruiz's story) and negotiated the students' demands with the school board.

I was very impressed with the blowouts. We knew that the schools were bad. Education was horrible for Chicano kids. They were put in shop classes all the time and not guaranteed a quality education. The schools pushed them out instead of promoting graduating and going to college. I admired Sal Castro for leading the students and for confronting the educational system. He had the courage, unlike the other teachers, to stand up for the students. David Sánchez many years later has asserted that he and the Berets led the blowouts, but in fact it was Sal and the high school and college students.

We in the Berets discussed participating in the blowouts, and we all agreed to do so. It was the biggest issue at that time. Some, including David, Carlos Montes, Fred López, Cruz Becerra, and Ralph Ramírez, got arrested for their involvement. They became part of the East L.A. Thirteen.[27] We demonstrated in support of them until they were released. All of this only added to the tensions between us and the police. I also went along with other Berets to the Board of Education meetings to further endorse the student demands. However, I didn't participate in the later sit-in at the board that fall to protest Sal's suspension from his teaching position. Fortunately, that protest forced the board to reinstate him.

I think that the blowouts were very important because it was the beginning of Chicanos forcefully confronting the educational system. Education applied only to the affluent and mostly white community, while the ghettos and barrios got just the crumbs. So we started demanding better education, with kids having the opportunity to go to college. It was an awakening. The students were awesome in leading the way. It was like a birth to see people get involved and do what they needed to do. It took great courage.

POLICE ABUSE

One of our priorities focused on police abuse, which had a long history in the barrios. Both the county sheriffs and the LAPD acted with impunity in harassing, arresting, beating, and violating the rights of Mexicans. Ironically, the worst cops were the Chicano cops. They were mean to other Chicanos. I think they felt that Chicanos, especially the vatos, embarrassed them as Mexican Americans, and so they really went after them. In fact, I once heard a Chicano deputy sheriff say that it was embarrassing to see somebody of their own race walking around with a flannel shirt and wearing big khaki pants, the usual dress of *cholos.*

Our role was to monitor such behavior. Since most of us didn't have cars, we didn't tail the cops. In fact, they tailed us when we drove. This usually involved my little VW, since I was one of the few Berets with a car. Our antipolice activity consisted of supporting families in the community on police-abuse issues. We helped to bring public and media attention to such incidents, as well as participating in marches and rallies against the police. When possible, we tried to arrange for attorneys. In our newspaper, *La Causa,* we often publicized stories about police violations, including those against us. I remember several times protesting in front of the "Glass House," the LAPD headquarters on Third Street.

At times these protests had to do with the horrific beatings suffered by Chicano inmates in jail. Some were actually killed in jail. I recall visiting somebody at the county jail and he told me, "See that cop over there coming this way?

"Yes."

"Don't look at him. He strangled a guy."

These inmates knew what was going on inside the jails, but no one outside cared. We protested such actions because jail killings were not uncommon.[28]

Police abuse and harassment of Berets was also not uncommon. They would stop us from time to time when we wore our uniforms. Sometimes they even arrested some of us. For example, in April 1968 county sheriffs arrested David and Cruz Olmeda for allegedly "disturbing the peace," as we peacefully protested. The usual sentence for such a charge is probation, but because David and Cruz refused to accept probation for simply exercising their constitutional rights, they were sentenced to sixty days in jail. We quickly mobilized to raise the funds to bail them out. But this was one of many other cases of police harassment against us.[29]

AFTER-SCHOOL PROGRAM

Because of our involvement in the blowouts, we were concerned about the kind of education that Chicano kids were receiving in the schools. The students, in part, demanded curriculum changes that would reflect the Mexican American contribution to American history and culture. This wasn't being done, and students, for example, were punished for speaking Spanish. While the EICC and the school board and school administration negotiated over such changes, we decided on our own to provide a learning enrichment for some of the Chicano students on the Eastside. We established an Escuela de Aztlán, or an after-school program. It included classes on Chicano history, Chicano politics, Chicano culture, and a class on "Knowledge" taught by David. The classes met on weekday afternoons, usually for thirty minutes or an hour, at the All Nations community center. David taught some of these classes, but the rest of us participated when we could. Instruction was informal and often amounted more to a dialogue between the Beret instructor and the students. We also called this rapping. No tuition was charged.

MARCHES

Besides participating in demonstrations such as the blowouts and protests against police abuse, we also marched in public from time to time. I'll never forget one particular time, when some of us marched in the annual September 16 parade in East L.A. This was in 1969. I was already a minister and the director of our free health clinic when I decided that we in the Berets should be part of this event commemorating Mexican Independence Day. Thousands of people attended and lined the main parade route on what then was Brooklyn Avenue in Boyle Heights. I felt that this was a good opportunity to emphasize that the Berets were part of the community, especially with respect to our clinic.

But I also knew that the parade organizers, mostly the merchants in the area, would never allow us to openly march as Berets in their parade. They considered us and the Chicano movement as a whole to be too radical and militant. So I decided I would tell them only that the clinic—El Barrio Free Clinic we operated—wanted to have a float in the parade. I didn't tell them that this was a Beret organization. They agreed to this.

I then approached a nearby army reserve unit to see if the clinic could borrow one of their training tanks to use as our float. Again, I didn't mention that I was a member of the Berets. They also wouldn't have supported the idea if they knew we were Berets. They bought it and so were just like "oh, cool!" To my surprise they agreed, and somehow we got the tank on a truck bed, because the tank couldn't be driven on the streets since its heavy tires would have ripped the street apart. One of the reservists agreed to drive the truck while I and the other clinic volunteers (many of them Berets) would ride on the tank with signs saying, "El Barrio Free Clinic" and "War on Disease," with the clinic's address and phone number. I drew those posters.

I was the only Beret minister on the tank. I don't know where David and the others were. But our plan all along was to go in disguise and then during the parade expose ourselves as Brown Berets. We wore ponchos over our Beret uniforms, with our berets in our pockets. We mounted the tank, and the parade started. We then took off the ponchos, put on our berets, and started shouting, "Viva la Raza! Chicano Power!"

After we exposed ourselves as Berets, to our amazement the contingent in the parade behind us was the LAPD! They gave us the nastiest looks, but we just laughed at them, especially Andrea with her insane laugh. And as we proceeded down the parade route, other Chicanos recognized us and jumped up on the tank to join us. The poor army driver got a little panicked because he saw all these Mexicans coming out of the woodwork on to his tank.

Then some of the people lining the parade route also started yelling, "Viva las gordas!" They were referring to my female Berets and me, since most of us were quite chubby. When I heard this, I started to shrink because I didn't like people calling attention to my size. But Andrea and the others were just laughing and having a ball! My brother, Bill, was also on the tank (he also was quite big), and he had a great time.

By the time we got to the end of the parade, the tank was completely covered with people. The poor driver just didn't know what had hit him. All you could see was that big cannon sticking out. Everything else was covered by Mexicans.

FUND-RAISING

To help us with our activities, we occasionally held fund-raisers. When I became a minister, I was in charge of some of these, as well as keeping our accounts. We didn't collect a lot of money, but it helped in our day-to-day operations.

There was one particular event that was memorable. We labeled it a "Zoot Suit Party." We used one of the community centers and put out the word for people to come dressed in the 1940s popular zoot suit. We didn't charge admission, but we sold beer. There used to be a beer factory, the 102 Brewery, off the 10 Freeway right before the downtown exit. Somebody told me since I was in charge of the event, "Go over there and get your beer. It's really cheap."

Well, it was this off-brand stuff, so what we did was buy all these trays of canned beer. Not only was it not very good beer, but people who drank it later complained of getting a lot of gas.

But because we wanted those who came to think we had good keg beer, we poured the beer into a cup in a back room so that when we brought the beer out it looked like it came out of a keg. But, of course, it didn't. It was really cheap and bad beer, but people bought it!

On the other hand, we did have one or two larger fund-raisers for our clinic, because we had more operating expenses. Rona Fields and her husband helped us make connections with physicians and other health professionals for our clinic and assisted us in raising funds. We knew Rona because she was doing a PhD program at the University of Southern California (USC) and had decided to do her dissertation on the Berets. As such, she hung around us quite a bit. I didn't particularly care for her, and after her dissertation was completed, I didn't like her depiction of the female Berets. She portrayed us as simply women involved to seduce the men.

Rona and her husband had money and lived in a mansion in Altadena, with a swimming pool, tennis court, and horses. It was a beautiful house. She invited lots of well-to-do white people, who pledged donations to the clinic. We attended in our uniforms, so these people knew that the clinic was a Beret operation. But they were liberal types and supported the idea of a free clinic in East L.A.

I remember just being bored at this event. I'm not impressed with people who have lots of expensive stuff. To this day, I'm not impressed. But we still ate Rona's caviar, and she didn't like it that we ate it all.

UNDERCOVER COPS, POLICE, AND THE FBI

All our activities, of course, were scrutinized by the cops. Federal agencies also were involved. The FBI, from what I know of those who have gotten access to their files on the Berets, extensively infiltrated all our chapters. I don't know who their agents were in our national chapter in East L.A., but there certainly had to be some. I've never requested my own FBI file and frankly couldn't care less what it contains. I didn't do anything illegal and was never arrested during my time as a Beret.

> FBI File, March 25, 1968: "[blank] Los Angeles Police Department Intelligence Division, advised on March 25, 1968 that the Brown Beret is a local militant organization, which has been loosely formed and which seeks more governmental positions for Mexican-Americans."[30]
>
> FBI File, Feb. 26, 1969: "The above [blacked out] signifies that the Brown Berets organization, which, heretofore had given indications of being a protective-type group for Mexican-Americans, established to attempt to better the living standards, employment opportunities and quality of education in its communities, now is developing into an organized, armed group."[31]
>
> FBI File, Nov. 16, 1970: "Captioned organization [Brown Berets] is an East Los Angeles–based Mexican-American youth group which has engaged in many militant activities resulting in violent confrontations with police authorities. The group has branches elsewhere in California. The Director has approved initiation of security investigations of leaders and members of captioned group because of its potential for violence."[32]

Because we suspected that police agents had probably infiltrated us, we read the following statement before each of our meetings: "Are there any representatives present in this meeting from any law enforcement agencies in the United States?"

"*IF NO:* Then we give notice that we are all witness to the fact that if you are from a law enforcement agency, you have refused to identify yourself and therefore any legal action on your part would be a clear act of entrapment."[33]

The one other guy who we later found out was an undercover cop for the LAPD was Robert Ávila who, it was later revealed, had also infiltrated the high school student groups during the blowouts. He looked really young. We never suspected Robert, and he was a nice guy. He seemed to be genuinely committed to the Berets.

I remember one occasion when, for some reason, this guy who was not a Beret started taunting us at the Euclid Center. Robert was there, and I could see that he was getting quite disturbed and doing everything to control himself. But then he just exploded. He jumped all over this guy and just dragged him all over the floor. That's what he was trained to do. We couldn't believe it. Here was this nice, quiet, young Robert, and all of a sudden he is beating up this vato. We were impressed, but then maybe this whole fight had been staged for this purpose and for us to fully accept Robert as a Beret.

But apparently Robert's assignment with the Berets also took a toll on him. One day I saw him in our office on Soto. He looked really sad.

"What's wrong with you?" I asked.

"Nothing, nothing. It's just hard."

"What's hard? What are you talking about? What's going on?"

He just looked really down in the dumps. All he kept saying was "it's really hard."

Soon he left the Berets. Apparently they pulled him out. What I think he meant by saying it was hard was that he had gotten attached to us and he actually liked the Berets. He got emotionally involved, not with female Berets, but with our members as a whole, and he probably began to support what we were doing. My guess is that he then found it hard to report on us, to be a Judas figure, to the LAPD. Either he requested to be transferred or they pulled him out when they began to realize that he was becoming sympathetic to us.

Robert just disappeared, but somehow we later found out he was a cop. In fact, I ran into him months later in downtown Los Angeles with his cop uniform on and walking his beat.

"So this is your reward for spying on us, Robert," I sarcastically said to him. "Wooo!"

La Causa also published an expose on Robert as well. It read, in part, "Through Brown Beret Intelligence, we discovered Robert Avila dressed in the black uniform of a *marano* (pig), packing his 38 caliber white solution piece *[sic]*, and wearing the badge of the Los Angeles Police Department. . . . And let Robert Avila be a lesson to all of us, 'the man is everywhere.'"[34]

Undercover cops were also involved in the so-called Biltmore Case in April 1969, when some of the Berets disrupted a speech by Gov. Ronald Reagan at the downtown Biltmore Hotel. I wasn't involved in this and, frankly, didn't even know this had been planned by David and the male Berets, or at least some of them. They had not only not consulted with me, but they hadn't done so with any of the female Berets. But, as earlier noted, this was typical of the men. They often didn't consult with the women because they saw such dramatic confrontations as "men's work," and therefore women didn't need to be involved. They saw women doing more "women's work," such as working in our health clinic. Although I did not participate in this action, I had no problem with such tactics. I think it was completely appropriate. You have to get your point across one way or another. Reagan was addressing a conference on education—the Nuevas Vistas Conference—and he and the conference had excluded representation from the Chicano movement, and, worse, their discussion was totally irrelevant to the problems in the schools that the blowouts had exposed.

The Biltmore incident, unfortunately, led to the arrests and prosecutions of some of the Berets as well as other non-Berets, but not David, on arson charges on claims by the police that as part of the disruption they had set fire to certain parts of the hotel. They became the Biltmore Six. The district attorney charged them not only with disrupting Reagan's speech but of deliberately attempting to firebomb the hotel and committing arson. However, it was later revealed that it was an undercover cop, Fernando Sumaya, who had done this, and not the Berets. Sumaya had infiltrated the Berets. I worked on their behalf to raise funds for their defense. One of the Berets arrested was Carlos Montes, who after being indicted fled and spend several years underground until he later returned. He was rearrested but was exonerated in court. Nevertheless, we lost a valuable Beret and one who was very supportive of the women.[35]

RELATIONS WITH BARRIO GANGS

Although we tried to be the main barrio- or community-based organization in East L.A., we had rivals. These consisted of some of the gangs or other barrio groups who didn't care for us intruding in their turf. This led to the firebombing of our Soto Street headquarters on Christmas Eve 1969 by the Primera Flats gang. While there was no proof that they did this, we strongly suspected them. We also had problems with a group called La Junta. Some believe that La Junta members were former Berets, but this isn't true. They were their own group, composed of former gang members of the Third Street Flats gang. Unlike gangs, La Junta had a purpose and goals like we did, especially with respect to confronting the cops. They didn't join the Berets because they didn't consider us as good a barrio group as they thought themselves to be. Their members also spoke more Spanish than we did, including those of us, like me, who couldn't speak Spanish at all. We often found ourselves at the same community meetings or demonstrations as La Junta. It wasn't that our goals in protecting and helping the community were different, but that each group felt that they were doing a better job. It was a rivalry.

We had similar tensions with an ex-con (*pinto*) group called LUCHA, which also didn't want us around. Interestingly, I also had no personal problem with this group because my own uncle was a member.

"You don't mess around with my niece," he told the other *pintos*. And they didn't.

SOCIAL LIFE AND RELATIONSHIPS

As Berets, we worked hard for the most part, but we also partied hard. We had good times among ourselves. It wasn't all politics. We developed relations with one another, and we laughed a lot. We'd have house parties at different homes. We didn't dance, or not much, at these get-togethers, but just ate and talked. It wasn't just Berets at these parties, but non-Berets as well. We once gave a big birthday party for David and even got a cake made in the shape of the La Causa symbol on our berets. It was really cool. I have a picture of it in my collection at Cal State, Los Angeles. We did dance when we hosted dances in our headquarters, especially after we moved to Olympic Boulevard. We didn't hire a band, but sometimes some musicians would come around and play for us. We also played records for dancing. On occasion we went to the beach and to the movies.

Although we had a policy against drinking liquor, there was some drinking at these social events, but it never got out of control. I also don't remember any drug use at these events. There may have been more drinking and drugs, but I was not privy to this. I occasionally drank, but I wasn't a drinker. I always had a thing because I'm a control freak about drugs and drinking and not being in control of my mind, so I always avoided getting high. I dabbled.

Perhaps the biggest social event that I was involved with as a Beret was the Brown Beret wedding. This was the wedding of two of our members: Bonnie López and Sabu, or Fred, Resendez. They wanted it as a Beret wedding, with some of us being part of the wedding party. So it became a Beret thing. Other female Berets and I were the bridesmaids, and the men were the ushers and our escorts. Ralph Ramírez escorted me. The selection of escorts was random and literally involved "I want you." Both the guys and we did the picking. The men, including Sabu, wore their bush jackets and berets, and the women, including Bonnie, made our dresses in a Beret style. We found this pretty Aztec pattern, or what we thought resembled one, and used it in sewing our colored dresses with the colors of gold and brown. We also wore our hair up, using these hair pieces that made our hair really big! I did all of the women's hair for the wedding.

The wedding invitations bore the name "Brown Berets" on the cover. The wedding took place at the Church of the Epiphany in Lincoln Heights. Father John Luce, an Episcopalian priest, officiated, even though most of us had been raised as Catholics. But Father John was one of the sponsors of the Berets, and so it felt perfectly right for him to marry Bonnie and Sabu. Father Luce, who recently died, was a wonderful person and championed the movement. He later baptized my first son.[36]

FIGURE 8. Gloria Arellanes and Ralph Ramírez at the Brown Beret
wedding, November 13, 1968. Courtesy of the Gloria Arellanes
Collection, John F. Kennedy Memorial Library, California State
University, Los Angeles.

In the wedding we carried candles and threw pinto beans instead of rice, so as
we walked out we could hear this crunchy sound as we stepped on the beans. My
mom attended. It was a great wedding!

Social relationships also included dating. We were all very young, and it was
only natural that some romantic affairs occurred within the Berets. Some of the
male and female Berets became boyfriend and girlfriend. There were a lot of people wanting to hook up with somebody, or they really liked somebody and had
crushes. For a female Beret to date a male Beret did not affect their roles within the
group. Actually, they were kind of respected a little bit more because it meant
"hands off" to other guys. At the same time, some of the other males had girlfriends who were not members of the Berets. Some of these women sometimes
hung around our headquarters. I, myself, dated a guy in the Berets, but I choose
not to discuss this.

Speaking of crushes, several of the female Berets had crushes on Carlos Montes,
especially one in particular. She was one of the younger Berets still in high school,
I think. But they never got together. The fact is that Carlos had many girlfriends.

These relationships, however, did lead in some cases to tensions as they intensi-fied, became traumatic, or fell apart. This was not aided by the immaturity of many of the men and women due to their youth. These dramas played themselves out within the group. At the same time, I never witnessed any abuse on the part of the men or sexual promiscuity. There was no "passing around."

Although most of us were single, a small number were married. This included David, who married a non-Beret woman. She would also come around from time to time, but I always felt that David didn't want her around. I actually baptized his first daughter. The baptism took place at La Placita church in downtown L.A.

However, David's views on social relationships within the Berets were often contradictory. It was more like "do as I say, not as I do." I remember one time speaking at UC San Diego, and a Chicana Beret from Oakland was there. She told me that on a visit to her chapter David had told them, "You're not to get involved with the opposite sex in the organization and blah, blah, blah." After hearing this, I just said, "really?"

The reason that I expressed amazement at what David had said was because he himself didn't practice it. He dated female Berets. I don't remember if this was before or after he got married, but he definitely did have relationships, especially with one of the women.

GENDER RELATIONS

These developing contradictions expanded into gender relations within the Berets. Men and women in the group got along fine for the most part, but underlying this was still the machismo of the men, which became destructive. The men tended to look at women as subservient and not as equal. There was a real division of labor. In that sense, there was never an equality or unity like we tried to say there was. It just didn't exist, and if it did it just kind of fell apart. There is no question in my mind that the one thing that broke up the Berets in time was the treatment of women.

It didn't start this way. In the beginning, when it was fresh and exciting, and we were busy trying to support the community in any way we could, everything seemed okay. But the problem became that the leadership didn't grow, and if this doesn't happen it stagnates, and that's when discontent settles in. I have seen this happen over and over again in organizations. If that leadership cannot grow any-more, it winds up doing the same old things. In the case of the Berets, the male leadership didn't seem to be capable of moving on from their machismo.

I think that part of the problem was that the men had socialized some of the machismo from their own families, in particular their fathers. They saw how their fathers behaved. I saw it in my own family. My father ruled over my mother, and he treated her unfairly. I never understood this, and often later as I grew up I pointed this out to my mother. But she always said, "well *mija,* I love your father, and you'll understand this when you fall in love." Well, I did fall in love, but I never accepted a man talking down to me. I will never accept this as long as I live.

Men believed that women's purpose was to have children and be a homemaker. There was a lack of respect for the female Berets. The men expressed this in the way they talked to the women. I think they also didn't trust us. However, some of us refused that niche.

The Beret men never openly expressed these macho attitudes, and that's why the other women and I weren't initially aware of this. And to be fair, not all the men acted macho. Carlos Montes and Ralph Ramírez, two of the ministers, were not like this. But that didn't prove to be the case with other leaders, such as David and some rank-and-file male Berets.

These macho attitudes were expressed in a division of labor that relegated women to second-class citizenship. Women did all the clerical, secretarial, and "domestic" jobs. I remember when we had a regional meeting of Beret chapters in Southern California at Father Luce's church that the women were all working in the kitchen, while the men sat around a table in the conference room discussing business. I refused to cook and, as a minister, insisted on sitting at the table. However, I did cook on other occasions because I enjoyed cooking. The women always did the cooking for Beret-sponsored events. But at most Beret meetings, the men dominated. In general, we as women were expected to do all of the dirty work while the guys talked politics, marched, and demonstrated. This was true even in the publishing of *La Causa,* our newspaper; and in the running of our free clinic.

On rare occasions machismo also involved physical violence by the men toward the women. One of our top leaders once slapped one of the women. I didn't see it, but I did hear about it from several people. If I had witnessed it, I would have been in somebody's face in a hot second. This female Beret did not leave as a result of this incident, but she did later when I and the other women eventually left.

I never personally experienced physical violence, but once it came close to this. I attended a Beret party with the Sánchez sisters and their brother. No sooner had we entered the house when David started screaming at me—and I mean scream-ing and jumping up and down. It was almost comical but yet threatening.

"You're nothing but a white women's libber," he shouted at me.

I just looked at him like, "wow!" The other men, including some vatos, tried to calm him down but couldn't. I just thought, I'm not going to get into an argument with this fool. I could tell that this wasn't David's normal behavior, so something was going on. He then asked to talk to me behind the house. I did this, but I knew that there could be no communication. He was spaced out and talking about very strange things up in the sky. So I just went along with it, "okay, okay, yeah, yeah, yeah."

But I lost a lot of respect for David, who had lost control and resorted to this immature emotional blank out for whatever reason.

David's behavior at that party only indicated to me how pervasive gender discrimination was in the Berets, because it came from the very top. In time the other women and I would have to confront this, and we did.

I never bought the notion that machismo was simply an expression of men protecting their families and community. If it was a form of protection, there wouldn't have been the hitting of females in the Berets or even possible attempted rapes (I will discuss this later). That's not protection. Actually, I never heard this weird definition of machismo within the Berets. I don't think the guys even understood how they were expressing machismo. On the other side of the coin, I certainly didn't understand the feminism that the other Beret women and I were actually going through or learning or about to give birth to. Machismo was an unfortunate cultural experience, and it would affect me in terms of relationships with men throughout my life.

MINISTER OF FINANCE AND CORRESPONDENCE

My confronting sexism in the Berets was enhanced when I became one of the ministers. I think this was early in 1968 or perhaps in the spring. I became the minister of finance and correspondence, which in a sense was at first nothing but a glorified secretary. I served as treasurer and press contact and also helped with security. I really don't recall how I became a minister. I wasn't interviewed. All of a sudden, David just informed me that he and the other ministers had decided that I should be part of them. I think that as more women joined the Berets, the men, despite their machismo, felt that they needed a female as a minister. I had leadership abilities and had already displayed some of this, for example, in recruiting other women. I think too, at first, they didn't see me as a threat or as someone who would be disruptive. The fact is that I've always gotten along with others, and I'm a hard worker in addition to being a leader. I'm a people person. It's only when I get pushed into a corner that I come out fighting. I think for all these reason, I became a minister.

I felt good and really proud of becoming a minister. I was the only female national minister, since the East L.A. chapter represented the national chapter. I also felt good because of the support of the other female Berets. They were proud of me, and I returned that pride to them. I worked hard to involve them and to make them feel important and a major component of the Berets.

As a minister, I then started meeting more with David and the other ministers. We didn't meet on a regular basis, but only when we felt the need to discuss particular issues. I at first had good working relations with David as the prime minister. It wasn't that he sought out my advice so much as it was just discussion and brainstorming. He never sat down with me and asked me, "What do you think about this?" or "How would you do this better?" We just talked about things.

I think that David respected me, as did the other ministers. I think they saw me and treated me differently than the rank-and-file female Berets. They knew and came to respect my work ethic and that I started taking on a lot of work. Part of this, I have to believe, was just my strong physical presence. I was a big woman with an imposing physique, and I think it made the men think twice about not treating me well, although that wasn't always the case. I'm an assertive person, and I used my physique to complement this. For example, at meetings, whenever I spoke out, I always stood up so I could display my physical stature and use it to my advantage in gaining attention and respect.

As minister of finance and correspondence, I dealt with keeping tabs on whatever funds we had, which was not much. I oversaw what funds came in from fundraisers, for example, and what funds went out. However, I was not in charge of our bank account and never signed checks for the Beret chapter. I would later do this for our free clinic, but not for the Berets per se. I think David signed the checks. As far as I knew, no Beret funds were used inappropriately, such as to buy guns.

I also handled a lot of the correspondence we received. People wrote in from all over California, beyond wanting information on the Berets. This included guys in the military and even in prison. Some wrote from Vietnam. They were intrigued and excited about the Berets and how they might be a part of us.

I would write back and send them our Ten-Point Program, copies of La Causa, and whatever other information we had. I did the same with the media when they requested it. I rarely did interviews myself. David always spoke to the press.

Part of the public-information work included helping to set up new chapters of the Berets. Chicanos would write in wanting to know how they could do this. I would send them our information. There was no formal process for establishing Beret chapters, but they had to be recognized by the national chapter and to acknowledge our leadership as the national chapter. Occasionally, at least in California, I would visit some of the new chapters that sprang up like wildfire all over the country, including Fresno, Palo Alto, San Francisco, Oakland, Santa Clara, Sacramento, Richmond, Sanger, Redding, Berkeley, Porterville, Stockton, Santa Barbara, Oxnard, San Diego, San Ysidro, National City, Imperial Beach, Seattle, Eugene, Denver, Albuquerque, Santa Fe, Detroit, Saint Paul, San Antonio, Houston, and Kansas City. By the fall of 1969 we had forty-four chapters throughout the country and adopted the slogan, "Occupied Mexico, Love It . . . Or Leave It."[37] We remained the only L.A. chapter; the closest to us was in Whittier. In California I traveled almost every week in my little VW bug to set up new chapters. I drove that VW to the ground. In these new chapters, I met mostly men but some women were also involved.

When I corresponded with other people, I would use our Beret letterhead, which included the Brown Beret and La Causa symbol. I didn't have my own office

FIGURE 9. Gloria Arellanes, circa 1969.
Courtesy of the Arellanes Collection.

or even desk to do this work. I just used whatever space was available. Later, when I directed the free clinic, I used my office there to do some of this Beret work.

After I became a minister, I became concerned about security issues and police infiltration. So even though we had a minister of defense, I initiated, with the approval of the other ministers, the security measure of having photos of all members, which I would keep. I didn't have a camera and neither did the other ministers or members, and so we started going to places that had those photo machines. For a quarter you could get four black-and-white photos of yourself, almost like a police mug shot. This is how I accumulated a lot of these photos of our members, including those of a couple of members who we later learned were cops. We'd wear our Berets since they were only head shots, and sometimes people would make funny faces to the camera.

However, my security project turned bad when some of these photos were stolen. I went to a friend's house and for some reason had some of these photos in my little VW bug. When I got back to the car, I discovered that the photos were gone. Nothing else was taken or done to my car. But clearly someone had broken in. It's possible it was the police, and they knew I had the photos. So much for security! But I still had some of the other pictures.

After I joined the Berets, I actively sought to recruit other women. Of course, the Sánchez sisters, Andrea and Esther, had joined with me, but we also reached out to others. By the time I left the Berets, we had several more women, perhaps around twenty or so. Women represented less than half of the Beret membership in the East L.A. chapter. Out of these, about six women represented what I call my core. They always supported me, and we did many things together. The other women tended not to be as active. Of the core, Andrea was my right hand. The core also included Esther Sánchez, Hilda and Grace Reyes, Yolanda Solís, Lorraine Escalante, and occasionally Arlene Sánchez.

I considered these core women to be wild women who believed in a revolutionary way. They were women warriors, fighters. They were all very strong women and committed. If I said we were going to do something, they would do it. We even went on a hunger strike once for two weeks to protest a case of police abuse in a county jail where some Chicanos were badly mistreated and in protest went on a hunger strike. Besides picketing the jail in support of the male prisoners, we, the female Berets, decided to also go on a hunger strike in solidarity with them. What was interesting was that the male Berets did not join us. I don't know why, but they didn't. So in this case, we took the leadership. Frankly, I didn't really care. We did what we as women felt needed to be done, and we did it. We didn't need the approval of the men, nor did we ask for it.

I think what aided us, at least in the case with the men despite their machismo, was that, in addition to myself, some of the other women were also big physically. I don't have an explanation for this other than we ate too much. Both the Sánchez sisters were big, as was Yolanda. On the other hand, some of the others weren't. Hilda and Grace Reyes were skinny, as was Arlene Sánchez, whom we called "chicken legs."

As I've mentioned, I used my bigness to my advantage. I learned body language. There's a way of talking to someone, where you kind of put your chin out that intimidates the other person. I would do this and put a hand on my hip, stand up at meetings, and look down on the men. It also helped that I wore my hair high, which probably added a good six inches to my five-foot-eight height; the other women did this as well. I absolutely used my physical presence to my advantage and encouraged the other women to do the same. I had learned from my high school days that if I asserted my physical side people didn't mess with me. This was different from my younger days, when I always did the opposite and tried to hide or shrink down so people wouldn't notice me. The fact was that while the Beret men were taller, we had bigger bodies.

While not all the women followed my lead on this, most of my core did. I was a leader and spoke up. They also spoke up, but at times the men shot them down. I encouraged them to stand up. They also tried to shut me down, but I just yelled a little louder and stood up.

One of the most important aspects of my role in the Berets had to do with the deep friendships and solidarity between the women. We supported one another, especially against the machismo of the men. But we also had wonderful times together. I cherish those memories. Andrea Sánchez once said, "There was a strong bond because we all basically liked each other and basically cared about each other and that's what made us strong. And we found out that we had to protect each other and unite with each other because we sure weren't getting any support from anywhere else."[38]

As a minister, I also developed contacts with other movement groups, especially those that had female participants. One such group was the East L.A. Welfare Rights Organization, led by Alicia Escalante, a dynamic leader. I respected her and her work immensely. I loved hearing her talk. We developed a good working and personal relationship. It helped that her daughter, Lorraine, became a Beret. Alicia would often call me to get support.

"Gloria, we're going to be picketing, can you get the Berets together? Come on down!"

The other Beret women and I would go and join whatever picket Alicia had organized on behalf of welfare Latina mothers. Any word Alicia gave, I would always honor. She did the same for me. She was amazing and a real major movement figure. She was a bit older than the rest of us, but that's also why she was respected and people looked up to her.

THE POOR PEOPLE'S CAMPAIGN

Within a short period after I became a minister, several other Berets and I decided to attend the Poor People's Campaign in Washington, DC. This demonstration by poor people focused on the plight of the poor and had been planned by Dr. Martin Luther King Jr. and the Southern Christian Leadership Conference (SCLC) prior to King's assassination in April 1968. After his tragic death, the SCLC pledged to continue the campaign, which would assemble in the nation's capital during the summer months. They reached out to all poor communities, including Chicanos. They contacted the Berets, and so we knew about the plans. While we didn't make a decision to attend as a group, some of us were motivated to attend and express our solidarity with other poor and minority communities.

I personally made that commitment. I knew I couldn't attend the entire summer due to my job, but I was able to get permission to go for two weeks. In fact, my boss and my fellow employees expressed excitement that I was going. This was Martin Luther King's dream. I could relate to that not only because of my role in the Berets but because in my job I worked in part in the black community of South Central L.A. I knew the problems and poverty there.

I told my mother that I was doing this and knew she would, in turn, tell my father, who I knew would not approve. I gathered enough clothes, including my Beret uniform, for two weeks and my sleeping bag and whatever money I thought I might need, although everything else was paid for, probably by the SCLC. This included transportation, housing, and food. I wanted to go because I thought this would be a valuable learning experience.

On May 15 we left L.A. for the cross-country trip.[39] The SCLC arranged for several Greyhound buses. Everyone going assembled at Will Roger's Memorial Park in Watts. My seven guy Berets and I left on one of them. Some other Berets would join us later. I was the only female Beret and the only minister on this trip. The other women couldn't go for a variety of family and work reasons. In our bus we were the only Chicanos; everyone else was black. For whatever reason, perhaps because we showed up late, the other Berets and I found ourselves sitting in the back of the bus. Most of the other people were older than us, including senior citizens. However, some were couples with young children, although not many kids went in our bus. But they were all super nice and grateful that we were joining them. We had a wonderful time with them. Only our bus left L.A. that night.

As we left California and entered other states, we were joined by other buses going to the campaign. It was like a caravan. Some of the buses contained other Chicanos, along with blacks and whites. The buses didn't go nonstop. In the evenings we stopped, and supporters put us up for the night and fed us. I particularly remember one evening in El Paso that turned out to be rather frightening due to police harassment. We were lodged that night in a convention center, and groups like the local MEChA students provided us with food. We were to sleep in the bleachers with our bedrolls. However, before we went to sleep, the police showed up and said that a bomb threat had been called in. The cops came in and checked the entire hall, but found nothing. In the meantime, they made us all stand together in the middle of the arena. I think that this was deliberate harassment, which might have even included the bomb threat. The MEChA students came to our rescue and offered to take us to their individual homes or apartments, although the rest of the group, composed mostly of blacks, were allowed to stay at the convention center. We decided, however, to go with the Chicano students. As we exited the convention center, we encountered a contingent of Texas Rangers. Everything you can think of a stereotyped Ranger—I saw. These were obese guys in uniform, drinking beer and laughing at us. They were taunting us. One of the students warned us, "Don't look at them."

I didn't need to be warned. I was raised with that warning: "Don't eyeball a cop," because that gives them a reason to stop you. All this was scary, not knowing what the Rangers might do to us.

But we left without any problems and spent the night with the students, although the Beret men crossed over to Ciudad Juárez and partied. I didn't have any interest in going with them. I guess the guys wanted to go have some fun. The next day, off we went into New Mexico. When we got to Albuquerque, we received a very warm reception, with Chicanos and Native Americans there too. We had a rally, and I was very impressed by an elderly Native American who spoke and who might have been a hundred years old! He spoke loud and clear in support of our efforts. He spoke in a Native American language, and one of his sons translated for him.

We spent the night there, and I was housed in the home of Reies López Tijerina, the by now legendary leader of the land-grant movement in New Mexico and one of the heroes of the Chicano movement. Tijerina wasn't at home, but his wife and children received me with much warmth. His home was almost like a bunker to protect him and his family from any kind of attack. Tijerina would join us later in Washington, where I, unfortunately, got a less than flattering impression of him.

From Albuquerque we headed to Denver and linked up with Corky Gonzales and the Crusade for Justice people. Corky, like Tijerina, was also becoming a major leader of the movement. He insisted that those of us from L.A. join the Crusade bus, which we did. We were now with a busload of Chicanos. There was only one poor, little, white guy on the bus, but he was really sweet and nice. We joked about his being the only white in a Chicano bus, but we accepted him.

Leaving Denver, we went into states like Kansas and Missouri. Our bus was part of a much larger caravan of buses, which included not only Chicanos but blacks and whites. We were going to go through Illinois, but some local police in that state wouldn't let us through, and so we diverted through Missouri. By contrast, we received wonderful hospitality everywhere we stopped for the night. Somewhere in Kansas, I stayed with a beautiful African American family. In other places, we were housed in community centers with cots. We passed through Saint Louis and then into Kentucky, where we met Rev. Ralph Abernathy, who had been Dr. King's right-hand man and who now led the SCLC and the campaign.[40] That evening we went to a church in Louisville, where King had preached. We had the privilege of listening to an inspiring choir with lively spirituals. The next day we drove through a black housing project. We had a big sign on the side of the bus that said "Chicano Power." People would stare at it, and we could see that they were trying to pronounce "Chicano." They had no idea what it meant or who a Chicano was.

Finally, after about almost a week in the bus, we arrived in Washington, DC. We weren't really that tired because we were so young and full of energy and excited to get to the Poor People's Campaign. When you're young, you can go three days without sleep. Upon our arrival, we did not go to Resurrection City on the National Mall, where thousands of mainly blacks had camped out in tents for the campaign. Instead, arrangements had been made for the Chicano contingents to stay at this private progressive school called the Hawthorne School. The school was conveniently located, and we could walk to most of the Washington sites, even the monuments.

We were housed in the basement because classes were still in session. But in the evenings we could roam around the school, including the cafeteria, where our meals were prepared for us by volunteers. I don't know who made the decision for us to stay there—perhaps Corky and the Crusade people. We had bunk beds and were divided by gender in different rooms. Women with women and men with men, even for married couples. We were all Chicanos from all over the Southwest and other places as well. We could use the gym showers and bathrooms, also separated by gender. Our meals were pretty basic. A lot of canned food had been donated, and I remember eating all these powdered eggs. One taste of these, and I said, "okay, I'm going on a diet now." But we all ate together. We were also allowed to use the school's laundry facilities so we could wash our clothes. While during the day we'd be out and about going to different protests, in the evening we returned for our meals and talked about our experiences and sang our songs like "De Colores," one of the farmworkers' songs that I learned there.

Although during the days I spent at the Hawthorne School everyone was supportive and cooperative in our living arrangements, there was one ugly incident that I personally got involved in. A young woman staying with us came up to me and told me that she was being sexually harassed. I don't think she used that term, but I got the point. Why she sought me out, I can't say. She may have heard that I was a member of the Brown Berets, and so she saw me perhaps as an authority figure or leader. So I asked her, "Who is he? Where is he from?"

He was from New Mexico and an older man. In fact, his wife was with him. After the young woman pointed him out to me, I confronted the guy. He denied it up and down. But I believed the woman. Other people gathered around us, as I continued to confront him and even threaten him.

"If I find out that you've touched this girl or you keep harassing her, you'll have to answer to me!"

I was yelling at him, and as I did so, other men got involved and, unfortunately, took his side. They defended him by saying that it was a matter of he said, she said. This pissed me off and so in front of these other guys, I repeated, "Maybe you got away with it now, but I'm telling you, you touch this girl or you harass her anymore, you personally will have to deal with me, and it's not going to be pleasant."

I made enough noise that his wife heard, and so I think he got it from her as well. He didn't bother the young woman anymore.

Each day the decision was made, probably by Corky and the SCLC and some of the other leaders like Father Groppi from Milwaukee, that we as Chicanos would go to a particular federal office to protest the conditions of Chicanos, such as poverty and the lack of educational opportunities. The most memorable protest occurred in front of the Supreme Court building. Mostly Chicanos protested, although we were joined by some whites. I also saw a Native American chief with his full headdress there. This was very impressive. In fact, we were protesting a recent Court decision that denied Native Americans in Washington State the right to fish in their ancestral waters.

The other Berets and I wore our uniforms and stayed together as a contingent. There must have been several hundred people protesting. We rallied at the steps of the Court, and various speakers, including Corky, addressed us. Tijerina came to the campaign, but he didn't speak at this rally. Everything was peaceful, although I heard later that some windows at the court building were broken. But I don't know who did it, and I didn't see the broken windows since they were apparently on the side of the building. We never entered the court building; we tried to but were refused entry. However, at the end, when we started to march back to the school, problems began. On our way, the local police confronted us. I have no idea why they did so. We didn't break any law; however, they justified it by saying that we didn't obey the traffic lights and that we walked through a red light! We had monitors in the streets, and they would say, "cross the street" or "stop." But we were told to keep going, even though at one of the intersections a red light had come on.

"No, you don't go," the cops announced.

That's when they attacked us. *El Gallo,* the newspaper of the Crusade for Justice, later recorded the police assault: "As the marchers left the Court to return to Hawthore [sic] School and Resurrection City the police marched along on the opposite curb. Finally, at the corner of 1st and Independence the police got what they'd long wanted—a chance to crack heads .... The police drove two motorcycles through the security line and into the mass of men, women, and children in an attempt to break up the march."[41]

They drew their billy clubs and started swinging away. I was walking with two other women from the Black Berets, and one of them had a young girl with her, about six years old. A cop came up to us, and instead of aiming his club against one of us adults, he raised it toward the little girl to hit her. I was next to her, and when I saw with horror what the cop was about to do, I freaked out and started yelling at the top of my lungs. My reaction immediately brought in some of our monitors, who quickly surrounded us and prevented the pig from bringing down his club. He might have seriously injured or even killed the little girl. I couldn't believe it. I then turned to the cop and screamed, "you would hit a child?"

I then turned to the other cops, who by now had pulled back into a line. I'll never forget the look on these huge cops because I was in their faces screaming at them. Some actually looked embarrassed and averted eye contact with me. Others looked at me with hate in their eyes. I could almost hear them say, "Oh, I'd like to tear your head off with my club." I just ignored these looks.

But the violence wasn't over. Some other cops jumped on Tijerina's son, Danny, who was about eighteen, and beat the hell out of him. I had never before seen someone physically beaten up, or at least not like this. They then handcuffed him and threw him into a paddy wagon. They later released him, and we had him treated for his injuries.[42]

After the violence stopped, the police still harassed us as we walked back to the school. They cruised by in their cars and took pictures of us. On a corner, they poked fun at us and tried to provoke us. This pissed me off and I was ready to explode again, but someone walking with me put their arm around my shoulder and said, "Okay, Gloria, come on, let it go, let it go."

I calmed down a bit, but my stomach was still turning at what I had just witnessed. For a cop, or anyone, to want to hit a child to deliberately hurt her? Who would do such a thing? And to beat up Danny the way they did for doing nothing? I felt like I had been socked in the stomach, and it took the air out of me. Somehow we made it back to the school.

The following day we all assembled in the cafeteria to discuss the police riot and what had happened. A few others in addition to Danny had been arrested, and we talked about this. I personally on my own talked to Corky about what had happened, and, of course, he sympathized with me and was just as upset and angry as the rest of us. After this I remember him calling me "our littlest Brown Beret," but in a joking and supportive manner.

While Corky was very much visible and supportive of all the Chicanos who came to Washington, Tijerina, by contrast, remained aloof and simply not around very much. But it wasn't just that he was distant; he seemed to see himself as some kind of VIP who desired to be treated as such. I witnessed this on the only occasion that I saw him, one evening when he came to have dinner at the school. Dinner was a time to relax and talk and laugh. We felt comfortable with one another. Our meals were not great, but they were okay, and what was important was the comradery. However, one evening after we had finished our meal, some of us decided to return to the cafeteria to talk and share experiences. That's when we saw Tijerina and his entourage enter the cafeteria and get served a meal unlike anything we had eaten. He was eating steak while we had powdered eggs and things like that. This elitist treatment of Tijerina, and perhaps it was that he demanded a better meal for himself and his bodyguards, only soured me on him. In my opinion, when you're a leader, you have to be humble and set an example for the people you lead. You don't wear an Armani suit when everyone else is wearing Goodwill clothes. You live as your people live. That's what I believe. You have to lose your ego.

Unfortunately, I've seen a lot of leadership do the opposite and just think that they're above everyone else and deserve better. Eventually, however, this ego betrays them and they fall. This was why seeing Tijerina assume this superior attitude and behavior was shocking to me. I expected more from a man who, given his exploits in the land-grant movement in New Mexico, was already a Chicano legend in 1968. But what was also disgusting is that no one confronted Tijerina that evening. Not only did he and his men sit alone, but they made no effort to meet the rest of us. He didn't go out of his way to say to us, "how's it going?"

That's why, by contrast, Corky exhibited such stronger leadership, which we could respect. He ate the same food with us and was always chatting with the people and thanking us for being there. He shook hands and hugged us as if he knew us personally. I was so much more admiring of Corky than I was of Tijerina.

I also admired the demands that Corky and the Crusade for Justice issued to the Johnson administration when we were in Washington, such as reforms on housing, economic opportunities, job development, law enforcement, and farm labor. They gave this statement on the redistribution of wealth: "That all citizens of the country share in the wealth of this nation by institution of economic reforms that would provide for all people, and that welfare in the form of subsidies in taxes and payoffs to corporate owners be reverted to the people who in reality are the foundation of the economy and the tax base for this society."[43]

Part of my experience at the Poor People's Campaign that I particularly enjoyed was networking with other Chicanos from different places. We all networked. At meals we sat with different people and exchanged information on where we were from and what kind of movement activities we were doing. Everyone, for example, wanted to know what was happening in L.A. They all looked up to the movement there in the wake of the blowouts earlier that spring.

Other Chicanos also went out of their way to meet us as Brown Berets, especially when we wore our uniforms. We felt like celebrities. Many women wanted to meet me, as the only Chicana Beret there. Everyone had heard about the Berets, and they wanted information on us. They wanted to know about our purposes and how we were trying to organize and what our goals were. We had brought with us copies of La Causa and of our manual with the Ten-Point Program, and we distributed these. People just grabbed them up. In this way, we set up a lot of contacts for possible new chapters. I carried my pencil and paper to get names and addresses to stay in touch and also to send them the additional information they requested. After the campaign, for example, people we had met there started up chapters in Albuquerque and, of all places, Milwaukee. To me the campaign was a big resource to meet people from all these different states and to see the interest they had in the Berets and in the movement in L.A., which was like the heartbeat of the movement.

There was also interest in the Black Berets, who were in Washington. They were from San Jose and were very similar to us, except that they wore a black beret. They expressed solidarity with us; we were not rivals. Sal Candelaria, the leader of the Black Berets, was there, and, of course, it was his young daughter who that cop almost hurt at the Supreme Court. I liked Sal. After I met Sal, I got to know him but lost track of him after both Beret groups began to disintegrate by the mid-1970s. However, years later I ran into him at a Native American ceremony. We had both rediscovered our Native American roots. He had become a bear dancer and had changed his name to Chemo. Unfortunately, the last time I saw him his knees were going, and so he couldn't dance anymore. I recently learned that he died in 2012 in Arizona.

While Sal attended as head of the Black Berets (I'm not sure if he was referred to as the prime minister), our leader, David Sánchez, never showed up. To this day, I have no idea why he didn't come. On the other hand, Carlos Montes and Ralph

Ramírez, two of our ministers, did make the trip, but arrived after I had already left. Alicia Escalante of the East L.A. Welfare Rights group also participated and brought along her seven-year-old son. But no David.

I visited a couple of museums, including a medical one. However, I never got to go to the White House or the Congress. We had the impression we weren't welcomed on the Hill. I walked around other parts of the city, but I never did get to Resurrection City. It was just never on our itinerary, although we should have paid a visit since there were thousands of people there.

While some think of the Poor People's Campaign as a failure because it didn't influence any new antipoverty policy or because of various disputes and tensions between the leaders, other Chicanos and I saw it as a major success, as I'm sure was the case with the thousands of others who participated, both blacks and whites, in the campaign. We saw it as a success because we got to express our views in the nation's capital, because we expressed our solidarity with blacks and other poor people, and because we got to network among ourselves as Chicanos, which would later be important in the Chicano movement. It was a success because we brought the Chicano movement to Washington and made it a national movement.[44]

All I know is that I saw what the campaign was all about and what I was exposed to and learned from it. I learned so much about different people that it expanded my perspective. This was not just the Chicano movement; it was all kinds of people coming together to try to change conditions. It was the black movement; it was the poor people of Appalachia's movement. Then it was the Chicano movement in Denver, in New Mexico, in the Midwest, and in many other places. So I came back with these kinds of experiences. It just influenced me not to be put in an L.A. hole. I was able to see something larger, a bigger picture. Just because you're from L.A. doesn't mean that everything is happening there. I learned that other Chicanos were doing things in other parts of the country and that some had unique circumstances in their communities. All of this didn't make me less of a Chicano nationalist, but it did give me an appreciation of this country's diversity.

After two exciting weeks in Washington, returning to L.A. was anticlimactic. Some other Chicanos and I boarded another Greyhound bus, and it was like an express bus because I don't think we stopped anywhere to sleep. Before we left, Corky came on the bus and very generously gave each of us five dollars to help us out.[45] The bus just went straight through with only some stops for meals. Unlike the trip to the campaign, there were no rallies or people meeting us along the way. We mostly just slept the long trip home, which took about a couple of days. Since we left earlier than most other Chicanos, the bus was not completely full. I'm not sure who arranged for it, probably the campaign organizers. I think most of us were from L.A. or at least from the Southwest because the bus didn't stop very much to leave people off. All I know is that I was pretty tired after two weeks of activity, although at the same time excited about what I had done. I just couldn't

FIGURE 10. Gloria Arellanes *(left, second row)*, memorial march for Senator Robert Kennedy, June 1968. Courtesy of George Rodríguez.

wait to share this with others back home. In fact, after I got back to L.A., I talked about my trip with anyone who would listen, both in and out of the Berets. Many expressed interest in what I did in the campaign and my feelings about it that, of course, were very positive. I've never regretted going, and it remains one of my fondest memories of my experiences as a Brown Beret and as a movement activist.

Shortly after I returned from Washington, Senator Robert Kennedy was assassinated after he won the California Democratic Party primary. While we were suspicious of most politicians, especially Anglo ones, we admired Kennedy, especially because of his support for César Chávez and the farmworkers and for the students involved in the blowouts. I think we also admired the Kennedy family and their relations with Chicanos. So we in the Berets participated in a memorial march for him in East L.A. along with several other groups. We marched in our uniforms. We felt it was the right thing to do. I had voted for Kennedy in the primary.

LA CAUSA

There is no question but that one of my major roles within the Berets was as the managing editor of *La Causa*, the Beret newspaper. The paper may have started before I joined the group, but it really took off after I became a Beret.[46] We published the paper once a month on average and aimed to allow people to read about what the Berets were doing and how we were spreading nationally, in addition to our position on issues and the philosophies we held. Our intended audience was anyone who had an interest in us and in the Chicano movement. Ironically, I'm sure a lot of law-enforcement agencies, including the FBI, had an interest. The paper stated, "News for the purpose of illustrating the many injustices against the Chicano by the Anglo Establishment."[47]

La Causa was a tool of communication. Of course, there were many other movement newspapers, not only in L.A. but throughout the Southwest and beyond. We didn't have a problem with these other publications. *La Raza* in L.A., which first began as a newspaper and then evolved into a monthly magazine under Raul Ruiz, was the most professional of all these papers. It was printed on glossy paper and well written and edited. Others were just mimeographed kinds of newsletters and about as grassroots as you could get. I think *La Causa* was somewhere in between. Financially, we were limited in our coverage as compared to *La Raza*; however, we still managed to cover a number of stories, especially about police abuse. We never felt a competition with *La Raza*.

There is also no question that the Beret women dominated the publication of our newspaper. Besides myself, many of the other women contributed to the paper. The women just decided, "let's do this," and took over the paper. This included my core female comrades—Andrea, Esther, Hilda, and Grace—but other women also contributed. We worked as a team.

Although David was listed as the editor in the beginning, I, for all practical purposes, served as the editor. I did almost everything in the publication process. I pretty much decided what stories we would focus on, as well as writing some of them. Some carried my byline and others didn't. Some of the other women, such as Andrea Sánchez and Lorraine Escalante, also contributed stories. These were radical stories and, as I look back, I'm struck at how radical they were. I particularly remember one that I wrote about Fernando Sumaya, the undercover cop who infiltrated us. After we discovered who he really was, I published a scathing piece on him. I wrote, in part, "White man's society may judge and award him as a hero, but members of this organization who had him around for several months know the syphilis infested mind of this perro [dog], who WOULD SELL HIS MOTHER FOR ANY PRICE, IF THE OPPORTUNITY PROVIDES!"[48]

As far as I was concerned, Sumaya was a real betrayer. At the same time, I felt a bit bad about denouncing him because he was actually quite likable. But that was part of the betrayal—that he gave us his "friendship" and then turned around and used us. I actually enjoyed being around him because he was so funny. But in my story, I also criticized his womanizing. He was very flirty. He always used funny but sexual innuendoes.

Still another article that I remember was a film review of the movie *Che,* about Che Guevara, which came out in 1969. I had seen the movie and decided to do a review of it. Che was such an icon to us, and I thought I should do it. Here in part is what I wrote:

> For those of us who saw the movie "Che" and let the capitalists take our money, I am sure that we will all agree that the movie was a very poor portrayal of El Revolucionario Che, the greatest revolutionary of our times.
>
> The movie Che, with Omar Shariff to take the role, made Che look like a sadistic, blood thirsty mongrel with his most contend [sic] initiative being only to kill and make revolution. The movie reeked with "American propaganda," implying that . . . Che's revolutionary ideas, philosophies and beliefs, which were not truly put forth on the big screen, were to blame for the american [sic] student unrests[,] ghetto riots, etc. The movie made sure that the CIA had absolutely nothing to do with the inhumans [sic] assassination of Che Guevara. . . .
>
> However, in parts of the movie, I felt that some of the Real Che was brought out, such as his love for people, especially oppressed people, and his hate for yankee imperialism.[49]

Occasionally, some of the men objected to my articles or those written by some of the other women. But I didn't care about their objections, especially since they chose not to work on the paper while the women did all the work. One time, one of the men came to see me about an article. For some reason, he felt we shouldn't be printing something. I can't remember what the piece was about. I just started yelling, "If I want to put the F-word on a full page, I'll do that if I feel like it."

And that was the end of that argument.

When anyone tried to censor me about *La Causa,* I just responded, "Oh, no, no, no. You don't come in here and tell me what to do."

As far as I was concerned, if you didn't work on the paper, then you had no reason to criticize it. I didn't value such critiques, and I had no respect for them.

The other women and I typed the articles before publication. I edited them, but I don't think I did a very good job. I'm embarrassed now when I look at the paper and see typos and misspellings. We weren't professionals, but we did the best we could.

While women did most of the work on the paper, this didn't mean that men didn't contribute to it by writing some articles. This even included my younger brother, Bill, who actually wrote a poem that we published. Obviously influenced by the concept of Aztlán, Bill wrote, in part, these lines:

A New Land Has Been Found
The Land of *Aztlán*

. . . .

I, A Chicano, Will Now Fight For
My Freedom, My Land In Aztlán.[50]

I also did most of the calligraphy for the paper. I had a talent for this. I used borders that had Aztec patterns for the pages. I did a few illustrations as well, but Andrea did most of them. She was a very good sketcher. One of her best was a large image of a female Beret dressed as La Adelita, the female revolutionary figure of the Mexican Revolution of 1910. In Andrea's sketch, the image wears a *bandolero* (cartridge belt), with bullets draped around her body. It was a great image and emphasized the revolutionary commitment of the female Berets, as well as their connection to their revolutionary female ancestors such Las Adelitas. Andrea really had talent. Others also contributed illustrations, such as Ramses Noriega, who I would get to know later in the Chicano antiwar movement. Ramses was not a Beret, but he was an accomplished artist and activist. We occasionally used photos, but not many. None of us, including myself, were photographers, and none of us even owned a camera. I took whatever photos people gave me.

Once we had the articles and illustrations or photos, we then did the whole layout before getting it published by a barrio printer. I still don't know how we published the paper, since we had little equipment, which was not very good at that. We had these old clunky manual typewriters since we didn't have electronic ones. Of course, computers and laptops were light-years away! We did everything in our office and then at our free clinic, when we started that service. We used the clinic's reception room after hours during the week and especially on weekends to put out *La Causa*.

Although David Sánchez was listed as the editor in the first issues of the paper, he really didn't edit it. I would touch base with him and ask him if he wanted anything in particular written up or if he was going to contribute an article. He would give me feedback and usually wrote a piece. Where David did play a more decisive role was that he had to approve the content of the paper. I would discuss the articles with him, and he usually approved of them. I don't recall him turning down any stories. We actually worked well together on the paper, even though the women and I did all the actual work.

Because women dominated the paper, we included a column, "Palabras para la Chicana" (Words for the Chicanas). It was a specific column for Chicanas about Chicana issues. We also used the column to recruit additional women to the Berets. In one column, I wrote the following:

> The Movement we are involved with is a serious matter. Women and men alike must drop and forget all their pettiness (there is no time for that) and put forth their strenghts *[sic]*, talents and efforts. Men must understand that because a woman wants to become involved, that he must not discredit her in the beginning for being a woman. When it comes right down to it, the women are the most important factor of the Movement, because it is the woman that gives birth to new life and gives knowledge to that new life, and not the knowledge of the dominated white schools, but that of La Vida Nueva [the New Life].[51]

Although this column had what I would consider a feminist perspective, there was also one very controversial article that appeared in 1969 that in retrospect went against this view. I don't recall that I had anything to do with it, and it may have been inserted when I was traveling and wasn't able to edit this edition. It's also possible that when this issue came out I was so involved in running the free clinic that I didn't edit it. This was an article on birth control. The title was "Genocide in the Chicano Family," and authorship was attributed to "By Concerned Chicanas." This is, in part, what it said: "Advice being denounced are all types of contraceptives which have been in experimental stages approximately 10 years. We demand that they start treating and respecting our people as human beings and not as 'guinea pigs' to participate in murderous experiments. For all types of birth control contraceptives, regardless of length used, threaten the life of this Chicana and all her unborn Chicanitos. Contraceptive[s] such as the pill, the diaphragm, the coil, and foam are all murder weapons invented for genocidal purposes."[52]

I can understand some of the concerns about birth control and especially about sterilization, but there is an irony and contradiction in this article. First of all, I'm not sure it was written by Chicanas, even though it references Chicana Berets. In fact, it might have been written by David and some of the men who wanted to make it seem like the Beret women supported these contentions. But the real disconnect is that in our free clinic we provided birth control, such as the pill, the IUD, and other forms, along with information on contraception. We also advised on abortions and connected patients with particular doctors for these matters. No one in the Berets, including David and the other ministers, to my knowledge, ever objected to these services.

We were amazed when we learned that *La Causa* was being read by others outside of Los Angeles, even by some in the military. We received one letter from a private, Larry Gonzales, stationed at Fort Polk, Louisiana: "I read La Causa and I fine [sic] it very interesting in what y'll say. The reason I'm writing is because I want to no [sic] more about the Berets and none can tell me about this better than y'll. Can The Berets send me more copies of La Causa. I'm in the Army now and I like [sic] to join The Berets."[53]

I'm very proud of the work I did on *La Causa* and of the other women who helped me with it. Without the female Berets, the paper would not have been published. But this work was typical of the contributions of the women. Unfortunately, it also spoke to the gender inequalities in the Berets. David and the men took the credit for publishing the paper as well as other activities, while we the women did a lot, if not most, of the work.

DENVER YOUTH CONFERENCE

Sometime, probably around February 1969, we heard about the first National Chicano Youth Liberation Conference to be held in Denver and hosted by Corky

Gonzales and the Crusade for Justice. The conference was scheduled for late March. The word spread like wildfire. The Crusade sent out a lot of publicity, telling everyone, "You must come!" Soon everyone in the movement in L.A. was saying they were going. It sounded like the place to be. We in the Berets—or at least some of us—thought that, like the Poor People's Campaign, this would be a good opportunity to make contacts.

On our own, Andrea, a few of our other female Berets, and I decided to go. We didn't clear this with David or any other Berets. We just decided on our own. In fact, I don't recall David or any of the other ministers attending. Some of the male Berets also went on their own.

I didn't want to drive all the way to Denver in my little VW bug; it was too far. We went on a regular bus, probably a Greyhound. We left a bit late for the conference and arrived the evening after the first full day. We went to one of the colleges in Denver where the Crusade had made arrangements for housing those attending the conference. I think this was during spring break, and so the students weren't around. But I also remember how cold and snowy it was upon our arrival. My friends and I weren't used to such cold or snow. We froze. All we had were our Beret blazers, which in no way protected us. I, for one, also had on a dress, which only made me feel even colder.

The next morning we went to the Crusade headquarters, where the conference was held. I couldn't believe how impressive the Crusade building was. It made our little office space in East L.A. seem like nothing. By comparison, it was a huge two- or three-story building with lots of offices and meeting rooms. At the same time, Crusade members warned us to stay away from the windows because recently someone, possibly the cops, had shot at the building. The Crusade was always under police surveillance. Still, we were welcomed with open arms. Corky and his people provided us and all in attendance with almost everything we needed, including lodging and meals. We paid for very little.

Corky, of course, was everywhere at the conference. There was no question that he was in charge. He remembered me from Washington and was happy to see me and my Beret companions. He thanked us for coming. I appreciated Corky's charisma and leadership even more by being there. We also learned a lot about the Crusade and all the educational and community work it was doing. It was impressive.

There were a number of workshops and panels, but I didn't actually attend that many. I don't even remember those that I did attend. Of course, the most controversial one became the women's workshop on La Chicana in the movement. This is one of the ones that I didn't attend because it took place on the day we missed. I say that it became controversial because I don't think it was controversial at the time. However, over the years, when people learn that I attended the first youth liberation conference, they want to know one main thing: "Did you attend the session where women voted not to be liberated?" What I understand happened at the workshop was that the Chicanas there discussed their relationship to the white women's feminist movement. As part of this discussion, they agreed that for several reasons they did not feel that that they wanted to be connected to that movement. In this sense, they did not want to be "liberated." I agreed with this. I had very strong feelings about the white women's liberation movement because they were burning their bras, and we were not going to do something like that. They also were separating themselves more and more from men, which I didn't agree with. By contrast, we Chicanas wanted to stay within the movement despite problems with the men. We wanted to keep unity within our community, although we felt frustrated due to the sexism. In a way, we were locked, but at the same time we didn't want to be like the white feminists and go our separate way.

As women we wanted to be recognized as women who had something to say. We didn't necessarily recognize ourselves as feminists, but in fact we were becoming a feminist movement; we just didn't know it. I can look back now and say, "okay, yeah." Because people always ask me, are you a feminist? Back then, I would say, "oh, no." You ask me that now, and I say, "yes." Yes, because I understand it now. I didn't then when I associated the term "feminist" with white women. I didn't want to be tagged a feminist because of this connection or what I thought was a connection. But even then as we were becoming feminists, this didn't mean that we were the same as white feminists. We came from our barrios, we identified with our families, and we struggled out of low-income conditions. This was very different from middle-class white women. I also likened the white feminist movement with the hippies, who seemed to be walking away from their earlier lives. They were like dropouts; we couldn't do this or afford to do this.[54]

The conference, of course, is best known for the drafting of El Plan de Aztlán, which became one of the major documents of the movement and of the concept of chicanismo. I witnessed the fact that only a small number of men wrote up El Plan. On one of the days of the conference, the other female Berets and I found ourselves sitting on the floor outside one of the meeting rooms. I don't know why we were doing this; perhaps we were waiting to attend a session, and there probably were no chairs to sit in. In any event, we started talking and laughing and carrying on quite loudly, and I guess disturbing the men who were in the room. One of them came out and told us to "shut up." "Oops," we responded. We asked if we could come in but were told that we couldn't. I think they didn't want women there. I don't know if he told us that they were busy writing El Plan or we found out later that they were doing this, but it did register to me that this was a men's-only meeting and a small one at that. They later presented El Plan to the concluding session of the conference for adoption, and it was embraced unanimously.

Somehow I also found out that Alurista, the poet, was at that meeting. He wrote the preamble to El Plan, called "El Plan Espiritual de Aztlán." Apparently, he

introduced the term and concept of Aztlán to the conference and to the movement. I got to like Alurista. He was a very small man, very sweet, and funny. But at
the same time he was very fiery and committed. I remember him reading his preamble at the closing meeting. It was very inspiring. The delegates went crazy for it.
This was the first time I had heard about Aztlán. For me, and the other Chicanos
there, Aztlán meant a homeland that we could claim. The idea of an ancestral
homeland, I believe, had the biggest impact at the conference, rather than the
theme of indigeneity. The conference was more oriented to Chicano identity and
culture rather than a strong indigenous leaning, although transferring Aztlán to a
claim of indigenous heritage would come soon afterward. But at the conference
the symbols were not yet apparent. There were no Aztec dancers or Aztec symbols.
Instead, there were more images of Che Guevara than anything else. Corky did
introduce *las tres caras de Aztlán,* or the three faces of Aztlán, as well, but this
stressed more the mestizo or mixed history of Chicanos and not just the indigenous. The conference presented cultural activities, but they were more Mexican
than indigenous. What was also interesting is that while Chicanos were rediscovering their Mexican backgrounds, all the sessions I attended were conducted in
English. I couldn't speak Spanish, and I suspect that many of the others in attendance couldn't either.

As in Washington, we met many new people, and they gravitated toward us
because of our Beret uniforms. We made a lot of contacts, many of whom wanted
to establish Beret chapters back in their places, and many did. I didn't see any
Black Berets in Denver, and so we were the only Beret show in town.

I also came away from the conference even more inspired by the Chicano
movement and proud that I was a part of it, even though we were told to shut up
outside of that meeting. Despite this, I think the conference was historic and very
positive. I also returned with a very favorable view of the Crusade and of Corky
and his group.

In fact, I was inspired enough that I went to the next Denver conference in
March 1970.[55] I don't remember as much about this one, but what I'll never forget
is the time spent driving all the way to Denver. The reason I drove had to do with
taking some high school students to the conference. One year after the blowouts,
students again walked out of Roosevelt High in further protests about the lack of
school reforms.[56] I attended some of the meetings about these problems at the
Euclid Community Center, where the adults highly praised the kids. However,
when it came time for the second Denver conference, no one suggested that some
of the high school students should be sponsored to attend it. I thought they should.
So I rented a truck. I didn't know how I did this, because I didn't have a credit card.
I must have just paid with cash. I do remember telling the car-rental agency that I
was only driving up to the mountains. I didn't mention Denver. I guess I was afraid
that if I stated my real intentions, they wouldn't rent to me for going out of state or

they would charge me more. They later got really pissed when I returned the truck and somehow they learned I had taken it to Denver. They wanted to charge me extra, but I refused to pay the additional costs.

I arranged for about four or five high school students to go with me, plus one of the Berets to help me drive. The kids were all young men. I tried to get some of the female students to go, but their parents wouldn't let them.

In selecting the truck, I made the mistake of renting a pickup with no cover on the back. I had forgotten how cold and snowy it would still be in Denver, plus crossing the Rockies in late March. The kids practically froze.

The students really appreciated the conference, and they learned a great deal. They also had a chance to meet other high school students there and exchange information. I pretty much left them on their own. I didn't feel I had to chaperone them, plus I was exhausted from the long drive, which is why I probably didn't attend many sessions. The conference for me might have also been anticlimactic in comparison to the first one. However, I'm glad I went, and in particular I was pleased to have taken these brave kids who had engaged in the Roosevelt walkouts. They deserved to be rewarded.

EL BARRIO FREE CLINIC

Without question, the most significant contribution of the East L.A. Brown Berets was the establishment of what we called El Barrio Free Clinic. This was our major service to the community during the history of the Berets as part of the Chicano movement. All the rhetoric, theatrics, marches, and so on pale in comparison. The clinic was a direct intervention into the community, with real and practical results. It was certainly my most memorable experience as a Beret. I was privileged and honored to have become the director of the clinic and especially to work with most of the other female Berets, who represented the backbone of the clinic. If I left any legacy as a Beret, it was my role in the clinic.

I have to credit David Sánchez with the idea of the Berets sponsoring a free clinic. It's possible that he was influenced by the successful free clinic of the Black Panther Party in Oakland, but I don't really know. I never heard David connect our clinic with that of the Panthers. He first discussed organizing a clinic in October 1968 with some very liberal and New Left–type medical professionals who were involved in the Fairfax Free Clinic in West L.A., one of the few such clinics in the city. These professionals organized into several groups: L.A. Physicians for Social Responsibility, L.A. Psychologists for Social Action, and the Medical Committee for Human Rights. Rona Fields introduced David to these people. Most of these, like Rona, were also Jewish Americans with politically active backgrounds. They counseled David on what it meant to organize a free clinic. David's main motivation, of course, was to provide a needed service to East L.A., since few medical facilities existed there and many untreated health issues affected the barrio. More-over, few of these facilities had Spanish-speaking personnel. Like the Fairfax clinic, ours would be a nonprofit.

I was not privy to David's discussions about a clinic, but I had heard that he was meeting with these groups. However, one day he came to me and just said, "Gloria, I want you to go to some meetings about establishing a free clinic."

"Okay," I replied, "but I'm not really interested."

The reason I said this was because I knew that the people that David was meet-ing with were all white and I thought I would be uncomfortable with them, besides the fact that they were professionals and older than me. I didn't want to engage with them, but David felt otherwise.

"Well," he said, "you need to be interested because you're going to run the clinic."

"I don't think I want to run it. I don't think I could work with these people."

"No, you're going to run it."

So, I did. At first I was slow to get into it, but once I did, I became very dedicated to it. It became my baby.

I also learned and appreciated that the white medical professionals were very committed and dedicated, and I worked well with them. This proved to be very important to me since I didn't know anything about running a free clinic. What helped in this relationship, and here I credit David again, was that he made it very clear to these outside groups that the clinic was to be a Brown Beret operation and that while we appreciated and desired their advice and support, the Berets would call the shots and not them. As I became the director, this gave me a certain auton-omy from this advisory group, even after some became part of our board of direc-tors. There was no tension over this relationship, at least not at first.

As we moved to open the clinic, we were guided by our goal of serving the com-munity. This was a central part of our identity as Berets. It was part of community empowerment and provided us with a positive self-image. It became a feather in our cap and softened our image as gun-toting militants. People found out that we weren't monsters. They realized that we wanted to help them.

The first step was to find a location for the clinic. We found an adequate place with enough room on Whittier Boulevard, which was perfect because this was the central avenue through East L.A. The rent was a bit high—about $200 a month—but with the grants that we got for the clinic, we were able to manage this. The storefront was sandwiched in between two bars that, to say the least, made for interesting neighbors. We even cared for some of our patients after brawls in the cantinas. The address of our clinic was 5016 Whittier Boulevard. We officially opened on May 30, 1969, as El Barrio Free Clinic.

Once we obtained space for the clinic, we started to organize it. It was a small space, so we had to be creative in setting up our operations. In a back room, we set up an examining room, as well as a restroom. We designated a side room as our lab. In the front, we had a reception and waiting room. In still another room we put in a hospital bed.

Once we had a sense of how we could use our space, we made arrangements through the professional organizations that were advising us to contact various physicians, nurses, and lab technicians who would be willing to volunteer their time. We were quite excited when a number did, including some of our advisers. We also established informal contacts with the Fairfax Clinic to get their advice. For a while we even had a group of Anglo priests and nuns from Mexico who were medical workers and nurses, and they volunteered at the clinic for a brief period. They had broken from the Church because they were unhappy with it.

One of the initial things I learned about setting up a free clinic was that I didn't have to get any kind of state, county, or city approval. As long as we had certified medical personnel working in our clinic, then we could operate it. I'm sure this is no longer the case. I think, too, that it was perceived that we were an extension of USC County Hospital, which supported us.

Two major contacts that I made involved USC County Hospital and the County Health Department. I met with the hospital administrator and explained our goals. He was very supportive and offered to give us whatever we needed, plus the use of one of his doctors, Dr. Craig McMillen, a pediatrician. County Hospital also provided us with the key inventory we needed, such as first-aid supplies, examining equipment, and microscopes for our lab, in addition to materials for blood tests and urine samples.

Then some of the Beret women and I negotiated with the County Health Department. "Look," we told one of the administrators, "we're going to start a free clinic here in East L.A., and we'd like you to participate by helping us. People don't go to your facilities because they're afraid. They're afraid of deportation. They're afraid of the police. They think that if they go to you, they might even get arrested. They just have that fear. Look at your own statistics on who you're serving, and you can see that you're reaching only a small percentage of Mexicans. But we can reach these people. However, we need your support in terms of giving us supplies."

The Health Department agreed to do so because I think they realized that what we were telling them was true. They weren't reaching the residents of East L.A., and they concluded that we could. That certainly was our intent.

We also got support from some businesses that contributed office equipment such as desks, chairs, and typewriters.

Even my father helped out. Since he was a welder, I asked him, "Dad, can you make me some frames for my clinic so I can upholster them for the patients to sit on?"

"I want to see your clinic first," he said.

"Oh, great," I thought. Finally he's interested in my work with the Berets. So he and my mom came over on a Sunday, and he walked through each room, kind of like going, "mhm, mhm, hum." No comment, just this sound coming out of him. He then walked out the door and said to me, "You're a communist."

I just said, "Okay, I'm done. I'm done." I couldn't deal with my father any longer.

What, I think, led him to call me a communist was that we had posters of revolutionary figures such as Che Guevara and Zapata on the walls. As far as he was concerned, they were communists and I must be one also. However, to my surprise, he still made those frames for me. He even let me have one of his big metal desks. We disagreed politically, but he was still my dad.

Besides these posters, we also decorated the clinic by painting murals on some of the walls. We wanted to give people the impression that we were a Chicano clinic that was sensitive and supportive of Mexicans. We painted a large Aztec calendar, as well as other Aztec-related symbols. I painted some of these, as did some of the other women. I also painted our sign outside our building. It wasn't that all of the walls had posters or murals, because we still wanted to provide an impression that we were a clinic. But it was a Chicano clinic, no doubt about this.

As we prepared to open the clinic, we also knew that we had to do a great deal of community outreach to inform people of the clinic and the services we could provide. We first did this outreach by literally going door-to-door and passing out our flyers or leaving flyers at homes. At first, people were afraid of us. Some of them wouldn't open their doors. But for those who did, we said, "We're trying to give you free medical services." In those days, nobody gave anything free. So you can imagine how they didn't trust us, first, because they didn't believe us and, second, because we were Brown Berets. To downplay the latter, we never canvased in our uniforms or our berets. In fact, we never wore our uniforms at the clinic. We wore regular street clothes. In time, we succeeded in getting people to come to our clinic. Not everyone, but enough. Satisfied with our services, these patients then spread the word by mouth, and they became our best advocates.

A second form of community outreach involved the media. I did a number of radio programs, including Spanish-language radio, where I struggled with my Spanish, but somehow spoke enough to get my point across. As the clinic went into operation, I was also interviewed by an English-language TV channel that was curious about the Berets sponsoring a free clinic. This shattered their image of us as firebrand revolutionaries. What were we doing with a free clinic? This wasn't their image of the Brown Berets. I especially remember being interviewed by Stan Chambers, a well-known TV reporter who, before he went on the air with the interview spoke to me in a normal voice, but as soon as the interview started, he went into this TV voice that was so different! I could barely control my giggles as we did the interview. So media also helped to publicize our effort.

Because of these outreach efforts, soon we were reaching more than a hundred patients a day.

FIGURE 11. El Barrio Free Clinic, East Los Angeles, circa 1969.
Courtesy of the Arellanes Collection.

Finally, we went to the East L.A. high schools to talk to the students, especially about the dangers of venereal diseases and how the clinic could help with this by providing useful information and treatment. We didn't go inside the schools because this was prohibited, but we met the students outside the entrances and passed out flyers. The fact was that the schools did nothing about sex education, even though Chicano teens—or at least some of them—engaged in sexual activities without any knowledge of how to protect themselves. I don't think we used the term "sexually transmitted diseases," which might have been confusing, but our flyers made it clear what we were referring to. The kids took our flyers but never talked to us in public. This wasn't something you talked about in public. It was a private matter. Unfortunately, there was a lot of sexual abuse in families, and they just didn't talk about these things. Our flyers encouraged the students to come speak to us in private at the clinic. Some did and some even became volunteers.

Running the clinic was a lot of responsibility on my shoulders, especially as director. I don't recall if that was my actual title, but there was no question that I was in charge. Although I felt somewhat intimidated by the responsibility, I welcomed the challenge. I felt that I was a good organizer and that I had people skills, so I knew that would be of great help. And it was. What helped also was that there was no micromanaging of the clinic by David and the other ministers, and there was no Beret clinic committee. I was pretty much left on my own. The fact of the matter was that David and the other male ministers chose not to become active in the clinic at all. They saw this as "women's work." They took the glory of having a free clinic, but they didn't do any of the work. This would prove to be a major problem in time. However, at least it meant for me that I didn't have David and the others looking over my shoulder. I organized the clinic along with my core of Beret females, especially Andrea, who was my right hand in the clinic.

Besides Andrea and me, our key staff consisted of other female Berets. We served as director, receptionists, secretaries, medical assistants, janitors, and anything else that was needed. We all did these kinds of work. I, for one, never isolated myself in my small office. I wore all of these different hats. The only paid staff member was me. From our budget based on fund-raising and grants, I was paid $350 a month, which I split with Andrea, who served as my codirector. At the same time, however, I kept my job at the antipoverty program.

Most decisions about the day-to-day operations of the clinic were made ad hoc as I discussed issues with Andrea and the other female Berets. Still, from time to time, when needed, I held staff meetings. There were never any tensions surrounding our collective work. Clearly, the clinic represented the most important contribution made by the female Berets, and we were proud of it and supported one another.

Of course, the clinic also involved the various doctors and nurses who volunteered, but these were always good relationships. Most were white but we had a few Chicano doctors and nurses. They made decisions about patients, not about running the clinic. That was a Beret responsibility. However, everyone was free to state their opinions, with the liberty to say, "I think we should do this or that." New ideas were weighed, and if we agreed, then we would do it. If not, then we wouldn't do it. But the ultimate decision was made by the Berets and me.

In addition to the Beret women, we also had a number of community volunteers, both men and women, including students. Most, if not all, were quite young, and so they brought a lot of energy to their work. I can still visualize most of them, even though I can't remember their names. I think that when you get a lot of young people together, it's a very comfortable kind of gathering. You are kind of growing together. I found that to be true with our volunteers, especially our students. The students included some high school kids, but mainly college ones. They came from Cal State, L.A., and East L.A. College.

Of course, we didn't just accept volunteers without any supervision. We interviewed them and decided who to accept. We also set certain regulations. They had to come properly dressed, although we didn't have a dress code. We cautioned them about not being loud or laughing too much or having a lot of fun. This was serious work, and they had to have a serious approach to their work. As volunteers, they helped out in office work, as well as assisting the doctors and nurses after they were properly trained. But they were all great people, and I thoroughly enjoyed working with them. They helped make the clinic a success.

While women represented the backbone of the clinic, some men, such as the volunteers and rank-and-file Berets, also helped out. The Berets, who did tend to be younger recruits, wanted to do something concrete and constructive. I never had a problem with any of them. But, as earlier noted, this was a totally different attitude from the older guys and especially from David and the ministers. They never helped out.

Administering the clinic also meant that I had to be responsible for record keeping and the budget. Record keeping was vitally important, because even though patient records were confidential, we still needed to maintain them for any future treatments. Moreover, these records provided me with the data that I needed to help document proposals for grants. Our budget was not very extensive—only between $1,200 and $1,500 a month. Still, I needed to account for every penny. I personally did not pay the clinic's bills, but sent them to the board as part of my monthly financial report.

I also had to be responsible for the clinic's schedule. This meant deciding the hours that we operated as well as scheduling the different services. I had to contact the doctors and nurses to see if they were available on certain days and times. I had to see who was going to be there or, if somebody cancelled, if I could replace them. So I had to sometimes juggle things. We tried to have a regular schedule for our patients, but occasionally we had to make adjustments. This involved arranging for doctors to be on call. All this was a new learning experience for me, but a very valuable one.

Running the clinic certainly tested not only my organizing skills but my overall leadership ones. I was a good organizer and administrator, but I also had to be strong in protecting the interests of the clinic. This challenge to my leadership skills sometimes involved potential dangerous situations. I'll never forget one example of this. The male Berets had a standing feud with a Chicano car club called the New Breed. I think it was also a turf and macho dispute; it involved the fact that car clubs had to have sponsors, and the county sheriffs sponsored the New Breed. So they, like the sheriffs, had no love for the Berets. In any event, one day the Berets and the car club got into a dispute, and some members of the New Breed chased the Berets into our clinic. For whatever reason, the Berets tried to hide from the car-club guys. At this same time, we had all these young boys like ages eight to twelve, mostly white kids, from Pasadena there to get physicals to play Little League baseball because they couldn't get their physicals closer to where they lived. They became startled and even scared at what appeared to be some sort of gang fight right there in the clinic. I had no choice but to confront the situation.

"There is a clinic going on here," I told two of the New Breed members who were camped right outside of our offices and looking for the Berets. "There are families in here. You need to take your stuff into the ally."

But these two guys, especially the one who appeared to be the leader, didn't budge and instead started in on me.

"You got some sissies hanging in there, and you're protecting them," he challenged me.[57]

So I yelled at him and kind of flipped out on him, at which point, this guy loses it and pulls out a big old German Luger on me. As he does this, I hear one of the Berets behind me in the office say, "Gloria, watch it! He has a gun!"

As if I didn't know this, *pendejo* (idiot)! I thought to myself, resenting the cowardice of the Berets.

Well, seeing this guy's gun only set me off worse. I gave him my back.

"Here's my back. Is that easier for you? Come on, come on, come on!"

Actually, this was more theatrics on my part. As I've mentioned, I had studied body language to learn how to assert myself. I always watched how a person reacts, and I could tell this guy by the way he was handling his gun and the way he was talking to me that he was all mouth. Thank goodness!

The other car-club member was also trying to get the guy with the gun to put it away. Finally, the guy with the Luger says to me, "I'm remembering you, and I'm going to be back."

"You do that. You do that big guy," I shot back at him. "You don't scare me."

All this drama was unfolding right before the eyes of all these young Pasadena kids, their parents and coaches, and some of our other patients. In their eyes, I had stared down this gangster and saved their lives, not to mention the clinic. They thought I was awesome. I became a big hero in Pasadena. Some later called me and said, "Wow, you are something else. You're a hero to us."

"No, I'm nuts," I thought to myself.

While I was the day-to-day director of the clinic, I also worked with our board of directors. We set up a board primarily to help in getting grants for the clinic as well as to advise me on running it. David had the idea of having a board, and he selected those on it. Most were part of the group of medical professionals who had initially helped plan the clinic. Some were volunteer doctors. Professional social workers also served on the board. Board members helped secure resources for the clinic. Sometimes, when needed, I suggested a name or two for the board, mostly on the basis that someone else had recommended them to me. Although it was clear that the Berets controlled the clinic, only David was a member of the board. We wanted a totally professional board that in a sense gave us cover for the clinic, as well as helping in obtaining grants. Looking back, however, we should have had more grassroots community representation on the board. I kept in close contact with the board, but I didn't often attend its meetings, which were not held that frequently anyway.

The fact of the matter is that the board of directors was indispensable in helping us secure grants. In this relationship, my role was to write the grants after the board or others identified potential sponsors. I didn't have any prior experience with grant writing, but somehow I did it. Once I wrote the initial one, the others were easier. Each foundation had certain directions on how to do the proposal, but they were all very similar. They tell you what they want, and you just write it up. I've always been a good writer, and this certainly helped. Once I wrote a proposal, then I would take it to the board, which would discuss it and in most, if not all, cases approve it. The proposal would then be submitted under the board's name. This was crucial because we didn't want it to go forth as a Beret proposal, knowing that as such it probably wouldn't be approved. This is what I mean by the board giving us cover.

Some of the foundations that approved our proposals and gave us funding included the Ford Foundation, United Way, the Mexican-American Opportunities Foundation, and the Los Angeles Regional Family Planning Council, because we provided such services in the clinic. Through David's connections with the Westside Jewish medical professionals, we also got a grant from the American Jewish Committee. The Catholic Church, through its Campaign for Human Development, likewise provided a grant, only to take it away when they discovered that we provided family planning and birth control. A priest came to the clinic, walked through it, and simply said, "Nope, we're done." Despite the Church's reaction, the other grants helped us with our operating expenses, such as paying rent, utilities, and my salary, and in purchasing whatever equipment wasn't donated.

The only place I drew the line in trying to get grants was with the federal government. I knew that it would place all kinds of restrictions on us and require bureaucratic paperwork, and I didn't want to get involved with this. I refused to give into this process. I remember one of our professional family counselors telling me, "You need to accept federal money."

"No, I don't," I replied. "This clinic runs without it, and it's doing fine so far."

We could have had a lot of federal money, but it would bring, in my opinion, a lot of constraints. I got pressure from some board members and others to go in that direction, but I resisted it.

As we settled into the clinic, we began to get patients. Most were poor working-class Mexicans, both U.S.-born and immigrants, including a lot of children in the summer for physical exams for sports activities. We also serviced a lot of elderly people. Men and women came to the clinic, but many more women, especially with their kids, came to us. Typically, men in the barrio don't like to go to doctors, period.

For our clientele, we provided a variety of medical services at no cost. They didn't have to pay a penny. Not a thing. We also promised complete confidentiality with respect to their records. They didn't even have to give us their real names.

This helped many of our patients, especially undocumented immigrants who feared that by going to the clinic they might be exposed to immigration officials.

We also made the clinic as available as possible and emphasized that we were a family clinic. We were open every day, even Sundays. On weekdays we were open from seven o'clock in the morning to ten at night, on Saturdays from noon to ten, and on Sundays from seven in the evening to ten o'clock.[58] In addition, we made appointments for those who couldn't make these hours. Most of this time, we made sure to have doctors and nurses available. The doctors always wore their white coats with their stethoscopes. We insisted that all our patients be treated with courtesy and respect. I wouldn't tolerate anyone not doing so, even if they were doctors. Fortunately, I never had to reprimand anyone for this.

The extent of the medical services that we were able to provide was amazing. Because many mothers came to us with their babies, we had a baby clinic within the clinic, and we had pediatricians available. We treated many sick babies.

We were located between two bars, and sometimes we provided first aid to guys (and they would always be guys) who got into fights. Of course, we had many others who used the clinic like a hospital emergency room when they had cuts or abrasions of one kind or another. I remember once seeing blood all over the handle of the clinic front door and on the sidewalk from guys who had been in fights and then came to the clinic. Once I had to assist one of our doctors in sewing stitches. I was asked to hold a flashlight, and I almost fainted when I saw this big cut on this vato. There was another case when a woman came in with her finger just hanging sideways; it was broken. I've never seen a bone hang off like that to the side. She had to have it stitched up.

Although drug abuse was not as rampant as it is today, we still dealt with many cases of drug overdose. Drug abuse involved whatever drug of choice was available in those days, especially with older guys, meaning in their twenties and thirties. Heroin was a big issue, along with reds, or barbiturates. Both have always been in East L.A. These are old drug choices. Angel dust was also just starting to come into the barrios. Most of these cases that came to us involved men. Some were brought in as an emergency; this could be any time during the day or into the evening. I remember one time I was at the clinic and some guy just dumped another guy at our door. He was in bad shape. We didn't have the facilities to deal with such a bad case, and so I just put him in my car and drove him to White Memorial Hospital. I think he was dying, but they gave him something, and it brought him out of his condition. Although we couldn't really treat drug abuse at the clinic, we did provide preventive services through our community programs. We had medical people and councilors trained in this area who worked with us. We counseled predominantly men about drug abuse.

We also did immunization drives. I would get the county to provide a van, a doctor, and a nurse, plus all the immunization medicine. The day before we went on these drives, we would go to a particular housing project and pass out flyers announcing that we would be back the next day for the immunizations and to have their kids available.

"Tomorrow we're going to be here between this time and this time. Please bring your children. If you have any health records, bring them. If not, we will give you something for your records."

Many parents—mostly mothers—responded and brought their kids to our van, where they would get their shots for measles, smallpox, mumps, rubella, and tetanus. It was amazing. Our Beret women, along with some of our young male volunteers, helped out in these drives. I never saw any of our Beret males doing this.

In turn, the county used our clinic for TB exams. They would park a big truck in front of the clinic. Inside the truck is where they had the X-ray machine for chest exams. We announced the availability of this service, and many took advantage of it.

As noted earlier, we also provided physical exams, especially for kids going out for sports. To play on the football teams, for example, the young guys had to first have a physical. Many came to our clinic for that. But, in addition, we gave general checkups to anyone else. Sometimes, if a doctor diagnosed a more serious problem, we referred the patients to the hospital or a specialist.

One of the most important services we provided, in my opinion, was family planning. Of course, this was controversial. We lost our funding from the Catholic Church because as part of our family-planning counseling we included birth control. This defunding didn't intimidate us or discourage us, even though almost all of us were Catholics. Many barrio women wanted information on family planning and birth control, and we gave it to them. In fact, when the Church threatened us with withdrawing their funding, I told the priests, "Look, if you were to take a survey of all our patients that come here, you would see that 98 percent of them practice birth control." This included the rhythm method allowed by the Church.

With the professional psychologists who worked at the clinic, we counseled patients as to their choices regarding family planning. We also had a gynecologist. We gave women the opportunity to make a decision to have a child or not and told them that if they chose not to, there were various forms of birth control available. People, again predominantly women, came to us and inquired about contraception.

These were mostly single women in their twenties, although there were some older married women. We provided them with the different methods of that period, such as the IUD, the diaphragm, various foams and jellies, and, of course, by the late 1960s, the pill. We never advocated just one way to go. We felt that we needed to provide all the information and then let them make that choice. Interestingly, most chose the IUD instead of the pill. I think that this was because it's not the same as taking a pill every day. It's something that's inserted and hassle free. We inserted IUDs when requested to do so. On the other hand, some requested the pill. Sometimes we had samples and distributed them free of charge. In other cases, our doctors would write out a prescription, because our own small pharmacy didn't have the pill. We encouraged them to go to Family Planning, where they could get the prescription filled at no charge. As for condoms, we didn't stock them, and, as mentioned, very few men came in for family planning or to see about getting condoms, which they could get at a pharmacy or even in a men's room in a bar, like our two neighbor bars.

As far as abortions were concerned, we sometimes had women who had become pregnant and were not sure that they wanted the baby. These were mainly teenagers. We counseled them and suggested that they might think about adoption as an alternative to an abortion, which by the late 1960s was legal in California. But if they insisted on an abortion, we referred them to Family Planning because they provided abortions.

Since many of our patients were women, we also provided gynecological services. These included pap smears as well as other forms of exams for women.

As part of our family-planning services, we focused on teen pregnancies. This problem was as widespread then as it was later and even today. Venereal diseases were also quite rampant in East L.A. I remember that a lot of the premarital blood work that we did revealed syphilis. We tried to address such problems. As mentioned, we did outreach to the high schools and passed out our flyers, in which I wrote, "Have you thought about venereal disease such as syphilis?"

As a result of our outreach, a number of young people, mostly girls, came in for consultations, especially if they were pregnant. We dealt with each case based on what the family situation was. Were the parents sympathetic or hostile? Did they even know? We referred some to St. Anne's, which housed and treated unwed mothers until they gave birth. In many cases St. Anne's arranged, with the mother's consent, to have the babies adopted. In extreme cases, we referred the young women to Family Planning to discuss abortions.

But we also were proactive and provided sex education classes to prevent unwanted pregnancies, especially teen pregnancies. We counseled "safe sex," although we didn't use that term either back then. The fact is that the younger generation of Chicanos were feeling the freedom to become more sexually active outside of marriage. I think we succeeded with many young people because we didn't judge them.

They were more fearful of going to a hospital or another type of clinic. We made them feel that it was okay to come to our barrio clinic and discuss their problems.

Although most of the clinic work dealt with physical problems, we did, at the same time, address emotional ones through psychological counseling provided by our professional psychologists and counselors. This counseling, of course, was highly confidential. They would meet in separate rooms. Most of these issues had to do with family planning, drugs, and alcohol abuse. Very few came in for advice on marital conflicts, including spousal or child abuse. Unfortunately, people just didn't talk about these things outside of the family, if at all. This was the reality then and now. Some people might think that if a woman is in an abusive situation, she can and should leave it. But the reality, especially among the working poor, is that they can't or won't leave. You just can't pick up and leave. It's not that easy.

For our physical cases, we were fortunate that we had the facilities to do some lab work in the clinic as well as professional technicians who volunteered their services. This wasn't anything fancy, just simple blood work and urine sampling. We would then send these samples to the County Health Department for analysis. We used some of our volunteers to take these samples to other facilities. Every morning we would deliver them. Some of these samples were to look for not only sexually transmitted diseases but diseases like diabetes, which among Mexicans was quite prevalent.

Finally, we had our own small pharmacy, where we could dispense some drugs free of charge. These were usually samples given to our doctors who, in turn, donated them to us. These were over-the-counter drugs that did not need a prescription, such as aspirin, cough medicine, and some children's medicines, along with first-aid supplies. We did have some antidotes for alcohol abuse as well as medicines for detoxing from heroin. Perhaps some of these drugs required a prescription, but if the doctors at the clinic okayed them, then we would give it to the patients. We didn't dispense the more serious drugs willy-nilly. And, as noted, we did provide some contraceptions. We kept all our drugs under lock and key.

Directing the clinic was my most fulfilling experience as a Brown Beret. Part of this had to do with a sense of community that enveloped the clinic as we worked together for a common purpose with real results. None of my other experiences with the Berets gave me this feeling. This sense of community had to do with my wonderful and supportive female Berets, plus our volunteers. We all became good friends, not only through our work but also because we socialized together. We partied together and did other things together. It wasn't all work.

CRISIS OVER THE CLINIC

The one major disappointment in running the clinic was the lack of involvement by David, the other male ministers, and most of the rank-and-file male Berets.

They all agreed with David that the clinic was "women's work." They took credit for it as a service to the community, but they didn't put in any work into it. This was a glaring contradiction. David occasionally came around and wanted to use my office for something else, and that was okay, but he was never really involved in the clinic. The men didn't want to do the hard work of operating it. Ironically, they stressed discipline in the Brown Beret manual, but they themselves, from David on down, didn't have the discipline to work at the clinic. So they didn't know the first thing about it or how it ran. Had they worked there and learned this, they would have been able to maintain the clinic even after the other Beret women and I left.

Our eventual leaving had to do with the attitude of David and the other men toward the clinic. While they refused to work there, they would still come around after hours and want to use the place to party. They brought liquor and women and would leave the place a mess and not clean it up. The other women and I had to do this in the mornings before we opened. This became an impossible situation. You can't have a clinic and keep it clean and sanitized when you have guys coming in and dirtying the place up almost every evening. You have sick people coming to the clinic, and you don't want them to get sicker.

"David, you have to put a stop to this," I told him.

But he did nothing. He either didn't want to, or, as I suspect, he had no control over most of the Beret males. To me, this spoke to his eventual lack of leadership qualities. And so the problem continued to fester until, after several months of directing the clinic, I couldn't put up with it any longer. I even went to my board of directors on this, and, regrettably, they also refused to act. They didn't want to confront David and the guys. I frankly think that they were intimidated or afraid of them because of what they perceived to be their militancy and gun toting. They didn't want to be caught up in this conflict. They didn't want to stick their necks out.

After several months of this tension, I became very frustrated and angry over these disruptions at the clinic. I warned David more than once: "You've got to clean it up or else I walk."

I went to a board meeting at the clinic and told the members that if they didn't change immediately, I was leaving the clinic. They seemed to be taken by surprise. But I also made it clear that I would likewise be leaving the Berets. I told them that I would be opening up another clinic and invited them to join me. David was not at this meeting. I was shocked at the response.

"Gloria, you're not indispensable."

I was shocked by this response, especially because it came from one of the doctors whom I very much respected. It wasn't a hostile response, but matter-of-fact.

I responded, "Okay, fine."

No one on the board tried to dissuade me, but even if they had, I was adamant about leaving. I believed that there was no going back and trying to make things better. I had tried this, with no results.

With no support from either David or the board, I quit and left the clinic. It was very painful for me because the clinic had become my life, my purpose. It defined me as a Beret. But I couldn't continue with the mess that the men caused almost every evening.

However, when I left, I didn't leave alone. I talked with the other women and the volunteers, and they all felt like I did. So when I left, I took everyone with me.

When we left, the clinic ceased to operate. David and the other Berets didn't know what to do with it. Since they hadn't participated, they had no idea of how to run it. They had no clue how to operate a free clinic.

We left everything in the building, even though David later accused me of taking items. This wasn't true. I didn't take a piece of paper or a pencil or supplies.

We left in February 1970. When we decided to leave the clinic, it also meant leaving the Berets. After what had happened at the clinic, there was no way we could resume being Berets. This wasn't easy, but there was no other way. David and the others, in effect, forced us out. However, we weren't just victims; we made the decision to leave, and it was the right decision.

David was devastated. He was also angry and resentful. But he got hit at the knees. He had no idea of how we felt. I don't think he knew how to recover from this blow. Not only was he losing the clinic, but he was losing the Beret women, or most of us. Yet it wasn't in him to say, "Come back, and I'll really clean it up. Don't let the clinic fall apart. Gloria, if you come back, I promise you this."

He didn't do this.

I never heard from David again for years. He never spoke to me after this.

I think that the free clinic may be the most important legacy of the Brown Berets, despite the fact that most of the men had nothing to do with it and that their unruly and sexist behavior led to its downfall. I can't think of any other major community contribution that the Berets—or at least the female Berets—did that equaled the role of the clinic. Despite its short existence, it helped many people in East L.A., and it became a role model for other free clinics in the city, including one that I would later become involved with. The free clinic was good for the community. It took care of people's health needs. It reached them. It was a very positive thing for the barrio. This is its legacy.

As for me personally, I loved what I did at the clinic. It became my passion. I learned a lot about myself. I learned a lot about medicine. I especially learned about giving to people and that I was strong and could run a project like this. I could organize people to work for me. So I learned that these were my skills—my organizing skills—and I've used them throughout my entire life. I still use them, even in retirement.

LEAVING THE BERETS

Let me say more about leaving the Berets. While the issue of the lack of real support by the men for the clinic represented one of the last straws, the tension between the women and the men had been building over sexism and gender relations. In addition, there were other factors that led to the split. David and the men, for example, seemed to be more and more employing the theme of violence and guns as opposed to social services such as the clinic. We had guns, but I was starting to realize that I was not a violent person. I could never hit anyone. If I had children, I would not want them exposed to weapons. I was already formulating these thoughts when I left.

Prior to the other women and me leaving, we had informal discussions among ourselves, as we usually did about most issues. It was in these meetings that it became clear to me that the other women felt like I did. They couldn't put up with the men's behavior anymore, so they were also willing to leave. This included my key supporters, such as Andrea. Some of the younger women also left. Arlene Sánchez, David's sister, who had not been active in the clinic, didn't join us. I'm sure she felt torn between her brother and me. She later left on her own. A few other women stayed, and the Berets recruited additional women, especially of high school age. When I see their photos, such as around the time of the Chicano moratorium, I can't identify any of these new female Berets. My brother, Bill, also soon left the Berets.

I think the last straw for me was when I was almost raped by the Beret men. This was while I was still at the clinic, but really beginning to criticize the men for their lack of work and support at the clinic. I was told that there was going to be a meeting of all the ministers at one of their homes; I don't remember which home this was. Although I was criticizing the ministers, I felt that, as a minister, I needed to attend.

I was ambushed. They set me up. When I arrived I became aware that besides the other ministers, there were additional male members of the Berets in attendance. In all about ten or fifteen guys were there, including David. They were all smoking weed. They tried to get me to relax by offering me some weed. I wasn't into drugs, although occasionally I used weed, and so to be part of the group I used some that evening. The meeting soon deteriorated when they started in on me about why I was being critical of the men and that I shouldn't do this because this was antirevolutionary. "Why are you a Brown Beret? What is it you want? What are you going to do after the revolution?" they asked me. These guys were living in a fantasy. But I soon began to get anxious, and maybe this was the effect of the weed that can make you paranoid, but I remember thinking, "they're going to rape me." Maybe this was just me, but I feared the worst and knew that I had to get out of there.

Fortunately, Carlos Montes, who had not yet gone underground, saved me. He knew what they wanted to do to me. He came up to me and said, "Hey, Gloria. Let me walk you to your car." And so I got up and walked out with Carlos. They didn't try to stop us. I drove home knowing that Carlos had saved me. I have the highest respect for him; he respected women.[59]

I didn't talk to anyone about this. You didn't talk about rape or things like incest or spousal abuse then. None of the other female Berets ever reported any rape or attempted rape by the Beret men to me. But it's very possible they were also faced with such threats. If they were prepared to do this to me as a minister, I can only imagine what they might have done or tried to do with the rank-and-file women. They, with some exceptions such as Carlos Montes, had no respect for women.

I knew then that I had to leave the Berets.

But this was not the first time that I faced a possible rape attempt. An earlier incident occurred when I had a confrontation with some Berets who belonged to the El Monte chapter. One night while I was in my car in El Monte, one of the leaders of the chapter came up to me. He was loaded. He had two younger guys with him. He tried to convince me to get out of my car. I knew what he wanted. When I refused, he told the other guys, "Help her out!" I knew what this meant, especially because there was an empty field nearby. Fortunately, the younger guys refused to follow his order.

"You don't want to do that," they responded to the leader. "We don't think you want to do that, man."

They knew that I was a Beret minister and that there might be repercussions if they attacked me. I had a liquor bottle in my car, for some reason, even though I didn't drink, and I was prepared to break the bottle and use it as a weapon to defend myself if I had to. Fortunately, I didn't have to, as the leader left with the two other guys. I didn't tell David or anyone else what had happened.

Many years later, I am now telling others, especially young women, about these rape attempts. They need to know about this other side of the movement—the dark side.

On February 25, 1970, ten other female Berets and I resigned from the Brown Berets. This wasn't a formal process. We just verbally informed David and the other ministers of our decision. There was no formal letter of resignation. I did write some letters to other Beret chapters outside of L.A., explaining what had happened and why the women were leaving. One of these letters to Aron Mangancilla of the Redwood, California, chapter has survived and is in my collection at Cal State, Los Angeles. In this letter, I wrote the following:

"*ALL* Brown Beret women have also resigned from further duties in the organization. We have been treated as nothings, and not as Revolutionary sisters, which means the resolutions that all our 'macho' men voted for have been disregarded. We have found that the Brown Beret men have oppressed us more than the pig system has, which in the eyes of revolutionaries is a serious charge. Therefore, we have agreed and found it necessary to resign and possibly do our own thing."[60]

I never heard from any of the male Berets, including David, after we resigned.

How did I feel about leaving the Berets? I felt very liberated. I had operated the clinic by myself with the help of the other women and the volunteers. So I knew what I could do and knew that I didn't need David and the Berets to do it. I knew that I could now move on to establish another clinic without the baggage of the Berets. So I felt very liberated. I never felt that I had failed or fallen down. I just felt that what I did was a good thing for me personally and for my mental health. I didn't feel bitter, although I was angry about having built up the clinic and then having to walk away from it because of the destructiveness of the men. I resented this. But if you stay in that resentment, it drowns you. If I've learned anything in life, it's being positive and trying to keep that negative energy away from me. I knew I had done a good job and that I had done other good work in the Berets, and I took off from that. As for the Berets, I did discuss the problems that led to my resignation after I left, but I didn't set out to destroy the Berets. That was not my intent at all. I would never try to destroy anyone.[61]

LAS ADELITAS

Prior to the time that the other women and I were planning on leaving the Berets, I began to organize a new group composed of the Beret women and other women in the movement who were also dissatisfied with the men. "Let's just start a women's group," we concluded. I was not someone who uncritically approached the issue of women in the movement. By that I mean that I observed how some women were what I call catty. They had their nails out for other women when they turned their back. Catty meant jealousies among women, especially over guys. Fortunately, we didn't experience this among the female Berets who worked closely with me. If somebody liked a man, there was a code that you didn't mess with that guy because she liked him. It has to do with respect. We supported one another.

I felt that we needed to establish and expand such a support group. I ran it by the other women, and they liked the idea. Some women from other movement organizations also liked it. It didn't mean that like us they had to leave their groups but that they could join us and still remain part of their organizations. We didn't see ourselves as a rival or competitive group.

I decided to call our new group Las Adelitas de Aztlán. I had come to learn more about the history of the Mexican Revolution of 1910 and was fascinated by the image of La Adelita, the female revolutionary who fought in the revolution. I had seen photos of Las Adelitas with their *bandoleros* and their rifles. They were not a separate group in the revolution, but fought alongside the men. This was part of the Chicana search for historical role models. We had used such images in *La Causa* patterned after Hilda Reyes, one of our Beret members, who somewhere acquired a *bandolero* and began to wear it along with her Beret outfit. In fact, a photo of Hilda with her *bandolero* was taken by Raul Ruiz, and it became and still is an iconic image of the role of women in the Chicano movement. So I thought that by using the name Las Adelitas, we would be conveying our women-warrior roles in the movement. I added Aztlán to also indicate that we were committed to the movement.

I associated La Adelita with the *corrido,* or ballad, by that name that came out of the Mexican Revolution. I remember looking for the words to the song and finally finding them. I then found an image of La Adelita in one of those Mexican calendars that are in Mexican restaurants and bakeries. I wanted to use such an image to publicize our new group.

So we adopted the name of Las Adelitas de Aztlán, along with the image of La Adelita. We envisioned strong women who would be supportive and always back one another up. Was this a feminist group? As mentioned, I didn't call myself a feminist, nor did the other Beret women, but in retrospect we were feminist in fact and in action. Now, forty years later or more, I see us and Las Adelitas as a group that helped give birth to Chicana feminism. That's a very powerful statement to make, and it has taken me a long time to accept this.

Las Adelitas became a place where women could "Come and tell how you've been treated. Let's talk about this," because I realized that it wasn't just the male Berets who were behaving badly toward women. It was something in the movement and in chicanismo that produced this macho mentality. Of course, it also came from the patriarchy associated with Mexican culture. Las Adelitas became a forum for Chicanas to get together and talk about all of this and to deal with it. It provided us with a sense that we were not alone in confronting these gender problems. In a way, we were also redefining *la familia,* or at least the traditional patriarchal family. We adopted the slogan, "Porque somos una familia de hermanas [Because we are a family of sisters]." Our goal was not to beat up on the men but, more important, to empower ourselves.

I also put out a flyer inviting other Chicanas to join us. I sent it out to different movement groups. The flyer read as follows:

> Chicanas, find Yourself!
> Do you have a part in the Movement?
> Are you satisfied?
> Are your ideas suppressed?
> Come & CREATE your ideas!
> HELP CREATE Las Adelitas de Aztlán.[62]

Las Adelitas was not a formal organization; I never intended it to be. We didn't have an office or regular meetings or officers. We just met from time to time in different places, including the second clinic that I organized as well as at the Euclid Community Center on Whittier Boulevard. We were a discussion and support group.

We made our first major public appearance as Las Adelitas de Aztlán when we participated in the so-called March in the Rain anti–Vietnam War demonstration on February 28, 1970, organized by the Chicano Moratorium Committee, led by Rosalio Muñoz. It became referred to as the March in the Rain because of the heavy rainstorm that day in Los Angeles. It was one of several Chicano antiwar marches that built up to the historic National Chicano Antiwar Moratorium on August 29, 1970. This early protest came just three days after the women and I had resigned from the Berets, which indicates that we had already been organizing Las Adelitas. We joined the two or three thousand protestors marching in East L.A. that day, but we marched as a separate contingent. I painted a large banner with calligraphy that read "Las Adelitas de Aztlán," and we carried it with us. It was a pink banner, and the letters were huge; it took up half of the street as we marched. This was how others became aware of our existence. Despite the rain, the banner held up pretty well, and the paint didn't run. There must have been about twenty of us who marched. We wore all black clothes, with *rebozos,* or shawls, as a sign of mourning. In fact the Moratorium Committee encouraged all women in the protest to wear black.[63] At my suggestion, we also carried white crosses with the names of some of the Chicano men from L.A. killed in the war. My cross had the name of my cousin, Jimmy Vásquez, who was killed in Vietnam. It was very moving to have all these crosses with the names of the deceased.

As we marched, we sang, or tried to sing, the *corrido* "La Adelita." We didn't know all the words, so we hummed parts of it. The march was filmed, and when I later watched the film, I could hear us humming the song. The Brown Berets also participated in the protest, but it didn't seem clumsy to me. I didn't feel anything but pride. We were tired of being put down by the men. We weren't going to be put down anymore, and they couldn't put us down. We had a lot of support during the demonstration.[64]

CHICANO MORATORIUM COMMITTEE

My involvement in antiwar protests actually commenced a few months before the March in the Rain. In October 1969 I participated in the large national moratorium in San Francisco. I went because for one of the first times in the short history of the anti–Vietnam War movement, there were going to be Chicano contingents, with speakers such as Corky Gonzales, Dolores Huerta, and Rosalio Muñoz. Of course, I had already met Corky in Washington and later in Denver, but I had not met Dolores or Rosalio. I also went to see how other people organized big gatherings. It was quite a show, with many thousands who attended. It was amazing. I really liked what I saw. I don't recall if I went with other Berets, but this was probably the case. I not only attended; I marched. At the end of the march, I went up close to the stage so I could listen to the Chicano speakers. It was an incredible experience and motivated me to think, "We can do this."

The Chicano antiwar movement in L.A. was actually started by the Brown Berets. I attended some of these early meetings, which included not just Berets but others who were also beginning to oppose the war. At first, I wasn't very active in what became the Chicano Moratorium Committee. While David and the Berets eventually drifted away from the committee, the Berets still should be credited for starting it, and it should be seen as part of the Beret agenda. The Berets opposed the war based on the disproportionate numbers of Chicanos casualties. Chicanos were being drafted, killed, and wounded in the war, totally out of proportion of what we represented in the U.S. population. The war impacted Chicanos more. Some of us also opposed the war because it personally affected our families. As mentioned, my cousin, my paternal aunt's son, Jimmy Vásquez, was killed in Vietnam. He was just a little older than me. I remember playing with him until we became cool teenagers. I don't remember going to his funeral. He was from Pico Rivera, and his high school later placed his name on a memorial plaque along with other former students, mostly Chicanos, killed in the war.

I personally opposed the war not only because of my consciousness but because of the senselessness of so many killed in the war, both Americans and Vietnamese. It was horrifying for me, Vietnamese children being killed and maimed. Then there were the lies about the war. "No, we're not going into Cambodia," and then they were in Cambodia. The costs of the war also disturbed me. If they had spent that money on education, we wouldn't still have so many problems in the schools today. I hated this war and all wars.

While David and the Berets organized the Chicano antiwar movement in L.A., others participated, such as Rosalio, who after graduating from UCLA publicly refused induction into the military. He then started a Chicano antidraft movement, which led him to join the Moratorium Committee. Rosalio had strong leadership qualities and soon emerged as a key figure in the committee. From my perspective, this did not sit well with David and the other Berets, who wished to dominate the group. I didn't agree with their animosity toward Rosalio. The Berets didn't care for him because he was such a go-getter. He surrounded himself with amazing people who were willing to go out and work, unlike some of the Berets. The Berets also considered Rosalio to be new to the movement, a newbie. But the fact was that there were a lot of newbies, including Berets.

I could also see the tension between David and Rosalio. They had a strained relationship. David, in my opinion, resented Rosalio's leadership. That was evident to me. I think that David was jealous of Rosalio's talents—which he didn't have—such as being articulate and a great speaker, as well as his intelligence and incredible memory for details.

I didn't know all the reasons why David and the Berets began to withdraw from the Moratorium Committee after having started it. They were still considered part of it, but into 1970 they played less of a role. Fortunately, Rosalio and his supporters took up the slack. I personally liked Rosalio and would go on to work with him after I became more active with the committee, following my resignation from the Berets. Rosalio was hardworking and very balanced in that he seemed to get along well with others and was friendly with everyone, even those who might not be in total agreement with him. He was always in control of his emotions. I recall some Berets confronting him over something after he became the leader of the committee. He just kept his cool and brushed them off.

Besides participating in the March in the Rain, I had actually also been involved in the Moratorium Committee's first staged demonstration against the war, on December 20, 1969. This, of course, was when I was still a Beret. In fact, since the Berets were chiefly responsible for the initial protest, I was asked by the committee to obtain permission from the LAPD to march on some of the streets in East L.A., including the main thoroughfare of Whittier Boulevard. I don't know why I was chosen to do this. It was probably because none of the men volunteered, and I said, "okay, I'll do it." But when I went to police headquarters to request permission, I chose not to go as a Beret but as a community person. I didn't want to get the cops all riled up about Beret involvement. I also didn't say that this was going to be an antiwar march, but instead one honoring Chicanos killed in the war. I requested only half of each street so that tying up traffic would not be an issue. To my pleasant surprise, the police commission, composed of civilians who gave these permits, had no objections. They didn't realize that this was an antiwar protest and certainly not one led by the Berets.

On the day of the march, we assembled at Obregon Park, where there actually is a war memorial with the names of all the Chicanos killed in wars such as World War I and World War II. Before we marched, we paid homage to these fallen veterans by reading their names, and there were quite a few. We knew that this initial protest would not be very large, but surprisingly we attracted about a thousand people or so. It was a local event, but its importance was that it was the first antiwar protest ever in East L.A. It also wasn't a very long march.

In this march the other Beret women and I marched as a specific contingent apart from the male Berets. In fact, I drilled the women to prepare for the march. Of course, we wore our uniforms. As I look back on it now, the fact that we marched separately indicated how unhappy many of us already were with the behavior of the guys. I didn't speak at the rally, nor did any of the Beret women. However, we were pleased that this first antiwar demonstration was successful.

I then, as noted, participated in the March in the Rain with Las Adelitas after we had left the Berets. Following this protest, I became heavily involved with the Moratorium Committee. I began to attend more meetings at its headquarters. By the spring of 1970, things really began to pick up after the decision was made at the second Denver youth conference to hold a national antiwar moratorium demonstration in East L.A. on August 29, 1970. This was to be a national demonstration for Chicanos throughout the Southwest and beyond. The L.A. Moratorium Committee, which now became the National Chicano Moratorium Committee, was charged with organizing what some at the time believed would bring in fifty thousand or more protestors. I just remember how the committee's headquarters was filled with activity and excitement. It was like Grand Central Station, with people coming and going. Committee meetings, which I attended, also took place. Rosalio and usually someone else chaired the meetings. By now David Sánchez and the Berets had pretty much pulled out of the committee, although occasionally they showed up to try to put their two cents into what we were doing. These would be annoying, rather than supporting, interventions.

I was joined in these meetings and in the committee by some of the other former Beret women. Hilda and Grace always participated, as did Andrea. Of course, Andrea and I were inseparable. We were like bookends. As women, we found ourselves feeling more comfortable in the committee's work. It was a better climate for women; we were treated much better and with greater respect.

I functioned in different capacities in the committee. At first, I did some clerical work such as handling phone calls. But I soon began to do other things. One that I really enjoyed was traveling on weekends up to the Bay Area to encourage Chicanos in Northern California to attend the moratorium. Each weekend I jumped into my VW bug and, usually with a couple of other committee members, both men and women, drove north. Through various contacts that I had made involving other Beret chapters in this area, I helped organize what we called "backyard meetings." We got someone to host us in their homes, and they, in turn, invited other people. These meetings averaged about twenty-five people per meeting. We met in the early evenings, so we could show the film that had been made on the March in the Rain. We'd show the film and then discuss the plans for August 29. We sometimes also showed the film *I Am Joaquin*, based on Corky Gonzales's epic poem about Chicano history. We passed out flyers for the demonstration. We held these meetings in San Jose, Oakland, Redwood City, Palo Alto, and several other communities. Over several weeks of these backyard meetings, we got the word out to a number of people who promised not only to go to the moratorium but to encourage others to go. So our efforts were cumulative.

Showing the film on the March in the Rain was interesting. It was a 35 mm film that we had to bring in a huge canister, along with a film projector. Each home provided us with a white sheet, which we hung up in the backyard to serve as the screen. We plugged the projector into an electrical outlet and showed the black-and- white film. Sometimes instead of a sheet, we'd project the film onto a white fence or structure. After the film, we talked about our goals and plans and answered questions.

In addition to this type of activity, I also was assigned to pay visits to various community organizations in East L.A. to inform them of what we were planning and to solicit their endorsement. Many of them responded positively. In addition, I helped make some of the flyers for the moratorium. I was good at this and always carried my calligraphy supplies with me, my pen, ink, and a ruler that I used for this work. We couldn't afford a copy machine, so we used a mimeograph to produce the flyers. We posted them all over. I went to some of the East L.A. merchants and tried to get them to post the flyers, but they wouldn't.

Using my Beret experience, I further helped write up press releases because I knew that they had a certain format that had to be followed.

But the most important activity that I did on the committee had to do with arranging housing for the many participants that we expected from outside of L.A. Of course, I worked with others on this issue. Our challenge was to get people in the city to agree to house some of these activists. One way was that we put notices in community newspapers to get the word out. "Can you house somebody coming from another area to the moratorium?" Then there was word of mouth, where we also asked, "If you can't house someone, do you know of someone who can?" When we went to meetings, we'd always bring up this need for housing. Many responded positively. "I'd like to offer my home," some replied. "I can take in this amount of people," or "I can house one or two or three people."

We estimated how many we had to house by the number of people from outside L.A. who contacted us by phone or mail about housing. I kept a list of these names. It's in my collection. We had inquiries from El Paso, Sacramento, and other places in California and from Milwaukee, Ogden, Utah, San Antonio, and Chicago, among many other areas.[65] As we got closer to August 29, the pressure on housing increased, but somehow in the end we were able to accommodate thousands of people. Those last few days, we worked well into the evenings on this project. This was a huge job, and it really tested my organizing skills.

We knew that the demonstration was going to be big, and so the committee did have security concerns. We planned for monitors, and I knew that Rosalio had met with the county sheriffs responsible for the area of the march and rally to assure them that this was going to be a peaceful protest. I wasn't involved in these matters, but I knew that we had concerns. But no one seemed to expect trouble. On the other hand, I learned that David had instructed the Berets that if they were going to participate in the demonstration not to wear their uniforms, which might incite the police. I think that the L.A. Berets obeyed this instruction; however, some Berets from other places did not. All I know is that David put out the word: "Do not wear your brown berets or bush jackets. Do not identify yourselves as Brown Berets."

I remember thinking that maybe David knew or felt that shit was going to hit the fan.

But as August 29 dawned, we didn't think about anything going wrong. My brother, Bill, who had also left the Berets, had planned on driving his truck in the march, and the committee approved it. It was a 1965 big blue Chevrolet truck. It used to belong to my father, who gave it to my little brother. It would help lead the march and would be right behind the large banner that we did identifying the demonstration as sponsored by the National Chicano Moratorium Committee. The truck was to be the only vehicle in the march. I decided to be on the truck along with other members of the committee. We drove the truck to Belvedere Park, the assembly point, and waited for the march to begin.

Pretty soon thousands of people streamed into the park, and we started what would be a momentous and fateful day. As we moved onto the streets, from my vantage point of sitting on the ledge of the truck right behind the back window and looking back, all I saw were Chicanos who had arrived for the demonstration. It was an incredible sight. People were yelling antiwar and Chicano movement slogans and cries. It was really very upbeat. People were happy. Whole families participated. As we moved onto Whittier Boulevard, the main artery of the march, I saw people coming out of stores and expressing support. I remember in particular some ladies coming out of a hairdresser shop and waving to us, even giving us the power sign! The whole atmosphere was very celebratory and exciting. As we went farther, I began to see just a mass of people, many carrying banners and signs, some of which indicated the group or places they represented. Unlike previous demonstrations, we occupied the entire street. We later learned that perhaps as many as twenty thousand or more demonstrated that day.

As we slowly proceeded toward Laguna Park, the site of the rally, the day got hotter and hotter. This was only made worse, because I don't recall that we had thought of bringing water on the truck. Perhaps we did, but it probably didn't help that much with the heat. I also didn't wear a hat or cap, and, boy, did I get an awful sunburn.

From the truck, I did see some police around, but nothing that seemed threatening. I didn't see any black-and-white police cars or any sheriffs with their helmets on. If you see them with helmets, you know something's cooking. When you see this, it's kind of, "Oh crap! What's gonna happen?" But I felt none of that. I'm sure they were around, but it wasn't intimidating.

When we reached the head of the march at Laguna Park, my brother parked the truck behind the assembled stage where the entertainment and speakers would face the crowd. Before he parked, he let the others and me off at the entrance to the park. When we arrived, some of the entertainment that we had arranged for had already commenced, since a number of people were already there, especially families and older people who didn't march. There was Mexican folkloric dancing and singing of *corridos*. It was all very joyful. It was a very high-spirited event. And as this was going on, marchers entered the park. It was an ocean of people.

I positioned myself next to the stage as part of the security so I could look at the large crowd. It wasn't long before the sheriffs attacked. I almost immediately went into like a trauma seeing what was happening. All I could make out toward the back of the park was a wave that began to move people out. This is when I started seeing the attack. Some were still entering the park. I really think I went into shock and later suffered post–traumatic stress syndrome. Everything was so happy and good, and then I'm going, "What happened?"[66]

I saw people running all over the place and screaming. I saw children and *abuelitas* (grandmothers) trying to escape the sheriffs. It was just very, very traumatic to see all this. It was horrible. Very quickly, the tear gas exploded. It burned my eyes and face. My face was already quite red due to my sunburn, and it now got only redder. I couldn't see or breathe. I felt someone grab my arm and move me out. As my eyes cleared a bit, I saw this young man. I can still see his face. He put me on a bus and laid a wet T-shirt on my face. I began to breathe and see better. I think he told me his name, but I can't remember it. I wish I knew who he was so I could possibly still thank him now after all these years.

I found myself on a bus with several other people. We were in a school bus, or it looked like a school bus, that had brought people to the march. The driver seemed panicked, and he drove out fast. We all jumped from our seats as he raced over the speed bumps. But before we got out of the park, Corky Gonzales and some of his people jumped on the bus and came inside. He recognized me and asked, "Are you okay?" But very soon Corky and his group must have changed their minds, because they started pounding on the doors, demanding to be let out. They wanted to go back into the park to help others. They broke the doors down and jumped out because the driver refused to stop.

I don't remember where I got off the bus, but somehow I found my way back to one of our committee offices on Brooklyn Avenue. This wasn't our main office, but another location we used. It was a storefront, and from there I could see the smoke going up around Laguna Park and the part of Whittier Boulevard where some Chicanos began to counterattack by burning buildings and setting fire to police cars. It was very frightening.

As soon as other committee members and I reassembled in this office, we immediately started helping others who somehow found their way to our location. Some were also very traumatized, as I was. Some had been beaten by the cops or were suffering from the tear gas. There was one guy who was high on acid, but it looked like his leg had been shattered. We called the paramedics, who put his leg in a plastic tube and took him to the hospital. Others just came in from the park, wanting to know what had happened. Why had the sheriffs attacked us?

I remained there the rest of the afternoon. People were calling us with reports about others who were injured or arrested and about the burnings. We also turned on a radio and listened to the news of the events around the park. Through all of this, I was very afraid. How far was the fire going to go? Was it heading in our direction? Were the cops going to raid us? What's going to happen? I was scared, but I knew better than to show this to others. If you do, they become very frightened. Instead, I tried to remain calm, as I comforted others and assured them that we were safe. I tried the best I could to do this, but I don't know how much I succeeded, because I was afraid.

Part of the trauma I suffered was compounded by the deaths of three persons connected with the moratorium, including Ruben Salazar. I learned about this through the news media, but not until the following day. A few days later I attended the funeral of Lyn Ward, a fourteen-year-old Brown Beret from El Monte. I knew him, and I felt the need to pay my respects not only because he was a Beret but also because he was from my hometown. At the funeral I saw police or plainclothes FBI standing apart in the bushes and shamelessly, and with no respect to Lyn's family, doing surveillance and taking photos of everyone there. I couldn't believe this! I was disgusted. Hearing about Salazar being killed by a sheriff only increased my fears.

These deaths forced me to focus on the value of life when I was still at a young age. They changed me. Here, I as a Beret had learned how to use a weapon, and now these types of weapons had led to the death of people like Lyn and Salazar. I realized even more that I could never kill a human being. I can't even hurt animals. I rescue animals. These deaths awakened me to the importance of life and how fragile it can be.

After attending Lyn's funeral, I never went back to the Chicano movement. I started a new free clinic, but it had nothing to do with the movement. The attack on the moratorium, the destruction, and the deaths just devastated me. I felt fear, and I just couldn't handle this very well. I never participated again. People kept calling me, "Gloria, are you going to march in the September 16 demonstration?"

"I'm done, I'm done," I think I responded.

The only thing I did later, in 1971, was to register votes for La Raza Unida Party in L.A., but not much more than this. I wasn't involved in Raul Ruiz's campaign.

I stayed in touch with some of the Beret women, but eventually that also went away. I never returned to the Moratorium Committee. Nothing. I left the *movimiento*. I excluded myself from all movement activities. It took me twenty years to go back to a movement reunion, and they had to twist my arm to go.

LA CLÍNICA DEL BARRIO

By the time I had decided to leave the Berets, I was also setting up my new free clinic that would be totally separate from them. In fact, the Beret free clinic folded right after the other women and I left it. So the need for a replacement was there, and with my experience, I organized a new one. I found a location at 274 Atlantic Boulevard in East L.A. At first I called it El Barrio Free Clinic. However, I soon changed the name to La Clínica del Barrio, but it was also referred to as La Clínica Familiar del Barrio (the Family Barrio Free Clinic). It took several months to put everything in order, and it officially opened on March 15, 1971. Unlike the cramped Beret clinic, this one had much more space. It was in a second-story building, which, in fact, used to be a mortuary. We had several examining rooms, a large reception area, and various offices, including my own on the second floor. Despite the tensions I had with the Beret board, I convinced some members to join my new board. It was through them that I obtained the initial funds to rent the building. We then acquired other grants for operating expenses. As with the Beret clinic, I didn't have to go through any county or state approval process, at least that I can remember. We just did it and, like the Beret clinic, it operated as a nonprofit. My title was program administrator. From the grants we got later, I received a salary of $350 a month. I was no longer working for the antipoverty agency, and so this was my only source of income.[67] However, because Andrea also helped me open the new clinic, I gave her $150 from my salary as my assistant. I felt I owed her something for her loyalty and hard work. We were the only paid staff; everyone else volunteered their services. Because I had this limited salary, I moved back in with my parents.

Although some of my board members were holdovers from the Beret clinic, I very consciously included new ones from the Chicano community. For the doctors and nurses who volunteered at the new clinic, I again went through the County Health Department. Once again, County Hospital donated equipment. Moreover, any lab work that we did was evaluated by county health facilities. We once again attracted many volunteers, mostly Chicano college students, who eventually became doctors, nurses, or lab technicians. This was great training for them. Another group of volunteers came from the East L.A. Health Task Force. These were mainly community people who wanted to bring health services to the barrio.

Our services compared well with and even exceeded what we did at the Beret clinic. We soon developed a strong clientele and particularly reached out to undocumented immigrants. We could treat even more patients due to our larger facilities and a larger staff. Probably more families came for our services. This included many *viejitos* (senior citizens). I loved talking to them because they would tell me about their folk medicines. I loved sitting in the waiting room with patients and listening to their stories.

As part of our services, we continued to provide birth control and advice on abortions. In this, we relied on our family counselors, including Family Planning ones. We had great counselors.

While we provided many, if not all, of the same services that we did in the Beret clinic, the main difference was that, I believe, we were even more efficient. We had more resources, more funds, more personnel, and all of this added up to a better-running operation.

One of the requests that I received as director of the new clinic was from David Sánchez. He wanted me to supply some first-aid materials for the so-called Beret occupation of Catalina Island in August 1972. David stated that he was taking back Catalina from the United States since, he claimed, the island had never been formally transferred from Mexico after the U.S.-Mexico War of the 1840s. This was a foolish action by David and the Berets, and I refused to give him the supplies. He did not request this personally; he went through some intermediary.[68]

Many of the same foundations and agencies that had previously supported us did so again for the new clinic. Again, I wrote and submitted most of the grant proposals. Most provided annual grants of funds. However, I applied only to funding sources that would not require us to share much, if any, of our patient information. I was especially sensitive to this due to our efforts to connect with the immigrants. That's why I chose once more not to apply for federal grants that we probably could have gotten. They would have involved providing too many patient details. I refused to violate our patient's privacy for the sake of those grants. Fortunately, we received sufficient nonfederal monies to operate. However, the pressure was always there to apply to the feds.

In fact, after almost two years at the clinic, those pressures mounted from my board and others to the point that I decided to resign. But it wasn't just this pressure. Some volunteers proved to be uncooperative, and that created tensions for me. I also worked very hard over this time to make the clinic successful, and I found that I was getting burned out. I wasn't happy, and I resented the pressure from some board members who felt that I was letting down the clinic by not applying for federal grants.

All of this convinced me to resign. I left with some bitterness. But I've always felt that in life when you're unhappy—and if you can't change the conditions—why stay under those circumstances? You need to move on. So I did, in 1972.

I felt bad about resigning, but I knew that I had to go on with my life. Some time later, the clinic, along with other social agencies, gave me an award, the Mexican-American Woman of the Year Award, but I didn't attend the event to receive it. I had gone on.

MOVING ON AND SINGLE PARENTHOOD

After I left the second clinic, I had to deal with my personal and family life. I had to make a living, but not just for myself. Although I never married, I had two sons, Cuauhtémoc Arellanes and César Greywind Arellanes. This is a part of my life that I have chosen not to publicly discuss. I was a single mother. I wanted to go back to school and get a degree; however, I also knew that I had to work. I got a clerical job with the city of South El Monte. At the same time, I started taking classes at Rio Hondo College in Whittier. My hope was to then go on to Cal State, L.A. I got my associate's degree and transferred to Cal State with the hope of majoring in history. But I never graduated because the Department of Social Services informed me that, according to its rules, as soon as my first son turned six years of age I was no longer eligible for support. My son was turning six, and so I had no choice but to drop out of school and go back to work full-time.

I then began a series of jobs over the next two decades. Most were temporary. A friend then gave me a tip about a job at the county jail for women, the Sybil Brand Institute, and so I applied and was hired. Having to deal with the different inmates was a hard job, but I stuck at it and was even able to make some changes there as I got more responsibility. I created, for example, a bodybuilding gym in the jail. By then I had gotten into bodybuilding and so knew its health and psychological benefits. I moved up the ladder and eventually achieved a managerial position in charge of training others. I also wrote up some proposals for the sheriff's department. So I worked for the County Sheriff's Office from the 1990s until my retirement in 2005. I retired early due to work-related injuries of one kind or another that especially affected my hands. Eventually I had three surgeries for carpal tunnel syndrome.

My life hasn't been easy, but I'm a survivor.

Being a single mother, of course, only added to the pressures on me. When I had my first son, I was living in Lincoln Heights, but I soon moved back in with my mother. My dad had died around 1970. He was only forty-nine. But after I had my second son, I briefly moved to South El Monte. When my mother died in 1979 at the age of fifty-four, I moved back into the family house, and I've been here ever since.

My eldest son went on to get a PhD at UCLA in physical chemistry. He never became an academic and works instead for a big insurance company in downtown Los Angeles. My youngest son has had more difficulties. He got partially paralyzed but was able to overcome most of this. However, his hands will never be the same again. He lives in Phoenix, where he is completing college through online courses in which he can use voice-activated computers. I have two grandchildren, Diego Papesar (which means red-tail horse) and Elisa April, from my oldest son.

INDIGENOUS ROOTS

After I left the Chicano movement, I began to rediscover my indigenous California roots from my mother's side. I knew a little bit that we had indigenous ancestors from the California tribes, but I didn't know much more. I remember growing up asking my mother about this, but she quickly shut me up by saying, "We're Mexicans." As I look back on this, it had to do with the fact that many indigenous people, like my mother, felt it was more socially acceptable to be of Mexican descent and thought that they and their children might be spared the discrimination and racism directed at Indian people. Was she ashamed of being Indian? Maybe. But there was no basis for this. Of course, the complication is that, because of the Spanish conquest of the indigenous people in California, we were also part Mexican. My father, of course, was Mexican American, or Chicano. That's why I grew up identifying as a Chicana and not knowing much about my California indigenous side.

But this changed for me after I left the movement. I guess I was searching for a new identity, a new sense of who I was after the difficulties I had in the movement, especially as a woman. I began to ask more questions of my mother and my maternal aunts about this. I discovered that we descended from the Tongva tribe of Southern California who were renamed Gabrieleños, the name given to them by the Spaniards. But we were really Tongvas, which means "people of the earth." I also read books about the Tongvas, as well as talked to some who I discovered were tribe members. In this process, you don't ask questions of tribe members and certainly not of the elders. They pass on this knowledge to you. This is the respectful way. I actually learned more about Tongva culture from listening to the elders than I did from reading.

In the course of these discoveries, I also came to know that the father of my two sons was Tongva, and this motivated me to make sure that my sons grew up appreciating their indigenous background.

Knowing more about my roots, I joined a Tongva community and became active with others of my tribe. I still am. Every weekend I attend meetings and social gatherings. In fact, I'm on the board of directors of the American Indian Healing Center in Whittier. It also serves as a health clinic. I first sought out health services from it, and after they found out that I used to direct a free clinic, I was invited to be on the board.

Now that I'm older, I'm also considered an elder of the tribe. It's my responsibility to pass on my tribal knowledge to the younger members. Everything I've learned I'm supposed to give away to others. So I work with a youth group and teach them about our culture and values. I tell them that we believe that everything has a spirit. We respect the land and water. Water is very sacred to us. We respect one another. We respect animals. Of course, this is the respect that we need in human society and for our environment, which we are unfortunately destroying. After this rediscovery of my indigenous background, I find myself very much at peace with myself. I'm very blessed. I used to be loudmouthed, outspoken, and angry, shouting out "Viva la Raza!" However, now I've found a new balance within myself, even though it took me a long time to get there. I tell young people that in life there is a negative and a positive, and then there's a balance. "Always try to achieve the balance," I counsel them.

REFLECTIONS ON THE CHICANO MOVEMENT

When I look back on the Chicano movement over forty years ago, when I became involved with the Brown Berets, I no longer feel any anger or bitterness. I did what I had to do, and I'm proud of my actions. I'm especially proud of what I did with the Beret free clinic. I think that this was the Berets' most important community contribution, and it was the Beret women who did this. I'm very proud of the other Beret women for their hard work and contributions. I don't feel any regrets about this part of my life because it was my choice to become involved with the Berets and it was my choice to leave. I don't knock the movement; it was what it was, and it empowered a whole generation of activists. Chicano Power started to become a reality then, and it has continued to expand. Our communities still face many problems, but we have much more of a voice and the force to back it up. This is the legacy of the movement.

While I did divorce myself from the movement, I still kept in touch with some of the Beret women for a short while. They had also left very hurt and angry, and many of them never overcame these feelings. I think I did because I didn't dwell on them; I moved on. Although I hear from others that the former Beret women don't want to talk about their experiences in the movement, I think that it's important to do so, and so I feel that I speak for them. We as women played an important role in the Berets and in the movement, and this has to be acknowledged. This motivates me to tell my story, but it's also the story of the other women as well.

I think in part this is why I decided to participate in the recent movement reunions that Rosalio Muñoz and others have organized. Rosalio had to coax me into doing this, but I'm glad he did. I've enjoyed being reunited with other activists whom I haven't seen for years. I'm shocked to see how they have aged, and this only makes me think how old I must also look to them.

There was one funny incident at one of these reunions. I had a sore throat that day, and so when I spoke to the group someone called out across the room, "Can you speak up?"

"No, I can't."

"Well, can you stand in the middle?"

"No, I won't," I replied, because my legs were hurting.

It turned out I was having this exchange with Lydia López, a former activist and just a great person. Lydia was there with her walker due to her own physical problems. I later told Rosalio, "I thought us old ladies were going to go out of that meeting and take on the world again, except this time with our canes and walkers!"

Despite our age, those of us at these reunions still have our commitment to our communities and still recognize that the movement represented the cradle of that commitment. I'm shocked at how many of the younger generations of Chicanos and Latinos know so little, if anything, about the movement and what we did.

FIGURE 12. Gloria Arellanes and Rosalio Muñoz, October 2013. Courtesy of Rosalio Muñoz.

That's why these reunions and panels at universities are so important. This is a history that can be used to empower our young people to also struggle for social change.

Do I see myself as a historical figure? I think I have come to accept that, although it's taken some forty or more years to do so. I've been moved at how at these retrospective events, people still remember me, and, fortunately, this includes a few young people who say that they have heard about me. I was amazed to discover that some young women have restarted Las Adelitas. When I was introduced to them, they said, "Oh, gosh! You started Las Adelitas!" They treated me like a rock star.

I was especially moved when, for the fortieth anniversary of the Chicano moratorium, Rosalio designed a commemorative T-shirt with my image on it. I think it was taken from a Raul Ruiz photo of me at the March in the Rain protest. I was honored. I've heard that I've also been mentioned in some books, which I didn't even know about.

So, yes, I accept myself as a historical figure, but not just because of what I did. It's because of what the other women and I accomplished and because of our mutual struggles. My story is also their story, and I'm proud to tell it.

3

Rosalio Muñoz

My parents came from very different backgrounds. My father's family emigrated from Mexico, and my mother's family has deep roots in the Southwest. Yet they both came together, and my siblings and I are the result.

When I think back on my family history, I begin to appreciate the roots of my political values and commitment in my parents' background and how they raised us. I was particularly reminded of this when my dad, Dr. Rosalio Florian Muñoz, died in 2004. He was a wonderful and inspiring father and a historical figure in his own right. My mother, María de Socorro Urias, made sure—like most mothers— that we grew up with a sense of respect and an awareness of the importance of giving to others. She died in 2005. My political story is very much a continuation of their tradition.

Where does it all begin?

My father's family came from Mexico to the United States in 1918. My dad was five years old at that time. But unlike many other Mexican immigrants who were poor or peasants or from the working class, my father's family was more educated and middle class. My paternal Spanish-speaking grandfather, Esau P. Muñoz, was a Methodist minister and poet. His Protestantism further differentiated him from the predominant Catholic character of most Mexicans. He was also proud of his Sephardic roots. My grandfather was from northern Mexico, specifically from Saltillo, Coahuila.

By contrast, my paternal grandmother, Febronia Florian, was from the interior of Mexico, from the state of Michoacán. She too was educated; in fact, she was a teacher. Like my grandfather, she was also a Methodist. My grandparents met in northern Mexico and got married. This, of course, was during the Mexican Revolution of 1910, and many Mexicans were dislocated.

Married and already with three children, my grandparents crossed into El Paso. They didn't stay there but moved to several small towns in west Texas before settling in Arizona. There my grandfather continued to move from time to time and was minister to different Mexican Methodist congregations in mining towns such as Ray and Miami. He knew several languages, including Nahautl, the language of the Aztecs. Eventually he had seven children. My father was the eldest and graduated from high school in Phoenix, Arizona.

On my mother's side, her extended family had probably entered into what is now Arizona before Mexico achieved its independence from Spain. They were artisans and small business people. Her father's family settled in Tucson in about 1788. My maternal grandmother, Ignacia Terrazas de Urias, used to have memories of some of the Indian conflicts in Arizona after the U.S. occupation following the U.S.-Mexican War of the 1840s. My grandfather, Antonio Urias, worked for many years as a dry goods salesman for a U.S. firm, traveling in northern Mexico and the Southwest.

On both sides of my family, education was always stressed. Indeed, both families were way ahead of their times in promoting college, even for the women. Besides graduating from high school, my father attended a junior college, Phoenix Junior College, and then attended Arizona State Teachers College (later Arizona State University), where he got his BA in 1935 and then an MA in education in 1938. That same year he became a U.S. citizen. This was all during the Depression years of the 1930s. He actually had gotten a scholarship to attend the University of Chicago for his undergraduate education but turned it down in order to work and help provide for his family.

My mother attended college at the University of Arizona, where she graduated cum laude and became a teacher. When she met my dad in the late 1930s, she was teaching at a public grade school in St. John's, Arizona, along the northern Arizona–New Mexico border. She had just started to teach. My father, at first, was working as a social worker in St. John's. Later, after being naturalized, he became the principal of my mother's school. They courted for a while and then got married in 1940.

This actually was my dad's second marriage. Although I don't know much about this side of his story, I know that he had married earlier and had one child, my half sister, Margaret. The marriage didn't work and ended in divorce. Whatever happened to his first wife, I know little. My parents and older siblings kept in touch with Margaret.

My father's divorce affected his marriage to my mother. My mother was raised Catholic in a very religious family. The idea was that they would get permission to get married in the Catholic Church. They even wrote to the pope for a dispensation, but they never heard from him or any other Church official. As a result, they eloped and got married in 1940 in a civil ceremony somewhere in New Mexico.

My parents complemented each other. The fact that they were both very well educated for that period, especially in comparison to other Mexican Americans, helped a great deal. My mother was also, for her time, a liberated and socially active woman.

One of the things I learned about my father's life in Arizona was that during the 1930s, he and a few other Mexican American students at Arizona State Teachers College, including his sisters Josephine, Rebecca, and Lucinda, organized a club called Los Conquistadores. The club held social events for Mexican American college students and, more important, raised money for scholarships to encourage, recruit, and retain other young Mexican American men and women. This club was similar to the better-known MAM, or Mexican American Movement, in Los Angeles, which was doing the same kind of work. There were conferences between both groups. Félix Gutiérrez, a UCLA graduate and one of the leaders of MAM, met and married my father's sister Rebecca, who became active in MAM. Their son, Dr. Félix Gutiérrez Jr., a well-known scholar at USC, is my cousin. MAM published a newspaper called the *Mexican Voice* and, in one of its late 1930s issues, reported on a speech my father gave in Arizona, titled "Our Place in American Democracy: A Heritage and a Challenge." In what the paper called an "inspirational speech," my dad stressed the fact that Mexican Americans should not consider this country a foreign country because our ancestors had settled in the Southwest well before the Anglo-Americans arrived.[1]

While living in St. John's, my parents started their family. My older sister, María Rosalia, was born in January 1942, and my older brother, Ricardo, was born later in December of that same year in Bisbee. However, World War II interrupted family life when my dad joined the navy.

Although he was a college man, my dad was not made a commissioned officer. I don't understand that. Instead, he was a chief petty officer in intelligence. He monitored phone calls from Mexico as well as worked on the navy codes. He didn't see any combat, although he served in the South Pacific. When the war ended, the navy offered him a commission, but by then my dad was ready to go home. Still, he was proud of having been in the navy.

I, of course, was part of the post–World War II baby boom. I was born June 29, 1946, in Flagstaff, Arizona. My family had moved there when my dad found a job as a social worker.

After being in Flagstaff for about a year, my father decided to move to Los Angeles to do graduate work at the University of Southern California. He took advantage of the GI Bill to help finance his graduate education. He was in school (while working) from about 1948 to 1957 and received both an MA in social work in 1949 and later a PhD in education. His dissertation was on school dropouts. He was one of the very few Mexican Americans with a PhD at that time. He began a career in school social work for the Los Angels city schools and continued to do so after he completed his doctorate. Eventually, he became a top LA city school supervisor, until his retirement. He also taught educational psychology courses at USC, San Fernando Valley State College (later Cal State, Northridge), and Cal State, Los Angeles.

COMING OF AGE

When we moved to L.A., where we had some relatives, we first lived in the Belvedere section of East L.A. on Fifth Street. We then moved to the Maravilla Projects and public housing. That's where my first memories are. I don't remember much, except that it was fairly multiracial then. You could hear country music coming from some homes and *rancheras* (Mexican country songs) from others. I was baptized at La Soledad Catholic Church.

While living at the Maravilla Projects, my younger brother, Carlos, was born in 1948. My mother, besides raising us, also from time to time worked as a secretary. She never went back into teaching. It was around this time, in 1951, that we moved to Lincoln Heights, close to downtown Los Angeles but still considered part of Greater East L.A.

With more income, plus the elimination of prewar housing covenants that had prohibited Mexicans from buying or renting in much of Lincoln Heights, my dad bought a home in the Heights. I still remember the address: 143 South Avenue 23. It's still there. A year later, Elvira, my youngest sister, was born.

Like other parts of East L.A. then, Lincoln Heights still had some ethnic diversity. Some parts were becoming predominantly Chicano. Some, like where we lived, had Italians and working-class whites.

I started my schooling when we moved to Lincoln Heights. I attended the Avenue 21 School and later the Gates School. In general, I have good memories of that experience. I particularly remember my first-grade teacher, but not her name. I was her pet. She would give me candies and stuff like that. My mother was quite involved in the Gates School and served as president of the PTA. Of course, my two older siblings were going through school ahead of me, and that helped a lot; I learned from their experiences. None of us faced a language problem since English was our dominant language at home. My parents were bilingual but deliberately spoke English at home, especially to ensure that we learned English well in order not to have problems at school. At the same time, my parents were proud of being Mexicans.

We children attended eight o'clock Catholic Mass with our mother and Methodist Sunday schools at nine thirty, where Dad went. Our whole extended family was active in both denominations, Catholic and Methodist. We read the Bible every night. My dad would read it to us. When my dad was not at home, my mother had us say the Hail Mary and the Lord's Prayer. I don't know that I was particularly devout as a kid, but I did like to be the one who memorized some verses best. Our religion gave us strongly held values and codes that influenced us. The Methodist church also stressed leadership, since the faithful exercised strong leadership in the church, and undoubtedly this influenced our socialization. I grew up thinking people were good. Human beings were good. We were God's children.

Of course, life also contained problems. Ricardo, for example, was in the church's Boy Scouts program but encountered some racism. He was being taunted and harassed by some of the older Anglo kids who were Scouts. Ricardo was very hurt and humiliated, but he fought back. He got together some of his friends (Chicanos, whites, blacks, and Asians), and they all went and confronted the Boy Scout leader. "You don't mess around with Ricardo," was the message they delivered. Ricardo had no more problems after that. This incident, as I remembered it later, showed that when you organize against a problem, you can overcome it.

I also later joined the Cub Scouts and Boy Scouts that were affiliated with our Methodist church. I think being a Scout helped develop my leadership traits.

It was good to have an older brother like Ricardo. He always looked out for me. Our family was a very close and tight-knit unit. Of course, my mom was the hub of the family. She was a wonderful mother and a great cook! She was also a wonderful pianist and loved to play the piano. She played both classical and some popular tunes, but not rock. My favorite was the swing tune "In the Mood."

Although family and neighborhood life in Lincoln Heights was good, I also recall that we boys would be afraid when we encountered the police. We were too young to be conscious of it, but this was a time of much police-Chicano friction. In Lincoln Heights in 1951 what came to be referred to as the Bloody Christmas incident occurred, when on Christmas Eve of that year police detained and brutally beat up several young Chicanos. This was also the time of mass raids by immigration officials in East L.A. and elsewhere in the Southwest against undocumented immigrants, which culminated in 1954 in Operation Wetback, when more than a million Mexican immigrants were deported to Mexico.[2]

We didn't then know all these facts. But even as young kids we sensed that the cops weren't our friends. So we became apprehensive when a police squad car came down the street.

My own parents weren't political activists then, although my dad did support Edward Roybal, the first Mexican American elected to the city council in the twentieth century. He was elected in 1949 and reelected several times; then in 1962 he was elected to the U.S. Congress, where he served for many years.

Overall, my elementary school years were good ones. I have many good memories. I did very well in school and received many As. My favorite subject was history, the subject I would major in later on in college.

HIGHLAND PARK

In 1956 we moved again. By this time my father was completing his PhD at USC, which he received in 1957, and was moving up the administrative ladder in the public school system. This meant a higher salary, which made it possible for us to afford better and larger housing. We also moved because new freeway construction was tearing up Lincoln Heights. So we moved to Highland Park, an area north of Lincoln Heights. It was a mixed working-class and middle-class district, with better schools. We bought our house in a middle-class neighborhood in the hills of Highland Park. It was predominantly a white area. My parents continued to live in that house on York Boulevard for nearly fifty years, until their deaths.

It felt strange to move into an unfamiliar neighborhood. We didn't know the kids, and they didn't know us. For quite a while I wasn't invited into another kid's house, nor did I invite them to mine. We continued, for example, to attend our Methodist church in Lincoln Heights.

I was enrolled at the Garvanza School, where I finished my elementary schooling. I had no friends there either. In fact, that was where I had my first school fight. Actually, these fights weren't at the school but at a nearby playground. My first fight was with a guy who was half Anglo and half Mexican. The next fight was with an Italian American. I think I may have fought one or two Anglos, but there were too many of them, so I gave up fighting. I became nonviolent.

In Highland Park I attended Luther Burbank Junior High. But, like my neighborhood, junior high was a completely new and estranged experience. It was predominantly white. If I go back and look at the yearbook I might discover some diversity, but I know that in my classes, which were the more advanced, it was mostly white students. I was one of the exceptions, often the only one.

Maybe because I felt alienated and discriminated against in junior high, I didn't do as well academically as in elementary school. I went from being an A student to receiving Bs and Cs. I think too that I lacked a certain experience that the Anglo kids had, especially coming from "white" schools.

Yet, interestingly, because I was bright, some of the other students copied from me. Yet while they received As, I still received only Bs and Cs. I think now it must have had to do with some level of discrimination or the classic low expectations by teachers of Mexican American students such as myself.

These low expectations—if that's what it was—ironically even included the sole Mexican American teacher at Luther Burbank, a Mr. Pacheco, our Spanish teacher. In one of my Spanish classes he gave me an AUU. This meant an A in subject matter, but unsatisfactory in cooperation and work habits. This was such a contradictory and ridiculous grade that even my homeroom teacher couldn't buy it. He forced Mr. Pacheco to change it. Pacheco, the first Mexican American Republican I ever met, changed it to ASS with a smile on his face.

At one point, despite the fact that I was bright, they tried to put me in the lower-level academic track with slower learners, including most of the other Chicanos in the school. I just remember what a disaster this experience was. There seemed to be no effort at teaching and learning in these classes. The teacher couldn't control the kids. Spitballs were flying all around. They would have us read out loud in class, and most of the students could barely do so. By comparison, I was an excellent reader. On top of this, when we were administered the infamous IQ test, I tested out with a 154 IQ, perhaps the highest in the school. And when they realized that my dad was a PhD and a rising administrator in the L.A. school district, they couldn't possibly keep me in the lower track. After just a short while, I was placed in the college track.

Fortunately, I received academic reinforcement at home. Besides my dad reading to us from the Bible, he would also read other books, such as those by Joseph Conrad as well as by other authors. I also did a lot of reading on my own. My dad had these books on naval history, such as the life of John Paul Jones, which I would read. My dad had also bought us a set of the *Britannica Junior Encyclopedia* just before we moved. I just about read it entirely. My teachers at Luther Burbank would sometimes be surprised that I knew certain things.

But, on the whole, junior high did not represent my most memorable years. I didn't do as well academically as I was capable of doing. I was a bit alienated and felt marginalized because of our move to Highland Park. Because of all of this and more, I wasn't very popular in school. I wasn't hated or anything like that, but I just didn't stand out. I wasn't an "in" kind of kid. Some students did like me and wrote in my yearbook comments like "very sweet" and "nice guy." Junior high was clearly an adjustment period for me.

HIGH SCHOOL YEARS

From Luther Burbank Junior High I went to Franklin High School, where my older brother and sister had also attended and from where they graduated and went on to college. I started high school in the fall of 1960. Franklin included the tenth, eleventh, and twelfth grades. It was a bit more working class, and so there were a greater variety of students, including more Chicanos. It probably was about 30 percent Chicano. However, this was not the percentage of Chicanos who graduated. That rate, unfortunately, was much lower.

High school was particularly memorable for me in a lot of ways. I stayed in the college prep classes and got decent grades, mostly Bs and As and some Cs.

I also began to participate in sports, especially basketball. That was my favorite sport, even though I was short. But I was quick player, a good dribbler, and a pretty good shot. There were three teams—A, B, and C. The A team was the varsity. I first played on the C team and was a starter the second year. Finally, in my senior year, I had a chance to play on the varsity. I actually had sprung up a bit more between my junior and senior year. I went from being five feet one inch to five feet six inches. I broke into the starting team during the season.

I got along pretty well with my teachers. However, there was one exception: Mr. Ferraro, my civics teacher. I referred to him as a "little Mussolini." He later was elected to the school board for several terms. He was a strict disciplinarian and a right-winger politically. He would tell us that the communists, including the FBI, infiltrated the government in Washington. He sometimes harassed me, probably because I was Mexican. But Ferraro was more of an exception, since there were many liberal white teachers who were influenced by the civil rights movement. It was some of these teachers who interceded for me and protected me from Ferraro, whom they very much disliked. Because of them, at my graduation I won the award for Scholar/Athlete.

Although I was mainly English dominant, my Spanish improved when my dad took a sabbatical leave from his job and we spent it in Mexico. This was during my junior year in high school, and I just took a leave from school for the year. Since I was a year younger than my classmates, taking a year off from school did not set me back with respect to my age cohort. We traveled throughout Mexico because part of my dad's intent was to study Mexico's school system to better understand Mexican immigrant students. He interviewed administrators in different Mexican states.

We, of course, took in the impressive tourist sites, such as the great pyramids at Teotihuacán. We went to the fabulous museums. I'll never forget going with my family to attend a performance by the Amalia Hernández Ballet Folklórico in the stately confines of Bellas Artes. I wasn't a Chicano nationalist then, but something ethnic stirred within me. All these sights and sounds impressed upon me a great pride in being of Mexican background, which I'm sure later played a role in my Chicano movement identity and politics.

While our visit to Mexico made me appreciate my Mexican heritage more, I didn't necessarily have a strong ethnic identity in high school. Back in Lincoln Heights my friends had been of different ethnic backgrounds. Moving to Highland Park did not significantly change my ethnic identity and certainly didn't lead to a greater Mexican or Chicano political consciousness. That would come later. Most of my friends were white.

At Franklin I wasn't in any kind of social group. Some of the Chicanos stuck together, but I wasn't into that. My own friends continued to be of different ethnic backgrounds, including some Chicanos. But this didn't mean I was ashamed that I was of Mexican descent. I knew that. At the same time, however, the other students called me "Ross" rather than Rosalio.

In high school I wasn't really interested in politics or political issues. I don't even remember that I had much of a reaction to the assassination of President Kennedy in 1963.

My heroes then were sports figures such as Elgin Baylor of the L.A. Lakers. I considered myself more of an intellectual in high school, especially by my senior year. Although I was not a full A student, I did get good grades and graduated with a 3.5. My teachers considered me to be a "smart Mexican." But I think I learned more out of class than in school. I became interested in ideas and began reading books not assigned in class. I read voraciously, especially history. This in large part was due to the influence of my brother, Ricardo, who was at UCLA. He lived in the dorms, but when he would come home on weekends, he would bring some of the books he was reading for his classes. I remember that he introduced me to the writings of John Dos Passos, especially his *U.S.A.* trilogy. When Ricardo finished reading them, I would read them. I've forgotten some of the other books he read, but some of them were, as I recall, pretty radical texts, especially in history and literature.

One highlight of my senior year was that some of my friends encouraged me to run for a student-body position.

"Ross," one of my friends said, "you should think about running for an office. You're going to college, and this will help you."

I wasn't at first sure of doing this. But after I thought about it, I told my friend, "Okay, I'll run, but I'm going to run for student-body president."

I didn't know about campaigning, but I got a lot of help from my friends and from my younger brother, who was a sophomore and convinced a lot of his class-mates to vote for me. I probably also benefited from the fact that my opponent was not a very strong candidate. He was a nice guy but didn't seem all that serious. The only real opposition, curiously enough, came from Mr. Ferraro, who had it in for me. I later learned that he went around the cafeteria telling students, "Don't sup-port Muñoz." Fortunately, Ferraro's tactics were countered by some of the other faculty and coaches coming to my defense and putting Ferraro in his place.

I won the election and became the first Mexican American student-body presi-dent of Franklin. In fact, another Mexican American was elected vice president of the student body.

My election, of course, gave me a certain stature in the school. I become better known and more popular. Being student-body president didn't carry much author-ity. It was mostly ceremonial. I presided over student-council meetings that dealt with student and campus issues, but nothing really substantial. I also opened for school assemblies and introduced guest speakers. I enjoyed it, and it certainly pre-pared me for future leadership challenges.

It was also in my senior year that I began dating. For the first time I had a girl-friend. She was an Anglo-Scottish girl, Julie McGuckim, whose family was from Ohio. She was new in the school. She once came up to me and said, "Hey, my name's Julie. What's your name?" She was actually part of the in-crowd. She lived in the Mount Washington area of Highland Park, which was one of the much nicer neighborhoods. She liked me, and we started seeing each other.

Because my brother and sister were already in college, I had no doubt that I would follow. Of course, my parents were college graduates and my father a PhD. As far as I was concerned, there was only one college for me: UCLA. It was the only school I applied to in my senior year. We had some college counselors, but they never made an effort to talk to me. I was accepted, although I didn't receive a scholarship or any kind of financial grant. I hadn't applied for a scholarship. My dad was paying for my brother and sister and fully expected to do so for me also, although we all worked during the summers.

At my high school graduation, I was glad that I was graduating because it meant that I would be going on to college and a more intellectually simulating environment. I was looking forward to what life had in store for me. Maybe I had a little bit of a sense of destiny. My developing worldview was to learn in order to make a better world. This came from my family's influence of helping people and wanting to know the truth. My parents and family, of course, were excited, and everyone came to the ceremony and took lots of pictures. But these large high school graduations are not very intimate or personal affairs since there are so many graduates. My name was almost lost among so many others. I was very conscious, however, to make sure that when they called my name out it would be my proper name— "Rosalio" and not the "Ross" that my friends knew me by. I don't think this was a political idea on my part. It was more a matter of pride in self and family.

UCLA

Going to UCLA in 1964 was, of course, an adjustment. It was quite a change from high school. To begin with, the campus was huge. But what helped was that my older brother and sister were already there. If I had my questions about the campus, where to go, who to see, and what classes I had to take, I just asked them.

In fact, I lived with Ricardo my freshman year. Ricardo, who was now a senior, was sharing an apartment in Westwood, right off campus, with two of his white friends. I enjoyed living with them. It was a lot of fun, and they introduced me to a lot of parties and girls. There were lots of beautiful women on campus, and it was mind-blowing.

Before classes started, I went to the orientation. I had decided to major in history, since I had always liked it and had read some of Ricardo's college history books. I went to the history-major orientation in Royce Hall with several hundred other students. The one thing that sticks in my mind about this meeting is that one of the history professors told us that we should take a foreign language, but it shouldn't be Spanish or another "minor" language. "The only two languages that you'll need as a history major," he said, "are German and French. These are the key intellectual languages." Somehow, I don't remember reacting negatively to what I now know was an absurd and even racist statement. But I didn't have a Chicano political consciousness yet. I knew Spanish, even though if I didn't use it, I became rusty. I had taken Spanish as part of my SAT tests and had gotten a 770. So I figured I really didn't need to take Spanish in college. I followed the professor's advice, and I enrolled in French.

One thing that was very noticeable to me as I started out at UCLA was how few other Mexican Americans attended. I saw some here and there and saw one or two in my classes, but there weren't very many. In fact, there were also very few blacks. Later, when I started working for the early affirmative-action programs on campus, I saw the figures. In 1964 there were no more than fifty-two Mexican Americans attending UCLA as undergraduates. The number went up a bit each year, but not by much. It wasn't until after the 1968 Chicano student blowouts or walkouts in East L.A. that these figures rose dramatically.

In fact, in a city where the largest minority was Mexican, there were more blacks at UCLA, especially athletes.

Mexican Americans, like myself, were not identifiable as a particular ethnic group on campus. Because other students never considered Mexican Americans to be students, I was asked several times during my undergraduate years if I, with my dark skin and straight black hair, was from India. Was I a foreign student? Even students from India asked me if I was from India! This was weird. People just didn't expect to see Mexicans at UCLA. I'm not sure how I thought about all this at first. I think that I was ambivalent. I didn't really think in ethnic terms yet. I was still Ross Muñoz. Rosalio Muñoz had not yet surfaced.

BECOMING AN ACTIVIST

Although I did well initially in my classes, I struggled the rest of my freshman year and into my sophomore one. It wasn't that my classes were too hard, but that I felt a certain alienation, some of it being personal and having to do with breaking up with my high school girlfriend.

However, things began to change for me in my junior year. This proved to be a turning-point year for me. Not only was I now an upper-division history major, but, more important to me, I became more of an activist on campus, even though my political consciousness was just barely being formed.

One of the first projects I got involved with was helping to organize a new experimental school completely controlled by students. This was a kind of "university without walls." I got involved because one day the editor of the *Daily Bruin,* Neil Reichline, whom I had met, invited me to a meeting to discuss establishing an experimental college patterned after a similar one at San Francisco State. The idea was for students to set up classes on their own on whatever topics they wished. While some faculty might participate, it would be students who would control the classes.

I liked the idea and went to the meeting. There was a lively discussion of the nature of such a project. We kept talking about the concept, but we never got down to discussing how to put it together. So at some point someone said, "Well, who's willing to do something?" I added, "I might want to organize a class. I wouldn't teach it, but I'd be willing to talk about things if other people will."

Others also said they would help put together classes, but someone was needed to coordinate all of this.

"Why don't you do it?" Neil, the editor, turned to me.

"Well, okay, someone has to do it," I responded.

The next day I was amazed to see an article in the *Daily Bruin* about the experimental college, with a quote from Ross Muñoz. The quote had to do with supporting the idea. I didn't remember if I had actually said this, or if Neil had just written it for me. With this article in the paper, I felt I couldn't back out of this project, even if I wanted to.

The student government agreed to support the experiment. They gave us a small budget and an office with a phone. The next step was to organize a series of classes for the rest of the academic year. Since we had the quarter system, these classes would be for the winter and spring quarters. We got the word out about needing students to volunteer to put together classes. These were noncredit classes. Students would attend them because they were interested in the topics. A student would get the discussion going, but they would be freewheeling classes.

Soon several classes were organized. I organized one called Affluence and Leisure. I was influenced by some of my classes, in which we discussed *The Affluent Society* and how the United States had achieved one of the highest, if not the highest, standard of living in the world.[3] But I was also influenced by my own reading, which pointed out that if we had such affluence, then we also could afford full employment and a guaranteed minimum wage. I argued that there didn't need to be scarcity and that we didn't have to wait for the "hidden hand" in the form of a market economy to take care of people more in need. These are the kinds of things we discussed in my class.

I remember someone else doing a class on parapsychology and another called Psycho-Sexual Paralysis and the Contemporary Syndrome. Then the W. E. B. Du Bois Club on campus, which was a Marxist group, sponsored a class on Marxism. Someone did a class on George Bernard Shaw. There were all kinds of classes, some serious and some not so serious. But they were opportunities for students to explore topics that interested them, away from the more traditional and less innovative classes offered in the regular curriculum. Classes were held, for the most part, in student apartments, in the dorms, and in churches or other off-campus facilities. The classes were like bull sessions, but they worked. There were no assigned readings, no tests, and no grades. We met once a week and discussed a variety of topics.

The experimental college was an extension of the free speech movement and of a new, more active student initiative about their education. This was the sixties at UCLA. We were saying that the students should not be seen as just passive learning subjects, completely dependent on a hierarchical academic structure. We could teach ourselves and learn from one another. Our chancellor, Franklin Murphy, had called UCLA a "marketplace of ideas," so we countered by calling our experimental college the "corner market of ideas." Other campuses developed similar projects.

I thought the whole experiment was a success, and I became identified with it. I also developed my abilities to interact effectively with a broad range of people.

During this time, I was hired part-time by the nonacademic counseling center to participate in the discussion of methods and perspectives for making the university a more human, fulfilling, and less threatening experience. It was really also a subsidy for my other pursuits.

My activities on campus further accelerated when, in the spring quarter of my junior year in 1967, I decided to run for student council. I hadn't thought of this myself, but one day when I was in my experimental college, the president of the student council, whose office was just down the corridor, poked his head in and started a conversation. We talked about the work I was doing.

"You know, we really need people to run for student council," he said. "Why don't you run? That way you can get even more resources for the work you're doing."

I thought about it, and I don't remember what I responded, but I did decide to run. Why not?

I still didn't know much about campaigning, but what really helped was that I got a lot of good coverage by the *Daily Bruin*. The paper had already featured me in some stories about the experimental college, so the editors knew me. Moreover, the staff was composed of fewer fraternity types and more independents, including a large number of Jewish students. By comparison, the student council was more "Greek" in orientation and more Anglo. There was a rivalry between the two. But the paper's coverage of my candidacy was crucial. I think people respected what I was doing and how the experimental college was meeting a felt need.

I was further helped by a lot of the students involved in the experimental college. They rallied behind me and encouraged others to vote for me. They helped pass out my campaign flyers and got the vote out on election day.

Election day, by coincidence, fell on May 5—Cinco de Mayo. This Mexican holiday was not yet big on campus, but I was aware of it, and so my campaign slogan became "¡Viva Muñoz, Cinco de Mayo!" I still didn't yet have a Chicano consciousness associated with a political movement, but my slogan did, looking back, represent my ethnic consciousness and even pride. Without making a big deal about it, my parents had socialized us to not be ashamed of our ethnic roots.

In the election there was only one opponent, a representative of one of the dorms. He was a nice guy, but I won handily, 54 percent to 46 percent. My election only increased my involvement in student politics in my senior year.

My first challenge in office was to help produce the students' first professor evaluation forms. In their registration packet, students were provided with computer cards, on which they could rate professors from zero to ten on several "objective questions." On the back, they could write responses to a few open-ended questions. My job was to summarize these "subjective responses." Though only a fraction of students filled out the cards and even fewer wrote comments, I still read the thoughts of thousands of students about their concrete educational experiences. I think that I did a good job, and the evaluation had a big impact. It gave students a voice and effective leverage for better responses to our thoughts and feelings. Personally, it gave me confidence and some respect among concerned faculty and administrators and many students as a voice for educational reform.

CHICANO STUDENT POLITICS

Besides my involvement in the experimental college and student council, I also began to get involved with UMAS, or the United Mexican American Students. This was one of the first Chicano student organizations, not only at UCLA but also at other California campuses. By my junior year, due to affirmative action, a few more Chicanos were being recruited to attend college, and this was true of other campuses in L.A.

It was Ricardo who initially made me aware of UMAS. He had been bringing some of the gang youth he was working with to visit UCLA, and when he did this he would try to get me involved. I would help show them around the campus. This was Ricardo's way of sensitizing me to Chicano issues and the vatos to greater social awareness.

As part of this, Ricardo invited me, somewhere in my junior year, to go with him to a meeting in East L.A. to discuss the organization of a Chicano student organization. This came to be UMAS. I somewhat reluctantly went. At the meeting there were just a few Chicanos, but they were all very excited about organizing Chicano students. I especially remember Monte Pérez, who I think at the time was a student counselor or recruiter at Cal State, L.A.

In the fall of 1967 UMAS formed at UCLA. I went to some of the initial meetings, which consisted of about twenty or thirty students, including undergraduates such as Moctesuma Esparza from Lincoln High School in East L.A., as well as

Ramses Noriega, Susan Racho, Roberto Sifuentes, and Evelyn Márquez. Then there were outspoken graduate students such as Juan Gómez-Quiñones and Ron López in history and Reynaldo Macias in education. They all spoke in Spanish. That intimidated me because my Spanish had become rusty again. Needless to say, I didn't say very much. I wasn't really going to the meetings to join, but more to observe and find out what was going on. I felt I should be there for moral support. I was also becoming a bit more ethnically aware, and so this also motivated me to attend. I think, too, that Ricardo was encouraging me to join UMAS. At the meetings, I wasn't too knowledgeable because the students discussed mostly community issues, and I, of course, was immersed mainly in campus ones.

Later that fall, I think, there was a general UMAS conference at USC that brought together the different UMAS chapters throughout the L.A. area. Although I didn't yet consider myself an UMAS member, I attended. There were a couple of hundred Chicanos there, which was impressive given the small number of Chicano students in college at that time. What was even more impressive to me was the discussion of what came to be called the Guzmán Report. This report was written by Professor Ralph Guzmán, a political scientist at Cal State, L.A., who had also been a member of a Ford Foundation–sponsored research project based in UCLA. In the report Guzmán documented the particularly high Chicano casualties in Vietnam. Chicanos made up about 10 percent of the population in five southwestern states, including California, and yet, according to Guzmán, they made up 20 percent of the casualties from the region. What also impressed me was how some of the student leaders were linking Chicano casualties in Vietnam to the lack of attention to the many social problems in the barrios, such as unemployment, high dropout rates in the schools, gang violence, and so on. "They're screwing us in Vietnam," one speaker exclaimed, "and they're screwing us in our barrios!" Whatever I might have already been feeling about the war then was now beginning to be influenced by the developing Chicano movement.

My involvement with UMAS increased sometime later, when I was asked as a member of the student government to request funds for a UMAS-sponsored symposium. I really should say I was encouraged to do this. Moctesuma Esparza, who had emerged as a key UMAS leader, cornered me one day and told me that UMAS wanted to organize this symposium on Mexican Americans. They needed funds to get speakers and for the other expenses of the symposium. They wanted the student government to provide the needed funds.

"You're the only Mexican American on the student council," Moctesuma told me, "so we want your support."

"How much money do you need?" I asked.

"Well, we're thinking of inviting Reies López Tijerina, Corky Gonzales, and a few others, so we have to pay their travel and give them an honorarium. I think we need several thousand dollars."

"Several thousand!" I exclaimed. "I don't know that I can get that much; that's a lot."

"Look, Muñoz," Moctesuma further cornered me. "Look at yourself in the mirror. You're an Indian. You are going to be in this movement whether you want to or not."

Somehow I didn't feel offended at Moctesuma's tactic. In fact, I agreed with what he was saying. I begin to realize that this was the direction I was heading—to identify with the new Chicano movement. I was becoming Chicano. The fact was that I also could really help.

We got the funds, and the symposium, held in mid-February 1968, was a huge success. We packed one of the larger halls on campus. We hired buses to bring in students from the East L.A. high schools. Community people also attended, as did Chicano students from other L.A. colleges. Corky Gonzales from Denver spoke, as did Tijerina from New Mexico, along with Luis Valdez and Bert Corona.

The speaker I remember the most, and the one who had the most impact on me, was Reies López Tijerina, the fiery and militant leader of the land-grant movement in New Mexico. I was particularly impressed because he spoke in Spanish. But it wasn't just his use of Spanish; it was his evangelical style of speaking. I learned later that he had been a Pentecostal preacher, and his speech showed that. It was incredible! I remember him saying, "This is our land, the Southwest; it was taken from us by the U.S. in its war against Mexico, but it's still our land." This statement in Spanish from Tijerina also hit me like a bomb. "Maybe he has something there," I thought to myself. "Our land."[4]

I was becoming more attracted to this type of nationalistic Chicano ideology, but with limits. When the concept of Aztlán became part of chicanismo—the cultural nationalistic ideology of the movement—I never became obsessive about that idea of the original homeland of the Aztecs somehow being the Chicano homeland as well. I think other students were more into that. My ethnic consciousness was beginning to stir, but I remained more focused on concrete and practical social change. I never fully became an ideologue.

As a result of the symposium, I became more involved with UMAS. I attended more meetings and was accepted as a member. I had always felt a bit tentative about UMAS because my Spanish wasn't that good and also because I didn't come from the hard-core barrio. But I soon discovered that the Chicano students in UMAS came from diverse backgrounds, and not all were fluent in Spanish either. I didn't become a big leader in UMAS, but I felt that I could contribute in my own way, especially with my connections to student government. I felt like other UMAS students came to respect me.

A couple of weeks after the symposium, the blowouts—in which thousands of Chicano students protested their inferior education and lack of access to higher education—occurred in the East L.A. schools. This was a defining moment for the

Chicano movement in L.A. It really got the movement going. I personally wasn't involved in the blowouts, but other UMAS students, such as Moctesuma, were. They helped organize and protect the kids who walked out. Part of the fallout that did affect me was that the blowouts shocked universities such as UCLA into recognizing how few Chicanos attended college in the L.A. area. Pressured by the blowouts to respond, UCLA, as well as the other schools, began to implement stronger affirmative-action programs to recruit Chicano and black students. In one year the Chicano enrollment went from a couple of hundred to more than two thousand!

After the students had walked out of the schools that March 1968, a couple of months later, in early June, thirteen Chicanos were arrested and charged with conspiracy to cause the blowouts. These were not the high school students themselves but some of the college students, including Moctesuma. Others arrested included Brown Beret leaders, editors of *La Raza* newspaper, and UMAS activists. The most celebrated arrest, however, was that of Sal Castro, the Mexican American teacher at Lincoln High School who had inspired the students to walk out. Those arrested became known as the East L.A. Thirteen.

Within a day after their arrests, a large rally was held in downtown L.A., I think at the city jail. I learned about it and went. It was impressive. The arrested Chicanos, the protesters claimed, were really political prisoners. I agreed with that and protested their arrests. I made a sign saying, "Viva Moctesuma Esparza."

I became further involved in the aftermath of the blowouts when UMAS appointed me as its representative to a new student-faculty-administrator task force established by the chancellor. Of the two committees under this task force, one was concerned with developing ethnic studies centers on campus, and the other focused specifically on Chicano and black student recruitment. I chaired the recruitment committee and worked through the summer. In this work, and as a result of the blowouts and the general civil rights unrest in the country, I emphasized that we needed to recruit Chicano and black students who might not meet the entrance requirements of the UC system, and specifically at UCLA, but who showed promise and potential. These included many of the students who had participated in the walkouts.

The administration was not too keen on this idea. They wanted to recruit more minority students but at the same time maintain the high requirements, such as in GPA and SAT scores. I, and other students on the committee, pointed out that this was impossible. It was the high and strict requirements that were part of the problem, in addition to the weaker schools in places such as East L.A. Affirmative action, as far as we were concerned, meant special-action admission for minority students. While some administrators remained doubtful, the chancellor accepted this recommendation, not just from us but also from faculty bodies, and began to implement special-action recruitment, referred to as the High Potential Program. Within a year this program helped lead to significant increases of Chicano students at UCLA. Despite problems over time, this type of student recruitment has paid dividends. Many prominent Chicano and Latino professionals and political leaders achieved their college education through such programs, not only at UCLA but at other campuses as well.

The increasing political activities of Chicanos on and off campus unfortunately led to some racial backlash as well. Toward the end of the spring quarter in 1968, some frat guys put on what they called a "Viva Zapata Party" to make fun of *mexicanos* and Chicanos. At their party they had a big replica of the Mexican flag, but instead of the eagle in the middle, it had a big middle finger. They were giving us and other Chicanos the finger! The UMAS members were mad as hell. We decided to protest and to demand that the chancellor expel the fraternity from campus. The chancellor listened to us, but in the end only temporarily suspended the fraternity. But this didn't end the issue. Several fraternities joined together to counterprotest the suspension of the one fraternity. They claimed that the frat party was all in fun and that we Chicanos had overreacted. A "Greek Power" rally of hundreds was held. On top of this, the Greek frats pressured the student government to go on record against the fraternity suspension.

This was the last straw for me. I resigned from the student government. I resigned out of principle, but it also gained me even more respect within UMAS. I'll never forget Ramses Noriega, whom I would come to develop a close political relationship with, coming up to me and telling me how much he respected me for what I had done. I was deeply hurt and angry with the student council. I realized how much anti-Mexican sentiment there was in Southern California.

During the summer of 1968, politics both on and off campus was steaming up. Of course, 1968 was a politically explosive year, with the Martin Luther King and Bobby Kennedy assassinations. I, along with other UMAS students, campaigned for Kennedy due to his support for the farmworkers and blowouts and African American issues as well. For the first time I got involved in supporting César Chávez and the farmworkers' struggle. There was a farmworkers' support group on campus, and several UMAS members participated in it. The group picketed our Student Union to stop buying grapes that the farmworkers' union was boycotting and offering these grapes in the cafeteria. I supported the picketing. Tension increased when one day the picketers decided to enter the Student Union and stage a sit-in. I was actually on my way to get lunch at the cafeteria when the protesters saw me.

"Ross, come join us. We're going to sit here until they get rid of the grapes."

What choice did I have? I supported the grape strike and boycott, so I sat down with the others and became their spokesperson. Fortunately, the manager of the union realized that not only would the sit-in be disruptive but it also would be in the news. He didn't want that and quickly agreed to stop buying the grapes. This impressed upon me the power of public protest.

STUDENT-BODY PRESIDENT

Although I should have graduated in the spring of 1968, I couldn't because I had cut back on credits and had some incompletes, and so I needed to stay on for another quarter. In a way, that was fortuitous because it opened up a new and interesting challenge for me.

That summer of 1968, before fall classes resumed, the president of the student council resigned. There had been some shady things going on with his administration since the previous year, including being involved in the destruction of thousands of copies of the *Daily Bruin* that endorsed his African American opponent during the Greek Power mobilization. As far as I was concerned, it was good that he was gone from student government.

I was present at the meeting when the president announced his resignation. Ramses Noriega was with me. We had gone to see if we could get council support for the farmworkers' boycott. Like everyone else, we were shocked by the resignation. Thinking out loud, I told Ramses, "I think I could win the election to replace the departing president."

The meeting adjourned shortly thereafter, and Ramses came with me to my apartment for wine and pizza. We discussed what had happened and he told me, "You have all the qualifications; it would help the *movimiento* if you were elected student president."

Ramses had just come in from working with the farmworkers on the grape boycott and didn't have a place yet. Ramses is a pretty persuasive guy, and I found it hard to resist him. He was making sense. My candidacy would be symbolically important, as well as advancing a more progressive agenda. After all that wine mixed in with good, solid political talk, I decided to be a candidate. But I added a stipulation.

"Ramses, if I run, you have to be my campaign manager, okay?"

What could he say? He agreed.

One advantage that we had is that we could start a campus farmworkers' support group as a base for the campaign. The students, who were picketing the Safeway stores for selling scab grapes, also began campaigning for my election that fall. My election, as Ramses had suggested, would be a victory for the grape boycott.

We had to move fast because the special election to replace the guy who quit would be in early October.

Besides the boycott group, Ramses got the endorsement of UMAS. In fact, from the very beginning my campaign had strong Chicano overtones. I ran as a Chicano. I was no longer Ross Muñoz. I was Rosalio Muñoz.

At the same time, I ran on a very progressive platform that was also intended to draw support from liberal white students. I called for more student independence from the administration, for more student initiatives in the curriculum and in campus planning, for disarming the campus cops, and for rent control in the apartments surrounding the campus. I also said that I was against the U.S. war in Vietnam, a growing issue on campus. But the main item was student power and independence, or what I called "academic freedom for students."

Ramses served as my campaign manager, assisted by Larry Weinstein, a strong supporter who had followed me in becoming the student educational policy commissioner. Ramses's initiative won support from the Black Student Union and a wide range of progressive students. Larry was effective with the educational reform constituency, with dorm groups, and even with some Greeks.

We were further aided when the *Daily Bruin* endorsed me. This actually wasn't easy. The editor, Mike Levine, was supporting a friend of his, whom he thought would be a better candidate to defeat the frat candidate. This was before Ramses pigeonholed him.

"What do you mean this guy has a better chance to win than Rosalio? Why can't a Mexican be president of the student council?"

Ramses raked Mike over the coals. I got the paper's endorsement.

It was a pretty tough campaign. Some of the fraternities again expressed their racism by passing the word out that if I were elected, it would really be UMAS calling the shots, and UMAS, they suggested, was a dangerous group.

On election day, we worked hard to get the votes, making sure all our supporters voted. I won 47 percent of the vote and was just a few votes short of a majority out of a field of seven. As a result, I had to be in a runoff with the next closest candidate, the frat guy. In that runoff a week or two later, I won, running away with some 60 percent of the vote. It was a great victory. It was the first time a Chicano was elected as president of UCLA's student body. What was great was that we got broad support. I ran as a Chicano, but there weren't enough Chicano and black votes to make up my margin of victory. We got support from many other students, including many of the white Jewish American students. It was the highlight of my UCLA years!

I was also proud that my election came a couple of years after my cousin Félix Gutiérrez was elected student-body president at L.A. State College, which later became Cal State, L.A. In addition, he helped organize UMAS on his campus.

I assumed the president's office right away. Since it was a year's commitment for sure, I had to now spend another year at school. It didn't take long for me to return to earth after my election. Winning the election was easy compared to being president. I entered into quite a mess. For one, the conservative Greek fraternities controlled the council. This meant that I faced opposition from the very beginning. On top of this, the outgoing president, with the conservatives on the council, to my amazement, had appropriated much of the budget already for the 1968–69 year. A lot of these funds were to go for big ticket causes, such as the sophomore sweetheart banquet or to the Bruin Belles for their events.

FIGURE 13. Rosalio Muñoz, student-body president, University of California, Los Angeles, 1968–69. Courtesy of George Rodríguez.

Fortunately, the resigned president had not had time to sign these allocations. So I decided not to sign most of them. All hell broke loose when I announced this. The conservatives on the council denounced me and threatened to impeach me. The affected sorority girls whose events I wouldn't fund even went to see Chancellor Charles Young. I got a call from him: "Rosalio, what the hell is going on? I have these sorority members in my office, and they're all crying because you won't support them!"

But he was only giving me a hard time. Chuck was okay then. He understood where I was coming from at that time.

In the end, I did support some of the Greek events, after Young came up with more money, but I used my veto as a threat to make sure I got some of my measures passed. "You scratch my back, and I'll scratch yours." In this way I was able to help get a number of good social programs funded. In a way, I was paying back my political supporters. This included support for the grape boycott, UMAS community projects, similar programs by black students, affirmative-action programs, and, among other things, antiwar projects.

Despite some of the frustrations and stress that went with my position, it was nevertheless worthwhile to be president. I felt, as I still do, that besides being a symbol of rising Chicano power on campus and in the community, I was able to improve the quality of life on campus. It wasn't fun, but I'm proud I did it.

Some of my other duties as president included speaking at different public events or welcoming various groups to campus. I was invited, along with other student-body presidents of the UC campuses, to meet with Gov. Ronald Reagan in Sacramento. There I reunited with a junior high school friend, Charley Palmer, who was half Mexican; he was the student-body president at Berkeley. We went to junior high together and then to rival high schools. Before we went into the meeting with Reagan, Charley leaned over and whispered to me, "Ross, whatever you do, don't let yourself get photographed with Reagan. He's having trouble with the student and Chicano communities and would love to get his picture in the paper talking with someone like you."

When we went into the governor's office, the first thing I observed was all these bowls filled with jelly beans, which Reagan liked and apparently always had available at meetings. Then Reagan and his staff came in, and the photographers swarmed toward him. But instead of going to the center of the room, Reagan began to circulate among us. He kept coming closer to me. As he did, the photographers kept shooting. I remembered Charley's warning, and I just put up my middle finger to ruin any photo taken with Reagan. I turned around, smiling, to tell Charley "mission accomplished," only to hear the sound of a camera clicking. And, sure enough, the next day, right there in the *Sacramento Bee* was my big face with Reagan looking toward me as if he was talking with me. I hadn't said a word to him, and he didn't even greet me. But that's not the way it came out in the photo. Score one for Reagan! I also learned a valuable political lesson: much of politics is timing and staging.

But I got back. Later at that meeting, in the question-and-answer session, I got up and addressed Reagan even though I was a bit nervous.

"Governor Reagan, you're a conservative, and conservatives pride themselves on knowing what ordinary people need and want. Well, if that's so, then when are you going to get down and try to understand the Chicano and black communities and relate to them? When are you going to support ethnic studies in the UC system so that the history and traditions of these communities are part of what our students learn? When are you going to do that?"

Reagan never responded to me because one of his staff jumped in and changed the subject, and soon thereafter Reagan was ushered out of the meeting.

THE DRAFT AND THE VIETNAM WAR

My five years at UCLA, from 1964 to 1969, of course, coincided with the escalated U.S. involvement in the Vietnam War. Initially, I was not very concerned about the war or its personal implications for me. When I graduated from high school in 1964, the war had not yet fully become a U.S. war, and the number of U.S. troops in Vietnam was still small.

This was the backdrop when I had to register for the Selective Service, or the draft, upon turning eighteen right after high school graduation. Registration was mandatory, but I don't remember how I registered. I may have just mailed it in. At the time, I didn't think much about it. I wasn't that political yet. I didn't want to go into the military, like a number of other high school seniors. I wanted to go to college, and that's what I concentrated on.

When I entered UCLA, the possibility of being drafted was the furthest thing from my mind. For one, I had a deferment because I was in college. I knew that at least for the next four years I couldn't be drafted. I don't even remember asking for a deferment.

Even into my first two or three years at UCLA, the war still remained a distant and vague issue for me. I didn't read newspapers because I was too busy with my classes and campus activities. I didn't watch the TV news because I didn't have a television as a student.

Of course, I wasn't completely sheltered from the war. Art Ershoen, one of my best high school friends who had enlisted in the army right out of school, was killed in Vietnam. I was saddened by Art's death; he shouldn't have died. He was a nice guy. Still, despite his death, the Vietnam War seemed very distant to me.

At the same time I was aware that guys were getting drafted if they didn't stay in school. The brother of one of my friends at UCLA was drafted because he had stopped going to school. He was attending USC, but having a rough time in his classes, so he decided to take some time off, perhaps work, and then return to school. No such luck. No sooner had he dropped out of school then he was drafted. He couldn't believe it.

I did begin to think about how I would feel about going to war. Could I go to Vietnam and kill? I even had dreams, or perhaps they were nightmares, about this. It was like a war movie. Sometimes I thought I could do it if I went with my high school buddies. But then the more I thought about it, the more I realized that I couldn't kill someone else, not even in war. That wasn't me. I'm not a fighter. At the same time, I didn't want someone else serving in my place, as occurred during the Civil War. When I'd occasionally think about this, I'd get chills. Still, this was only occasional. For the most part I went about my life.

I was aware that some were resisting the draft. I knew this one guy, Joe Maizlish, who did not drop out of UCLA, but he refused induction when drafted. He went to prison for that. He was a very gentle and soft-spoken guy. I really respected him for his convictions. He was a hero for me, and I'm proud that we are still friends. It made me think, Could I do the same? Would I have the courage?"

There was, of course, group opposition to the war, both on and off campus. I think I was either a sophomore or a junior when Ricardo invited me to go with him to an antiwar protest at MacArthur Park in L.A. Actually, the reason Ricardo wanted to go was because the Chambers Brothers, the then popular psychedelic black rock group, was going to play at the protest. Ricardo was really into music. So was I, for that matter. I didn't hesitate to join him. It was a large demonstration, but somehow I didn't really feel like a part of it. I didn't see myself as antiestablishment at that point. But I enjoyed the music. This was my first antiwar demonstration. I was against the war, but not an activist.

What really began to bring the war and the draft closer to me was when, around junior year, all the other students and I were ordered by the Selective Service to report for physicals. There were rumors and efforts by some to end college deferments, and so this was part of the reaction. The deferments didn't end, but we still had to report for physicals. I was assigned to report to Pasadena City College for my physical. There were hundreds of other students there. It was awful. I felt like I was already being drafted and reporting for duty. The officers there barked out orders just as if we were already recruits. We had to strip to our shorts and endure a battery of tests. It was dehumanizing. Besides the physicals, we had to fill out these questionnaires about ourselves. I left that place like I had been liberated. I knew even more then that I wouldn't go to the military, much less to war.

UCLA was not like Berkeley. There wasn't as much intense antiwar activity on our campus. The antiwar movement was mostly in the community. However, some protests did occur on campus. I didn't participate in them, but I observed them.

Probably the most dramatic action involved the protest against the Dow Chemical Company for its job recruitment on campus. Dow was the manufacturer of napalm, which the United States was using indiscriminately in Vietnam and causing countless civilian casualties. Antiwar protesters by the hundreds surrounded the Dow representative's table until they forced him out.

Clearly, the opposition to the war was growing, and by the time I was elected student-body president, I identified with the movement. I not only did not want to go to Vietnam, but I was against the war in general. I wasn't steeped in all the arguments for why the United States should not be in Vietnam, and I did not know much about the history of this involvement. But I knew enough to know that I was against a war that the United States should not be involved in; that was causing injury to young men, including many Chicanos, as I had learned in the Guzmán Report; and that was dividing the country.

I had become more antiestablishment. I did my senior history paper on a Chicano-*mexicano* lettuce strike in the Imperial Valley in the early 1930s. It was documented in what became known as the La Follette Report of a U.S. Senate investigation of corporate antilabor activities during the Great Depression. It showed police and media collusion with violence, blackmail, libel, red-baiting, and racism across the nation and against Chicano and *mexicano* farmworkers in particular. My concern for social justice matured into commitment.

As I prepared to graduate in the spring of 1969, I couldn't help but now give more thought to the very real possibility that I would get drafted. I saw that this was happening to other graduated seniors. Some were drafted and went. Others refused and went to jail. Some became moral conscientious objectors and were still drafted but placed in noncombat service. Still others left the country, many going to Canada. What would I do? I respected those who opposed the war by practicing passive resistance, but now that I had also become more involved in the Chicano movement on campus and saw what high school kids had done in the blowouts, I felt that if I were going to resist the draft and the war, it would have to involve a more militant response. Passive resistance was not in keeping with the militancy of the Chicano movement. I wasn't sure what this action would be. All I knew was that it would be dramatic and public. I would use the occasion—if it came—to advance the movement. I did not want to just get out and have another Chicano or poor person take my place.

Of course, I did have the option of going to graduate school and maintaining my deferment. I had thought of that and, in fact, applied to law school at UCLA and was accepted. But my heart wasn't into going to law school. I didn't really want to be a lawyer. I wasn't sure what I wanted to do, but I knew I was distancing myself more and more from the system. I didn't accept the law school offer.

Graduation came that June. I couldn't believe I was graduating. I didn't have the highest GPA in the world. It was a bit under 3.0, but I had made it. I don't know if I had learned more inside than outside the classroom; I actually learned a lot in both. They had been an interesting five years. The world looked different to me in 1969 than it did in 1964 when I started at UCLA. I had grown and matured a lot. I had entered as Ross Muñoz, and I was leaving as Rosalio Muñoz. I had also seen a major institution go through dramatic changes from top to bottom for students, including minority ones, and I had been a part of it. These intense five years, of course, had been capped by my election as student-body president. I felt like I had made history.

BEING DRAFTED

After graduation I wasn't sure what I was going to do. I was tired of going to school. I wanted to do something else. At the same time, I had the issue of the draft, which would now loom over my head since I no longer had a deferment.

However, one day, Ron López, who had helped me with my senior seminar paper on the 1933 lettuce strike in the Imperial Valley, called me up.

"Rosalio, I've just been named as director of the new Mexican American Studies Center at the Claremont Colleges, and I need an assistant director. Are you interested?"

"That sounds good, Ron. What would I be doing?"

"Don't worry," he assured me. "You'll be doing mostly outreach with the students. It's right up your alley."

I accepted. I needed a job, and the salary was good.

I had moved back with my parents, but now that I had a job I looked for an apartment closer to the Claremont Colleges. I found some other guys who worked at the colleges and who were also looking for roommates.

I enjoyed my work, although it was summertime, so not many students were on campus. But one of my duties was to contact Chicano students to make sure they were returning in the fall and to see if they had any particular problems that I could perhaps help them with. I found that I shared one of the guys' main concerns—the draft. A good number of the Chicano students had been recruited to the Claremont schools from the Coachella and Imperial Valleys. These students told me that their local draft boards were telling them that even though they were in college, they didn't have a deferment. This was a way to fill the draft quotas without the Anglo rancher kids having to be drafted themselves.

I pointed out that what their draft boards were telling them was a bunch of bullshit.

"Of course, you have a deferment. That's national policy. Your draft board can't go against that. They're only trying to intimidate you because you're Chicanos. They want you to drop out of school and enlist."

These conversations with the students made me more aware of how unfair the draft was. It had a greater impact in minority communities, where draft boards tried to fill their quotas. All this only increased my own anxieties about my draft status and what I was going to do when I received my induction notice.

My concern continued to fester into the summer. On a visit to some Anglo friends who had graduated with me at UCLA and who still lived close to the campus, the conversation turned to the draft. Some of them said that they had hired attorneys to get them out of the draft. One guy said he was going to act insane to avoid being drafted. And another guy said he would injure himself to make sure he didn't pass the physical. This discussion reinforced my resisting the draft. I saw the race and class differences of how the draft affected the white middle-class guys who had access and resources and the poor Chicanos who were being funneled to the front lines. My decision to take a strong stand against the draft and the war solidified.

Then, too, I had conversations with Ramses, who was also looking at the draft himself if he stopped going to school. I remember one particular conversation, where it was either Ramses or me who said, "What we need in the Chicano movement is someone like Muhammad Ali who publicly resisted induction based on his opposition to the war." We both had been influenced by Ali's resistance speech when he said, "Why should I go to Vietnam? I don't have a quarrel with the Vietnamese. What have they ever done to me? They never called me a nigger. If I have a quarrel, it's with the white crackers who discriminated against me growing up in Kentucky. If I'm going to fight anywhere, it's going to be in Kentucky." That was a powerful statement, and Ramses and I both agreed that we needed someone in our movement to do the same. Fate turned out to make it me.

The more I thought about it—like almost every day—the more I concluded that I had to do something like Ali did. I knew what I had to do. "I'm going to refuse induction," I told my girlfriend. This was the first time I had said this to anyone. Saying it, mouthing the words, only empowered me. "I'm refusing induction."

I didn't stay very long with the Chicano studies program because another and better job opened in the Claremont schools. It was for a student recruiter, and I applied for it and got the job. It involved recruiting specifically Chicano students to the different Claremont Colleges. Since it was still late summer, there wasn't much yet to do, but I looked forward to going to different high schools in Southern California to encourage Chicanos to apply.

I was just easing into my job when my mother told me that a relative had passed away, and she wanted Ricardo and me to escort her to the funeral. We did. When we got back home, I went out to get our mail from the mailbox. One of the letters stuck out. It was from the Selective Service. I didn't even have to open it up. I knew exactly what it was. When I did open it up, I was intrigued that my induction date was set for September 16, 1969. Was that someone's idea of a joke? Or was it just circumstantial? I couldn't believe I was being inducted on the *dieciséis de septiembre*—Mexican Independence Day! Needless to say, I wasn't too thrilled.

REFUSING INDUCTION

Maybe it was the confluence of my induction notice and Mexican Independence Day, but I now more clearly realized what I wanted to do. Yes, I would refuse induction, but I would do it publicly, like Muhammad Ali, and here is where the opportune date of September 16 would help. I would use the historical date to link my refusal with the Chicano movement. This was not going to be just about me but about the movement. I would help make the draft and the way it unfairly targeted Chicanos part of the movement's agenda.

But I also needed to have all the facts about my legal status in refusing induction. One morning, before I got the induction notice, I had gone to see an attorney in Santa Monica who was doing a lot of draft cases. I told him of my idea of legally challenging the draft as discriminatory.

"Mr. Muñoz, I understand what you're trying to do," he said, "but I don't think I can help you. I'm only taking on cases where we can get people out of either being drafted for family, health, or other circumstances or else arguing for conscientious objector status on religious or moral grounds. You don't seem to fit any of these categories. You want to make your draft status into a political issue. I sympathize with you and wish you luck, but I can't help you. What I can advise you is that when you leave this office you should immediately send a telegram to your draft board at least raising the issue of conscientious objection to protect yourself legally."

This attorney knew this was serious business. Middle-class kids were paying to get out of the draft by hiring attorneys like him, and, as a result, Chicanos and blacks filled the quotas more and more. This was a growing problem, an epidemic of "genocidal" proportions.

I left and went to the nearest phone booth and sent the telegram. This later saved me from prison. At that very moment the draft was preparing to mail me, and many others, draft notices the next day. My timely request for conscientious objection gave me full due process in court, which would be important later. Draft law had become a growing industry, and lawyers knew what draft boards were doing and could help, for a fee. Although I gave myself some legal cover, I was still prepared to take on the draft system. Unknowingly, my draft board had given me the perfect occasion to do so. I could use Mexican Independence Day to my advantage. That would bring media attention. The fact that I had been student-body president at UCLA would also bring attention. I looked forward to that day.

But if I were going to politically protest my induction, I would need help. The first person I turned to was Ramses Noriega. He had masterminded my campaign for student-body president; he could do the same for my induction protest. Not only was Ramses politically astute, but he had been trained as an organizer by the farmworkers and had organized the grape boycott back East in Pittsburgh as well as participated in organizing the Coachella strike.

Immediately after seeing the attorney and sending in my request to my draft board, I drove to Hollywood, where Ramses now lived.

"Ramses, I want to do something about the war, and I need your help. Do you remember what you said to me about running for student-body president? How this would be important for Chicanos to have a Chicano president? Do you remember that? Well, now it's important for a Chicano to publicly refuse induction so that it can inspire other Chicanos not to go to war. But to do this, I need your help. I have some ideas, but I don't know about organizing the community. You do. I need you, guy."

We went back and forth. Ramses wasn't convinced I should do this. "This is really serious, Rosalio. We could get killed. Are you willing to die?"

But, in the end, Ramses was in. I knew he would be. He liked to fight injustice too much to stay out. We had been a good team on campus. We could do it again on the draft issue.

As we discussed the strategies further that day and other subsequent days, we concluded that my protest would be built around three themes to gain maximum support and stress the legitimacy of what I was doing. First, we had to confront and redefine the traditional machismo that led to too many Chicanos joining the military or allowing themselves to be drafted. They mistakenly believed that one could better prove his masculinity through the military. By my stand, I would be redefining machismo to mean having the courage—the *huevos,* balls—to take on the system. The real macho, my message would convey, doesn't wage war on Vietnam; he fights for his community at home.

The second theme we would stress is that I wasn't some wild-eyed radical or some drugged-up hippie. I was serious about what I was doing. It's true that I had grown my hair somewhat long, but then that was the style of that time. More important, I would emphasize my college background at UCLA and, of course, especially that I had been student-body president.

Finally, as I had already planned, we would link my induction refusal to the sixteenth of September and Mexican Independence Day. This linkage would stress my Chicano background and, hopefully, connect with the larger Mexican American community. I would literally wrap myself around the flag—the Mexican flag!

Before we proceeded further, I knew I had to talk to my parents and my family about my decision. I knew that Ricardo and the rest of my siblings would support me. My real concern was with my parents, especially my father. My father, of course, was a World War II veteran. Would he understand? How would my mother react? I sat down with them at home and explained the situation.

"Dad, you know how I got my induction notice to report on September 16? I've been giving it a lot of thought, and I've decided to refuse induction and to publicly protest the draft, how the draft is unjust to Chicanos, and my opposition to the war. I hope you can understand."

My dad at first didn't say anything. Then, without raising his voice, he started to ask me questions.

"Are you sure? Are you sure you're not just trying to avoid military service? Are you sure you're not just trying to escape your duty?"

He seemed discouraged at my decision, or at least that's the impression I got.

Turning to my mother, I added that what I wanted to do was call attention to the social injustices that Chicanos faced and how the draft was a part of this. As we talked more, they began to realize that what I wanted to do was part of the struggle for social justice. I'll never forget my dad at that moment. There he was in the living room, listening like an Indian and looking very Indian-like with his dark skin—the very skin that I also wear.

"Well," he finally said. "If that's what you want to do, we're with you. We'll support you."

And they did. If nothing else, I knew that they were with me, as they always were and always would be.

STRATEGY

I had received my induction notice around early September, so we didn't have much time to plan a strategy for my public rejection on September 16. Ramses and I sat down and plotted out what we should do.

We knew that we would need support from Chicano students and other movement activists. We decided to go back to our student base at UCLA and inform the Chicano students there, who had now renamed UMAS to MEChA to conform to the statewide call for Chicano students to unify based on the new name. This call came from El Plan de Santa Barbara conference held at UC Santa Barbara in April 1969. We met with the students and told them about my decision and that we needed their help for the protest in September. The students on campus then supported me and said that when other students returned in September, they would inform them about the protest.

We knew that my main support would come primarily from L.A., but we, at the same time, wanted to reach out to other activists. This was in keeping with our decision that my protest would be organized not as a personal statement but as a part of the Chicano movement. So far, the movement had manifested itself on different issues: farmworkers, land grants in New Mexico, education, electoral politics, police abuse, welfare rights, and so on. The one big gap was the war and the draft. We wanted to fill that gap. My protest, we hoped, would start an antidraft and antiwar component of the Chicano movement. The movement was challenging institutional racism, and we felt that taking on the draft and the military was furthering the challenge. That was our goal.

Because we wanted to integrate our issues with the rest of the movement, we decided to contact and possibly visit some key movement leaders. In early September Ramses and I took off on a whirlwind trip through California to do that. We first drove to Delano to meet with César Chávez. He wasn't in his office, but we found him taking one of his walks on the Forty Acres, the farmworkers' compound. He sympathized with us. Although he didn't offer any concrete support, he did wisely counsel us.

"You're going to go through a lot of struggle and even pain," he said, "but this will make you stronger. It will prepare you for the long, hard struggle. People will appreciate your struggle and respond favorably to you."

César was sharing his own experiences with us, and we appreciated that. He gave us his own personal support but didn't commit to actually going to the protest or sending some of his people. We didn't really expect that anyway. What we wanted to do was just inform him of our action.

From Delano, we drove up to Fresno, where we met with Eliezer Risco. He had worked with César earlier and then gone down to L.A., where he started La Raza, an early movement newspaper in L.A. Risco was Cuban but identified with the movement. Besides supporting what we were planning on doing, he helped us by giving us other names of key people to visit on our whirlwind tour. These included Armando Valdez, Sophie Mendoza, Luis Nogales, Froben Lozado, Delfino Varela, and Professor Ralph Guzmán, who was now teaching at UC Santa Cruz. All these people we visited sympathized and expressed support, which they followed through on.

We covered a lot of ground on that short trip, and we felt good about it. Now some key movement leaders in the state knew what we were going to do, and they would tell others as well. This networking, we felt, would also be important if and when we would move to organize a wider movement on the draft and the war.

We didn't have the time and money to travel out of state, so Ramses communicated with Corky Gonzales in Denver and Reies López Tijerina's organization in New Mexico by phone about our plans.

"I ACCUSE"

Following the trip, our next step was to draft my statement refusing induction. This was key because the statement would provide my reasons and link them to broader issues in the context of the movement. We had a group session to discuss my statement, with my brother Ricardo, Doug Smith, and a few students from UCLA and the Claremont MEChA. I appreciated their input. I then wrote it, and Ramses looked it over and approved. I wanted my statement to be dramatic, especially to get media attention. I also wanted to link my protest with history. Since I knew modern European history best, I drew on this background and resurrected the Dreyfus case in France in the late nineteenth century. Alfred Dreyfus was a French Jew who was persecuted mostly because of increasing anti-Semitism in France. His became a celebrated case and foreshadowed what would happen in Germany with the rise of Hitler and the persecution of the Jews there and in German-occupied Europe. The Dreyfus case received worldwide attention also because the famous French writer Émile Zola used a defense of Dreyfus, titled

"J'Accuse," or "I Accuse." In his statement, Zola accused the French government of genocide against French Jews. It was a powerful statement and accusation.

I wanted to do exactly what Zola had done. I wanted to issue a similarly powerful accusation. So I also titled my statement "I Accuse." Except that in my case, I accused the U.S. government of genocide against Chicanos, not only through the draft and the war but also by neglect of Chicanos within the country. Here, in part, is what I wrote:

> Today, the sixteenth of September, the day of Independence for all Mexican peoples, I declare my independence of the Selective Service System.
>
> I accuse the government of the United States of America of genocide against the Mexican people. Specifically, I accuse the draft, the entire social, political, and economic system of the United States of America, of creating a funnel which shoots Mexican youth into Viet Nam to be killed and to kill innocent men, women, and children.
>
> I accuse the education system of the United States of breaking down the family structure of the Mexican people. Robbing us of our language and culture has torn the youth away from our fathers, mothers, grandfathers and grandmothers. Thus it is that I accuse the educational system of uneducating Chicano youth. Generally, we are ineligible for higher education, and thus are ineligible for the draft deferments which other college age youth take for granted, which is genocide.
>
> I accuse the American welfare system of taking the self-respect from our Mexican families, forcing our youth to see the army as a better alternative to living in our community with their own families, which is genocide. . . .
>
> I accuse the United States Congress and the Selective Service System which they have created of recognizing these weaknesses they have imposed on the Chicano community, and of drafting their law so that many more Chicanos are sent to Viet Nam, in proportion to the total population than [sic] they send of any of their own white youth.
>
> I accuse the entire American social and economic system of taking advantage of the machismo of the Mexican American male, widowing and orphaning the mothers, wives, and children of the Mexican American community, sending the Mexican men onto the front lines, where their machismo has given them more congressional medals, Purple Hearts, and many times more deaths and casualties than any of the other racial or ethnic groups in the nation, which is genocide. . . .
>
> I have my induction papers, but I will not respect them.
>
> I will not respect the papers UNTIL the United States government and people can provide the funds and the willingness to improve the educational system so that all Mexican youth, the intelligent, the mediocre, and the tapados [closed-minded], just like the white youth, the intelligent, the mediocre, and the tapados, have the opportunity to go to college and get deferments. . . .
>
> I will not respect the papers UNTIL the Armed Forces, the largest domestic consumer of California table grapes, recognizes the United Farm Workers' Organizing Committee. Until that time, I cannot recognize the Armed Forces, or any of its polit-

ical uses of the American people. Until they begin to boycott the sellers and growers of California table grapes, I must boycott them.

CHALE CON EL DRAFT![5]

The evening of September 15 we organized an orientation meeting at UCLA's Zapata Center in Boyle Heights for some of the students and other supporters. In L.A. we had contacted the Peace Action Council, which was the major antiwar group in the area. They supported me and sent some people to the later demonstration. At the meeting, attended primarily by MEChA students, I went over why I was doing this and gave them a copy of my statement. We encouraged them to go to the protest the next day, and some of the Chicano students volunteered to pass out copies of my statement at the big Sixteenth of September parade in East L.A. Students such as Pat Tamayo, Teresa McKenna, Antonia Hernández, and María Elena Yepes helped mobilize the other students.

We also had made arrangements for my friend Neil Reichline, who had been editor of the *Daily Bruin* and a film studies student, to make a 16 mm film of my protest. Neil wound up taking quite a lot of footage of that day. The film effectively introduced the issue and me to the people. Neil later became an award-winning documentary filmmaker.

We were up early that morning of the sixteenth. I hadn't slept very much that night, just thinking about the next day. I had to get up quite early because my induction was scheduled for about seven or eight in the morning. I got dressed and wore a turtleneck and corduroy jacket with a peace sign around my neck, but instead of socks and shoes, I wore my huaraches, my Mexican sandals. After all, this was Mexican Independence Day, and I was a proud Chicano.

I picked up the young woman, Beatrice Winchell, I was seeing then and drove downtown to the induction center by Olympic and Broadway. We met Ramses there. When we got there, there was already a small crowd of supporters, which continued to grow. There must have been about a hundred people. I would have liked more, but it was early in the morning. They carried handmade signs, some of which Ramses had done, protesting the draft and the war.

We had contacted both the print and the electronic media, and, to my surprise and delight, we got excellent media coverage. There were reporters from both the *Los Angeles Times* and the *Herald-Examiner*. At least one of the TV stations, as I recall, covered it. *La Opinión,* the Spanish-language newspaper, didn't cover it, to my knowledge, nor did channel 34, the sole Spanish-language TV station.

After the crowd assembled and the media was present, I stood before the entrance of the induction center and read my "I Accuse" statement. We also handed out copies of it. From time to time my statement was interrupted by applause and shouts from my mostly Chicano audience, although some black and white supporters were also in attendance. At the end of my speech, the crowd

FIGURE 14. Muñoz protesting his draft induction, September 16, 1969. Courtesy of George Rodríguez.

broke into even more applause and shouts of support: "Viva la Raza! Chicano Power! Bring the Troops Home!"

While I was reading my statement, a number of other guys, mostly Chicanos and blacks, showed up for their induction. They and their families were waiting for the draft office to open. They read my statement, but no one heckled. They didn't say anything. Instead they displayed a stern pensiveness. No one—but me and the other demonstrators—seemed happy to be there. It was a liberating experience for me.

When the doors opened, the draftees just silently walked into the center. I knew I had to follow them. Fortified by my speech and my supporters, I walked in as well. I got in line in front of the reception desk. After we checked in, we then had to cross the line where the military officials would sign us in and give us a physical and other tests. Once we crossed the line, we were in. I had no intention of crossing the line. My plan was to go to the line and tell the officials that I refused induction.

I never got the chance that day. When I went to the reception desk, the guy behind the desk, after taking my name, told me that my induction had been postponed. I found this almost too coincidental. They had learned about my intention to publicly reject my induction and were trying to undercut me by changing the date.

I was a bit pissed off at that, but, at the same time, I felt good that my protest did become a public event, as we had planned it. The day, as Ramses agreed, was a success.

That night, although I didn't see it myself, I was shown reading my statement on one of the TV channels, and the next morning both the *Times* and the *Herald-Examiner* reported the story—not on the front page, but not far from it. The *Times* quoted Ramses as saying, "There is an overwhelmingly disproportionate number of Mexicans dying in Vietnam. We have the highest percentage of any race being killed. This is a class accusation. He [Muñoz] is doing this for La Raza."[6] The Associated Press likewise picked up the story, and it appeared in some newspapers in other parts of the country.

We made our point, and we were on the way to making not only the draft but also the war into one of the major issues of the Chicano movement.

NEXT STEPS

Although we had received some media coverage on my protest, I particularly wasn't pleased with the *Times* coverage. I decided to call the *Times* to complain. Ruben Salazar got on the phone. I had never met Salazar, the lone Chicano reporter on the *Times* and a pioneer in Latino journalism.

"Mr. Salazar? This is Rosalio Muñoz. I wanted to tell you about our protest the other day when I refused induction. Did you hear about it?"

"Nice to talk to you. Yes, I did hear about it, and I read the *Times* story on it. I'm afraid I was out of town that day. What can I do for you?"

"Well, we didn't like the *Times* story, and we thought that you might do another one."

"I'm afraid I couldn't. The event is over, and I can't correct the reporter who was there. Do you have any other protests planned?"

"Well, we hope to use our protest to build up an antidraft and antiwar movement within the Chicano movement. Too many Chicanos are being drafted and killed in Vietnam. We have to stop it."

"Listen, I wish I could do something now. But if you do what you say you're going to do, you'll get coverage. I'll guarantee that. Just keep me posted. Good luck."

We weren't completely satisfied with Salazar's response, but we figured that at least we had made the connection, and we could follow up on it.

We did get some additional media attention, when I got a call from Jesús Trevino to be on a new TV program he had on Chicanos on KCET, the public television station.[7] I gave a version of my "I Accuse" statement. The show ended with the camera going down a long list of Spanish-surnamed soldiers killed in Vietnam. It had a big effect. Some friends who watched the live program said that I came across pretty well.

One of the things that we worked on right after the protest was the film that my friend Neil shot of that day. Neil edited it, and Ramses and I did the narration. It turned out to be a good short film. It was in black and white, 16 mm, and Neil cut it to about eleven or thirteen minutes. It showed me reading my statement, and the crowd picketing the induction center. I narrated in English, and Ramses did a separate version in Spanish. We also added music. I've always enjoyed the music and *corridos* of the Mexican Revolution of 1910, so we used some of this music, including a guitar version of "La Cucaracha," as well as the "Marcha de Zacatecas" and "El Adiós del Soldado." The film proved to be important because we used it at later antidraft workshops that I conducted.

It was on October 20 that I was called in to meet with my draft board. This was preliminary to my having to go to my postponed induction. I think the board wanted to see if I was going to continue my protest. Ramses and I decided to use this occasion to again protest the draft.

I had to go to the draft board on San Gabriel Boulevard. We didn't organize a protest as we did on the sixteenth of September. It would be just the two of us. Our strategy was to make fools of the draft board members.

We took a tape recorder. I was to speak in Spanish, and Ramses was to translate in English. This was funny enough since my Spanish still wasn't the greatest and Ramses's English was heavily accented.

We walked into the meeting, and we sat at one end of the table. I turned on the tape recorder and said, "Hola señores. ¿Qué quieren de mí? [Hello, sirs. What do you want with me?]"

"Now, Mr. Muñoz," this tall, thin Anglo guy at the other end of the table said, "You can't do this. We know you went to UCLA and that you speak English."

"No, señores. Yo soy Chicano y voy hablar en español. Eso es mi derecho. [No, sirs. I'm Chicano, and I'm going to speak in Spanish. That's my right.]"

"Mr. Muñoz, turn off that tape recorder. You can't have this gentleman translate for you."

They brought in a young Chicana or Latina to translate. Actually, she did a pretty good job. Ramses turned off the tape recorder.

I proceeded as best I could in my *pocho* (Anglicized) Spanish to summarize the key points of my "I Accuse" speech, pointing out how the draft and the war was a form of genocide against Chicanos. This really got them upset.

"Mr. Muñoz, you're wrong. We don't discriminate against anyone. We're just doing our job."

"Well," I shot back in Spanish," that's what the Nazis said at the Nuremberg trials."

That got them even angrier, and they just ended the session right there.

It was drama, but we drove our point home.

Earlier in October I also attended a national conference of college recruiters in Chicago. The Claremont Colleges gave me a nice expense account to go, and so I was able to take Ramses with me. I didn't tell this to my supervisors. In Chicago, in between my attending sessions on student recruitment, Ramses and I set out to make contact with other Latinos there. We told these guys about my draft resistance and that we were organizing an antidraft movement. They told us that a *puertorriqueño* resister would be out of prison soon, and he would be our liaison. His name was Fred Avilos. These contacts paid off later, when we moved in this direction and beyond.

After returning from the conference and talking more with Ramses on our trip, I decided to quit my Claremont job. For one, I had the cloud of my induction refusal hanging over me, and I didn't know whether six months down the line I might actually be in jail and then wouldn't be able to do my job. More important, I had now concluded that I was going to plunge full-time into building an antidraft and antiwar movement within the Chicano movement. I knew that this would have to be a total commitment. Fortunately, I could continue living with my parents, and that would help me with expenses. If I had to, I would find a part-time job, but my focus now was on my political work. Ramses was with me, and we would go from there.

CHALE CON EL DRAFT

Ramses and I decided we would organize an antidraft grassroots organization to not only denounce the draft but also begin to counsel other Chicanos on rejecting induction or avoiding getting drafted. Some groups were already doing this, but very few were in East L.A. We didn't formally name our group, but because one of our slogans was "Chale con el Draft," which roughly means "To Hell with the Draft," others began to refer to us by that title.

We approached Joe Razo, one of the editors of *La Raza* newspaper, about getting office space. Joe introduced us to Rev. Antonio Hernández, who was the staff person for the Congress of Mexican American Unity, funded by the Southwest Council of La Raza and the Ford Foundation. He had his own offices and others at the Euclid Community Center. Reverend Hernández provided me with a desk in the same room Joe Razo had one, no rent, but we had to pay for our own phone. We were now a legitimate community group. Joe Razo, as an early movement leader, also shared insights and advice and moral support. He is an unsung hero of the movement.

At first, I started to attend different community meetings to talk about the draft. When possible, I showed our film. Everyone was very sympathetic and supportive. I also began to attend Chicano movement conferences in different locations. I was invited to be part of an antidraft workshop at a movement conference in Kansas City, Missouri. I guess people had heard of my protest. With my own savings and help from Joe Razo, I flew to the conference. This was the first large movement conference I had ever attended. I was very impressed. There were activists from all over. There were people from the Mexican American Youth Organization (MAYO) in Texas who wanted to build La Raza Unida Party in communities such as Crystal City, Texas. The Brown Berets from L.A. and elsewhere sent representatives. Corky Gonzales's people from the Crusade for Justice in Denver were there. Many campus MEChA groups also attended. César Chávez came and spoke at the conference, after which we all marched out of the meeting hall and picketed a Safeway store in support of the United Farm Workers' (UFW) grape boycott.

At the antidraft workshop, I showed the film and informed those in attendance of what I was doing and why. It was well attended, and my presentation was well received. People came up to me after the session, and I made several new contacts. The key contact I made was Roberto "Bobby" Elias. He really liked my presentation. He was also from L.A., but I had never met him before. He said that he wanted to get involved with what we were doing. He and I spent a whole night just talking about the draft and the war and what the movement should be doing on these issues. Bobby also told me that the following week he was going to another movement conference in Albuquerque and encouraged me to attend.

"I'll meet you there," Bobby said, "and one of the things we can do is try to get Corky's people involved in what we want to do."

Bobby was very impressed with Corky and felt that if he got involved in the draft issue, this would give us a great deal of credibility in the movement. I agreed, as did Ramses, and told Elias that I would see him in Albuquerque.

Through contacting the Albuquerque conference organization, I was able to put together an antidraft workshop. Again, people expressed support, including members of the Crusade for Justice. Together with Corky's input, we called for a meeting in Denver the following week.

I returned to L.A. elated because we had established "Chale con el Draft," and we were beginning to promote our message and integrate ourselves in the movement. Things were moving fast.

Prior to these conferences, I also got a call inviting me to speak at the national antiwar mobilization scheduled for San Francisco on November 15. I was stunned at the invitation. Since the mid-1960s, when the United States escalated its military presence in Vietnam and thousands of U.S. combat troops began streaming into that civil war–torn country, the growing antiwar movement began to organize national demonstrations against the war. In the fall of 1969 there were two major antiwar efforts. One was called the moratorium movement, with demonstrations across the nation in scores of cities to reach deeper into local grassroots levels. These protests were held on October 15. The second effort involved two centralized mass demonstrations, one in Washington, DC, and the other in San Francisco, which were held on November 15. The October 15 moratoriums were so successful all around that the term "moratorium" became the term used for antiwar demonstrations. As a result, the November 15 demonstrations were popularly called moratoriums.[8]

I was invited to speak at the November 15 San Francisco demonstrations. I had just started organizing full-time, but I guess event organizers heard of me as a Chicano antiwar leader and invited me just before the moratorium. I think that the Peace Action Council in L.A., which had supported my draft protest, had given them my name. I quickly accepted the invitation. This would be one additional way to call attention to the disproportionate number of Chicanos being drafted and dying.

Ramses and I drove up a day or so before the moratorium, which was scheduled on a Saturday. On our way up, we stopped and visited César again, who, in his way, blessed our actions. From there we attended a Chicano antiwar meeting in Hayward. Corky Gonzales was one of the speakers. At some point in the meeting, I was asked to speak, and although I don't recall what I said, it was probably about the antidraft and peace work we were doing. On the other hand, Ernesto Vigil, a Denver activist, recalls that I proposed a separate Chicano antiwar moratorium.[9]

Before the demonstration, we stayed with Armando Valdez. That next day, on Saturday, we joined a Latino feeder march that assembled in the Mission District and went to Golden Gate Park, the site of the rally and where many others and I would speak. I mostly remember a sea of people streaming into the park—people as far as the eye could see. There must have easily been 250,000 people.

When we got to the stage area, the cast of the musical *Hair* was performing: "Let the sun shine, let the sun shine in, the sun shine in." I wasn't the only Chicano speaker. Corky Gonzales and Abe Tapia from the Mexican American Political Association (MAPA) spoke much earlier that afternoon. Dolores Huerta was an emcee. I was scheduled to speak almost at the end of the program. I was totally energized by the scene and the speakers. By the time I was to speak, it was getting dark, and way in the distance I could see bonfires being lit in the park. The program was running late, and I was told that I might not be able to speak. This upset me, but before I could protest my treatment, Buffy Sainte-Marie, the folk singer who was scheduled to end the program by singing, told the organizers, "I'm not singing until this guy gets to speak."

So, thanks to Buffy, I was introduced as an antidraft organizer in L.A. and brought up to speak. It was incredible. In front of me were all these demonstrators. To the side of the microphone and me were these huge amplifiers that sent out my voice. So even if people in the crowd were talking, my amplified voice just drowned them out. I spoke only for two or three minutes and pretty much repeated my "I Accuse" statement. I was nervous at first, but the sound of my amplified voice, I guess, empowered me, and I gained confidence as I went along. I didn't read my statement but spoke directly to the crowd. I ad-libbed my closing by referencing the UFW struggle and the battle with the Defense Department.

"I'm not going to serve in the U.S. military, if I ever serve, until the Defense Department stops buying nonunion grapes as a way of breaking the farmworkers' struggle. ¡Viva la Huelga! ¡Viva la Raza!"

Dolores Huerta rushed up to me and gave me a huge *abrazo* (hug). "Gracias," she said. "César will really appreciate this."

I was on quite a high as others congratulated me. It was an occasion I'll never forget.

We spent that night at Armando Valdez's house, where we watched the TV news and its coverage of the demonstration. My rap, of course, wasn't covered, but what we noticed and what bothered us was how the other Chicano speakers, such as Corky and Dolores, were also ignored. It was like Chicanos weren't there that day. We talked of how even though it was important to have Chicanos speak at these national moratoriums, it wasn't a successful way to reach Chicanos on the issues of the draft and the war. "We need our own Chicano antiwar moratorium," we told one another. I didn't know how we would do this, but the genesis of the Chicano antiwar movement that Ramses and I would help organize was an idea whose time had come.

It was also around the time of the San Francisco moratorium, or perhaps just before it, when I received my second formal induction notice. It instructed me to appear at the downtown induction center on November 18, as I recall. I, of course, was not going to obey it. With Ramses's help again, we quickly organized another protest outside of the induction center and put out a press release to this effect. We had a pretty good turnout, although most of the media didn't cover it. The *Los Angeles Times* published a short piece that quoted me as saying, "If Nixon wants war, then let him send his daughters to fight it."[10] In that article, Ramses was also quoted as saying that the people were talking of having a "Chicano moratorium." Unlike the first protest, however, I decided not to enter the building and inform the Selective Service people inside that I was refusing induction. Since I was on a fast (emulating César Chávez, who did it to strengthen himself spiritually), I didn't want them to use it as a way of undercutting me. They might just decide to eliminate my issue by not drafting me because I was physically unfit due to my fast.

THE CHICANO MORATORIUM COMMITTEE

Besides going to conferences and the San Francisco moratorium, Ramses and I talked about organizing a Chicano moratorium, but hadn't gotten around to that yet. In the meantime, I attended a Chicana women's conference at UCLA before Thanksgiving, where a Chicana Brown Beret announced that a committee to hold a Chicano moratorium was being formed and that a meeting on such-and-such date would take place. Unfortunately, I had to be out of town at the New Mexico conference, but Ramses attended. He later briefed me that the Berets had called for the committee and that David Sánchez, the prime minister of the Berets, served as chair of the first meeting. In fact, Ramses was also invited to cochair that meeting.

The intent was to organize a Chicano moratorium march and protest later in December against the war in East L.A. It would be the first such moratorium led and organized by Chicanos.

I was excited about the developments and saw the opportunity to merge our antidraft movement with the work of the Moratorium Committee. The next meeting was held at the Berets' headquarters on Fourth Street in East L.A., just across from Roosevelt High School. About twenty or twenty-five people attended, packed in the small storefront office. Again, David and Ramses led the meeting. They ran it as a community meeting, not a Beret one. Different people gave reports based on the work of the first meeting. I remember seeing Alicia Sandoval there, who was very involved in educational issues and had her own TV show on channel 11. Another Chicana, Hilda Reyes, reported on collecting food from local merchants to feed some of the people who would attend the demonstrations from out of town. Of course, a number of Berets were also present. I didn't recognize a lot of people because I was just starting to get involved in the community. At the meeting, the committee selected December 20, a Saturday, for the moratorium. All of us would work over the next several weeks to encourage others to attend and to plan for the speakers and other details.

I couldn't get completely involved in the Moratorium Committee because we, at the same time, had continued our discussions with the Crusade for Justice in Denver about holding an antidraft-antiwar conference there. We agreed to hold it on December 6–8. This would be the first national antidraft conference organized by Chicanos. Bobby Elias, with his contacts with Corky Gonzales and the Crusade, was key in putting together the conference along with Ramses and me.

A number of activists attended from different states. The largest contingent, of course, was from the Crusade in Denver. Our group from L.A. was the second largest, and then some came from Texas, New Mexico, Northern California, and a few other places. Fred Avilos, the Puerto Rican activist who had served prison time for refusing the draft, came all the way from Chicago. Overall, perhaps about 150 people attended, and I was very pleased with this since the conference had been organized on short notice.

This was also the first time I met Corky. I couldn't help but be impressed with him. He voiced support for all that we were doing and pledged to do whatever he could to advance the antidraft-antiwar movement.

Although we focused on the draft at our meetings, pretty soon the discussion shifted to protesting the war. People believed, and rightly so, that the war was now the major issue. As a result, although we agreed to continue draft counseling in our communities, we also decided to begin to build a national Chicano antiwar movement. Since the L.A. people, including the Chicano Moratorium Committee, were already ahead of others in their work, we in L.A. would take the lead in organizing initial antiwar demonstrations. David Sánchez and the Berets did not attend, but

Ramses and I told the conference that we believed that the Moratorium Committee would be in support.

In Denver we further determined that we would use a stage-by-stage approach to build a national moratorium. This would start with encouraging people to attend the December 20 demonstration in East L.A. Of major significance, we agreed that at the second National Chicano Youth Liberation Conference scheduled in the spring in Denver that our group would organize a major workshop on the war and that we would introduce a resolution calling for the conference to endorse a national Chicano antiwar movement. This would be crucial because we wanted to have wide support, certainly from throughout the Southwest but hopefully from outside of the region as well. The Denver youth conference would give us this wider imprimatur, or endorsement. In the meantime, we all agreed to go back to our communities and begin to build the antiwar movement. No specific national demonstration was projected as yet.

When Ramses and I began discussing having a Chicano moratorium in mid-November, we were already raising the antiwar issue. The antidraft theme had resonance, but the antiwar focus got to the essence. The Denver conference was the transition point for our national antidraft work to be converted to antiwar. "Raza Si! Guerra No!" became the main slogan now.

Around this time I also arranged to consult an attorney to handle whatever legal action the Selective Service might take against me. I discussed my case with Michael Tigar of the UCLA Law School. Tigar already had a growing reputation for defending people, like me, who refused induction, including one of César Chávez's sons. He also had gotten a lot of press coverage from being one of the defense attorneys for the Chicago Seven case, which had resulted from the massive demonstrations at the Democratic Party National Convention in Chicago in 1968. He had also defended Angela Davis in some of her legal battles from her political activism. Tigar was a top guy.

"Rosalio, I admire you for your protest," he told me. "I'll help you in your case."

I was, of course, delighted. But any thoughts about my legal condition would have to wait. I could only totally concentrate now on the Chicano antiwar movement.

MARCH AGAINST DEATH

We didn't have much time to organize the first moratorium, scheduled for December 20 in East L.A. I myself wasn't too involved with this work due to the time I spent putting together the Denver conference. Ramses, of course, was much more involved, as was David Sánchez and the Brown Berets, including Gloria Arellanes, the only female Beret minister. Most of the organizing work had to do with just getting the word out, literally mouth to mouth, as well as informing other movement groups and older Mexican American organizations about the march and demonstration. The Moratorium Committee also sent out a press release I wrote and invited a number of speakers. I was asked to be one of the speakers.

The committee also decided to focus the demonstration on the theme of bringing attention to the Chicanos, especially from L.A., killed in Vietnam. The committee selected the theme of "March against Death." We borrowed this theme from the November national antiwar demonstration in Washington, DC. The flyer we put out read, "IN HONOR OF OUR CHICANO BROTHERS, RELATIVES, FRIENDS AND LOVED ONES, WHO HAVE BEEN CHANNELED INTO THE DEATH PITS OF VIETNAM."

December 20 was a cold and overcast day. The assembly point for the march was Cinco Puntos, or the Five Points section of East L.A. The committee appropriately selected Cinco Puntos because a memorial to those from East L.A. who had died in World War II, including some Medal of Honor recipients, was located there. Because the committee had not been able to secure a permit from the county to march on Brooklyn Avenue, the main street, we used Michigan Avenue. We marched until we reached Obregon Park, where the rally would take place.

It was a spirited crowd, predominantly of young people. However, at first I was disappointed at the turnout. At the beginning of the march, it didn't seem like a large number. We marched by this little church where a wedding was taking place, and I remember thinking to myself that there seemed to be more people at the wedding than in the march. But at a later point, when the march went downhill, I raced ahead to get a better view, and as I looked back all I could see were hundreds of marchers filling the street. It looked impressive. In the end, we had about two thousand people, which we felt was a big success, given that it was the first Chicano protest against the war and that it was organized on such short notice.

At the rally, a number of people spoke, including myself. We used a flatbed truck as our stage. We all spoke in English, but some added in Spanish too. Oscar Zeta Acosta, the activist attorney, gave his rap. Alicia Escalante of the welfare-rights movement also spoke, as did a Mr. Domínguez, who had been a recent victim of police abuse. David Sánchez, of course, said a few words, as did several others, representing a variety of different community groups, including Joe Cerda, the leader of the L.A. Farm Workers' boycott. The speakers were very impressive. The Moratorium Committee had put together a true coalition. People spoke about the war and how it was damaging the Chicano community. They integrated their political issues, such as the farmworkers' struggle, the schools, police abuse, welfare rights, conditions in the barrios, and other issues, to the protest against the war. What was impressive to me was that these different movement groups were comfortable fitting these issues in with the antiwar issue. This held the key to the future organizing of the Chicano antiwar movement.

My own rap reflected this. Ramses had wisely counseled me to make the talk personal, to tell a story. So I talked about myself, in particular, about my fight with the Selective Service. I linked this to the general protest against the draft and the war. But I also linked these issues and my personal struggle with the racism and discrimination that we witnessed in the barrios.

"Our struggle is here, in the barrios. If we're going to fight anywhere, it's here at home and not in Vietnam."

I wasn't aware at that moment that at this first moratorium we were developing what would become the key theme of the Chicano antiwar movement: "¡La lucha está aquí!" (The struggle is here!) This theme was inherent in my "J'Accuse" proclamation. It began to be a slogan at the December 20 demonstration.

We didn't get much media coverage, but we didn't care. The moratorium had been a success. Channel 34, KMEX, covered it, and interviewed several others and me.

Everyone was elated and excited about the day. We sensed that it was the first step in making the war a central issue of the Chicano movement. "Let's have another one!" one of the excited Berets said at the end of the rally. We hadn't talked about another one soon, but we instinctively knew that we would.

MARCH IN THE RAIN

I now began to work more directly with the Moratorium Committee. By the end of the year, we decided that the next demonstration would be on February 28, 1970. It would again be in East L.A., but we planned it as a statewide demonstration. Going statewide was the natural thing to do. We had developed contacts throughout the state and even outside the state. We knew more people wanted to get involved. This meant more work for us, but we were ready for it and excited by the challenge.

Part of this work involved my assuming the cochair of the Moratorium Committee. Ramses, who was serving as cochair along with David Sánchez, wanted to get back to his classes at UCLA, and while he would continue to work with the committee, he felt he couldn't continue as cochair. As a result, I was asked to assume this position. David, who recommended me to the committee, agreed. I accepted.

In becoming cochair, I began to work almost full-time on the committee. Bobby Elias, who had joined the committee, also worked about as much. In between organizing for the February 28 demonstration, I worked for the UCLA Counseling Center as a consultant on the draft issue. I was hired that fall, and since I didn't have a job, I accepted the part-time position to have some income and not be too dependent on my parents.

These were busy and hectic times for me. The Moratorium Committee met every week to discuss our progress in organizing the February protest. We held our

FIGURE 15. *Left to right:* Mr. Ayala, Muñoz, and Chris Cepada at the Greater Los Angeles Press Club, February 1970. Courtesy of People's World, Labor Archives and Research Center, San Francisco State University, www.peoplesworld.org.

meetings mostly at the Euclid Community Center. David Sánchez and I chaired the meetings. I didn't know David very well, but we developed a good working relationship at the time. It was a goal-oriented relationship. David ran a good, organized meeting. I thought I did the same. We had different takes here and there, but there was room for some diversity of opinion. Part of this diversity had to do with the fact that our backgrounds were different. David was not centered on the college campuses. His emphasis was on working with high school students and with vatos locos and trying to recruit them into the Berets. By contrast, my political experience, such as it was, had been with college students at UCLA. But what tied us together, in addition to our antiwar views, was that we were all young people. We were a new generation—the Chicano generation.

In between our meetings, I spent a lot of time speaking at different community and campus groups about supporting and mobilizing for the February demonstration. Bobby Elias and I would often go together. We'd go to MEChA meetings, community organizations, antipoverty groups, and church groups. We would tell them about the inordinate number of Chicanos dying in Vietnam at the same time that antipoverty and educational programs were being cut or losing funding that instead went to pay for the war.

We were well received at these meetings. Most Chicanos and even those who called themselves Mexican American were against the war. Too many of their brothers, cousins, and sons had been killed or had returned either physically or emotionally wounded or both. We were also helped in that by 1970 what had been LBJ's war had now become Nixon's war. Most Mexican Americans supported the Democratic Party, and those who had held community positions due to their Democratic Party allegiance had been timid about voicing opposition to the war as long as the Democrats controlled the White House. After Nixon took office in 1969 and the Republicans continued the war, these Mexican American Democrats found it easier to criticize U.S. policy in Vietnam. These previous political buffers for the Democrats now became anti-Nixon opponents.

In addition, Mexican American labor union leaders endorsed and supported us. This was especially true of progressive unions such as the United Electrical Workers and the United Auto Workers. We also spoke to many church groups, both Catholic and Protestant. Some of the priests and ministers were a little cautious, but they didn't resist, and many supported us. Mexican American women were interesting. The women didn't have to hide behind any pro-war machismo. As mothers and sisters, they knew the sacrifices of their sons, brothers, cousins, husbands, and boyfriends. They weren't ashamed to cry, like my mother, when we talked about casualties. They fully endorsed our cause.

While Elias and I concentrated on these groups, David focused on mobilizing all the Beret chapters throughout California. By now there were Beret chapters in a variety of locations, such as Oakland, San Jose, Richmond, Santa Barbara, Riverside, Pomona, and San Diego, as well as many other cities and towns. Beret members numbered in the several hundreds, and they constituted a core support for the moratorium.

In addition to Chicano and Mexican American organizations and leaders, we also received support from some of the left groups in Los Angeles. The Peace Action Council continued to endorse our movement. The council had different progressive members. Sam Kushner, a reporter for the *People's Daily World*, the West Coast newspaper of the Communist Party, gave us good publicity for the moratorium. The Socialist Workers Party, the Trotskyite rival of the Communist Party, likewise endorsed us and through their paper, the *Militant*, provided more publicity.

After just a few weeks of hard work and organizing, the day of the march dawned. What a day! It was one of the worst days of our California winters. I awoke to a steady and cold downpour. California rains are not sporadic. They go on and on. That's the way it was on February 28, 1970. I was apprehensive as I drove to the staging area at Atlantic Park in East L.A. I didn't know what to expect. Surely the rain would discourage attendance.

Boy, was I surprised! When I arrived, there were already a large number of people, and the crowd continued to grow despite the rain. I could see that this was already going to be a larger demonstration than the one in December. That's what we hoped for and that's what we got. Some of our group estimated later that there were between three thousand and five thousand people. It felt like five thousand to me. I was elated. We had gone from almost nothing to this. We knew by now that we were getting our message out.

From Atlantic Park the march went on a few blocks and turned west on Whittier Boulevard, the main route of the march and the main artery of East Los Angeles. We then marched to Laguna Park (now Ruben Salazar Park), a distance of about two and a half miles. And we marched in the pouring rain. Ramses yelled out to Tlaloc, the Aztec rain god, "We are here!" Some people had umbrellas, and others had rain gear. In fact, some people who were not marching came out of their homes and stores and gave their umbrellas to some of the marchers. I wore a light jacket and a Mexican straw hat that I had bought in Mexico when I lived there. My clothes, however, were entirely inadequate. The rain went right through my hat, and I froze with my light jacket.

Despite the inclement weather, it was a spirited march. We had gotten permission to march in the streets, so we filled the streets with protesters. The mostly young marchers carried a variety of homemade signs, which soon wilted with the rain, and the lettering began to run. Some of the signs read,

"Hasta la Victoria Siempre [Until Victory, Always]"

"Learn to Read, Not to Kill"

"Mi Raza Primero"

"Chicano Power"

The UFW flag with the black eagle was also visible.

As we marched on Whittier Boulevard, Chicanos also shouted out a variety of movement chants as well as antiwar ones:

"Que Viva la Raza"

"Hell No, We Won't Go"

"Chicano Power, Chicano Power"

"Raza Sí, Guerra No"

"Raza Sí, Vietnam No"

"Bring Them Home"

There were contingents from a number of campuses and MEChA groups in L.A. and from other parts of California. Froben Lozado from Merritt College in Oakland came down with some of his students. Community groups also participated. But there's no question that the most visible and dramatic contingents were the various Brown Beret locals who marched with us. They wore their by now recognized brown berets and their khaki military-style jackets. The female Brown Berets, a contingent from Santa Barbara, wore their miniskirts and calf-length boots. They marched in tight military step: "left, left, left, right, left."

Also very dramatic were a number of young women who called themselves Las Adelitas de Aztlán (borrowing the term—Las Adelitas—from the women revolutionaries of the Mexican Revolution of 1910) and who dressed in black and carried short white crosses symbolizing the Chicanos killed in the war. This was very impressive and effective. Actually, these were former female Brown Berets such as Gloria Arellanes, Hilda and Grace Reyes, and others, along with Chicana welfare-rights activists. At the time I didn't know that these women had left the Berets or were in the process of leaving due to the sexism of the male Beret members.

I don't remember seeing many police along the route. There were some squad cars here and there, but not many. Where their presence was felt most was at the gas stations where the sheriff's department (in charge of unincorporated East L.A.) had apparently told the station owners or managers to lock their rest rooms to inconvenience us.

When we got to Laguna Park it was still raining steadily and getting even colder. We had planned for a rally with speeches and entertainment for at least a couple of hours, if not more. But we quickly realized that this was going to be impossible. We couldn't keep these thousands of people long under these awful conditions. As people trampled into the park, it became a sea of mud. We decided to cut the rally short.

Still, the speeches were good. I can't remember all the speakers, but we once again had Alicia Escalante. She was introduced as the *"adelita de todas las adelitas."* Alicia, unlike most of the other speakers, chose to speak in both English and Spanish: "It is an injustice that our Chicanos are sent to fight the war in Vietnam while our people here are denied welfare and other rights. ¡Ya basta!"

Then there was Oscar Zeta Acosta, the activist attorney. Oscar wore a cowboy hat, and all I can remember about his rap was that he sounded like Reies López Tijerina on the issue of Chicanos regaining their lost lands.

"This is our land! This is our land! Goddamn it! This is our land!" Oscar's voice boomed out. "This is not our government."

Sal Castro, the teacher and leader of the East L.A. blowouts, also spoke. Besides speaking out against the war, Sal called attention to the lack of Chicanos on Selective Service boards and made the point that this was one of the reasons why so many Chicanos were being drafted. He concluded by shouting out, "This has to change! ¡Viva nuestra raza de bronce [Long live our bronze race]!"

When David Sánchez spoke he accused the U.S. government of genocide against Chicanos because it was "destroying our *raza* in Vietnam."

I don't remember whether I spoke at the beginning or toward the end. Clinching the megaphone tightly and speaking directly into it, here is some of what I said:

> Before the moratorium in December, very few Chicanos were taking advantage of our draft counseling. Then, after the moratorium, when we walked down the streets of East L.A., the number of Chicanos who went in for draft counseling doubled and tripled. And after today, this is only going to increase. Just think of it, what if they gave a war *y no vino la raza* [and the people didn't go]? Que viva la raza!

FIGURE 16. Muñoz speaking at the March in the Rain antiwar demonstration, February 28, 1970. Courtesy of Victor Alemán.

I remember that I also, somewhat tongue in cheek, said, "Today we are all *mojados* [wetbacks] and proud of it!"

Although our moratorium was one of the largest held in L.A. against the war, it did not receive much media coverage. The Chicano press and the left press, of course, covered it, but not the mainstream one, although the Spanish-language channel 34 was there. On the other hand, KCET, the public television outlet, did send Claudio Fenner-López, one of their staff persons, with a crew to film the march. With a grant we purchased twenty copies of the film, which included interviews that we were able to use in our later antiwar efforts. Seeing the film showed others how to organize their own antiwar demonstrations. It also provided the image of our movement to the masses.[11]

DENVER YOUTH CONFERENCE

Following the March in the Rain, the next step toward organizing an even larger national moratorium involved going to the second Denver Youth Liberation Conference, scheduled for March 25–29, 1970. Inspired by our earlier demonstrations, we now came to the idea of organizing the national antiwar demonstration that we had talked to Corky Gonzales about in December. We planned to propose to the conference the idea of endorsing and supporting a national Chicano antiwar moratorium to be held in L.A. later that summer. We communicated our idea to Corky, who approved of this, and with his key help we felt confident that the participants at the conference would also endorse it.

Bobby Elias, Ramses, and I went to Denver representing the Moratorium Committee. David Sánchez chose not to go, although some Berets did attend. To this day I don't know why this was. However, we later picked up on rumors that some tensions existed between David and the Berets on one side and Corky on the other. But I don't know the nature of these tensions. David never talked to me about it, and I never heard Corky refer to it either.

Some two to three thousand Chicanos attended the conference. I had not attended the historic first one a year before that had issued El Plan de Aztlán. I was impressed with the turnout and the commitment to the Chicano movement displayed by the activists who went. Many others went from the L.A. area. Of course, people, men and women, mostly young, from throughout the Southwest and some from outside the region also attended.

I chaired the peace workshop that discussed our proposal for the national moratorium. To my surprise, there was spirited debate at the workshop concerning the proposal. Everyone supported the idea of holding a national moratorium. All opposed the war in Vietnam. The debate instead focused on the details of the moratorium. Where should it be held? What date? Adding to the debate and not being particularly helpful was a contingent of Chicano Trotskyites, members of the

Young Socialist Alliance. They emphasized that they preferred the conference to endorse a number of moratoriums on July 26 in different locations. This didn't go very far. We were going to have our own demonstration, independent of any other groups.

The debate became more involved about the location of the moratorium.

"We're already planning a moratorium in our city," some delegates said, "and we don't want to give that up for one in L.A."

In fact, several cities represented at the conference were organizing moratoriums.

We dealt with the issue with Corky's help by proposing that all these groups planning demonstrations continue to do so, but that they hold their moratorium earlier as a way of building up for the national demonstration in L.A. This satisfied everyone.

The next issue had to do with the date of the national moratorium. Several supported September 16, Mexican Independence Day, because it would allow us to build on this widely celebrated event. It would provide us with a ready-made audience. I could see their argument, but I didn't buy it.

"Look," Ramses pointed out, "the sixteenth of September is a Mexican holiday. We're Chicanos. We need our own history."

The distinction between Mexican nationalism and Chicano nationalism made a difference. We ruled out September 16.

We wanted a date before Labor Day, when most people were still on vacation and not yet back in school. We also needed a date late in the summer to allow us sufficient time to organize for the moratorium. I don't remember who proposed August 29. It might have been me, but it could have been someone else. In any event, the date seemed logical. It was the last weekend in August and just before Labor Day. It was a Saturday.

"¡Órale!" someone said. "Let's vote on this."

We did, and by a unanimous vote of the workshop we adopted the proposition that the conference endorse a national Chicano moratorium against the Vietnam War to be held on August 29, 1970, in Los Angeles. In addition, we proposed that the L.A. Moratorium Committee be in charge of coordinating the mobilization. To facilitate this we also adopted the name of the National Chicano Moratorium Committee. The plenary session, composed of all participants, in turn also passed these proposals unanimously and with great enthusiasm.

I, needless to say, was elated. We had succeeded in making the war in Vietnam into one of the major issues, if not the most important, of the Chicano movement. But this was only a partial success. Our challenge now was to pull it off by organizing as large a demonstration as possible.

As a result of this decision, a key slogan at the conference was, "Chale No, We Won't Go!"

Ruben Salazar, who covered the Denver conference and wrote a short front-page story on it for the *Los Angeles Times,* conveyed our elation. He interviewed me for it. In his article, Ruben noted that we were planning for as many as one hundred thousand demonstrators at the national moratorium. I don't remember using that figure—or anyone else using it either. On the other hand, we hoped to attract thousands, and if we could get even fifty thousand that would be great! It wasn't a bad goal to aim for.[12]

Recalling talking to Salazar in Denver makes for an eerie feeling today. How could we have known that when we selected August 29 as our moratorium date that we were also selecting the date for Ruben's murder?

BUILDING FOR THE MORATORIUM

Soon after returning from Denver, the Moratorium Committee met to discuss the conference and to begin to lay plans for the national protest on August 29. Prior to this meeting, somewhat to my surprise, David Sánchez told me that he was stepping down as national cochair of the committee. He gave as his reason that the Berets had many other issues, such as police brutality, that they were working on and couldn't afford to concentrate just on the moratorium. He also mentioned differences with Corky. I say that I was only somewhat surprised because I had noticed that David had not been as involved in the committee over the past few months. His not going to the Denver conference was part of this.

"I'll continue to support you, and the Berets will organize for the moratorium," David said, "but I can't personally be cochair. I'll propose that you be named the sole chair of the committee."

David's suggestion was accepted, and the committee passed it. I accepted the nomination, knowing it would be a lot of responsibility on my shoulders. It was a tough assignment, but by now I was fully committed to the struggle. I looked forward to the challenge.

As national chair, I stressed along with the committee that the focus of the national moratorium would be the toll that the Vietnam War was having on Chicanos. We were dying and being wounded disproportionately to our numbers in the United States. This issue of disproportionality in turn addressed what I had been saying about genocide and institutional racism. This suffering caused by the war was what attracted Chicanos, both young and old, to our cause. Grandsons and sons had been killed in Vietnam. Without this focus, we wouldn't have succeeded.

I stress this point because today some historians suggest that the moratorium was more of an effort to use the war issue as a way of highlighting Chicano domestic grievances such as the lack of job training, education, cutback in social welfare, and so on. Instead of the single issue of the war, they claim, the moratorium was really a multi-issue movement.[13] Now, I don't discount that the war impacted a

range of Chicano domestic concerns. Of course it did. But we could not have succeeded in recruiting people to our struggle if we approached them on a multiplic-
ity of issues. It was the war, and the war alone, that drew us support. I knew that
this had to be our focus, and I worked to make sure that we kept it and weren't
drawn into other issues that would distract us.

After the Denver conference, we in the committee resumed our weekly meetings. We had a good, committed, and regular group that came each week. Our usual
attendance was between fifteen and thirty people. Former female Brown Berets led
in this. Some older Mexican American leaders also participated. Everyone came to
work. At our meetings, we'd decide who was going to work on what aspect of the
moratorium, and then we would get weekly reports. Some people worked on publicity, some on arranging for food and housing for those coming from out of town,
some contacted other groups, and so on. As chair, I oversaw all these activities.

We were fortunate that we could operate out of an office. We had been using an
office in the Euclid Community Center on Whittier Boulevard, provided for us by
the Congress of Mexican American Unity, but this space soon became too small.
Fortunately, we got a break in June after the California primary when George
Brown, a liberal antiwar Democrat, who was running for the U.S. Senate against
John Tunney, a more conservative Democrat, lost the election. He had a large field
office in East L.A. on Brooklyn Avenue, and after his defeat he decided to let us use
it. This gave us much more room, not only for our meetings but also for our daily
work. It gave us a separate identity.

Besides a petition drive, endorsed in Denver, to get signatures against the war, we
went out and spoke to other Chicano and Mexican American groups to let them
know about the moratorium. We were aided in our presentations by a copy of the
March in the Rain film. Father John Luce of the Episcopalian church in Lincoln
Heights helped us by securing funds from the local National Council of Churches to
make some twenty copies of the film, as well as to rent some projectors. Armed with
the film, some of us would go to do our rap for these other groups. After we talked
about the war and the moratorium, we'd show the film. Sometimes we also got a copy
of the film *I Am Joaquin,* produced by the Teatro Campesino and based on Corky
Gonzales's poem by the same name. Our speakers would usually be Ramses, Bobby
Elias, Gil Cano, Gloria Arellanes, Gonzálo Javier, Lupe Saveedra, Jacobo Rodríguez,
and me. Instead of all going together, we split the work up. Ramses, based on his
experience with the farmworkers, always reminded us, "Take a collection." So we did
at the end of our presentations. We used the funds we collected for office supplies and
other related expenses such as long-distance calls. We found that what César Chávez
said was true: "when poor people give you their money, they give you their hearts."

Our most successful speaking engagements, however, came on the Cinco de
Mayo of that May. By this time, the Cinco de Mayo had become the one big cultural event associated with the movement and sponsored by MEChA and other

FIGURE 17. Muñoz at a protest at Roosevelt High School, 1970. Courtesy of Devra Weber.

Chicano student groups on campus and in communities. What was important about these engagements was not only speaking to large student groups but getting paid for it. The MEChA groups had access to campus funding, and so they could pay us anywhere from $100 to $500 to speak. We added these funds to our committee account to pay for our expenses.

It was around this time, the beginning of May, that the Cambodian invasion by Nixon took place. The campuses erupted in protest. Strange as it may seem, we in the committee really didn't take part in these actions. We were too busy with organizing the moratorium, although, of course, we supported and sympathized with the protests. The Cambodian invasion and the widening of the war, in turn, only seemed to bring more attention to our specific antiwar activities as we looked toward August 29. The moratorium had now become the priority of the *movimiento*.

Besides speaking to different groups, we also sought their endorsement of the moratorium. This meant that in our publicity, as well as in our contacts with other groups, we could list those who had endorsed the planned demonstration. In addition to the various student groups that endorsed us, we also went to some specific community groups for their support. Very early on, the Congress of Mexican American Unity, led by Esteban Torres, supported us. This was big because the congress represented more than two hundred Mexican American groups. I attended the convention of the Community Service Organization, a longtime Mexican American civil rights group, led by Tony Rios, and got its endorsement. Bert Corona, one of the founders and leaders of the Mexican American Political Association, invited me to speak at the MAPA convention in Fresno. They, too, endorsed the moratorium. Several other Chicano groups, both movement and nonmovement, such as the United Auto Workers of the L.A. area, also supported us.

In addition, we received endorsements from white antiwar groups such as the Peace Action Council, faith groups, the Communist Party, and the Socialist Workers Party. Both of the parties in turn publicized the moratorium in their papers.

Some black groups also endorsed us. These included both student and community ones. Angela Davis, who was then at UCLA, gave us her personal endorsement and participated in the moratorium as part of the Che-Lumumba Club sponsored by the Communist Party.[14]

In these efforts, we were also fortunate to recruit a number of volunteers who helped staff the office and supported our different activities. The former Berets were of great assistance and proved to be effective organizers. In addition, many MEChA and local area groups sent representatives to our weekly meetings. A strong San Fernando Valley Chicano Moratorium Committee was formed. Older grassroots activists from the zoot-suit days were committee members, such as Rudy Tovar, Rudy Salas, Carmen Vera, and Lillian Villegas.

There is no question that in addition to what we were doing in L.A. to build support for the moratorium that the strategy of Chicano antiwar moratoriums in other cities proved crucial in getting the word out about the national demonstration and getting people inspired to go to Los Angeles. There must have been as many as twenty such moratoriums that spring and summer. In some cases these were arranged by local Brown Beret chapters or by other groups such as MEChA or MAPA. We sent representatives from the committee to as many of these as possible. These protests were held in places such as Fresno, Oakland, San Diego, Santa

FIGURE 18. Muñoz at the San Fernando
Chicano Moratorium, July 18, 1970.
Courtesy of People's World.

Barbara, San Bernardino, Coachella, Bisbee, Chicago, McAllen in Texas, and other areas. I personally went and spoke at moratoriums in Oxnard, San Pedro, San Fernando, San Francisco, Oakland, and Houston. The turnouts varied but in some places reached five hundred, one thousand, and two thousand.

In mid-July we held a big fund-raiser for the moratorium. We didn't organize it. The Peace Action Council did it for us. They rented a venue in West L.A. and invited singers like Pete Seeger, Arlo Guthrie, Earl Robinson, and several other protest singers. Lots of people, mostly liberal whites, attended.

At the event, I spoke, as did my attorney, Michael Tigar. Other antiwar activists also spoke, mostly Anglos. Actually, Tigar introduced me as a draft resister and as the head of the Chicano antiwar movement. I was flattered, but I was more impressed with the amount of money raised for us. I was actually given this amount in cash and checks and just stuffed them in my pockets.

In addition to going to other moratoriums, we built for the August 29 date by keeping in contact with many other Chicano groups, inside and outside of California. From my trips in the fall to Kansas City, Albuquerque, and Denver, I had gotten a fairly long list of names and phone numbers. Most of these people were affiliated with student or community organizations. That summer we started calling them to encourage them to come to the demonstration.

"How's it going? I'm just calling to see if you guys are thinking of coming to the moratorium. We can help with housing and food."

"Yeah, some of us are going. We'll be taking some vans. We're looking forward to it."

We called all over the place. Many of the funds that we collected in fact went to paying for our long-distance calls. Almost everyone was encouraging and expressed support for the moratorium.

Through these calls we got an indication that many were coming from outside L.A. and from other places in the Southwest. Unfortunately, one of the groups that did not formally respond was La Raza Unida Party in Texas, led by José Ángel Gutiérrez. Carlos Guerra, a MAYO activist from Texas and La Raza Unida leader, did come to the moratorium to speak. It's possible that in time La Raza Unida Party from Texas might have joined us.

ROUTING THE MARCH

Part of our concentration, in addition to getting the word out, was to plan for the event itself. We all agreed that, as in the previous two other antiwar protests in East L.A., the moratorium would be in Boyle Heights, the heart of the barrio. But we had to decide just where the march would take place and where the rally would be. In this discussion, one of the Berets suggested that the principal location of the march be on Soto Street and that the rally be at Hazard Park on Soto.

"We've done the other route before, *ese*," he said. "Let's do something different."

But the others and I didn't agree. Soto Street is more of a side street. Instead, we wanted to use Whittier Boulevard principally again because it was the main thoroughfare through East L.A. It was the largest commercial center of the barrio. Everyone went there to shop, eat, and just hang out. We also eliminated Hazard Park for the same reason—it was not adjacent to the center of the barrio. Instead, we again chose Laguna Park due to its proximity to Whittier.

One change that we made was to choose a larger staging area for the march, where everyone would first congregate. We felt that we would get a very sizable crowd. We chose Belvedere Park, which would provide this space. This meant that the initial part of the march would be on Atlantic Boulevard and then intersect with Whittier, where we would march until we got to the entrance to Laguna Park. The specifics of the entire route were from the park down East Third Street,

Beverly Boulevard, Atlantic Boulevard, and Whittier Boulevard. The distance was about three and a half miles, and we figured it would take at least a couple of hours for the marchers to reach the park.

Having decided on the route, we then requested a permit to use the streets for the march. This meant going to the board of supervisors for permission. Since this section of East L.A. is an unincorporated area, it was and is under the jurisdiction of the county and the County Sheriff's Department. All we had to do was fill out a form. In a few days, we received permission, but with a stipulation that we could march only on one side of the street. We didn't make a big deal about this because we knew that we weren't going to abide by that restriction anyway—it was ridiculous. Imagine tens of thousands marching in two lanes and cars going on the other side in the opposite direction. This wasn't going to happen.

Besides obtaining the permit, we maintained contact with the sheriff's department up to August 29. We wanted to make sure that they knew what we were doing and our plans for the march and for the rally. One thing that we were concerned about was having too many officers visible during the march; we wanted to avoid any reaction to their presence. They assured us that whatever force they might have that day would remain some distance from the marchers. I got no indication that we might have some trouble with the sheriffs. They seemed very accommodating. This was perhaps naive on our part, or maybe we just had so many other things to deal with.

SÁNCHEZ COUSINS

During July our efforts had clearly intensified. However, it was around this time that we briefly paused to join in a community-wide reaction to a case of police abuse. Without any reason, the Los Angeles police had killed two innocent Mexican nationals, the Sánchez cousins. The police had busted into their apartment allegedly on a drug raid and without provocation killed the cousins. It was never proven that they had been involved in drugs. The Chicano community reacted with outrage.

One of our volunteers, an undocumented worker, upon hearing the news on the radio began urging us to do something about what had happened. Our activists and volunteers were for it. We called around to our support groups, and people wanted to react by organizing an all-day and all-night vigil and picketing the police headquarters. Consequently, we shifted gears and integrated this strategy into our mobilization.

We all went downtown, where we joined hundreds of other Chicanos picketing the police and calling for an investigation and justice. Congressman Edward Roybal joined the protest. We picketed and held our vigil until about five in the morning. Sometime before then I drove to Boyle Heights to pick up one of our volunteers, only to be arrested by the cops. It was like they had been waiting for me. They charged me with not having paid some parking tickets. But the fact that they used the vigil to arrest me for these minor charges was too coincidental. This was clearly a political arrest. From having been outside Parker Center, I was now taken inside and booked. I was going to be put in jail, but fortunately—and I don't know how this happened—Rose Chernin, one of the leaders of the Communist Party, bailed me out. Needless to say, I was very much indebted to her.

Despite our protests, the police did not investigate the killing of the Sánchez cousins. Ruben Salazar, now the news director for KMEX, the Spanish-language television station, gave priority coverage to the case. Eventually, the liberal U.S. attorney in L.A. brought charges against the police officers involved; however, he was soon removed from his office.

As I look back on all these events leading up to the moratorium, it's very likely that the police, the sheriffs, and even the FBI infiltrated our group. We later learned that this kind of surveillance was being done on the movement as a whole.

But we again didn't focus on this, and we certainly didn't obsess about it. We were doing nothing illegal. In fact, we were exercising our constitutional right of peaceful protest.

The fact of the matter was that police repression against the Chicano community was becoming a major movement issue even before the moratorium. Its importance was substantiated by the U.S. Civil Rights Commission and emphasized by leaders such as César Chávez and Bert Corona. Ruben Salazar, now as news director of KMEX, gave priority coverage to it. The Sánchez cousins only added to growing grievances against the police.

ORGANIZING AND PUBLICIZING THE RALLY

One of the tasks we had to finalize was the list of speakers at the rally. There was no controversy about the list. There were the obvious speakers such as César and Corky. We also invited Luis Valdez and the Teatro Campesino. Others outside of L.A. included Enriqueta Vásquez, a writer from New Mexico, and Carlos Guerra, a representative from MAYO in Texas. Then there would be other speakers from L.A., including some of the same ones from previous demonstrations such as David Sánchez of the Berets, Oscar Zeta Acosta, and Sal Candelaria of the Black Berets from San Jose. We also arranged for some Puerto Rican and Native American speakers. I would speak as chair of the committee. Finally, we invited some singing and Mexican *folklórico* dance groups to provide entertainment. It was a full schedule of speakers and performances for the rally.

Once we completed the agenda for the march and rally, we then turned to publicity. We needed a poster that would call attention to the moratorium and that we could distribute everywhere. We placed Ramses, since he was an artist, in charge of this. I told him that I thought it would be a good idea to have images of key people such as César, Corky, Luis Valdez, and David Sánchez.

"I think this will reflect the leadership of the movement and that they endorse the moratorium," I said.

Ramses didn't disagree with me, and so I didn't give it much thought, believing that he agreed with me. A few days later, Ramses shows up with the poster.

"Here it is. I hope you like it."

I couldn't believe it. Instead of César, Corky, Valdez, and David, there was only one image. Me!

"What the hell? What am I going to do with this poster?"

"*Cálmate, ese,*" Ramses told me to calm down. "It's important that the moratorium speak with one voice and that it reflects leadership. You're the chair of the committee, and you should be on the poster. Don't you like it?"

It was a good poster, and outside of my image it provided all the necessary information that people needed about the moratorium. I tried to convince Ramses to change the image, but he wouldn't hear of it. In fact, the other members of the committee thought it was fine. So I went along with it, still fearing a negative reaction from the others.

I was pleasantly surprised when no one attacked me for promoting myself as a cult figure. There were a few rumblings from the Berets, but no real criticism. But just to be sure, we put out another poster done by a Mexican artist, Adolfo Cevallos, which was a bit more abstract, featuring an Aztec pyramid with these brown hands coming together. It was a good poster.

In addition to distributing posters and mailing them to our contacts outside of L.A., we also contacted the media about the moratorium in the hope that they would mention it and cover it. We sent out press releases to all the media: newspaper, radio, and television. This was the Anglo media. We knew that the Chicano media, such as the movement newspapers, would give us publicity.

As a result of our press releases, we got a number of requests for media interviews, including local television news. The media coverage intensified as we got closer to August 29.

Of course, we made a special effort to contact Ruben Salazar. By then he had left the *Times,* although he still wrote an influential column for the paper. As significant, if not more, he had accepted a new position as news director of KMEX-TV, channel 34, the only Spanish-language station in L.A. at the time. In this capacity, Salazar was increasing the station's coverage of the Chicano community and doing hard-hitting investigative stories, especially about police abuse. We wanted to reconnect with Salazar to make sure that he and his TV crew covered the moratorium.

We knew that Salazar would cover it. He had promised this back at the time of my draft protest. But it was also clear by now that Salazar was becoming more outspoken on Chicano issues, including the war. In an interview with Bob Navarro of KNBC-TV, filmed before the moratorium but shown only after his death, Salazar openly criticized U.S. policy in Vietnam and used our argument about the disproportionate number of Chicano casualties.

We called Salazar and arranged a meeting with him. He suggested that we have lunch at a restaurant close to the station.

"Can I bring some of my committee members?" I asked.

"Sure," he replied, "bring whomever you want."

Ramses and Gonzálo Javier went with me.

At lunch, we briefed Salazar on our preparation. He listened intently. When we were finished, he then peppered us with questions about the route of the march. How many people were we expecting? He wanted to know, more or less, how marchers would line up—would they be random or by contingents? He wanted to know the setup of the rally. Where would the platform for the speakers be? What kind of a sound system would we have? How long would the rally last? Then he wanted to know the list of speakers. Who would speak first? Was it certain that César and Corky would be there?

By the questions he was asking, I got the sense that he was trying to picture what the scene would look like and how he would film it, including how many cameras he would need. At that time, videotape was not widely used, so he would use regular film that would be edited for the news program. He really wanted to feature the event.

We finished lunch, with Salazar's assurances that he would definitely film the moratorium. This was not just a reporter telling us this. It was also a Mexican American who was proud of what we were doing and why we were doing it. He wished us luck.

"*Hasta luego, muchachos.* I'll see you on August 29."

I would see Ruben Salazar one more time on that fateful day.

Besides the posters and press releases, we also provided bumper stickers and buttons calling attention to the moratorium. Home meetings hosted by community people and campus rallies furthered our efforts to get the word out.

EVE OF THE MORATORIUM

August 29 was almost on top of us. As we came closer to the date, we began to get more indications of a sizable turnout. More people were calling to tell us they were coming and bringing so many people in cars and vans. It looked like it was going to be big. We hoped for fifty thousand. With all the notices that we were receiving by August, I felt that we had a good chance of getting that many. I knew it would be in the thousands and that it would dwarf the other moratoriums. Gloria Arellanes took on the challenging task of arranging housing for those from out of town.

Two things happened, however, prior to the demonstration that were disturbing and, in retrospect, chilling. The first concerned the Berets in L.A. criticizing our efforts. In their newspaper, *La Causa*, they raised questions about our leadership and about the credibility of the committee. It also had a snide reference to Corky Gonzales. It was a cheap shot, and provocative.

What was of further concern were statements that there might be a riot at the moratorium. In fact, these came from the Berets. They didn't say that they were going to riot, but one Beret told me, "Rosalio, we need to have a riot like the blacks. That's the only thing that whites pay attention to."

Then some young vato told me, "There's gonna be a riot."

"No," I said, "there's not going to be a riot."

"But the people want a riot," the vato persisted.

"No," I replied with some irritation, "the people don't want a riot."

I must have been temporarily distracted by this kind of talk, but we were so busy on the eve of the moratorium that I couldn't dwell on it. It's only now, many years later, that I look back on that prophesy—if that's what it was—with questions. Did someone already know what would happen?

I should say that during all this time preceding the moratorium, my parents were very supportive, as were my siblings, although, understandably, they were worried about something happening to me. I appreciated their support, even though by that summer I no longer lived with them. I had a new girlfriend then, Alicia Saucedo, and I moved in with her. I didn't see my parents much because I was running around all over the place. I was very pleased when my parents said that they would be attending the moratorium. My older sister, with her infant son, would be coming down from Oregon, and my brother Ricardo would drive them to the rally. It would be a family event. My younger sister, Elvira, and my cousin Sylvia Díaz would sit with them.

I don't think I got very much sleep the night before the moratorium. I kept thinking about my speech and what the next day would be like. I was too anxious and nervous to sleep. Everything seemed to be falling into place. We had worked hard over the past few months, and it appeared that our work would now be rewarded. Key people all had their responsibilities: Ramses, Gloria Arellanes, Bobby Elias, Grace Reyes, Jacobo Rodríguez, Carlos Reyes, Gonzálo Javier, Gil Cano, and many others.

❦   AUGUST 29

August 29 dawned early. I could already feel the heat of the day. I went to the office around eight or nine o'clock, but most everyone had already left to go either to the staging area at Belvedere Park or to Laguna Park, where the rally would take place. On the way to Belvedere, I saw a lot of Chicanos who had arrived for the demonstration. Our office at 4629 Brooklyn Avenue was about a half mile from Belvedere.

When I got there, a large number of people had already gathered, and more were arriving. We had put on our posters and had stated in our announcements that the starting time of the march would be at ten o'clock. We didn't expect to start quite then. We were going by Chicano time—when the people were ready, that's when we would start. Ten o'clock was just a way of assuring that people had a sense of what time they should assemble. I immediately started running into people I knew. "How are you," they would say to me. "We've brought a large contingent with us." A lot of people were arriving, but I could tell it wasn't going to be a hundred thousand or even fifty thousand. But still my sense was that it was going to be big.

When I got to the park at Third and Laverne, some of the speeches were already under way. We had arranged for some speakers at the commencement of the march because it would be a way of keeping people together and keeping spirits up as more people arrived. Some of the speakers included members of our committee or representatives from outside of L.A. The big names would speak at Laguna Park.

When the park got packed with people—a crowd that would later be estimated at between twenty thousand and thirty thousand people, mostly Chicano but about 15 percent non-Chicano—it was time to march. There was no logic or order as in a parade. With the exception of a lead banner by the Moratorium Committee, everyone else just fell into line depending on his or her proximity to the start of the march. While there was no set order, people tended to march with the group they came with. For example, there was a sizable UFW contingency. Some belonged to various political or community groups, while others were linked by the places they represented such as Fresno, Tucson, El Paso, and so on. At this point I wasn't involved in directing the march. Others were doing that. My focus remained just on what I would say. I was still agonizing over this as the march commenced. I was always nervous—still am—just before I have to speak in public. I didn't want to read a speech, so I kept going over in my head just what I would say.

We began leaving Belvedere Park somewhere closer to eleven o'clock. I'm not certain of the actual time, but that's my best guess.

The route of the march was a bit different from the previous ones, since this was the first time we had gathered at Belvedere Park. We had needed a bigger assembly point. As we exited the park, we went on Third Street and then south on Atlantic Boulevard on our way to Whittier Boulevard, which would be the main part of the march until we got to Laguna Park.

On Atlantic, we encountered a wedding party out of St. Alphonsus Catholic Church, one of the largest parishes in East L.A. The wedding party came out and joined the march! But that was no coincidence. It had been planned. The guy who was getting married was an activist by the name of Miguel de la Peña. He was a MEChA leader from USC, a real militant guy at the time. I witnessed all this because I was marching toward the front. The encounter with the wedding party only added to the festive and deeply cultural character of the demonstration, at least at that point in the day. It was quite a sight to see the bride and groom with the wedding party all dressed up and marching with us.

Shortly after that, I encountered Ruben Salazar with his channel 34 TV crew at the corner of Atlantic and Whittier. Sam Kushner, the reporter from *People's Daily World,* was walking with him. I could see that Ruben was in a good mood and excited about the great turnout. People had hoped for but not expected such numbers. Ruben spotted me and came up to me.

"*Viejo,* congratulations! You did it!"

He gave me a big *abrazo.* I could feel he was sincere about his feelings. He had promised us months before that if we pulled off a large antiwar demonstration, he would cover it. And here he was. Ruben wasn't just covering the moratorium; he believed in what we were doing. We smiled face-to-face. I later learned that he wore one of our moratorium buttons. This was the last time I talked to Ruben. I don't even remember what I said to him. It didn't matter. What he said was what mattered. Ironically, as we marched down Whittier, we passed the Silver Dollar Café, a hole-in-the-wall bar that would become immortalized later that day.

As we marched, everyone was having a good time. We filled the streets. We felt empowered. There were some people on the sidewalks, but not many. It was mostly the marchers on Whittier that day. As in the other marches, people spontaneously chanted and called out slogans:

"¡Viva la Raza!"

"¡Raza Sí, Guerra No!"

"¡Raza Primero!"

"¡Viva la Chicana!"

Many carried signs indicating what groups or locations they represented. Other signs read:

"Be Brown and Be Proud"

"Our Fight Is in Aztlán, Not in Vietnam"

"Brown Is Together"

"Aztlán: Love It or Leave It"

People were meeting people and exchanging greetings. It was kind of like a picnic.

On the other hand, I heard from some of our people and others that large contingents of county sheriffs could be seen on adjacent streets. I saw a few, but not many, along the route of the march. They were not super obvious. But I did get reports that in fact there were many around, some in buses, and that they were armed. A later news report mentioned five hundred fully armed county sheriff's deputies. They were staging, so I heard, as if for a fight or something. I was particularly concerned because that's the way the sheriffs and cops in general acted when there was a large demonstration. We had told them that this was going to be a peaceful moratorium, and so my feeling was that there would be no problems, at least not from the people.

We had, of course, taken certain precautions to ensure order, so as not to provoke the sheriffs. We had organized a number of monitors to control the march and the rally. Many of them were Chicano law students such as Richard Cruz and his people from Loyola Law School. They had been involved earlier with Católicos por la Raza.[15] At one point Richard took on a dissident Brown Beret who wanted to disrupt the march. Richard quieted him down. With the monitors' help, I felt confident, as the march proceeded toward Laguna Park, that everything was going as planned. The march was a success, and now we would move on to the rally and the speakers.

It took us about an hour or an hour and a half to do the march. This covered about three and a half miles. We weren't goose-stepping or running, but we were walking at a deliberate pace. At different points, part of the march might get a bit ahead of the rest, but the monitors soon connected them.

It was a long march, and it seemed longer due to the temperature. It was one of those hot, smoggy L.A. summer days. The temperature must have been in the high eighties or low nineties, with a bright sun out. We all got tired and, of course, thirsty. Small individual water bottles weren't as available then as now, so most marchers carried no water or other drinks. We had anticipated that and had stationed stands along the way with containers of water and paper cups.

It wasn't until we got to the entrance into Laguna Park that we encountered our first problem of the day. There was no direct entrance into the park from Whittier. The park is set back about a block or so from the boulevard. There are one or two small streets that lead into the park, but they're very narrow. Our plan was to keep the marchers moving as we passed these small entrances and instead go a bit farther down Whittier and enter the park from the back or west end, where it was more accessible. To ensure that the marchers continued moving in the direction we wanted, we arranged for the sheriffs to install some barriers to block those other entrances. However, when we reached that point, there were no barriers. Why weren't they there? As a result, some people started leaving the march to enter the park through those side streets, while others continued. All this caused congestion and stalling, until some marchers got too impatient and tried to find other ways to enter the park on their own. This caused some confusion and disorganization. It also meant that our monitors couldn't keep an eye on everyone. In retrospect, this was a problem.

Since I was at the front of the march, I was part of the contingent that first entered Laguna Park. There were already a number of people inside the park who had opted to go directly to the rally rather than march. Many of them were older, like my mom and dad, or had young children, like my sister. Upon entering, I went to the makeshift stage that we had assembled earlier in the day. We had gotten the use of a flatbed truck from somewhere, which we used for the stage, where the speeches and entertainment would take place. Behind the truck, and as a protective backdrop to the stage, we had also positioned two or three yellow school-type buses. The idea for this had come from Corky Gonzales and his people, who had told us that for Corky's security we needed to do something like this. The buses protected our rear. No one could position themselves behind the stage. We had no money to rent such buses, but fortunately some contingents from places like Long Beach and Riverside came in buses. We knew ahead of time that they would so we arranged to borrow the buses for our stage.

From the stage I could look out at the already-assembled crowd, now being joined by the marchers. What struck me was that the people who hadn't marched seemed to be families with small children. The presence of families with kids only added to the festive atmosphere. It seemed typical of a weekend in the park in East L.A., when families go to have a picnic or barbecue and let the kids enjoy the open spaces. I knew my parents and siblings were out there somewhere, but I couldn't make them out. Laguna Park isn't that big, but with several hundred people already in the park and thousands more arriving, it soon became a sea of faces. These included courageous undocumented immigrants whom Bert Corona and Chole Alatorre had brought.

I don't remember the exact time that the others and I reached the park. I guess it was around one o'clock, and it was getting hotter. When I got there the entertainment with groups like the Trio Aztlán had already started, which was good since there were those people, like my parents, who had arrived earlier. We had scheduled *conjuntos,* or small musical groups, who would sing the *corridos* of the Mexican Revolution. We also had *folklórico* dancers, seven- to twelve-year-olds, who would do traditional Mexican regional dances. Again, the music and the dancing further contributed to the peaceful, nonviolent character of the moratorium.

As a chair of the Moratorium Committee, my charge was to open the program by welcoming the crowd and delivering my speech. I was even more nervous as it came time to do this. We had to wait a while, until all the marchers entered the park. In the meantime, the singing and dancing went on. One activist read, "El Plan Espiritual de Aztlán." We had no fixed time schedule. Whenever we were ready to start, we started.

Then it was time for me to step up to the stage. It was perhaps sometime after two thirty in the afternoon. I had carefully planned for this moment. I didn't want to appear too informal, so I wore my nice white *guayabera* shirt that I had bought either in Mexico on our trip when I was still in high school or when I was a college student. I can't remember. In any event, here I was with this sparkling white shirt that looked even whiter contrasted to my quite dark Indian-looking complexion, which had only gotten darker due to the hot sun that day.

FIGURE 19. Muñoz speaking at the National Chicano Antiwar
Moratorium, August 29, 1970. Courtesy of George Rodríguez.

But I was nervous. I had spoken to an even larger crowd at the San Francisco
moratorium, and I was nervous then, but I was even more nervous in East L.A. I
think because this was our moratorium, I felt an even stronger responsibility to it.
At one level, I was thrilled and proud that we had pulled off what would amount to
the largest demonstration during the Chicano movement. But I didn't have time to
savor this because of my being nervous about my presentation.

Fortunately, we had installed a decent sound system with a microphone,
so I wouldn't have to shout into a megaphone, as I had to do in the earlier
moratoriums.

I saw no cops around. All I could see was a sea of faces—mostly Chicano—sitting and standing in the park. I welcomed them on behalf of the Moratorium
Committee and all those who had worked with us.

I went into my prepared remarks that I had tried to memorize:

You know, about a year ago, when we started *organizando* against the war, when I got
my induction notice for the sixteenth of September, there were very few of us, but the
few of us knew that our people were tired of this war, knew that our death rate was
twice that of all other service personnel, and knew that if we moved and dedicated
our lives to this struggle, that the people would respond. In fact, they would take
leadership, and that is what you have done today. You have taken the lead for our
people.

But it's only, only the first step in the organizing of the chain so that our people
have self-determination. It's like a child, a baby, learning how to walk. Many times we
stumble, many times we fall, but we get back up, and we know we have time on our
side, that we're going to have a whole lifetime of La Raza before us. If something hap-
pens that seems to be discouraging at one point, knowing that time is on our side, we
can use it to our advantage. This is the power that we have as La Raza.

You know we Chicanos have the best architects, the best artists this world has
ever seen, and our movement already has the structure there for a powerful force for
social change, but we are like a *familia separada* [separated family] in the issue of the
war and our pride in our love of working. They take advantage [of us] in Vietnam, in
the fields, and in the factories. But we have to come together and put our family
together as we have begun to do *hoy* [today], and we're going to be doing that.

One of the things we have to stress is unity. We can no longer really tolerate the
backstabbing that we have seen in many of our organizations. We have to come
together as a *familia* to make a strong force for *cambio social* [social change]. And in
beginning, on this issue of the war, we have to bring the war here in the struggle for
social justice. The Moratorium Committee and many people after this organizing on
the war will begin organizing on the issue of police brutality. But we also, all of us,
have to join in the struggle of the campesinos. We have to back Chicano candidates
like Ricardo Romo [candidate of the Peace and Freedom Party]. We have to support
all of our groups because they are all moving on their own levels, and we'll bring an
end to this oppression.

¡Que Viva la Raza![16]

I got a huge applause in the form of a Chicano clap. This is a slow-developing
applause that then builds to a crescendo and ends with everyone clapping very
rapidly and loudly. Some shouted out, "¡Que Viva la Raza!"

I was relieved at the end of my speech, but at the same time feeling empowered.
I drew from the strength of the crowd. Speaking into the microphone, I could feel
the power of my voice. But I was also drained at the end. It was a great feeling.

Out of, I guess, vanity, I didn't wear my glasses when I spoke. I'm somewhat near-
sighted and have worn glasses since high school, but I chose not to wear them as I
addressed the crowd. I could see faces, but not very clearly. But even with my poor
vision, as I finished my remarks, out of the corner of my eyes, I glimpsed some movement that seemed out of sorts, but I couldn't readily identify it. I also detected, as I was

finishing my speech, a certain restlessness at the back of the crowd. At first I thought that it was because I was going on too long. "Get off the stage," I said to myself.

THE SHERIFFS' ATTACK

After I finished speaking, I went down the backstairs of the platform, where some reporters from Mexico and Europe were waiting for me. As I descended the stairs, I heard the next speaker, Gonzálo Javier, proclaim that Chicanos should refer to Laguna Park as Benito Juárez Park. This got a rousing applause. The reporters I talked to had not been able to make our press conference, so they wanted to interview me after I spoke. This didn't take very long. In the meantime, one of the singing groups started up again.

The interviews concluded. I went back up to the stage area. It was then that the commotion started. It started at the back of the park on the west end. This is where I had detected some movement as I had finished speaking. One of our guys, Gonzálo, kept telling the people to settle down, that there would be no problems. He spoke in Spanish: "Aquí están nuestras mujeres y nuestros niños. No queremos pedo [Our women and our children are here. We don't want any shit]." But now this was more than just some minor movement. There was disruption. The people in the back were stampeding toward the front. It was kind of wavelike. As the people in the back advanced, the next row of people joined them. They kept coming toward the front. Why were they fleeing? It didn't take long to see the bopping helmets entering the park, and as they advanced I could see the khaki uniforms of the sheriff's deputies. It wasn't just a few. It looked like a hundred or more. As I looked closer, I could see that they had their billy clubs out, and some had what appeared to be shotguns, which turned out to be tear-gas weapons. They were soon joined by the Los Angeles police.

All of this was happening in seconds. As some of our people and the monitors quickly realized what was happening, they got up on the stage and tried to restore order.

"Sit down, sit down," they shouted into the mike. "Sit down, sit down."

But they didn't sit down. It was a panic.

Realizing this, our people then turned to try to get the sheriffs not to advance farther into the park.

"Back up, police!"

"Hold it up!"

"Police, hold your line!"

"Hold your line, hold your line, hold your line," they appealed.

But this didn't work either.

At that moment, I had no idea what had provoked this attack or whether it was a calculated, preplanned attack. How could so many cops be there so quickly?

It wasn't until later that day that I learned some of the details, or at least the argument by the sheriffs, as to why they attacked. According to them, before entering the park some of the marchers had deviated from the march and entered the Green Mill Liquor Store on Whittier, around 3:25 P.M. They claimed that some of the Chicanos started stealing stuff from the store and that the owner called in the sheriffs. When the squad cars appeared, again according to the sheriffs, some of the Chicanos started pelting them with rocks, bottles, and other materials. As they chased these Chicanos down toward the park, the sheriff called for reinforcements and made the decision to declare the rally an "unlawful assembly."

I never bought all this crap. We heard later that the store owner stated he never called the cops. But assuming that what happened at the liquor store was true, there was no justification for attacking the entire twenty thousand–plus in the park. And how was it that on the spur of the moment what appeared to be hundreds of cops showed up? Was it possible they were there already and that the attack had in fact been planned? Was the incident at the store provoked by an undercover cop to justify the attack? We may never know, but I'm convinced, and I'll go to my grave believing that the sheriffs, the LAPD, and the FBI had every intention that day of destroying the moratorium. They couldn't allow Chicanos to successfully mount such a show of force. We had to be attacked.

The police moved on the crowd. However, some of the Chicanos began throwing rocks and sticks, whatever they could get their hands on, at the cops as a way of resisting. As they moved on the sheriffs, the deputies retreated.[17] Then more police arrived and moved forward again. Some of our monitors, such as Professor Rudy Acuña, moved in between the cops and the people. This took a lot of guts to be in between the firing lines. But this only temporarily halted the attacks on both sides.

While this was going on, I was on the stage witnessing the ensuing battle, while people—elderly ladies and young moms with their babies—were climbing over the stage or going around it to vacate the park. For all I know, one of these women might have been my mother. Fortunately, as some of the cops moved into the park, my brother had quickly escorted my parents and my sister out of there. Ricardo knew his way around this area and got them out without any problems.

In the meantime, there was chaos in the park. The closest thing to what was happening was a soccer riot. People were running all over one another. But getting out of the park wasn't easy. The east end of the park, where they ran to, was almost like a cul-de-sac. There were very few exits.

But what helped was that as some of the more courageous Chicanos attacked the sheriffs and forced their temporary retreat, this created a space and an opportunity for many of the people to move back and leave the park without having the cops right on top of them. Blocked by the Chicanos and the monitors, the deputies started lobbing tear-gas projectiles over them and onto the people. Some Chicanos picked up the hot projectiles and with their hands threw the tear gas back onto the cops. Again, this provided time for people to flee.

All this went on for several minutes. I urged people to remain calm, but then lost complete track of time. I was almost in a kind of daze, witnessing this battle and seeing our successful moratorium crushed by the cops. I thought I heard someone calling me.

"Rosalio, Rosalio, come on, you've got to get the hell out of here. The cops might be looking for you."

As these words became clearer to me, I realized that this was Ramses ordering me to leave the park. He believed that I might be a target of the police attack.

"Find somebody you know to take you somewhere safe, and we'll see you later. Go!"

Reluctantly, I followed his order, and as I left the stage, I ran into this guy, Rafas, who was part of the cultural collective that published the barrio magazine *Con Safos*. He was an Eastside *veterano* (old-timer).

"Rafas, is your car nearby so I can get a ride with you out of here?"

"*Sí, ese*," the movement *compañero* replied. "Come with me."

He took me to his old VW a couple of blocks away, and we drove out. Behind us I could see and even smell the tear gas. People were scattering all over the place. I asked Rafas if he would take me to my girlfriend's house, several miles away. She was at the march, but I lost sight of her inside the park. Her place probably wasn't the safest place in the world, but it was where I was living, so that's where I went.

My girlfriend wasn't home. She was still out there somewhere. After a while I turned on the TV to see if there was news about the moratorium. There was. "Riot in East L.A." This is what was being reported. They were showing the burning of cars, the breaking of storefronts, and what seemed like a war zone. I had left before some of this destruction took place. But this wasn't what the moratorium was all about. The news suggested that the moratorium had caused the violence. But this was bullshit. We were peaceful and nonviolent. This wasn't shown. The moratorium was about the war, and that wasn't shown. I watched further, but after a while I couldn't stomach the distortions.

I decided to leave and go to our office. This was about five or six in the evening, because dusk was coming. I had left my car at my girlfriend's, so I drove to the office. My concern was not only to get more details about what happened at the park after I left, but, more important, to remove our files before the police possibly raided us. I remembered how, after the blowouts, the cops had raided the office of *La Raza* newspaper and carted off all their files. I didn't want that to happen to us. We had nothing subversive in our files, but they were our files and the cops had no right to them. They might also use them to arrest some of our people on trumped-up charges.

When I got to the office a number of our people were there, and they briefed me on the events in the park, including the beatings and arrests that the cops did to the people. As a result, some of the Chicanos fought back by destroying property on Whittier Boulevard. I later heard that they broke the windows and looted the stores owned by whites only.

We were also getting reports about injuries and arrests. But before we acted on these, we gathered up our files and prepared to move them out. Fortunately, through our contacts we were able to transfer our files to a friend's office about a block away.

I then went over to the nearby Legal Aid Foundation, which became the central spot to deal with those arrested that afternoon as well as to provide first aid. Bert Corona and some of his people were taking the lead on this. We went there to do what we could. If we knew for sure that someone had been arrested, we called bondsmen to arrange their bail. But families were also calling in to tell us that they didn't know where their sons or daughters were and if we could help locate them. In these cases, we called hospitals and the sheriff substation in East L.A. to inquire about them. We learned later that some two hundred people were arrested.

Later that evening, around midnight, as we continued making our calls, someone announced, "Ruben Salazar's been killed. We just heard it on the news!"

"Salazar's been killed?" we all instinctively responded. "When, how?"

It was one more bombshell after the destruction of the rally. It was around that time or later that we also heard rumors that two other Chicanos had been shot that afternoon.

One was Lyn Ward, a teenager, who was a Brown Beret from El Monte. He was fatally injured after the riot spilled over to Whittier. Then there was another fellow, Gilberto Díaz, who supposedly ran a barricade later that day and was shot down. Both died two days later.

Part of me was stunned at this news, especially that of Salazar, but I was so focused on the calls that I was making that I had no time to ponder this news or to grieve. That would have to come later. We had to help those in jail now and locate the missing.

Sometime much later that night, drained and exhausted, I found my way back to my girlfriend's and just collapsed.

POSTMORATORIUM REACTION

That Sunday we had planned to gather at Cal State, L.A., to host a follow-up informal conference on what directions we would follow after the moratorium. This would be open to any and all who had participated in the moratorium. Of course, this was before the events of Saturday. But now that we had been attacked, it was even more important to meet. Unfortunately, the Friday before we were notified that the university administration had withdrawn its permission for us to use their facilities. They claimed that they had not been told that perhaps several thousand might participate and that they couldn't provide adequate facilities. But this was a lie. It was obvious that the administration didn't want to allow us to use the campus.

Instead, others and I went back to the Legal Aid Foundation to continue our work on bailing out those arrested and locating others who might have been arrested. Although the Legal Aid Foundation, like our office, was some distance from Laguna Park, we could see cops all over the place. They also had ordered a curfew in unincorporated East L.A., so everyone had to be off the streets by six or seven o'clock. They also banned meetings of any kind in the evening.

I personally didn't go to see the destruction along Whittier Boulevard that day. Perhaps I should have. But my focus was on the work of helping those arrested.

One of those arrested was Corky Gonzales. It was a setup. The cops charged him with armed robbery simply because he had $370 on him to pay for expenses for the Colorado contingent. He was then released on bail. That Sunday evening I went to see him at the home of Oscar Zeta Acosta.

"Corky, what do you think we should do now?" I asked him.

"You have to get the Chicano middle class involved so that there's a more general community reaction to what the cops did. They're going to try to isolate you guys as violent and responsible for what happened. But if you can get the businessmen and the professionals to support you, this will help against those charges."

I thought this was good advice and hoped that we could get such help.

As part of the tactic, as well as a response to the activity, we quickly arranged to have a press conference on Monday. We focused on what the true nature of the moratorium was and about what we had to do now after the attack by the police. I told the press, in part,

> The National Chicano Moratorium Committee, along with all major Chicano organizations, planned and prepared for a large, lawful and peaceful demonstration to protest the injustice that the war has brought on the Chicano community. This opportunity was used, however, by the Los Angeles County sheriff's department as an excuse to viciously and maliciously attack Chicanos, not only the many at the demonstration, but the Chicano community of Los Angeles in general and throughout the Southwest. . . .
>
> Using a minor and isolated incident off from the rally site as justification, the deputies, without any warning whatsoever, charged, clubbed and gassed the peaceful crowd of not only men but women, children, and elderly persons. . . .
>
> But perhaps the most indicting of the actions of the police involved the death of Ruben Salazar. . . . His death resulted from the overzealous efforts of the Los Angeles sheriff's department, who bombarded a location solely on an alleged rumor that there might be armed men in the place. The rumor was without foundation, but Ruben Salazar still died [of injuries to his head].
>
> Since the incidents of the 29th, the community of East Los Angeles has been turned into a state of armed siege. A virtual police dictatorship exists in the area and

FIGURE 20. Muñoz speaking at a press conference, September 1, 1970. Courtesy of the Los Angeles Times Photographic Archive.

the situation is worsening daily. Civil rights have been abolished and police terrorism of the community prevails. . . .

This occupation of our *barrios* by the racist, cowardly police must be terminated immediately. The persons arrested and jailed on ridiculous and manufactured charges must be released. All charges must be dropped.

Furthermore, an investigatory body must be composed as soon as possible to find the murderers of Ruben Salazar and ensure that police riots of this kind do not occur again. . . .

Let us make our stand a little clearer. We demand an immediate end to the occupation of the Chicano community by the repressive forces of the Los Angeles County sheriff's department, the California highway patrol, and all other so-called law enforcement agencies. . . .

We further call for the formation of a commission to investigate the police riot which took place last Saturday, August 29, 1970, and to determine the role of L.A. County Sheriff Pitchess, L.A. police chief Davis, the L.A. County Board of Supervisors, and the mayor's office, in conspiring to create this police riot and the subsequent murder of Ruben Salazar.[18]

Although I didn't say it at the press conference, I also believed and continue to do so that the FBI and CIA and other federal and military agencies in all likelihood were also involved in the breakup of the moratorium.

Ironically, that same day I received notice that a grand jury had indicted me on my draft case. Although I couldn't think much then about my own legal problems, I did issue a press release linking my indictment to the repression of the moratorium.[19]

After we had helped bail out those who had been arrested, we started talking within the Moratorium Committee about how we should react to the attack and the imposition of the curfew.

More immediately, we decided to participate in the wake of Ruben Salazar to also defy the police. At the mortuary, the people filed by the open casket to pay their respects to Ruben. For some reason I didn't go up to the casket. I can't remember why I didn't. Perhaps I'm hung up about death.

SIXTEENTH OF SEPTEMBER MARCH

The issue of the curfew and occupation, plus what the cops had done to us on August 29, infuriated us (and still does). We wanted to strike back. But how?

"What about marching at the Sixteenth of September parade?" someone proposed.

"Of course! That parade goes right through parts of East L.A. That's perfect!" I responded.

The traditional and annual Sixteenth of September parade celebrating Mexican Independence Day had been held for who knows how many years. It was a cultural event, never a political one, except for cars of politicians, dignitaries, and military contingents. There were floats with pretty girls, including a queen of the parade, along with high school marching bands. It was under the auspices of the Comité Cívico Patriótico (Patriotic Civic Committee), which went back at least to the 1920s.

We didn't know how to go about getting permission to march in the parade. The idea was that we would participate as the Moratorium Committee. Ramses and I met with Esteban Torres, the head of the Congress of Mexican American Unity, to see if Esteban could help us. He thought it was a good idea and offered to go with us to discuss this with the Comité. We discovered that the Comité had decided to cancel the event, no doubt due to what had occurred on August 29 and pressure from the county sheriffs. We urged them not to do so, and they finally agreed.

At that meeting, however, the leaders of the Comité at first expressed reservations about us marching as the Moratorium Committee. However, with Esteban's help, we impressed upon them that we adhered to nonviolence and that nothing harmful would happen. I think in the end they also appreciated the fact that many more Chicanos would attend the parade if we were included. We got the permission to march. This was what we wanted. We would return to the streets of East

L.A. As far as we were concerned, the Sixteenth of September would be a continuation of the August 29 moratorium.

We put the word out that we would be marching. We made a big banner, "Chicano Moratorium Committee," as well as one that read, "Remember Ruben Salazar." I had no idea what kind of turnout we would have. When we got to the assembly point, we were told where our place in the march was. At first I was disappointed. We started out with about fifty people, most related to our committee. But soon, and to my delight, more movement activists started arriving, many with their homemade signs and banners. As we entered into the main part of the march, we must have had two thousand or more. It certainly didn't rival the turnout on the twenty-ninth, but given everything that had happened, this was a great turnout. It was also a very spirited and even angry congregation. We shouted out all our antiwar slogans, but, of course, now we had a couple of new ones:

"Remember Ruben Salazar!"

"Down with police brutality!"

We literally took over the Sixteenth of September parade and transformed it into an antiwar and antipolice march.

It turned out that the Comité had good reason to be nervous. The cops were waiting for us again. At the end of the march, some of the demonstrators, many of whom I didn't know, veered off toward the Atlantic Square shopping area. Others of our committee and I didn't follow. What happened next was another police attack. Claiming later that the demonstrators had hurled rocks at the deputies, they retaliated with tear gas and their batons. Several Chicanos were injured and others arrested. It was August 29 again, except on a more limited scale.

I believed then and still do that this was one more setup by the cops. I'm convinced that there were police agents in the march who provoked the attack.

The end result of the Sixteenth of September march, unfortunately, led to more violence, but at the same time we had shown that we were not going to be intimidated by the police. We had taken back the streets and continued our struggle.

SALAZAR INQUEST AND POLICE ABUSE

The death of Ruben Salazar, of course, captured the attention of movement activists. His death at the hands of the county sheriffs, in addition to the police attack at the moratorium, dramatically shifted our attention within the Moratorium Committee. Prior to August 29, we had already been thinking of going beyond the antiwar issue to other areas such as police violence and building La Raza Unida Party in L.A. But the ferociousness of the police onslaught against us, plus Ruben's death, convinced us that our number one issue now had to be that of police abuse.

There was an inquest on Ruben's death conducted by the district attorney that started on September 10 and lasted a couple of weeks. I didn't attend any of these hearings, although many other Chicanos did. I didn't have much faith in this process, and the results bore me out. Nothing came of the inquest. The deputy, Thomas Wilson, who fired the fateful shots, was not indicted or penalized. The district attorney decided not to prosecute the case. Our appeal that the federal government investigate the case was not acted on. Nothing was done about Ruben's death.

This callousness and insensitivity to the death of a respected Chicano journalist only further impressed on us on the Moratorium Committee that our war at home had to be with the police. This was our Vietnam! We now had to mobilize, as we had done against the war, on the issue of police brutality in the Chicano community. I knew that this would probably, indeed predictably, lead to further conflict with the cops, but it had to be done. The police had declared war on us, and we had to fight back nonviolently.

The time of the Salazar inquest also coincided with my hearing to appear in court on my draft case. Since I had been indicted for refusing induction, I had to go to court to enter a plea. But a problem arose when the presiding judge, Judge A. Andrew Hauk, refused to allow my attorney, Michael Tigar, to represent me. Judge Hauk was an extreme right-wing judge who didn't like Tigar because of his activist politics. The judge wanted to appoint an attorney for me. I refused. Because I couldn't have my own attorney, I also refused to enter a plea. This outraged Hauk, but he had no legal recourse but to postpone my case. As a result, my case would drag on for a couple of more years.

As we refocused, we also began meeting with Armando Morales, a local social worker and scholar activist, who had already been documenting police abuse in East L.A. He later published his findings in a now-classic book called *Ando Sangrando* (We Are Bleeding).[20] Armando shared his research with us and advised us as well. All of this reinforced in us the sense of how critical and historically important the issue of police abuse was. With Armando's help, we began to draft proposals for police reform.

As we met with Armando, we planned our new strategies. With our supporters, we launched our first action against the police by organizing picket lines in front of the county sheriff's substation in East L.A. We focused on the sheriffs because they had attacked our moratorium, aided by the LAPD, and it was they who had killed Salazar. For a few weekends we had from fifty to one hundred people picketing and shouting out, "Who killed Salazar?" And the response was, "Wilson," the deputy who had fired into the Silver Dollar. This would be followed by still another yell:

"Who gave the orders?"

"Pitchess [the county sheriff]."

The picket was successful in keeping attention on what the deputies had done on August 29. However, the East L.A. Berets, minus David Sánchez, began to grumble that our focus should really be the LAPD, since they had an even longer history of police abuse. They wanted us to move our picket line to the LAPD Hollenbeck station in Boyle Heights. Other members of the committee and I disagreed and rejected the proposal. It wasn't that we disagreed about the ruthlessness of the LAPD toward Chicanos. But we had built momentum around the sheriff's station, and we didn't want to lose that. Besides, the sheriffs had led the attack on us and killed Salazar, and we wanted to keep reminding people about that.

Our rejection of the Beret's proposal coincided with growing unruliness on their part, as they came to the office, which now consisted of an old house next to the Euclid Community Center that had served as the grape-boycott office but that had been donated to us. They started drinking more there, as well as making long-distance calls from our phones. As a result, we had to institute strict rules against such behavior. This didn't endear us to the Berets.

"This is the people's place," they responded. "You shouldn't make these rules."

Besides their antagonistic rhetoric, some openly started toting guns as they came to the office.

Things were coming to a head between the Berets and us.

The Berets began to demand that, because we had betrayed the "people," we turn over the office to them, and they would assume leadership of the Moratorium Committee. To stress their point, they came en masse to one of our meetings fully armed, including rifles. It was ludicrous. It was a scene out of some B movie. These guys actually thought they were revolutionaries, even though they were acting like thugs.

I conferred with Ramses and Gil Cano. We had our supporters there, but we decided that we didn't want any provocation or violence. It wasn't worth it.

"Okay," I told the Berets. "You guys want the office, and you want to use the name of the Moratorium Committee—okay, go ahead. We don't think that it's that important. What's important to us are the issues and the people. We'll go work somewhere else."

And we did.

The Berets wound up electing or selecting a crazy guy by the name of Frank Martínez, who proved to be a federal and police undercover agent. He had been in Vietnam and on his return was diagnosed as having severe psychotic problems. He couldn't speak well, was a lousy organizer, and had no interpersonal abilities. I now also believed that the Berets had been infiltrated by the FBI.[21]

RENEWED PROTESTS

Because we no longer had an office, we went back to Esteban Torres, who then arranged space for us at the East L.A. Community Union, in the offices of TEL-ACU, a community-revitalization program. From there we decided that we would pursue the same kind of strategy that we had planned for the moratorium. We decided to have a march and demonstration against the county sheriffs, which we would call La Marcha para Justicia (the March for Justice). We had learned how to organize a large demonstration, and we wanted to use this experience to do a similar one now on the issue of police brutality.

As Ramses, Gil Cano, and I, along with some of the remnants of the Moratorium Committee, planned our strategy, we concluded that we would build the demonstration on two key issues. The first would stress the long history of police abuse of the Chicano community. This was something at a personal level that many Chicanos could relate to. Second, we would stress the political aspects of police brutality. By this we meant that the police clearly had set out to attack and destroy the Chicano movement in Los Angeles. We would remind people of police actions against the students in the blowouts, against Católicos por la Raza at their Christmas Eve demonstration at St. Basil's in 1969, and, of course, their vicious attacks against us on August 29. "We face genocide not only when they shove us onto the battlefields," I later told the press, "but also when the police repress us on the streets of our own barrios. Some cops inspire more fear and hatred in Chicanos than the Viet Cong."

With these two items, we then worked on building up support. We believed that there were four main areas in the county where Chicano activists were quite strong and where we could get support. These areas included Pomona, the San Fernando–Pacoima area, Venice on the Westside, and San Pedro and Wilmington in the harbor area. We went and talked with grassroots leaders in these areas, who expressed enthusiasm and support. Some of these groups were Brown Beret chapters, but they were not aligned with the East L.A. Berets who had given us problems. Once we knew that we had support from these four areas, we then came up with our master plan for the demonstration. Rather than focus just on East L.A., we wanted to stress the entire county of L.A., since this was the sheriff's jurisdiction. The plan was for the march to originate from these four areas. Instead of one march, there would be four. Each of the marches would traverse through their particular county neighborhood, where many Chicanos lived in small and large barrios. All four would then converge in East L.A. and on the sheriff's substation there. It would be like the four spokes of a wheel.

We set the date of the rally for January 31, 1971, with all four groups starting together, three days earlier.

In the meantime, the East L.A. Berets called for their own mass demonstration against the LAPD and set the date for January 9. We, of course, had planned our demonstration for later in January, with a focus on the county sheriffs. We had no expectation of supporting the East L.A. Berets, especially after what they had done to us. However, sometime in late December, David Sánchez finally surfaced again and came by to see us. He said that he had been traveling since September around the Southwest and other regions, establishing new Beret chapters.

"I know what happened here," he commented, "and I didn't approve of it. But I'm back in charge now, and I've kicked out these troublemakers. But the January 9 demonstration has already been set, and it would be damaging to the Berets if we canceled. But I need you guys to support it. We need to be united in this. We need your help to ensure that it is peaceful."

Well, we discussed this further among ourselves, and we finally decided to participate in the January 9 protest. But we would still continue organizing our demonstration. We had only a couple of weeks to get the word out on the Beret event, and we did what we could. Interviewed by the *Los Angeles Times*, I said, "We are marching to prove that we can protest peacefully and that we will not be intimidated by the police."[22]

Regrettably, it turned out to be still another conflict with the police. Somewhere between one thousand and two thousand people showed up for the march and rally. We assembled at Hollenbeck Park and then marched one and a half miles to the downtown central LAPD headquarters at Parker Center, where the rally would take place. I don't remember if there were speakers. The main intent was to form a picket line around the building, which we did. However, some began occupying an empty construction site across the street. The cops demanded that these guys leave the construction site, and when they didn't, the police moved in. They declared the demonstration to be an unlawful assembly and broke up the picket line. Chicanos began to disperse everywhere to avoid arrest. Some ran down to Broadway Street, toward the commercial section, and some began to hurl rocks against storefront windows. This included breaking the windows of the nearby *Los Angeles Times* building. This may have been—and probably was—a police setup through the use of provocateurs again. From where I stood, the police did not have to break up the picket line to deal with the situation in the construction site. Whether intended or not, this began to turn the *Times* against us. The newspaper, after August 29, seemed more supportive of our efforts to call attention to police brutality. After all, one of their own, Ruben, had been killed by the deputies. However, after the attack on the *Times* building—and this may have been planned by the cops themselves—the *Times* began to criticize us as rabble-rousers and the movement as violence-prone.

The police arrested about thirty demonstrators. We knew the dangers and pitfalls of organizing a mass protest under these conditions. But we had no choice. We wouldn't retreat from the streets. That's all we had—the streets and our bodies.

We received warnings from several people and groups about going through with our demonstration. We appreciated their concerns, but we were committed to our protest. We certainly didn't want the police to attack us, because, even though it would be additional evidence of police brutality, that's not how it would be received. Instead, the onus would fall on us as provoking the violence.

From another less friendly source, the media, we received more pressure not to demonstrate. Well, this was even less reason for us to adhere to what the establishment wanted.

Then there was red-baiting. Some accused us of being communists and of trying to foment a communist revolution in L.A. This was ludicrous but indicates the threat that we posed to some and hence their efforts to destroy us.

To try to prevent a conflict with the county sheriffs, or at least to cover ourselves in case of a police attack, we arranged to meet with both Sheriff Peter Pitchess and LAPD chief of police Ed Davis. As we had done for August 29, we assured them that our demonstration would be a peaceful one. We didn't trust either of them, but politically we had to assure them of our peaceful intent—that, of course, was genuine. We didn't advocate or condone violence. In fact, the violence had come from the cops.

JANUARY 31 MARCH

We continued to organize for January 31. Despite the pressures and warnings, we received a lot of support. We used many of the same strategies to get the word out that we had employed for August 29. As with the moratorium, I knew that it would be a large demonstration—not as big as the twenty-ninth, but sizable. I wasn't disappointed.

Because the march would emanate from four distinct and separate areas of the county and as far away as San Pedro, we planned it so that the march, or marches, would commence three days before they all converged in East L.A. at Belvedere Park, across the freeway from the sheriff's East L.A. substation. These three days would also allow for the number of protesters to grow. Each march staged different mini-rallies as they traversed through their areas, all with the intent of calling attention to the issue of police brutality and of adding people to the march. "We are planning a nonviolent demonstration," I told the press, "but if the [sheriff's] officers attack, there will probably be some civil disobedience."

On January 31 the four marches converged on Belvedere Park. "Who killed Ruben Salazar?" many of the marchers called out. Estimates were as high as ten thousand people, or perhaps close to half of the August 29 turnout, and this was a local event. This was the largest protest ever against police brutality in L.A. history and perhaps even in the nation. Chicanos had clearly regained the streets! We were, of course, all delighted and proud of our work, but at the same time leery of what the cops might do. Although we had originally thought of holding the rally right outside of the sheriff's substation, we finally decided not to, especially after what had happened to the Beret demonstration. We didn't want to invite a police attack. Instead we used Belvedere Park, across the 60 Freeway from the station, which would keep us apart from the sheriff's headquarters. From the park, we could see machine guns mounted on the station's roof.

Everything went well at the rally. Different speakers addressed the crowd. Many of these were community people who gave powerful testimonies to particular cases of police abuse. The police had attacked some personally. Mothers, especially, talked about how the cops had killed their sons. It was all powerful stuff. I was the last speaker, and I was worried about confrontation with the county sheriffs. I concluded by warning the demonstrators to disperse peacefully: "I hope you're going to respect those who came a long way."

The rally came to an end. It had been a successful and peaceful demonstration. We had pulled it off and had now made police brutality one of the major issues of the movement.

Unfortunately, we weren't able to rest on our laurels. At the completion of the rally, as people were departing for home, some Chicanos—it couldn't have been more than a hundred—started to march on their own toward the sheriff's substation across the freeway. We tried to stop them, with the aid of some of the Catholic priests in attendance. We slowed them down but couldn't persuade them to turn around. These were not Chicanos from our group. I didn't know them, and it's very possible undercover cops led them. Who knows? When they reached the substation, they started throwing rocks and then marched on to Whittier Boulevard. At this point, the deputies came out in force and fired into the unruly crowd, using real ammunition. One Chicano fell and died. Others fell, wounded. Many were arrested. From a distance I, along with some of our group, watched this next chapter of police violence against the movement. But in this case, the Chicanos involved had clearly provoked the cops. This doesn't excuse what the police did. They had no right to fire into the crowd, and certainly they had no right to kill someone.

We held a press conference the following day. We tried to focus on the success of our demonstration, but all that the media wanted to ask concerned the conflict with the sheriffs.

"Will you demonstrate again?" they asked.

This question put the rest of our group and me in an awkward position. We were beginning to rethink our strategy about demonstrations that put us in direct confrontation with the police or made it easy for police undercover agents to provoke a confrontation.

"We denounce the violence used by the deputies, and especially their killing of one of the demonstrators. We won't be having demonstrations for a while. But this doesn't mean that the issue of police brutality will go away. We intend to continue struggling for this issue until both the sheriffs and the LAPD stop waging war against the Chicano community."

LA MARCHA DE LA RECONQUISTA

There's no question but that we were at a crossroad following the January 31 incident. We were getting pressure from all sides not to organize another demonstration for fear of further police violence. The pressure didn't come from movement activists, but from the more established Mexican American leadership, such as the Congress of Mexican American Unity, as well as individual community leaders. Some of them who worked for federal agencies, in turn, were being pressured by the Nixon administration not to participate or support us, lest they lose their jobs. Things seemed to be getting out of hand. On the other extreme, police violence spawned the Chicano Liberation Front, which endorsed violence against the police.

We found ourselves right in the middle of this controversy. For over a year we had represented the leading force of protest in the movement in Los Angeles. All eyes were on us about whether we would continue the struggle or give it up.

We weren't about to be intimidated by the cops. On the other hand, we had to be realistic. It was clear that further demonstrations would trigger off police assaults on us. The cops were now dead set in destroying not only us but also the movement. This probably included the FBI. We felt constrained and, of course, frustrated. The cops seemed to have the upper hand.

Certain things, however, soon began to come together. We heard that movement activists in the Coachella and Imperial Valleys, centered on Calexico, wanted to be involved in a major protest action. They had felt isolated in comparison to what we were doing in L.A. Second, others on the Moratorium Committee and I felt that after our protest against police brutality, the time had now arrived to shift support to the building of La Raza Unida Party. Others, including myself, also believed we had to begin to target Governor Reagan for his right-wing attack on minorities and working people. Finally, David Sánchez and the East L.A. Berets wanted to march again, but not necessarily in L.A.

There were all these ideas floating around. We held a meeting with David and other activists. At the meeting we agreed that we would continue as the National Chicano Moratorium Committee, even though we were no longer focusing just on the war. The committee had name recognition, and we didn't want to lose this by starting still another group. We also agreed that we wouldn't be intimidated by the police, but, at the same time, we didn't want to play into their hands by demonstrating right away in L.A. again. After a few hours of intense discussion, we came up with a plan.

We would march again—after all, this is what we did best—but we would link ourselves with the activists in the Coachella and Imperial Valleys and organize a march starting there to go through Los Angeles and on to Sacramento. We would march mainly through rural communities. What would be our focus? Well, we brought together some of the issues being thrown around and decided that this would be a march against Reagan and what he stood for. To stress this anti-Reagan theme, we would borrow from César Chávez and march to Sacramento, but we would commence at Calexico, on the U.S.-Mexico border. Besides attacking Reagan's policies, we would also use the march to build La Raza Unida Party. To qualify for the ballot, the RUP in California needed several thousand signatures. We would get these signatures, or as many as we could, during the march. Bringing in all the issues under the umbrella of attacking Reagan, we then came up with five key sub-issues: the RUP, welfare, education, the police, and the war.

We would address each of these issues in a march that would take a few weeks and commence on the Cinco de Mayo of that year. This schedule would allow us to stop in different communities and speak to as many people as possible, including the farmworkers in the rural areas.

With our plan in hand, we then approached a number of people and groups to get their support, similar to our previous actions. The students and other movement activists were with us. The older and more moderate Mexican Americans were against it or timid about supporting us. More militant but older leftists, such as Bert Corona, endorsed us. Tony Rios, the head of CSO (Community Service Organization) in L.A., also supported us and went further by letting us use one of the CSO offices. We didn't communicate with RUP leaders about the march, but we knew that we could rely on Raul Ruiz and others. We also knew that we could count on Beret chapters.

With these preparations, we set out to march again.[23]

We assembled on Cinco de Mayo 1971, in Calexico. There were about eighty to one hundred of us, mostly from the Moratorium Committee and the East L.A. Brown Berets, along with movement activists from the Coachella-Indio area, MEChA students, and some from La Raza Unida such as Raul Ruiz. Of course, I was also there, with Ramses, Gil Cano, and David Sánchez. We started to march on a hot day, knowing that it would only get hotter as we moved on. We had no idea how long it would take to reach Sacramento, but we aimed at an August arrival. We didn't expect everyone to march the entire way, although some expressed a desire to do so. The idea was that some would march for a period, be replaced by others along the way, and then, after a rest, some of the marchers would rejoin. Our purpose was to attract marchers as we moved up the state, primarily through the central valleys, and in this way add to our numbers. "This march will be a sacrifice for the people," I told a college reporter. "It will take approximately three months, and we will walk eight hundred miles through some of the hottest parts of the state."

Besides the Mexican flag and the banner of La Virgen de Guadalupe, we also carried the American flag.

We marched alongside highways and occasionally alongside a few freeways. Mostly we followed highways rather than freeways, not only for our safety but because there were few freeways yet in the central valleys. We had contacts with the highway patrol, and, for the most part, they didn't bother us. We felt that they wouldn't want to call attention to our march by attacking us.

Of course, we needed provisions, primarily food and water. We borrowed or rented, I don't recall, an old school bus. Inside the bus we carried canned food and

FIGURE 21. Muñoz marching from Calexico to Sacramento, La Marcha de la Reconquista, summer 1971. Courtesy of Allen Zak.

water, which we would periodically replenish. But we also hoped that as we stopped overnight in different communities along the way, the people, the *mexicanos,* would feed us. In fact, this did happen, and we were highly grateful for a good warm meal.

Overnight, we camped out under the stars with our bedrolls, or some slept in the bus. The bus was also useful because people could ride in it if they got tired. But most marched steadily every day. These were mostly young people with lots of energy.

As the march advanced and entered more populated areas, we planned rallies at the end of the day. These gatherings would give us the opportunity to attack Reagan and his policies, as well as register people for the RUP. Our first big rally was in Coachella. About a thousand people attended, mostly from that area, although some came from L.A. Bert Corona, for example, came with some of his people, and he spoke at the rally. Although we were tired, this first rally reinforced us and made us feel that the march, so far, was worth it.

Our projected route took us west toward L.A., and the decision that we had to make, as we got closer, was whether we would march into L.A. or skirt around it toward the San Fernando Valley. I strongly argued that we needed to once again march in L.A., even though we knew that the police wouldn't let us. "Fuck them," I said. "We can't avoid L.A. We'll lose credibility if we don't march there."

Well, I was pretty much a lone voice among the leadership of the march. Even my good friend Gil Cano didn't support me. He believed that we would be attacked again, and La Marcha would not be able to continue. David Sánchez felt the same way. I don't recall that Ramses took a position on this. I was outvoted, but I thought it was a huge mistake.

Instead of going into L.A., we stopped in San Gabriel and held a small rally. From there we marched into the city of San Fernando in the valley the next day. We had a huge rally in the park there with well over a thousand people. We had some media coverage, including from a young Frank del Olmo for the *Los Angeles Times,* who had kind of taken over covering Chicano issues after Salazar's death.[24] Besides the speeches, including my own, again attacking Reagan, we got several hundred people to register for La Raza Unida Party. In my opinion, the San Fernando rally, in retrospect, was the highlight of La Marcha.

From San Fernando we marched on to Oxnard, where the local chapter of the Berets welcomed us. Here too we had a pretty good rally. But it was also at Oxnard that tension with the East L.A. Berets began to surface. All of a sudden they began to say that they did not support the RUP and that they wouldn't march on its behalf. This was ludicrous. We in the Moratorium Committee were marching in support of the RUP, and the Berets were mainly against it. I talked to David about this.

"What the hell is going on? I thought we had all agreed that the march, besides taking on Reagan, would support the RUP."

"We're not into politics," David responded. "Besides, there are too many communists and Marxists involved in the RUP, and we don't want to be a part of that."

Despite David's position, we worked out an agreement to continue the march, and if the Berets didn't want to sign up people for the RUP, that was up to them.

But after Oxnard, as we turned east and into the San Joaquin Valley on the way to Bakersfield, everything began to go downhill. As I see it, this primarily had to do with the Berets.

For one, there were constant fights all along the way, even before we got to Oxnard. Rivalries with gangs along the way or fights over girls or drugs only added to the tension. The potential for even greater violence lay in the fact that some of the Berets carried guns. This was, of course, not unique to the Berets; others in the movement also carried weapons. We in the Moratorium Committee did not and had no use for guns.

Added to the weapons was the heavy use of drugs by some Berets. They used all kinds of drugs, such as acid.

We were disturbed about their behavior, but we couldn't seem to communicate with them. David would come and go, and there would be days without him. Consequently, the problem with the Berets continued and even got worse as we marched up the Central Valley toward Sacramento.

It should be said, however, that despite these problems, there were bright spots. The rallies were effective, and we received a lot of community support from the different towns and cities that we entered, including local leaders and members of the Catholic clergy. In Fresno, we had a good-sized rally. Some of the places, primarily the smaller areas, had never had a Chicano rally, so they welcomed us with a lot of enthusiasm and attentively listened to the speakers. Some even signed up for the RUP.

But the problems with the Berets continued. About two weeks before we estimated arriving in Sacramento, we had finally had it.

"We're dropping out. We can't continue with all these problems with your people," I told David.

"Rosalio, you can't drop out now. It wouldn't look good. We need you guys. There won't be any more problems. I promise you. You have to continue."

I talked with Ramses and Gil, and we concluded that, politically, we had to finish the march.

"Okay," I told David, "we'll continue, but the rest of the march has to be nonviolent or else we will drop out. After Sacramento, it'll be all over, and we'll go our separate ways."

David agreed, and there were no more problems for the next week.

At the end of the first week of August, I think it was August 9, we finally reached Sacramento, after three long and arduous months of marching. I, personally, didn't march all the way. I didn't march, for example, from Oxnard to Bakersfield. There were also a few other times when I got a ride back to L.A. That was the case for most of us.

Despite the hardships, we concluded the march with the biggest rally of all at the state capital in Sacramento. Several thousand people attended, many of them students and movement activists. Over these three months, people had heard about the march, and many wanted to be there at the end, especially those who hadn't marched. It was an event and happening that they didn't want to miss.

We gave our final speeches. David Sánchez surrounded himself with Berets as he addressed the crowd because he feared that someone might try to shoot him. At the end, some Berets moved over to the flagpole and took down the U.S. flag and raised the Mexican one. The cops showed up, but nothing happened and the rally ended.

REFLECTION ON LA MARCHA

At the end of La Marcha, rather than being uplifted, I was tired, frustrated, and critical of the experience. As I returned to L.A. and over the next few days, I reflected on La Marcha as a failure. We had not achieved our objectives, and the end result was the breakdown and ending of what we had organized after my challenge to being drafted.

La Marcha failed, at one level, because we didn't register that many people into La Raza Unida Party. What frustrated me further was that, while we were busting our backs off for the RUP, party leaders in the state did very little. Other than when Raul came to the commencement of the march, he and other party leaders didn't help much, if at all. Perhaps they didn't want to be associated with the crazy Berets. Who knows? But the fact of the matter is that we were trying to help the *partido* get off the ground, and its leadership, such as it was, ignored us and didn't even acknowledge our help.

La Marcha also failed because it represented the death of the Moratorium Committee. The committee had started as a coalition between student activists, such as Ramses and myself, and the Berets. The history of this coalition had always been shaky, but in one form or another it had survived. La Marcha represented a last effort to resuscitate the coalition. In this it failed. There's no question in my mind that the final collapse of the committee resulted from the antics and questionable behavior of the Berets.

It's hard for me not to blame David Sánchez for many of the problems with the Berets. His lax leadership and his absence from the march allowed these troubles to fester and grow. David is a historical figure, and it's hard for me to completely judge him. While he could display charismatic leadership some times, he also could be withdrawn and irrational at other times. He seemed to be more interested in promoting his cult of personality than contributing to the movement as a whole.

But the failure of La Marcha and the termination of the Moratorium Committee was, in retrospect, not just David's and the Berets' fault. The rest of us in the committee also could be faulted for not developing a real political base. By this I mean that we didn't have a geographic center. In a way, we worked in the community, but we really weren't an integral part of the East L.A. community. We seemed to be in and out organizing our marches and demonstrations but not focusing on building a more permanent place in the barrios. Perhaps we couldn't, given our energies and the enthusiasm of our youth.

Feeling down after La Marcha and the end of the Moratorium Committee, I wasn't sure what I would do next. I knew I would recover from this experience and continue to be politically active in the movement. But just where and how, for the moment, I didn't know.

LA RAZA UNIDA

It didn't take me long to become involved again. I had returned to L.A. to immerse myself in some facet of the movement, and, fortunately for me, as I did, the first significant Raza Unida campaign was under way. Even though I had been disappointed in our efforts during La Marcha to register more people for the RUP and I felt that we didn't get much support from the party itself, still I believed in the idea of an independent Chicano political party that would not be beholden to either the

Democrats or Republicans. I believed that the RUP would be an effective electoral vehicle to advance the movement.

So I was excited that the RUP in East L.A. was contesting for the Forty-Eighth Assembly District of the state legislature. This was a special election for an open seat. There were several candidates, from the Democrats, Republicans, Peace and Freedom Party, and RUP. Raul Ruiz, the publisher and editor of *La Raza* magazine, was the candidate for the RUP. Both Gil Cano and I volunteered to help in the campaign. The election would be that November.

Of course, I had known Raul a little from previous movement actions in L.A. He was a respected part of the movement and, in fact, was a movement heavy. He was especially known as publisher of *La Raza*. He had given us support and publicity in the moratorium, but I didn't know him very well. In fact, to be honest, Raul and I never quite hit it off. Our personalities never meshed. Perhaps we both felt some rivalry of each other's leadership. I don't know. But I never felt that Raul thought that much of me, and, as a consequence, I maybe didn't think that much of him. At the same time, I supported what he was doing in organizing the RUP. That's where I was.

At first we did whatever Raul and Richard Martínez, Raul's campaign manager, wanted us to do. Every day we went to *La Raza* office, which was also the campaign headquarters. We even swept up the office in the morning and then put things back together at night.

But our most important work was to go out into the community and go door-to-door passing out Raul's literature and talking to people. We'd knock on doors and ask to talk about the campaign. Many invited us in and expressed an interest in the RUP. I enjoyed this, although I had to work at being more affable. I tend to be too serious. By contrast, Gil and Danny Zapata, another volunteer, were very good at talking to people and making them feel comfortable. We got support from the people. Some would say, "I've been a Democrat all of my life, but I'll support you."

The campaign didn't have a lot of funds, even though the Democrats accused us of taking money from the Republicans. If this was so, we didn't see that money. We just used our legs and our feet and walked precincts every day.

Overall, Raul had a pretty good campaign organization. Richard Martínez seemed to have a good strategy on how to effectively use volunteers. There were a good number of volunteers. A core of about fifteen to twenty came around four or five times a week, if not more. Then five to ten of us worked long days. As the campaign came to a close, the number of volunteers, mostly young Chicano people, increased. Because I had experience as an organizer, I sometimes proposed to Richard or to Raul how we might do some things differently. For one, I thought the issues they focused on were too narrowly defined around the party rather than having a broader appeal. I felt that most of my ideas were not accepted. I didn't feel bad about this—or at least not too bad—because I had come to the campaign late, and I didn't feel that I could push my ideas on what others had been working on. I accepted my secondary role.

From what I could tell, the goals of the campaign were to win the election. I believe that Raul sincerely believed that he could win. I also believed in this—or at least had high hopes. I knew that we worked hard to get as many votes as possible, not just for Raul but, more important, for the RUP.

Election day came with a lot of excitement and expectations on our part. The results came in, and we learned that while we didn't win, we had gotten a sizable percentage of the vote for a third party. Raul's percentage, in fact, denied Richard Alatorre the victory in what had been a safe Democratic seat. Siphoning votes away from Richard allowed Bill Brophy, the Republican, to win. I wasn't thrilled that a Republican won, but that wasn't our intent. At the same time, the others and I got some pleasure in teaching the Democrats a lesson—that they couldn't take the Chicano vote for granted. Raul's performance really scared the California Democrats, and they soon made stronger appeals to Chicanos, including sponsoring additional Chicano candidates. Part of me also thought that Raul would have gotten more votes if he and Richard Martínez had listened to me about running a broader campaign, but that wasn't the most important factor. As far as I was concerned, we—the RUP—had not lost the campaign.

Raul, however, felt differently, or at least that was my impression. From what I could tell, he was disappointed that he hadn't won.

My involvement in Raul's campaign represented a transitional phase for me. I supported the RUP, but I thought during the campaign that working with the RUP wasn't what I really wanted to do. I wasn't cut out to be a candidate myself, and, in addition, I wanted to work on more community issues rather than just electoral politics. Moreover, I was having doubts on the viability of RUP.

WORKING WITH FATHER LUCE

I didn't have to wait long to move on to my next involvement. Father John Luce, the pastor of the Episcopalian Church of the Epiphany in my old neighborhood of Lincoln Heights, approached me about working with him.

"Rosalio, there's a lot of community issues here that need attention," he said, "and I'd like to talk with you about them and see if you'd like to help."

I respected Father Luce. Early on, he had championed the Chicano movement in L.A. by providing a space and support for some of the first groups, such as *La Raza* newspaper and the Brown Berets. I visited with him and talked about a number of community problems that needed attention. He asked me to think about working with him. I wasn't sure about this, but I finally agreed.

I organized some meetings with community activists, some of whom were movement activists as well. Out of this came an understanding that the number one issue facing the Lincoln Heights area was jobs and better jobs. We formally organized what we called Unemployed Chicanos of La Raza Unida. We weren't affiliated with the RUP, but we took that name anyway. Father Luce was short on space in his church, so we made arrangements with the nearby Methodist church to work out of their facilities. I had attended this church as a young boy, although at that earlier time whites composed most of the congregation. The minister was a very progressive guy, who readily provided office space for us.

We didn't have much staff, and we had no salaries, but working with Gil Cano and a few others, we began to explore some of the new federal job programs coming out at that time. Chicanos didn't know about these programs, and we made an effort to alert the community about them.

We also became concerned that city jobs, some of them linked to these federal programs, were not going to Chicanos. Many more African Americans were being hired than Chicanos. When we investigated this, city officials only said that not many Chicanos applied. The fact that these officials made little effort at outreach only compounded the problem. We decided to test these officials by organizing a demonstration at city hall. We gathered a good number of people and marched to city hall, where we held a rally. We then en masse entered the building and lined up to apply for jobs. Some of us weren't serious about these applications, but we wanted to drive home our point that Chicanos were interested in city jobs, and the city had to reach out to them so that they knew about the jobs and how to apply.

Following this demonstration, we decided to change our name to Casa de la Vecindad, or Neighborhood House. We felt a name in Spanish that reflected our interest in the community would better serve our purposes. We continued to focus on jobs and related issues. For example, we assisted people with welfare problems. We had some Legal Aid workers who also started using our office to assist people in Lincoln Heights. The Model Cities program was a big urban renewal program that I had problems with, but it did provide jobs. We tried to place people in these jobs.

We were doing some good, but at the same time I was getting frustrated. I was doing a lot of administrative work, and this wasn't my thing. I'm more issues oriented, and, as a result, I felt stifled politically by having to immerse myself so much in basic administration to run the program. This frustration led me to make a huge mistake. This Chicano guy came around and fast-talked me into believing that he was a great administrator and fund-raiser and that he wanted to help out. Without checking him out, I foolishly agreed to take him on and turned over the administration of the program to him. This proved to be a disaster. He was a shyster and perhaps a police or FBI agent. He ruined the program and lost the support of the people we were trying to serve. A few years later I learned that this guy got busted for counterfeiting or some such crime. I couldn't believe that I had made such a huge mistake.

During this period, I myself didn't have a job. Fortunately, I moved in with my parents, and my dad supported me. I should have been working to help them out, but with my youthful energy and enthusiasm, I wanted to continue my political work, and I did.

MY DRAFT CASE

Part of the reason that I made this mistake about Casa de la Vecindad had to do with my preoccupation in early 1972 with my draft case. I had been indicted right after the moratorium for refusing induction with the armed services, even though the draft had ended. I had submitted a request for conscientious objector status earlier, but my draft board hadn't honored it because, they argued, they hadn't received it on time. On top of this, the local federal court where my case would be heard refused to accept my attorney, Michael Tigar, as my attorney. The judge argued that Tigar had a history of disrupting court proceedings and, as a result, he could not represent me. This was a lie and a political move by the attorney representing the government to get rid of Tigar, whom they feared. I offered to represent myself, but the court refused and wanted to appoint an attorney for me. I turned them down and insisted on my right to have my own lawyer.

It took over a year for us to appeal my request to have Tigar represent me. The federal appeals court agreed with my petition, and my case began in January 1972. In fact, the U.S. Supreme Court let this decision stand after the U.S. district judge appealed it. The Supreme Court didn't actually rule in my case but refused to hear the appeal. Instead of a jury trial, we requested a judge, because the case was assigned to a fairly liberal judge, Warren J. Ferguson, a Democrat. The first phase of the proceedings was the discovery phase, where evidence would be assembled and examined by both sides. The prosecuting attorney, this guy named Fox, brought in this ex-student, who probably was an informant for the FBI, to testify about my activities at UCLA. This had nothing to do with my draft status, but it was an attempt, I guess, to discredit me.

On our side, Tigar requested my FBI files. I remember this guy—ironically, by the last name of Muñoz—coming into court or the chambers where discovery was taking place with these boxes of files. I couldn't believe it. Here I was, only twenty-five years old, and I already had an extensive FBI file! As we proceeded to examine the material, we discovered it was mostly press clippings about my induction refusal and about the moratorium. But this material was important to us because we were planning to argue that I was being prosecuted, not because I had refused induction, but because the government wanted to punish me for my politics. This was not a legal case but a political one.

But we never got this far. Judge Ferguson began to question the time line around my request to be considered for conscientious objector status. He noticed that I had submitted my request via telegram a full twenty-four hours or so before my draft board sent out its statement to me that I was in violation of being inducted. When questioned about this, the draft board officials claimed that they had not received the telegram before they sent out their notice. But the issue now became not when they had received my request but my intent.

"Mr. Fox," Judge Ferguson told the draft board's attorney, "when Mr. Muñoz sent his telegram from Santa Monica twenty-five miles to San Gabriel, did you think that he expected it to be sent by Pony Express?"

The judge had them! On the basis of my intent to comply with the draft board by submitting my request to have my status reexamined as a conscientious objector within the appropriate deadline, the judge dismissed my case. The board, according to Judge Ferguson, had violated my right to appeal the board's rejection of my claim of conscientious objector status. The government had no response, and since the draft had ended anyway, it didn't appeal. We had won!

We didn't get a chance to use my case to argue the injustice of the draft and of the war, but at the same time we were relieved. This cloud hanging over my head, after almost three years, was now removed. Michael Tigar was brilliant in all these legal proceedings, and I still can't thank him enough.

In a way, the ending of my case was anticlimactic, although I must say it freed my spirits. Of course, my family was relieved. But my attention was no longer on the draft. In fact, the draft had now been replaced by a new lottery system. But my concern had turned to trying to build a power base to address community issues. In a way, as I look back on it now, I was moving from movement politics to community politics. It's hard to distinguish between the two, other than to say that much of the movement had addressed broader issues such as the war or electoral politics. I now felt it more important to focus on specific community issues that would involve not only movement activists but also ordinary community people. This change would affect my activities into the 1970s and beyond.

THE POLITICS OF URBAN RENEWAL

My draft case was over and I had removed myself from La Casa de la Vecindad, so I found myself once again between activities. Fortunately, Father Luce again came to my rescue. He informed me that some of the Protestant denominations had recently organized an ecumenical organization called COMMIT, or Center for Metropolitan Mission In-Service Training. It was a social-action center that was in part aimed at socializing ministers who were going to be working in the Chicano community. They needed someone to be in charge of this, and Father Luce said that if I wanted the job, he would make sure that I got it. It seemed perfect for me and, on top of that, it paid a salary that I needed. I quickly agreed to do it.

What was even more perfect about my COMMIT position was that Father Luce assured me that I could, at the same time, continue to do my other community organizing. In fact, the group encouraged it as outreach to the Chicano community.

As part of COMMIT, and with a small office at the Church of the Epiphany, I not only began to do workshops with the ministers but began to turn my attention to a growing crisis in the community: urban renewal.

After the moratorium experience, my thinking on Chicano empowerment and equality focused on a few major obstacles as related to Los Angeles: urban renewal projects, both public and private; mass deportation of undocumented Mexican immigrants; and electoral gerrymandering that undercut our ability to sustain large and stable communities on which to build effective electoral peoples' power. Bert Corona, Chole Alatorre, and others were building the historic struggle for immigrant rights and against deportations. MALDEF (Mexican American Legal Defense and Education Fund) and civil rights activists such as Hermán Sillas were strategically taking on the gerrymandering issues. However, while there were important struggles around people and park-removal projects in various areas of Greater East Los Angeles, there was no strategic approach to the chronic barrio destruction and dispersal associated with urban renewal.

In the early seventies the city and county began developing metropolitan-wide master plans on a neighborhood-by-neighborhood basis. At that time I saw the opportunity for a strategic approach, starting with the Northeast L.A. Neighborhood Plans proposal to change the residential zoning of the small Albion community in Lincoln Heights from residential to industrial. The area was an Achilles' heel for larger plans to "recycle the inner city," a major slogan for county-wide planning.

All of Los Angeles south of the downtown area, except for three city council districts, had poor housing. East and northeast Chicano concentrations could elect two council members, with another one in the San Fernando Valley. Together, these predominantly black and Chicano areas held the possibility of creating a major black-Chicano political coalition in the city if they were not destroyed by urban renewal.

The Albion industrial-zoning proposal used the lie of housing recycling and opened the door to exposing the potential of land-grab removal projects.

I elicited the help of Gil Cano, who was beginning to assist Latino Catholic priests in building the PADRES organization throughout the Southwest to promote Chicano issues within the Church. We convinced the pastor of Our Lady Help of Christians Catholic parish in the Albion area to open the church for a community meeting on the industrial-zoning plan. The meeting was packed, and we formed an organization to take on the industrial and other land-use aspects of the Northeast Plan, which threatened Latino and other working-class areas. We began leafleting and knocking on doors in the greater Lincoln Heights area. Parishioners convinced the pastor of the large Sacred Heart Church there to host further community meetings for our newly formed East/Northeast Committee to Stop Home Destruction. The name was designed to counterpoise us to the East/ Northeast Model Cities Program, which comprised many worthy programs, but which we also perceived was intended to soften up the neighborhoods for recycling projects. These programs were also used to provide more local patronage for conservative councilman Art Snyder, who represented this area, and his ally Mayor Sam Yorty, who faced reelection in the spring of 1973.

The Northeast Plan had yet to be taken up by the Yorty-selected City Planning Commission. We targeted the Model Cities Housing Corporation as the main threat and the Achilles' heel of the Model Cities project.

We held meetings, which grew in attendance, of homeowners, renters, and activists at the Sacred Heart Girls High School hall. Not only Chicanos but also Italians and Asians, old-timers, who lived in the Lincoln Heights area came to the meetings. To facilitate communication, we translated discussions on issues like the bylaws of the Housing Corporation into Spanish, Italian, and Mandarin.

Once organized, we intervened at one of the so-called meetings of the Housing Corporation, with about 100–150 community residents. The corporation was supposed to have an official membership made up of such residents who, in turn, were to select the board of directors, but none of this had occurred.

At the meeting, we demanded to elect members of the board. The bureaucrats there countered by saying, "Okay we'll have an election, but we can't now because we don't have members yet. We first have to get members."

"Well, what do you think we are?" I shot back. "We're here as members and we're going to elect the board. Here are our applications for membership." We already had these prepared.

"Yes," one of the bureaucrats responded defensively, "but state law says that the members first have to be notified of an election, and we haven't done that yet."

"What are you talking about?" I defiantly countered. "All of us just turned in our applications. Have you seen anyone leave the room? All the members are here right now, and we've been duly notified. Let's vote!"

And we did! There was nothing they could do about it. We could fill only some vacancies since the mayor and the city councilman for the district, Snyder, could also appoint board members. But we now had half of the board and could stymie the Housing Corporation efforts of recycling Lincoln Heights as part of urban renewal.

Meanwhile, for obvious political reasons, the Yorty administration had shelved further Planning Commission action on the Northeast Plan during the 1973 mayoral election. Yorty had continued Los Angeles's historical "any development goes" policy for twelve years, which had overzoned the city's residential areas. His opponent, liberal African American Tom Bradley, promised to procedurally downzone thousands of high rise–zoned lots throughout the city, including the Eastside.

When Yorty and Bradley emerged in a runoff race for mayor, we decided to invite them to discuss the master plan for our areas at the Lincoln High School auditorium, which seated more than one thousand. It was packed. Yorty didn't show up. Bradley did and pledged to include our proposals in a new plan if elected.

Bradley's vote on the Eastside significantly increased, and he won the election. Later that year he returned to Lincoln High with his new Planning Commission to hear our concerns. Our proposed changes were approved by the commission and in 1974 by the city council, and then Mayor Bradley signed off on them. We now had a mayor whose interest was to foster a growing Chicano vote on the Eastside and who challenged, as best he could, the establishment's effort to dilute our strength.

We still did not have power to elect our own, but we could affect local and city policy. Chicano power was moving forward.

The incorporation campaign also proved to be the swan song of the RUP in L.A. The fact was that the party was faltering, not only locally but throughout the Southwest as well. The party's short history had been highlighted by its national convention in El Paso in early September 1972. I didn't attend because I wasn't a delegate and because of my growing engagements in the housing issues.

GETTING MARRIED

In the summer of 1973 I undertook a big personal change in my life. I got married. Since college I had several girlfriends, but none of them developed into a serious or stable enough relationship in which I contemplated marriage. Besides, I was too busy in my political work to think of getting married. I also, of course, had my draft situation hanging over my head.

But by 1973 I felt differently. I had been dating Doraine, my girlfriend, for a year. She was Japanese American, from Hawaii, and even though we were from different ethnic backgrounds, as minority people we had a lot in common. I had met her on a double date with my brother. We got married in Hawaii, and Gil Cano served as my best man. Getting to know her family was interesting. At first, they had no idea what a Chicano was. "Is this someone from Chicago?" they asked. But they quickly accepted me, and over fourteen years of marriage, we would often visit my in-laws in Hawaii.

Doraine had an MA in Spanish and taught for many years. She taught English as a second language in adult education in the Eastside schools. She worked very closely with her predominantly Mexican immigrant students, especially the young women. She recognized the problem of unwanted pregnancies, and to combat this she invited representatives from Planned Parenthood to speak in her classes. Her students ranged in age from eighteen to twenty-two. She had no idea the fury that would be unleashed against her by school authorities for her action. They tried to fire her. We mobilized some of our community people in her defense, and we put pressure on Julian Nava, the only Chicano member of the school board, to intervene. Eventually the issue calmed down and she continued her teaching, although she no longer invited Planned Parenthood into her classes. Instead, she directed her students to seek such assistance at the agency itself.

With my wife's teaching salary and what I was getting paid from COMMIT, we were able to get along. We rented a house in Lincoln Heights to remain close to our work. Marriage did not change my political commitments, and I was grateful that my wife supported me in them.

TEMPLE BEAUDRY

In the spring of 1974, Chicano students at USC, led by Sy (Silas) Obrego, came to see me about still another urban renewal problem affecting Mexican residents. Sy was also the director of Centro Chicano. I had known Sy from the moratorium days, when he had been head of MEChA at Long Beach State. It was good to see him again.

"Rosalio," he informed me, "there's an attempt to remove many of the Mexican residents of the Temple Beaudry area downtown, just across the Harbor Freeway from the Music Center. We need your help."

Sy and the students knew of our earlier work on combating urban renewal on the Eastside. Sy further explained what was happening. Mexican immigrants, two hundred families, many undocumented, lived in this area, which was characterized by dilapidated housing composed of wooden structures or classic L.A. courts. They did not own their homes but rented from absentee landowners. The firm of the renowned architect Welton Beckett that had designed the Music Center and had close ties to the Chandler family, which published the *Los Angeles Times,* owned most of this area. In turn, the Security Pacific Bank administered the properties. The Bank of America wanted to build a large banking complex in the Temple Beaudry area and had made arrangements with Security Pacific to do so. This, of course, would dislocate the resident *mexicanos,* with no compensation. This private urban renewal plan was up before the city council for approval that was pro forma since the councilman from this area, John Ferraro, supported the plan.

The downtown area had not been part of our urban renewal project, but after listening to Sy and the students, both Gil and I agreed to help out. We first met with some of the families involved to get a sense of what they wanted to do.

"If we fight this issue, there's no guarantee that we can win," I told them in Spanish.

"Señor Rosalio," they replied, also in Spanish, "we have no choice but to fight. We have nowhere else to live. We can't afford other housing."

Inspired by the commitment and spirit of the residents and the innate leadership of some of the families, Gil and I plunged further into the fight.

Because some of the families had already displayed leadership, we didn't want to just come in and take over. Unlike the previous struggles, where Gil and I had been more up-front as leaders, we decided to take a different approach in Temple Beaudry. We assisted the residents in forming committees responsible for different tasks. This way more families would be involved and organic leadership would be further developed. These committees, in turn, operated under what the residents and we called the United Neighbors of Temple Beaudry.

We also attempted to get media attention, especially television, on what was happening to the immigrants. Rather than call a press conference and risk only one station or reporter showing up, we contacted individual stations and newspapers and stressed their covering the human drama of these people being kicked out of their homes by the powerful Bank of America. This strategy worked, and as stations and papers wanted to cover the story, we accommodated them by setting them up with individual families. This way, rather than one story being reported, we had several stories in different media outlets.

As in our other struggles, we reached out to develop a broad coalition to assist the immigrants. Although the priest of the local Catholic church nearest to Temple Beaudry refused to help—in fact, he was in the pocket of the bank—other Catholic priests and nuns, including auxiliary bishop Juan Arzube, joined the effort to stop the rezoning. We even linked up with an environmental group in Santa Monica called the No Oil Project, which was fighting against offshore oil leases. They wanted Chicano support because in other environmental issues, the oil companies and developers would often pit minorities against environmentalists with the argument that development would lead to jobs for minorities and that environmentalists opposed such jobs. Gil and I met with the group, and we reached a mutual understanding that the Temple Beaudry group would support No Oil and, in turn, the environmentalists would support the immigrants by raising funds for them and putting pressure on Mayor Bradley and the city council.

The ultimate fate of Temple Beaudry, of course, would rest in the hands of the city council. We knew that we couldn't affect the councilmen, since they all scratched one another's backs on development proposals. However, since we had helped elect Mayor Tom Bradley in 1973, we believed he would support us. Although Bradley, in general, supported the Chicano community, the Temple Beaudry issue proved to be a complicated one for him. He had friends and supporters among the bankers and the Chandler family. We knew this and tried to influence him by going through Manuel Aragón, one of his deputy mayors. But Manuel, who had supported us on other issues, also shied away. In the end, we finally exerted pressure through some of the Westside councilmen, who were more responsive to our environmental supporters than to the developers. They arranged access for us meet with Bradley. The mayor did not endorse us fully but did promise to broker a compromise that would assist the immigrants. We weren't pleased with this, but we took a realistic position.

The agreement allowed the rezoning to take place. The residents would be removed, and the Bank of America could build its center. However, the Bank of America would provide a reimbursement for the residents that would help in their relocation. Each family would receive a substantial amount to pay for their moving costs and for them to find new housing. Some families actually used their funds to help finance the purchase of a home. Moreover, during the time they looked for new housing, they would be exempted from paying rent.

The agreement did not achieve our goal of saving these people's homes, but we believed that the struggle, really led by the immigrants themselves, forced the bank and the city to compensate a considerable amount for the dislocations suffered by these people. I didn't think that I was violating any of my political principles by accepting the agreement. I was not an absolutist. I was beginning to realize that sometimes compromise is needed. Anyway, what was satisfying to me was not what was important. The goal was what worked for the immigrants, and the agreement proved to be beneficial to most of them. However, I realized that more and more low-cost housing was being lost, and rents were going up.

WORKING WITH IMMIGRANTS

Working with the immigrant families at Temple Beaudry impressed on me even more the plight of the undocumented. This impression, in fact, began to shift my attention more and more to working with them. It was also around this time, 1974–75, that Jean McDowell, from one of the antipoverty programs, alerted us to efforts to deny undocumented immigrants and their U.S.-born children various state and federal welfare programs. Working with Jean, Gil Cano and I organized what we called the Interreligious Committee on Human Needs. Gil had been working with many of the Catholic parishes, and I had my connections with the progressive Protestant ones. The purpose of the committee was to serve, on the one hand, as a lobbying group against the efforts to deny the undocumented public services and, on the other, to provide what services we could. To legitimize the work of the committee, we got Bishop Arzube to serve as the chair.

Through the committee we protested and helped defeat the proposed Rodino bill in the U.S. Congress, which, because of pressure from many other such groups, was not enacted. The bill would have further sanctioned mass roundups of undocumented immigrants and penalize employers for hiring the undocumented. We didn't sympathize with employers who exploited the immigrants, but we knew that this would lead to employers firing not only the undocumented but also all Mexican immigrants and perhaps also Mexican Americans. The undocumented would only suffer more as a result of such legislation. This was not a legal issue, but a human issue.

These were tense times for immigrants, especially due to the INS raiding workplaces and agencies serving the immigrants. On one occasion, while our committee was meeting, we got word that the *migra* (INS) was raiding the Lincoln Heights welfare office. We quickly called some of our lawyer friends to go there and assist. But what really worked was getting Bishop Arzube to call the INS. Hearing from the bishop, the INS officials quickly left the welfare office, leaving the immigrants alone.

LA ORGANIZACIÓN DEL PUEBLO

In 1975, while still employed by COMMIT, I helped start yet another organization. This was the Lincoln Heights National Client's Council, affiliated with the Legal Aid Foundation. The council provided legal assistance to immigrants, whether documented or undocumented. These different committees sometimes blended into one another, especially since many activists participated in more than one.

As with the earlier groups, we succeeded in getting a number of volunteers. One of them would come to have an important influence on me. This was Joel Flores. I had known Joel through the Moratorium Committee. He was an activist from the San Pedro area. One day he showed up at my office at the Church of the Epiphany.

"Rosalio, how you doing? It's been a while."

"Yeah, good to see you, Joel. What are you up to?"

"I'm no longer working in San Pedro. I want to get involved in working-class issues here in L.A. I'm now a Marxist, and I'm joining the Communist Party. I've been looking into what you've been doing recently, and I think I could work well with you."

"I have no problem with that, Joel. I respect the work you've done, and we need all the help we can get. Welcome!"

It was through Joel that I began to get more interested in Marxist thought. As a history major at UCLA, I had learned something about Marx and socialist movements both in Europe and in this country, although I had never systematically studied Marxism. I had also had some contact with the left groups, such as the Communist Party, that had supported the moratorium. I didn't think too much of some of them, especially the Maoists and Trotskyites. I also thought that some of the Chicano-movement Marxists were too dogmatic. By contrast, I had always had good relationships with some communists. Because of this, I had no problem when Joel joined the party.

I further learned more about Marxism and class analysis through conversations with Joel. He never tried to recruit me to the party, but he did make an effort to convert me to Marxism. He gave me three volumes of the selected works of Lenin, which I took with me when my wife and I went to Hawaii for Christmas in 1975. I read them thoroughly and was quite impressed with Lenin's thought on revolution, philosophy, and political economy.

I had never considered myself a revolutionary. I was a Chicano activist. I was concerned about racism and—as I served working-class people, including immigrants—with class exploitation. But I certainly was not a Marxist. In fact, I had even contemplated becoming an Episcopalian priest. I admired Father Luce and thought that I could continue my community work as an ordained Episcopalian like him. It wasn't religion or spirituality that drew me in this direction, but more the influence of Father Luce as a role model. I even started taking some classes on Episcopalianism. But I soon concluded that I wasn't cut out to be a priest of any kind. Still, I knew that my democratic values had some of their roots in my religious upbringing. As I studied Marxism, I saw no contradiction between Christian values and a Marxist perspective. The two influences aided me as I began to focus more and more on identifying with the poor and against the wealthy and powerful.

As I moved politically in a Marxist direction, I, along with Joel, concluded that it would be best to form an organization that had no links to agencies such as the Legal Aid Foundation, which, while doing good, was not a grassroots community organization per se. Moreover, because it had a board of directors spread throughout the county, it was beholden to others besides working-class people and immigrants. We felt that it would be better to have an organization that would work with agencies such as Legal Aid but at the same time be a grassroots group with its base in the community. This is how the National Client's Council evolved into La Organización del Pueblo (the People's Organization) by the spring of 1976. It was composed of many of our former supporters, including Father Roger Wood, who had taken over for Father Luce when he decided to leave L.A. and work in New York City.

La Organización del Pueblo was deliberately named in Spanish because we wanted to really reach out to the Mexican community in the Eastside. The Organización was planned as an umbrella group that would assist Spanish-speaking people in a variety of areas, including quality education, full employment rights, legal aid, immigration rights, health care, adequate housing, and consumer rights. "La Organización del Pueblo is for Justice," one of our flyers read. "It strives to help the people in their struggle against all forms of discrimination and economic oppression." At the same time, we would not exclude other working-class people in similar need. We made a concerted effort, with some success, to include not only Chicano activists but also community people as members. We had biweekly meetings, usually at the Church of the Epiphany. To reach out and inform people about who we were and what we were doing, we also published and distributed literature.

At the same time that we put together La Organización, the debate on immigration was still hot and heavy. Our group took the lead in protesting what was called the Eilberg bill in the U.S. Congress, which drastically reduced legal immigration from Mexico. This bill would only compound the movement of undocumented immigrants into the United States and further feed the anti-immigrant hysteria. The bill passed Congress, so we linked up with Bert Corona and the Hermandad Mexicana Nacional to pressure President Gerald Ford to veto it, especially since this was an election year. We thought that Ford might be trying to reach out to the Latino vote, and he might be susceptible to our pressure. In this struggle, we further linked up with other progressive groups and actively participated in a broad coalition to stop the Eilberg bill and the persecution of undocumented immigrants. Ford eventually signed the bill, but we had put up a strong fight and laid the groundwork for a coalition of pro-immigrant groups, which would in time have success, such as the amnesty bill signed by President Reagan in 1986.

One of the more exciting struggles that we in La Organización got involved with concerned tenant rights. A movement activist informed us that a number of fellow tenants—some seven hundred—in one of Lincoln Heights's federally subsidized apartment complexes, called the Mission Plaza Apartments, were going without heat because a gas line had broken and the owner had not fixed the rupture, nor had they reported it to the county officials. Winter had set in, and the people were suffering. This group wanted to know if we could help.

We agreed to meet with the tenants. While most were Mexicans or Latinos, a few were Vietnamese, and even some poor whites were involved. They had already informally organized among themselves. That made our job easier.

"We're going to try to help you," I explained to them. "But if the landlords don't listen, we may have to do something more drastic. Are you willing to do that?"

"Yes, Mr. Muñoz, we'll do what we have to do. We can't go on like this without heat."

Well, we got little, if any, response from the landlords, and the county wasn't any more helpful. So we decided to do a rent strike. We met with the tenants and proposed the idea, and they unanimously approved. They organized themselves into a tenants' rights committee and elected leaders to conduct the strike. Instead of paying their rents, they put the money into a common fund, which we used to pressure the landlords. We had several hundred people involved in the strike.

The landlords fought back, but we got Legal Aid attorneys, who obtained restraining orders to block any evictions. All the tenants hung in, and after several months the landlords finally caved in and agreed to do the repairs needed. Out of the collected funds, we then paid the accumulated rent.

Our success in this rent strike led to our involvement in others. Tenants whose rents were being unreasonably raised started coming to us. This resulted in several small rent strikes. At one point we had as many as seven rent strikes in different parts of the Latino communities going on at the same time. At each location the people formed individual tenants' rights committees. In all these cases, the tenants won.

Out of these rent strikes, we realized how important tenant rights were becoming, especially in Southern California. As a result, we joined our efforts with a broader L.A.-based coalition, the Coalition for Economic Survival, which began, at our urging, focusing on rent control and working to get local governments to pass laws to protect tenants from exorbitant rents. In fact, I was elected chair of the coalition for a year. Modern rent control in L.A. came from a barrio initiative. As a result of these efforts, other Southern California communities adopted such laws, although it continued to be a big issue, and it still is.

SUMMING UP

The focus of this testimonio has been my life prior to and during the Chicano movement. Some contend that the movement died off by the mid-1970s, especially with the conclusion of the war in Vietnam in 1975. But for me the movement continued and in a way continues even today, as it does for thousands of others. I am still committed to bringing about social change for the Chicano and Latino community. I could further elaborate on my activism at some length, but to maintain the emphasis of this volume on the key years of the Chicano movement, certainly between 1965 and 1975, I will just summarize the rest of my political life to the present. This is important to give readers the sense that most of us who became movement activists didn't just go away after 1975. Many of us maintained our political work, although in new ways and under new circumstances.

Into the mid and late 1970s, for example, I continued, as I had since the early 1970s, to work in the barrios, developing community-based movements and coalitions. As noted earlier, I had learned that one of the weaknesses of the movement was the inability, or even unwillingness, to develop actions based on the concrete needs of the people, such as housing, health care, jobs, and other basic issues. Hence, I continued to move in this direction, using my base with COMMIT and La Organización del Pueblo.

However, in 1978 I shifted gears a bit and decided, at Joel's urging, to enter electoral politics as an extension of my grassroots work. I did this not because I believed I could actually be elected to office but because I felt I needed a larger forum to raise the issues that I was concerned about and build a voting constituency on these issues. I announced in late 1977 that I would run against Supervisor Ed Edelman, one of the county supervisors who was up for reelection. He represented the Eastside, but his Third Supervisorial District also encompassed part of West L.A., including Beverly Hills. I chose to run against Edelman because I lived in his district and because he had not done much for the Chicano community and other working people. He had not been supportive of extending health care to either immigrants or working people who didn't have it, and he had been against rent control and other issues I was working on. My platform called for tax justice, human services, jobs, and housing.

While I made the decision to challenge Edelman, I was also encouraged to do so by some of my progressive friends, such as Joel and members of the Communist Party. I wasn't a party member, but I knew a number of them in Los Angeles. In fact, it was really the party that proved to be my main supporter for my campaign. Of course, members of La Organización del Pueblo as well as colleagues from the moratorium years also supported me. But, overall, I had limited funds, and we couldn't mount much of a campaign. I concentrated much of my effort on the Eastside, where I believed I could obtain more of a hearing and votes. I didn't do much door-to-door campaigning. Mostly we put out my literature on my issues and attacked Edelman for not supporting them. In addition, I got some press coverage, including the *Los Angeles Times*. The supervisorial election coincided with Proposition 13, which would radically reduce property taxes and would hurt the schools and other public programs. I strongly opposed it, as did Edelman, for that matter. But because of the controversy of Prop 13, the supervisorial election and other critical issues received a lot of attention.

My campaign was also made more difficult due to another Mexican American, who also ran for Edelman's position. This was a guy by the name of Gonzálo Molina. I suspected then that he was a stooge for Edelman, who got him to run to split the Chicano vote. That's exactly what happened. In the election, Molina wound up getting a few more votes than me and, of course, Edelman won reelection. At first I was disappointed at the results and about my campaign, although I got thirty thousand votes. I thought we didn't do a good job of getting my message out and using the election as a politicizing tool. However, I learned a lot about electoral politics. On the other hand, my votes and Molina's showed a lot of opposition to Edelman and a lot of support for progressive issues.

The election, however, did empower the coalitions and issues that I favored. Rent control, for example, was passed by the city and county when landlords, contrary to the Proposition 13 propaganda, raised instead of lowered rents. Edelman and Bradley joined forces with the Coalition for Economic Survival and other groups to get it passed. On health care for the undocumented and legal guarantees against cutting health services, Edelman changed his neutral stand and supported the issues. I learned what Joel had argued, that elections are not really a winner-take-all reality but that new and oppositional constituencies can result from them. He told me, "you are now more than a neighborhood and coalition leader, so when you lobby politicos, they also see you as thirty thousand votes on the issues, at least until the next election."

During the campaign all but one of the Protestant churches represented on the COMMIT board had voted to retract their funds from the organization, including the Episcopalians with my home church, Epiphany. I was not informed until after the election. I was almost devastated. However, the lone dissenting group, the Church of the Brethren, was so disgusted with this cowardly concession to the board of supervisors that they funded my activities to work on immigrant issues for a full year. With the help of Joel and others, like Lou Negrete, Rev. Bill Ruth, and Mary Seigfried, COMMIT continued. We started a project to get local, regional, and national church groups to back a program for immigrant rights that would oppose employer sanctions and family separations and support amnesty and public services for undocumented immigrants. The Methodists provided funds to organize Latino Methodist clergy on these issues, and I worked with other denominations. Progress was made on all levels. A number of Protestant church groups passed resolutions in favor of our agenda. I am proud of what we achieved.

But this paid position was for only a year, and I needed an income. Fortunately, I got a job as a reporter for the *People's Daily World,* the West Coast paper of the Communist Party. I wasn't a party member, but I had already been thinking of joining the party, except that my wife had reservations. However, in early 1981, shortly after I started working for the paper, both my wife and I joined the party. Working for the paper was not based on being a party member; I wanted to be in the party. As a member of the staff, I covered a variety of issues, including globalization, as industries, like the auto plant, closed in the L.A. area and relocated in Mexico and other third world countries. Although I did not have a background in journalism, I had taken some journalism courses at UCLA and had worked closely with the *Daily Bruin* office on campus.

I felt fortunate in getting the newspaper job, since I needed an income. Joining the party was more my reaction to the election of Ronald Reagan as president and my feeling that I had to be part of the fight against him and the ascendance of extreme conservatives to power in Washington. I had already been close to party members for some years, and I had become a convert to Marxist philosophy. I came to understand that institutional racism and other social ills were tied to the capitalist system. In addition, I was impressed that the party had a good number of Chicano and Latino members and outreach programs, including the Instituto del Pueblo, led by Evelina Alarcón, which provided classes in Marxism and other related topics in L.A. I had attended some of these lectures prior to making the decision to join the party. I had also been an avid reader of the *People's Daily World.* I believed that among the Left, the Communist Party had the most realistic and ideologically consistent program and policies, at least for me. I also didn't see that becoming a communist was a break from my involvement in the Chicano movement. For me, it represented an extension of my movement activities and my own political evolution. It wasn't a choice of being a Chicano or a communist. I could be a Chicano communist. At the same time, I have to say that I didn't discuss this with my parents. They knew I was working for the *People's Daily World* and in time realized that I was a party member. But they never raised objections, and they always supported me.

My history with the Communist Party has been very extensive and even hectic. It's had its ups and downs, but I have remained a party member and today am a member of the national committee. My life as a party member could fill another volume, and maybe it will some day. Suffice to say that, in addition to my continued work with the paper, I also ran again in 1982, stressing Chicano representation for county supervisor. I was supported by the party and other groups, such as MAPA. I was also involved in many other struggles, including the movement against Reagan's war policies in Central America, the antiapartheid movement with respect to South Africa, the nuclear-disarmament efforts, and the growing anti-immigrant hysteria into the 1990s, highlighted by Proposition 187, aimed at severely restricting and curtailing public services, including education, to undocumented immigrants and their children. The struggle for immigrant rights is one that I remained very much involved with into the next millennium. I also actively supported and campaigned for the growing number of Latino politicians running for city, county, and state positions, including the campaign of Antonio Villaraigosa and his election in 2005 as the first Latino mayor of Los Angeles since the nineteenth century. Of course, I opposed and helped mobilize opposition to Bush and Cheney's war on Iraq. I supported the election and reelection of President Barack Obama. All told, I have been a party member for more than thirty years.

Although being in the party has allowed me to remain an activist, it has also had its difficulties. In the later 1980s, for example, I began to have a drinking problem, which plagued me for several years. My health was further affected when I came down with a lung problem that knocked me down for almost a year, until I recovered. In battling my alcoholism, there were periods into the 1990s when I didn't work for the party or when my party participation lapsed. Instead, I had to try to find other means of employment. But I finally overcame this illness and by the mid-1990s was once again able to resume my political work.

In 1986 Doraine and I separated and later divorced by mutual agreement. Her participation in many of the civil rights and progressive causes that I championed was substantial for some fifteen years. In 1995 I married Rosalyn Grennan, a progressive activist and highly talented nurse, as my recovery from alcoholism was starting. My activism was reduced for a period when I dedicated a lot of time in helping to raise her three preteen and adolescent children, whom she had custody of. We also had two foster children in our care, and it was a wonderful experience. Though we divorced in 2005, we remain friends and I am close to her children and one of our foster kids. This is one of my joys.

All of this affected my relations with the party, in addition to some internal, not ideological, divisions that led me to effectively leave the party between 1999 and

FIGURE 22. Muñoz and Raul Ruiz, Los Angeles, 2006. Courtesy of Oscar Castillo.

2003. But I returned when the party invited me back and when I recognized that the internal problems were on their way to being solved.

I want to say something about the legacy of the Chicano movement. I have been politically active for more than forty years. In this time, I have been engaged in a number of struggles, some successful and some not. But throughout this period, and this is part of the movement's legacy, I have been joined or been able to call on some of my political allies who first joined me in protesting the Vietnam War. These activists from the movement continue to be involved and committed to social change for the Chicano, and now broader Latino, communities. I have never felt alone. Many of my colleagues from the movement years, or at least the most intense movement years, are with me; we still form a community, even though we are older and, hopefully, wiser. None of us have ever rested on the laurels of those earlier years. And out of this commitment, we have achieved quite a bit for our people. I disagree with those who say that this isn't the case and that Chicanos are still really poor and at the bottom of the barrel in many places. Well, not quite. Politically, economically, and culturally, Chicanos and Latinos are much more empowered than they were forty years ago. Unfortunately, the U.S.-based global corporate elite has grown in power as well.

I guess that I will always be associated with the Chicano Antiwar Moratorium. I have no problem with this. As a matter of fact, I am proud of what others and I did to protest the war in Vietnam and its consequences on the Chicano community. On the twentieth anniversary of the moratorium in 1990, I was interviewed on my feelings about August 29. And what I said then, I still believe today, forty-five years later:

> You have to measure the impact of the Chicano Moratorium with its own aims—to unite the Mexican-American community in the growing opposition to the war in Vietnam and to strengthen the Mexican-American struggle for equality and social justice. This was achieved despite the police repression and media distortion.
>
> The unity that was developed against the war in our community was unprecedented. At that time, we made up about 3 percent of the nation, so the turnout of 30,000 was proportionately equal to a demonstration of 1 million.[25]

Another part of the movement legacy concerns the false notion that the Chicano movement is dead. My response is, here I am. I'm not dead, yet. Nor is the movement. It continues in changed form, but it's still, in my opinion, the movement. We might call ourselves Latinos now to be inclusive of other Latin American groups, but the objectives are still very much the same. We are still struggling to control our lives and our own destinies. That's what the Chicano movement was all about, and that's what we're still struggling for.

From a personal perspective, the movement empowered me. In a way, I kind of married the movement. I made some personal mistakes, but most had to do with my own weaknesses that I let the movement compensate for. At the same time, the movement allowed me to do what I wanted to do. I think this has been positive. My politics and life have been out in the streets and in the neighborhoods, and that's what I want. Over all these years, it's been a fulfilling experience. It's kind of like Faust. I made my deal, and I had my chance—instead of being a history writer, to be a history maker—and I took it. That's who I am.

Am I a hero? Yes and no, just like thousands of other progressive activists with lifelong commitments to social justice. It is a heroic life in many ways; it entails conscious decisions to forgo some things and make personal sacrifices, but the gratifications are many. It's like what César Chávez told me at the start of the moratorium movement, looking at my dirty scratched VW bug: "It looks like you're struggling, but that's good, because the people will see you struggling and will relate to it."

Do I have any regrets about the course of my life? Politically, no. Personally, I have made errors. I have treated some people wrongly. I still have a lot of amends to do for my own sanity and sobriety. But, despite this, I don't have any regrets at all. I have not acted with malice toward anyone or anything except a social system that I think is unjust and outdated. I find inspiration in a psalm I learned when I was young: "The earth is the Lord's and the fullness thereof. God looked at the world He created and it was good." I still believe in this.

I've made my share of sacrifices, but there have been compensations as well. So I remain very positive. I want to go on. There are a lot more battles to fight, and I want to be a part of these, along with many others.

Epilogue

I want to conclude this testimonio on a personal note. First, I want to thank Raul Ruiz, Gloria Arellanes, and Rosalio Muñoz for sharing their stories with me. I hope I have done justice to them.

The Chicano generation of which Raul, Gloria, and Rosalio are representatives is also my political generation. Although I was not as active as they were, still the movement changed me. I became Chicano as a result of the Chicano movement. At the same time, I have learned much about the movement through these testimonios. I have learned how the movement affected personal lives in ways both good and bad. The movement had many faults. Activists had their own personal and political problems and paid a price for their commitments and actions. The price was personal, in terms of the disruption of relationships, and professional, in terms of careers set aside and negatively affected because of political engagement. This is as true today as it was then. Yet I have come away from this project with a great deal of admiration for my subjects. I admire their idealism, pragmatism, courage, persistence, and commitment. Taking the long view of history, movement activists such as Raul, Gloria, and Rosalio were committed to achieving a more democratic and egalitarian society in the United States. They struggled for civil rights and community empowerment. They also fought to be themselves—to be proud of who they were as Chicanos and of their culture and community. In a way, they sought to redefine American society in a more humane direction. Perhaps this was utopian, but without hopes and dreams, it is hard to imagine constructive social changes.

The Chicano movement, above all, was the collective and individual stories of activists. And indirectly my story is also embedded in these testimonios. As a

Chicano during the movement years, I witnessed the ups and downs and aspirations and frustrations of the movement that were also my own. In the postmovement years, I have also seen both the positive and negative legacies of the movement. By positive, I mean, for example, that the movement's history continues to inspire new struggles for social justice by new generations of Chicanos and other Latinos. By negative, I mean that for some, even today, the Chicano movement remains largely a cultural and ethnic nationalist movement, without any new sense of reaching out to non-Chicanos and Latinos to form political alliances. In addition, as the years have gone by, I have seen and participated in the evolving evaluation of the Chicano movement. Some of these evaluations are one-sided and unfair. For example, especially with the increased interest in issues of gender and sexuality in Chicano studies, there are some scholars who are applying a litmus test to the movement. How did the movement treat women? How did the movement treat the gay population? These are valid issues, and this book addresses at least the issue of gender relations. Sexuality, as it pertains to homosexuality in the movement, was not an open issue; for the most part at that time, gay Chicanos and Chicanas were not open about their sexual preference. What I object to is basing one's entire assessment and judgment of the movement on one or both of these issues. Such a litmus test does not contribute to our full understanding of a complex social movement and tells us more about the person raising the question or questions than it does about the movement. At the same time, what is more positive and encouraging is the growing number of new studies on the movement, especially by graduate students who are focusing on the movement in various local communities and how it operated in these different locations. I am certain that such research will only add to our appreciation of the movement as heterogeneous and complex.

For now, I leave it to readers and critics to deconstruct the meanings of the lives I have presented here, but I sincerely hope that this book will influence other scholars and graduate students to explore the lives of still other Chicano movement activists. Through biographies and oral histories we can put more human faces to this historic struggle.

There is some sadness in bringing closure to a study that I commenced more than twenty years ago. Knowing the importance of publishing these stories, however, my persistence and commitment did not falter. Raul, Gloria, and Rosalio have been my companions throughout this journey. The journey is completed now, and we must move on. But it has been a pleasure to be with them all these years. I shall miss them.

NOTES

NOTES

INTRODUCTION

1. The Berets in San Jose were referred to as Black Berets, as opposed to the better-known Brown Berets of Southern California and elsewhere.

2. See, for example, what is perhaps the best-known testimonio, Elisabeth Burgos-Debray, *I, Rigoberta Menchú: An Indian Woman in Guatemala* (London: Verso, 1984). See also John Beverly, *Testimonio: On the Politics of Truth* (Minneapolis: University of Minnesota Press, 2004); Georg Gugelberger, *The Real Thing: Testimonial Discourse and Latin America* (Durham, NC: Duke University Press, 1996).

3. Jeremy D. Popkin, *History, Historians, and Autobiography* (Chicago: University of Chicago Press, 2005), 72.

4. See Cynthia E. Orozco, *No Mexicans, Women, or Dogs Allowed: The Rise of the Mexican American Civil Rights Movement* (Austin: University of Texas Press, 2009).

5. See John R. Chávez, *The Lost Homeland: The Chicano Image of the Southwest* (Albuquerque: University of New Mexico Press, 1984).

6. On César Chávez and the farmworkers' struggle, see Jacques Levy, *César Chávez: Autobiography of La Causa* (New York: Norton, 1975); Richard Griswold del Castillo and Richard A. García, *César Chávez: Triumph of Spirit* (Norman: University of Oklahoma Press, 1995); Mark Day, *Forty Acres: César Chávez and the Farm Workers* (New York: Praeger, 1971); Susan Ferris and Ricardo Sandoval, *The Fight in the Fields: César Chávez and the Farmworkers Movement* (New York: Harcourt Brace, 1997); John C. Hammerback, Richard J. Jensen, and José Ángel Gutiérrez, *A War of Words: Chicano Protest in the 1960s and 1970s* (Westport, CT: Greenwood, 1985); Peter Matthiessen, *Sal Si Puedes: César Chávez and the New American Revolution* (New York: Random House, 1969); Ronald B. Taylor, *Chávez and the Farm Workers* (Boston: Beacon, 1975); Frederick John Dalton, *The Moral Vision of César Chávez* (Maryknoll, NY: Orbis Books, 2003); Marco G. Prouty, *César Chávez, the Catholic*

Bishops, and the Farmworkers' Struggle for Social Justice (Tucson: University of Arizona Press, 2008); Randy Shaw, *Beyond the Fields: César Chávez, the UFW, and the Struggle for Justice in the Twenty-First Century* (Berkeley: University of California Press, 2008); José-Antonio Orosco, *César Chávez and the Common Sense of Nonviolence* (Albuquerque: University of New Mexico Press, 2008); Mario T. García, *The Gospel of César Chávez: My Faith in Action* (Lanham, MD: Sheed and Ward, 2007); Miriam Powell, *The Union of Their Dreams: Power, Hope, and Struggle in César Chávez's Farm Worker Movement* (New York: Bloomsbury, 2009); Powell, *The Crusades of Cesar Chavez: A Biography* (New York: Bloomsbury, 2014); Frank Bardacke, *Tramping Out the Vintage: César Chávez and the Two Souls of the United Farm Workers* (London: Verso, 2011); and Matt García, *From the Jaws of Victory: The Triumph and Tragedy of César Chávez and the Farm Workers Movement* (Berkeley: University of California Press, 2012). On Dolores Huerta, see Mario T. García, *A Dolores Huerta Reader* (Albuquerque: University of New Mexico Press, 2008).

7. See Rudy V. Busto, *King Tiger: The Religious Vision of Reies López Tijerina* (Albuquerque: University of New Mexico Press, 2005); Richard Gardner, *Grito! Reies Tijerina and the New Mexico Land Grant War of 1967* (Indianapolis: Bobbs-Merrill, 1970); Michael Jenkinson, *Tijerina: Land Grant Conflict in New Mexico* (Albuquerque: Paisano, 1968); and Peter Nabokov, *Tijerina and the Courthouse Raid* (Albuquerque: University of New Mexico Press, 1969). See also Tijerina's English-language autobiography, Reies López Tijerina, *They Called Me "King Tiger": My Struggle for the Land and Our Rights*, trans. and ed. José Ángel Gutiérrez (Houston: Arte Público, 2000).

8. See Rudolfo A. Anaya and Francisco A. Lomeli, eds., *Aztlán: Essays on the Chicano Homeland* (Albuquerque: University of New Mexico Press, 1991). On Corky Gonzales, see Ernesto B. Vigil, *The Crusade for Justice: Chicano Militancy and the Government's War on Dissent* (Madison: University of Wisconsin Press, 1999).

9. Rodolfo Acuña, *Occupied America: The Chicano's Struggle toward Liberation* (San Francisco: Canfield, 1972); Robert Blauner, *Racial Oppression in America* (New York: Harper and Row, 1972); Anne Fountain, *José Martí, the United States, and Race* (Gainesville: University Press of Florida, 2014).

10. Carlos Muñoz Jr., *Youth, Identity, Power: The Chicano Movement* (New York: Verso, 1989); Mario T. García and Sal Castro, *Blowout! Sal Castro and the Chicano Struggle for Educational Justice* (Chapel Hill: University of North Carolina Press, 2011); Dolores Delgado Bernal, "Chicana School Resistance and Grassroots Leadership: Providing an Alternative History of the 1968 East Los Angeles Blowouts" (PhD diss., University of California, Los Angeles, 1997); Henry Joseph Gutiérrez, "The Chicano Education Rights Movement and School Desegregation, Los Angeles, 1962–1970" (PhD diss., University of California, Irvine, 1990).

11. See Chicano Coordinating Council on Higher Education, *El Plan de Santa Barbara: A Chicano Plan for Higher Education* (Oakland, CA: La Causa, 1969).

12. On the Mexican American Youth Organization, see Armando Navarro, *Mexican American Youth Organization: Avant-Garde of the Chicano Movement in Texas* (Austin: University of Texas Press, 1995).

13. See Juan Gómez-Quiñones, *Mexican Students por la Raza: The Chicano Student Movement in Southern California, 1967–1977* (Santa Barbara, CA: La Causa, 1978); Muñoz, *Youth, Identity, Power;* José Ángel Gutiérrez, *We Won't Back Down: Severita Lara's Rise from*

Student Leader to Mayor (Houston: Arte Público, 2005); and Marguerite V. Marin, *Social Protest in an Urban Barrio: A Study of the Chicano Movement, 1966–1974* (Lanham, MD: University Press of America, 1991).

14. On the Brown Berets, see Ernesto Chávez, *"¡Mi Raza Primero!" Nationalism, Identity, and Insurgency in the Chicano Movement in Los Angeles, 1966–1978* (Berkeley: University of California Press, 2002), 42–60; and David Montejano, *Quixote's Soldiers: A Local History of the Chicano Movement, 1966–1981* (Austin: University of Texas Press, 2011).

15. Benedict R. Anderson, *Imagined Communities: Reflections on the Origin and Spread of Nationalism* (London: Verso, 1991).

16. See Mario T. García, "Religion in the Chicano Movement: Católicos por la Raza," in *Católicos: Resistance and Affirmation in Chicano Catholic History* (Austin: University of Texas Press, 2008), 131–70; and Mario T. García, ed., *Chicano Liberation Theology: The Writings and Documents of Richard Cruz and Católicos por la Raza* (Dubuque, IA: Kendall Hunt, 2009).

17. See Chávez, *Mi Raza Primero*, 61–79; Lorena Oropeza, *Raza Sí! Guerra No! Chicano Protest and Patriotism during the Vietnam War Era* (Berkeley: University of California Press, 2005); and Jorge Mariscal, ed., *Aztlán and Viet Nam: Chicano and Chicana Experiences of the War* (Berkeley: University of California Press, 1999).

18. On La Raza Unida Party, see Ignacio M. García, *United We Win: The Rise and Fall of La Raza Unida Party* (Tucson: Mexican American Studies and Research Center, University of Arizona, 1989); Armando Navarro, *The Cristal Experiment: A Chicano Struggle for Community Control* (Madison: University of Wisconsin Press, 1998); Armando Navarro, *La Raza Unida Party: A Chicano Challenge to the U.S. Two-Party Dictatorship* (Philadelphia: Temple University Press, 2000); José Ángel Gutiérrez, *The Making of a Chicano Militant: Lessons from Cristal* (Madison: University of Wisconsin Press, 1998); and Chávez, *Mi Raza Primero*, 80–97.

19. Mario T. García, *Memories of Chicano History: The Life and Narrative of Bert Corona* (Berkeley: University of California Press, 1994), 286–320.

20. See Ignacio García, *Chicanismo: The Forging of a Militant Ethos among Chicanos* (Tucson: University of Arizona Press, 1997); and Richard Griswold del Castillo, Teresa McKenna, and Yvonne Yarbro-Bejarano, eds., *Chicano Art: Resistance and Affirmation, 1965–1985* (Los Angeles: Wright Art Gallery, UCLA, 1991).

21. See Alma M. García, *Chicana Feminist Thought: The Basic Historical Writings* (New York: Routledge, 1997); Bernal, "Chicana School Resistance"; Lara Medina, *Las Hermanas: Chicana/Latina Religious-Political Activism in the U.S. Catholic Church* (Philadelphia: Temple University Press, 2004); M. T. García, *Dolores Huerta Reader*; Dionne Espinoza, "Pedagogies of Nationalism and Gender: Cultural Resistance in Selected Representational Practices of Chicana/o Movement Activists, 1967–1972" (PhD diss., Cornell University, 1996); and Maylei Blackwell, *Chicana Power! Contested Histories of Feminism in the Chicano Movement* (Austin: University of Texas Press, 2011).

22. Mario T. García, ed., *Ruben Salazar, Border Correspondent: Selected Writings, 1955–1970* (Berkeley: University of California Press, 1995).

23. See Muñoz, *Youth, Identity, Power*.

24. Jorge Mariscal, *Brown-Eyed Children of the Sun: Lessons from the Chicano Movement, 1965–1975* (Albuquerque: University of New Mexico Press, 2005).

25. Ibid. I take the concept of radical liberalism from Kevin Mattson, *Intellectuals in Action: The Origins of the New Left and Radical Liberalism, 1945–1970* (University Park: Pennsylvania State University Press, 2002).

PART ONE: RAUL RUIZ

1. See Mario T. García, *Desert Immigrants: The Mexicans of El Paso, 1880–1920* (New Haven, CT: Yale University Press, 1981).

2. See Carey McWilliams, *North from Mexico: The Spanish-Speaking People of the United States* (1948; repr., New York: Praeger, 1990).

3. See Frantz Fanon, *The Wretched of the Earth* (New York: Grove, 1966).

4. On Students for a Democratic Society, see Kirkpatrick Sales, *SDS* (New York: Random House, 1973).

5. On Chicano students in the movement, see Muñoz, *Youth, Identity, Power;* and Marisol Moreno, "Of the Community, for the Community: The Chicano Student Movement in California's Public Higher Education, 1967–1973" (PhD diss., University of California, Santa Barbara, 2009).

6. On Sal Castro, see García and Castro, *Blowout.*

7. On the Brown Berets, see Chávez, *Mi Raza Primero.*

8. Ibid.

9. Ruiz uses the terms *sheriffs* and *sheriff's deputies* interchangeably. Both refer to county sheriff's deputies.

10. On César Chávez and Dolores Huerta, see M. T. García, *Gospel of César Chávez;* and M. T. García, *Dolores Huerta Reader.*

11. See Mario T. García, *Mexican Americans: Leadership, Ideology, and Identity, 1930–1960* (New Haven, CT: Yale University Press, 1989).

12. On chicanismo, see I. García, *Chicanismo.*

13. See "Lázaro Q.," *Inside Eastside* 1, no. 5 (1968): 4.

14. On the blowouts, see García and Castro, *Blowout.*

15. On the time difference, see ibid.

16. On the origins of the term *blowout,* see ibid.

17. On the Educational Issues Coordinating Committee, see ibid.; and Jesús Salvador Treviño, *Eyewitness: A Filmmaker's Memoir of the Chicano Movement* (Houston: Arte Público, 2001).

18. On the sit-in, see García and Castro, *Blowout;* and Treviño, *Eyewitness.*

19. On Corky Gonzales, see Vigil, *Crusade for Justice.*

20. See A. García, *Chicana Feminist Thought.*

21. On the Chicano homeland theme, see Chávez, *Lost Homeland.*

22. On Católicos por la Raza, see M. T. García, *Chicano Liberation Theology.*

23. See Oscar Zeta Acosta, *The Revolt of the Cockroach People* (1973; repr., New York: Vintage Books, 1989). Also see Acosta, *The Autobiography of a Brown Buffalo* (New York: Vintage Books, 1972).

24. See Oropeza, *Raza Sí.*

25. Raul Ruiz, *La Raza,* December 1969, 7.

26. On Ruben Salazar, see M. T. García, *Ruben Salazar.*

27. Raul Ruiz, *La Raza,* no. 3 (n.d.): 5.

28. On La Raza Unida Party, see I. García, *United We Win;* and Navarro, *Raza Unida Party.*

29. *Justicia O!* 1, no. 8 (n.d.): 1.

30. Raul Ruiz, "An Analysis of a Campaign," *La Raza* 1, no. 3 (1973): 4–5.

31. PRI stands for Partido Revolucionario Institucional (Institutional Revolutionary Party). The PRI was not significantly challenged until the 1980s by the leftist Partido Revolucionario Democrático.

32. On Frank del Olmo, see Frank Sotomayor and Magdalena Beltrán–del Olmo, eds., *Frank del Olmo: Commentaries on His Times* (Los Angeles: Los Angeles Times Books, 2004).

33. PRD stands for Partido Revolucionario Democrático (Democratic Revolutionary Party).

PART TWO: GLORIA ARELLANES

1. See quote in Mike Ward, "Relationships More Human," *Sunday Tribune Valley Life,* May 26, 1963, 4, in folder 7, box 2, Gloria Arellanes Papers, Special Collections, University Library, California State University, Los Angeles; hereinafter cited as Arellanes Papers.

2. For Sal Castro, see García and Castro, *Blowout.*

3. See Ward, "Relationships More Human," newspaper clipping, in folder 7, box 2, Arellanes Papers. See also copy of El Monte High School newspaper, *Lions' Trail,* November 6, 1963, 1, in folder 7, box 2, Arellanes Papers.

4. According to FBI records, the Berets opened La Piranya in December 1967 and operated it until February 28, 1968, when it was closed by the Los Angeles County Sheriff's Department; see FBI, "Young Chicanos for Community Action, aka Brown Berets," April 17, 1968, Los Angeles 100–71172, in Main Bureau File 105–178715, Washington, DC. FBI files on Brown Berets obtained through the Freedom of Information Act.

5. For a history of the Brown Berets, see Chávez, *Mi Raza Primero,* 42–60. The Berets' origins can be traced to 1966 with the formation of Young Citizens for Community Action, which was later changed to Young Chicanos for Community Action.

6. In her study of the Brown Berets, Marguerite Marin notes that one had to be eighteen years of age, of Latino descent, and pass a written and oral test on Chicano and Mexican history to join; see *Social Protest,* 148.

7. See David Sánchez, *The Birth of a New Symbol: The Brown Beret Manual,* February, 1968, reproduced in Rona Marcia Fields Fox, "The Brown Berets: A Participant Observation Study of Social Action in the Schools of Los Angeles" (PhD diss., University of Southern California, 1970), 300.

8. David Sánchez (lecture, Los Angeles, January 30, 2005), taped by L.A. Social Posse.

9. A later history of the Berets notes that the logo was designed by Manuel Parsens; see "Brief History of the Brown Berets," in the author's possession. See also Chávez, *Mi Raza Primero,* 46.

10. Carlos Montes has stated that the Berets were closely patterned after the Black Panthers; see Monica Sánchez, "The Brown Berets and the Chicano Movement with an Introspective with Carlos Montes" (unpublished term paper, July 28, 2003), 4, in the author's

possession. Montes further recalls that one of the Berets went to an army surplus store and bought a number of berets that happened to be brown. In his own book on the Berets, David Sánchez wrote that he was responsible for ordering twelve brown berets on December 3, 1967, for the group; see *Expedition through Aztlán* (La Puente, CA: Perspective, 1968), 2.

11. See *Greater Los Angeles Urban League Ghetto Awards,* program, August 26, 1968, in folder 1, box 2, Arellanes Papers.

12. "Brown Beret Ten Point Program," *La Causa,* May 23, 1969. Ten-Point Program also available in FBI, "Young Chicanos," July 16, 1970, Los Angeles 105–206966, in Main Bureau File 52–88699. FBI files indicated that Brown Berets were under FBI surveillance since early 1968.

13. Sánchez, *New Symbol,* in Fox, "Brown Berets," 6.

14. Ibid.

15. See *La Causa,* May 23, 1969, 2.

16. Ibid., February 28, 1970, 1.

17. David Sánchez, *La Causa,* May 22, 1970, 17.

18. In his history of the Berets, Chávez contradicts Arellanes by noting that "the Berets expressed a fondness for Marxism," especially as articulated by Mao Tse-tung and the Chinese communists; see Chávez, *Mi Raza Primero,* 50.

19. Sánchez, *New Symbol,* in Fox, "Brown Berets," 288.

20. See *La Causa,* March 1970, 7.

21. Ibid., May 23, 1969.

22. In her study of the female Brown Berets, Dionne Espinoza observes that sometimes the men and women met separately; see "'Revolutionary Sisters': Women's Solidarity and Collective Identification among Chicana Brown Berets in East Los Angeles, 1967–1970," *Aztlán* 26, no. 1 (2001): 17.

23. Fox notes that the drill practices were on Saturdays; see "Brown Berets," 146.

24. Fox asserts that at first only the male Berets drilled, but soon the women were also required to do also; ibid., 146.

25. In her study of the Berets, Fox also identifies this drill instructor as Robert Acosta; ibid., 75.

26. See García and Castro, *Blowout.*

27. On the East L.A. Thirteen, see ibid., 194–220.

28. For Chicanos killed in jail, see *LA Free Press,* July 10–16, 1970, 1.

29. See *Eastside Sun,* May 5, 1968, A1–2, and *Chicano Student,* April 25, 1968, 2. For the police raid on the Beret headquarters on East Olympic Boulevard, see *L.A. Free Press,* May 30, 1969, 14.

30. See FBI, "Young Chicanos," March 25, 1968, Los Angeles 52–11746, in Main Bureau File 52–88699.

31. Ibid. That same month, the FBI further alleged, "While the Brown Berets was ostensibly organized as a legitimate student organization it has been seized by rabble rousing members of the Mexican-American colony as a focal point for potential racial violence thereby posing a definite threat to the security of the country." See FBI, "Young Chicanos," March 26, 1968, Los Angeles 105–178715, in Main Bureau File 52–886993.

32. See FBI, "Young Chicanos," February 26, 1969, Los Angeles 105–178715–36, in Main Bureau File 105–178715.

33. See FBI, "Young Chicanos," November 16, 1970, Los Angeles 105–178715–92, in Main Bureau File 105–178715. The view that the Berets were violent terrorists was given expression in a 1971 book by Patty Newman, *Do It Up Brown!* (San Diego: Viewpoint Books, 1971), 253.

34. See "Wanted—Robert Avila as a Traitor, Vendido, and Dog," *La Causa,* May 23, 1969, 4–5, in folder 4, box 2, Arellanes Papers.

35. On the Biltmore incident, see Fred Hoffman, "Police Informer Rats on Chicanos, 14 Arrested," *LA Free Press,* June 13, 1969, 3, 24. For the Biltmore incident trial, see "Police Agent Tells Work in Brown Berets," *Los Angeles Times,* August 10, 1971, C-12; "Brown Beret Infiltration Laid to Crime," August 20, 1971, B-3; and "Brown Beret Denies Setting Fire," August 21, 1971, C-12.

36. The wedding took place on November 13, 1968. See copy of wedding invitation in folder 3, box 1, Arellanes Papers.

37. *La Causa,* May 23, 1969, 2; September 16, 1969, 2, in folder 4, box 2, Arellanes Papers. FBI files quoting from *La Causa,* December 10, 1970, listed fifty-one total Brown Beret chapters, with thirty-five of them in California. See FBI, "Young Chicanos," March 11, 1968, Los Angeles 100–71172, in Main Bureau File 105–178715. On November 2, 1972, the *Los Angeles Times* noted that there were ninety chapters with five thousand members (Dial Torgerson, "Brown Beret Leader Quits, Dissolves Units," 2:1). In 2006 David Sánchez recalled that the Berets had sixty chapters, including one in New York City composed of both Chicanos and Puerto Ricans and one in Hawaii; see (lecture, Los Angeles, January 30, 2005).

38. Espinoza noted that through conversations, gatherings, celebrations, and friendships, the female Berets created a sense of community for themselves; see "Revolutionary Sisters," 38; Sánchez quote on page 39.

39. In his study of the Poor People's Campaign, Gordon K. Mantler notes that five hundred Chicanos participated in the campaign in Washington, DC; see "Grassroots Voices, Memory, and the Poor People's Campaign," *American Radio Works,* accessed September 16, 2014, www.americanradioworks.publicradio.org.

40. See Arellanes's notes from Poor People's Campaign, in folder 1, box 1, Arellanes Papers. See also Corky Gonzales, "Poor People's March Instructions," n.d., in folder 8, box 1, Arellanes Papers.

41. *El Gallo,* July 1968, 4. After the encounter with the police, Ralph Ramírez of the Berets encouraged a march to the White House, where the contingent was attacked by police. Those arrested included Ramírez and Carlos Montes.

42. In his autobiography Tijerina notes that it was his fifteen-year-old daughter, Raquel, who was hit by the police. See *King Tiger,* 112.

43. *El Gallo,* July 1969, 10–11, folder 3, box 2, Arellanes Papers.

44. Arellanes's view that the Poor People's Campaign was a success coincides with Gordon K. Mantler's thesis in *Power to the Poor: Black-Brown Coalition and the Fight for Economic Justice, 1960–1974* (Chapel Hill: University of North Carolina Press, 2013). See this work for coverage of the Chicano role in the campaign.

45. See Gloria Arellanes, interview by Virginia Espino, October 11, 2011, unedited UCLA Oral History Project, 132, El Monte, CA, in possession of Arellanes.

46. Chávez notes that *La Causa's* first issue appeared on May 23, 1969; Chávez, *Mi Raza Primero,* 51.

47. *La Causa*, September 16, 1969, in folder 4, box 2, Arellanes Papers.

48. Ibid., July 10, 1969, 3.

49. Ibid., 6.

50. Ibid., May 23, 1969, 6.

51. Ibid., July 10, 1969, 6.

52. Ibid., March, 1969, 3.

53. Larry Gonzales to Brown Berets, n.d., folder 1, box 1, Arellanes Papers.

54. Espinoza uses the term "feminist nationalism" to describe the type of feminism that Arellanes and other Beret women were evolving into; "Revolutionary Sisters," 42.

55. The conference took place March 25–27, 1970; see *El Gallo* 2, no. 6 (1970), 8, in folder 3, box 2, Arellanes Papers.

56. See *La Causa*, May 22, 1969, 4.

57. Arellanes, interview by Espino, October 11, 2011, 124.

58. *La Causa*, July 10, 1969, 4.

59. I draw on this rape story from Gloria Arellanes, interview by Jaime Pelayo, Los Angeles, July 5, 1996; I am grateful for Mr. Pelayo's sharing an audio tape of this interview with me. Arellanes also mentions the potential rape situation in the interview by Espino, October 24, 2011, 238–40.

60. See Gloria Arellanes to Aron Mangancilla, February 25, 1970, in folder 1, box 1, Arellanes Papers.

61. In 1972 David Sánchez either resigned from the Berets or was forced out. There are contending accounts. Different and opposing Beret groups have existed since then. See "Brief History of the Brown Berets." Sánchez went on to work for liberal Democratic Party groups. Chávez notes that the Central Committee of the Berets fired Sánchez on October 21, 1972, on charges of stealing funds from the Berets. According to Chávez, Sánchez responded by resigning; see Chávez, *Mi Raza Primero*, 57. Sánchez himself claimed that he was resigning as well as dissolving all Beret chapters because he wanted to avoid strife in the Chicano movement and avoid others from using the Berets for their own political purposes; see *Los Angeles Times*, November 2, 1972, B-1. For later efforts to reorganize the Berets, see *Los Angeles Times*, July 12, 1993, B3.

62. See Arellanes, "Chicanas!," flyer, in folder 6, box 1, Arellanes Papers.

63. See ad for the "National Chicano Moratorium," in *L.A. Free Press*, February 27, 1970, 15.

64. For coverage of the March in the Rain, see Della Rossa, "Chicano Protest March," *L.A. Free Press*, March 6, 1970, 12.

65. See list of names, in folder 1, box 1, Arellanes Papers.

66. In 2005 David Sánchez stated that five hundred police officers attacked the assembled crowd in Laguna Park; see Sánchez (lecture, January 30, 2006).

67. Arellanes stated that she was still employed by the Neighborhood Adult Participation Project while working in the free clinic; see interview by Espino, October 17, 2011, 151.

68. Arellanes, interview by Pelayo.

PART THREE: ROSALIO MUÑOZ

1. *Mexican Voice*, n.d. Clipping provided by Rosalio Muñoz. On the Mexican American Movement, see Muñoz, *Youth, Identity, Power*.

2. On Bloody Christmas, see Edward J. Escobar, *Race, Police, and the Making of a Political Identity: Mexican Americans and the Los Angeles Police Department, 1900–1945* (Berkeley: University of California Press, 1999); on Operation Wetback, see Juan García, *Operation Wetback: The Mass Deportation of Mexican Undocumented Workers in 1954* (Westport, CT: Greenwood, 1980).

3. See John Kenneth Galbraith, *The Affluent Society* (London: Hamilton, 1958). Galbraith's book points out the disparities in wealth in the United States.

4. On Tijerina, see Busto, *King Tiger.*

5. Rosalio Muñoz, "Chicano Moratorium," *La Raza,* December 1969, 6.

6. Ramses Noriega, quoted in "Former UCLA Student Chief Refuses Draft," *Los Angeles Times,* September 17, 1969, C-10.

7. See Treviño, *Eyewitness.*

8. On the antiwar movement in general, see Tom Wells, *The War Within: America's Battle over Vietnam* (New York: Holt, 1994).

9. See Vigil, *Crusade for Justice,* 115.

10. Muñoz, quoted in "Youth Again Refuses Draft," *Los Angeles Times,* November 19, 1968, 29.

11. *March in the Rain,* directed by Claudio Fenner-López (Los Angeles: KCET, 1970), in Rosalio Muñoz's private collection.

12. Ruben Salazar, clipping, *Los Angeles Times,* n.d., in Muñoz's private collection; the article, although written by Salazar, has no byline.

13. Oropeza argues that the Chicano antiwar movement was more of a multi-issue one; see *Raza Sí.*

14. Patrice Lumumba was the African leader of the independence movement in the Congo in 1960. After becoming the first president of the Republic of Congo, he was assassinated by Belgian- and U.S.-sponsored counterrevolutionaries.

15. On Católicos por la Raza, see García, *Chicano Liberation Theology.*

16. Tape recording of Muñoz's speech, August 29, 1970, Los Angeles, in Muñoz's private collection.

17. Muñoz also uses the terms *sheriffs* and *sheriff's deputies* interchangeably. Both refer to county sheriff's deputies.

18. Muñoz's speech, August 31, 1970, Los Angeles, in Muñoz's private collection.

19. Ibid.

20. See Armando Morales, *Ando Sangrando: A Study of Mexican American–Police Conflict* (La Puente, CA: Perspectiva, 1972).

21. FBI files, Muñoz's private collection.

22. Muñoz, quoted in clipping, *Los Angeles Times,* n.d., in Muñoz's private collection.

23. See D. Sánchez, *Expedition through Aztlán.*

24. On Frank del Olmo, see Sotomayor and Beltrán–del Olmo, *Frank del Olmo.*

25. Muñoz, quoted in *People's Daily World,* August 25, 1990, 23.

INDEX

Abernathy, Rev. Ralph, 163
Acosta, Oscar Zeta, 253, 258, 269, 283
Acuña, Dr. Rudy, 104, 280
Alatorre, Richard, 87–90, 300
Alurista, 7, 58, 175–76
Arellanes, Gloria, 1–17, 113–210, 263, 271–72, 321–22
Arellanes, William César (Bill), 132, 149, 171, 192, 201
Arzupe, Bishop Juan, 308–10
Avila, Robert, 150–51
Aztlán, 4, 7, 15, 58–59, 81, 94, 132, 138–39, 171, 176, 196, 226, 274

Biltmore Six, 152
Black Berets, 1, 165, 167, 176, 269
Black Panther Party, 7–8, 36, 49, 70, 132–35, 139, 177
Black Power, 3–5, 7, 14, 70, 110, 139
Blowouts, 3, 8, 11, 15, 40–49, 145–46, 226–28, 281, 289
Bonpane, Fr. Blas, 64
Borjon, Patricia, 56
Bradley, Tom, 306, 308–09, 314
Brophy, Bill, 87, 89, 90, 300
Brown Berets, 8, 11–12, 14–15, 36–38, 40–41, 43, 50, 72, 84, 113, 129–210, 227, 248, 250–51, 255–58, 260, 262–263, 265, 267, 270, 272, 275, 287–91, 293–94, 296, 298, 300

Cano, Gil, 272, 288–89, 294–95, 299, 301, 304, 306–09
Camp Hess Kramer, 126–27
Candelaria, Sal, 167, 269
Castro, Fidel, 32, 52–54
Castro, Sal, 8, 11, 15, 36, 41–42, 44, 49, 50–52, 126, 145–46, 227, 258
Católicos Por La Raza, 9, 12, 15, 61–69, 275, 289
Center for Metropolitan Mission In-Service (COMMIT), 303–04, 307, 310, 313–15
Chale con el Draft, 247–50
Chávez, César, 2, 5–6, 7, 15, 38–39, 41, 47, 52, 59, 63, 93, 130, 169, 228, 240–41, 248–49, 250, 252, 263, 269–71, 293, 318
Chicano Press Association, 56, 60–61
Chicano Renaissance, 3, 10
Chicanismo, 4–5. 10, 14–16, 39, 59, 94, 138–39, 141, 195, 226
Chicano Law Students Association, 62
Chicano Student Movement (CSM), 40–41, 45, 49, 50, 52, 55, 70
Chicano Studies, 2, 8, 11, 13, 16, 103–06, 111
Chicano Youth Leadership Conference (CYLC), 12
Communist Party, 16, 54, 140, 265, 269, 310, 314–16
Congress of Mexican American Unity, 247, 265, 285, 293
Corona, Bert, 10, 15–16, 37, 226, 265, 269, 276, 282, 294–95, 304, 312

Cuban Revolution of 1959, 32, 52, 55, 81
Crusade for Justice, 55–56, 165, 167, 174, 176, 248, 251
Cruz, Richard, 61, 63, 66, 68, 275

East L.A. Thirteen, 49–50, 146
Educational Issues Coordinating Committee (EICC), 12, 46–51, 146–47
El Barrio Free Clinic, 12, 148, 177–189
El Plan Espiritual de Aztlán, 7, 58, 175, 276
Elias, Roberto "Bobby," 248, 251, 254–56, 260, 263, 272
Escalante, Alicia, 39, 131, 161, 168, 253, 258
Escalante, Lorraine, 131, 160–61, 170
Escuela de Aztlán, 147–48
Esparza, Moctesuma, 37, 49, 70, 224–27

Fanon, Frantz, 33, 140
Franco, Victor, 34–35, 40

Gómez-Quiñones, Juan, 37, 225
Gonzales, Rodolfo "Corky," 38, 55–56, 59, 71, 85–86, 93–99, 130, 163–68, 174, 176, 196, 199, 202, 225–26, 241, 248–51, 260–63, 269–72, 276, 283
Guevara, Che, 14, 32, 52, 81, 139–40, 171, 176, 180
Gutiérrez, Dr. Félix, 213, 230
Gutiérrez, José Ángel, 59, 86, 88, 93–99. 267
Guzmán, Dr. Ralph, 33, 72, 225, 241
Guzmán Report, 225, 235

Harding, Tim, 31–33
Huerta, Dolores, 5–6, 196–97, 249–50

I Am Joaquin, 55, 199
Inside Eastside, 11, 34–38, 40–41, 52, 70
Internal colonialism, 4, 15

Javier, Gonzálo, 263, 272, 279

Kennedy, Robert, 169, 228
King, Dr. Martin Luther, 32, 94, 128, 161, 163, 228
Kushner, Sam, 256, 274

La Adelita, 5, 172, 194, 195, 257
La Causa, 139–40, 147, 151, 156, 167, 169–73, 195, 272
La Clinica del Barrio, 203–05
La Marcha de la Reconquista, 292–98
La Organización del Pueblo, 310–14
La Piranya, 38–40, 129–31, 142
La Raza, 8, 11–12, 14, 34–36, 40–41, 49–50, 54–55, 60, 62, 64, 69, 71–73, 77–81, 84, 86, 88, 91,
    100, 102, 104, 106, 110, 140, 170, 227, 241, 247, 281, 299, 300
La Raza Unida Party (RUP), 3, 8, 10, 12, 14, 59, 85–103, 111, 203, 248, 267, 286, 293–301, 306
La Virgen de Guadalupe, 5, 39, 121, 294
Las Adelitas de Aztlán, 194–96, 199, 209, 257
López, Ron, 225, 236
Lozada, Froben, 241, 257
Luce, Fr. John, 34–36, 38, 40, 50, 132, 153, 263, 300–01, 303–04, 311

Malcolm X, 8, 140–41
March Against Death, 252–54
March in the Rain, 196, 198–99, 254–60
Mardirosian, Vahac, 47–48, 50, 52
Martínez, Elizabeth "Betita," 52, 60
Mexican American Student Confederation (MASC), 8, 58
Mexican American Youth Leadership Conference, 126
Mexican American Youth Organization (MAYO), 8, 86, 248
Mexican Revolution of 1910, 5–6. 172, 194–95, 246, 258, 276
Montes, Carlos, 37, 49, 134, 138–39, 142–43, 146, 152, 154, 156, 167, 193
Movimiento Estudiantil Chicano de Aztlán (MEChA), 8, 12, 58, 62, 162, 240–41, 243, 255, 257, 263–65, 273
Muñoz, Carlos, 8, 33, 49
Muñoz, Ricardo, 213, 215, 219–20, 224–25, 234, 237, 239, 241, 272, 280
Muñoz, Rosalio, 1–17, 72–73, 84, 113–14, 196–99, 208–09, 211–319, 321–22
Muñoz, Dr. Rosalio Florian, 211–18, 220, 239–40, 272, 275, 280, 315–16

National Chicano Antiwar Moratorium, 3, 9, 12, 114, 196, 261, 272–82, 318
National Chicano Moratorium Committee, 72–73, 84–85, 113, 196–203, 250–298, 310
National Chicano Youth Liberation Conference, 7, 55, 85, 93, 173–77, 252, 260–62
Nava, Dr. Julian, 48, 51, 307
Noriega, Ramses, 73, 172, 225, 228–30, 237–41, 243–52, 254, 257, 260–61, 263, 269–72, 281, 285, 288–89, 294, 296–98

Peace Action Council, 243, 249, 256, 265–66
Plan de Aztlán, 55, 58–59, 175, 260
Plan de Santa Barbara, 8, 58, 240
Poor People's Campaign, 14, 145, 161–69, 174

Ramírez, Ralph, 37, 134, 143, 146, 153–54, 156, 167–68
Razo, Joe, 37–38, 43, 45–46, 49, 60, 68, 73, 75–77, 79–80, 247
Reichline, Neil, 222, 243, 245–46
Resendez, Fred "Sabu," 153
Restrepo, Guillermo, 76
Reyes, Grace, 131–32, 160, 170, 199, 258, 272
Reyes, Hilda, 131–32, 160, 170, 195, 199, 251, 258
Risco, Eliezer, 35–37, 40, 49, 52, 55, 136, 241
Rodríguez, Jacobo, 263, 272
Roybal, Edward, 39, 44, 215, 268
Ruiz, Raul, 1–17, 18–112, 136, 170, 195, 294, 298, 299–300, 317 *fig.*, 321–22

Salazar, Ruben, 10–11, 74–78, 80–84, 203, 245, 262, 269–71, 274, 282–88, 290–91, 296
Sánchez, Andrea, 129, 131, 145–46, 149, 156, 159–61, 170, 172, 174, 182, 192, 199, 204
Sánchez, Arlene, 131, 160, 192
Sánchez, David, 36–38, 49, 72–73, 130, 132–44, 146–48, 151–53, 155–58, 167–68, 170, 172–74, 177–78, 182–85, 189–94, 197–201, 205, 250–56, 258, 260, 262, 269–70, 287, 289–90, 293–94, 296–98
Sánchez, Esther, 129, 131, 156, 159–60, 170
Silver Dollar Café, 76–77, 80–81, 83, 274, 287
Socialist Workers Party, 54, 140, 256, 265
Solis, Yolanda, 131, 160

Southern Christian Leadership Conference (SCLC), 161–64
Spanish-Speaking Youth Leadership Conference, 126
Students for a Democratic Society (SDS), 33–34
Sumaya, Fernando, 170

Teatro Campesino, 263, 269
TELACU (The East Los Angeles Community Union), 100, 102, 288
Tigar, Michael, 252, 266, 287, 302–03
Tijerina, Reies López, 6–7, 70, 96, 145, 163, 165–66, 225–26, 241, 258
Torres, Esteban, 100, 265, 285, 288
Trevino, Jesus, 245

United Farm Workers (UFW), 5–6, 248, 273
United Mexican American Students (UMAS), 8, 12, 34, 40, 43, 50, 58, 62, 224–230, 240
Urias (Muñoz), María de Socorro, 211–15, 237, 239, 256, 272, 275, 280, 315–16

Valdez, Armando, 241, 249–50
Valdez, Luis, 226, 269–70
Varela, Delfino, 241
Villa, Pancho, 5–7, 98

Wilson, Thomas, 76, 80, 83, 287

Zapata, Emiliano, 5, 98, 180